D1002022

INDIA'S
SECOND
REVOLUTION

INDIA

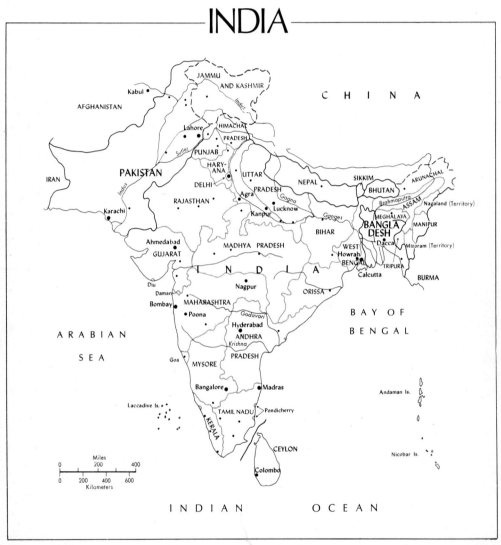

From *Geography of Mankind,* second edition, by Jan O. M. Broek and John W. Webb. Copyright © 1973 by McGraw-Hill, Inc. Used with permission of McGraw-Hill Book Company.

INDIA'S SECOND REVOLUTION

The Dimensions of Development

LAWRENCE A. VEIT

A Council on Foreign Relations Book

McGRAW-HILL BOOK COMPANY

NEW YORK, ST. LOUIS, SAN FRANCISCO, DÜSSELDORF
KUALA LUMPUR, LONDON, MEXICO, MONTREAL, NEW DELHI
PANAMA, PARIS, SÃO PAULO, SINGAPORE, TOKYO, TORONTO

For Nancy and David

Copyright © 1976 by Council on Foreign Relations, Inc. All rights reserved. Printed in the United States of America. No part of this publication may be reproduced, stored in a retrieval system, or transmitted, in any form or by any means, electronic, mechanical, photocopying, recording, or otherwise, without prior written permission of the publisher.

LIBRARY OF CONGRESS CATALOGING IN PUBLICATION DATA
Veit, Lawrence A. India's second revolution. "A Council on Foreign Relations book." Bibliography: p.   Includes index.
1. India—Economic   policy—1966–   2. India—Economic conditions—1947–   3. India—Foreign economic relations.
I. Title.   HC435.2.V425   338.954   76-853
ISBN 0-07-067395-0

123456789 RRDRRD 75432109876

COUNCIL ON FOREIGN RELATIONS BOOKS

Founded in 1921, the Council on Foreign Relations, Inc., is a nonprofit and non-partisan organization of individuals devoted to the promotion of a better and wider understanding of international affairs through the free interchange of ideas. The membership of the Council, which numbers about 1,600, is made up of men and women throughout the United States elected by the Board of Directors on the basis of an estimate of their special interest, experience, and involvement in international affairs and their standing in their own communities. The Council does not take any position on questions of foreign policy, and no person is authorized to speak for the Council on such matters. The Council has no affiliation with and receives no funding from any part of the United States government.

The Council conducts a meetings program to provide its members an opportunity to talk with invited guests who have special experience, expertise, or involvement in international affairs, and conducts a studies program of research directed to political, economic, and strategic problems related to United States foreign policy. Since 1922 the Council has published the quarterly journal Foreign Affairs. *From time to time the Council also publishes books and monographs which in the judgment of the Committee on Studies of the Council's Board of Directors are responsible treatments of significant international topics worthy of presentation to the public. The individual authors of articles in* Foreign Affairs *and of Council books and monographs are solely responsible for all statements of fact and expressions of opinion contained in them.*

This book was set in Baskerville by University Graphics, Inc. It was printed and bound by R. R. Donnelly & Sons Company. The designer was Ellen Seham. The editors were Nancy Frank and Cheryl Love. Milton Heiberg supervised the production.

CONTENTS

LIST OF TABLES

UNITS OF MEASURE AND RELATED INFORMATION

A. *General Measures*
one lakh = 100,000
one crore = 10 million
one ounce = 28.3495 grams
one hectare = 2.47105 acres
one kilometer = 0.62 miles
one kilogram = 2.205 pounds

B. *Time*
Calendar year (CY): January–December
Indian fiscal year (IFY): April–March
Crop year: July–June

C. *Rates of Exchange*
Predevaluation (pre-June 6, 1966): Rs. 4.7619 = $1
Postdevaluation: Rs. 7.50 = $1

D. *Abbreviations*
AICC: All-India Congress Committee • CD: Community Development • CENTO: Central Treaty Organization • COMECON: Council for Mutual Economic Assistance • CPI: Communist Party of India • CWC: Congress Working Committee • DGTD: Directorate General of Trade and Development • EEC: European Economic Community • GAO: General Accounting Office • GATT: General Agreement on Tariffs and Trade • GOI: Government of India • IBRD: International Bank for Reconstruction and Development, or World Bank • IDA: International Development Association • IFY: Indian Fiscal Year • IMF: International Monetary Fund • NDC: National Development Council • OECD: Organization for Economic Cooperation and Development • PL 480: Public Law 480 (Food for Peace Program) • RBI: Reserve Bank of India • SEATO: South East Asian Treaty Organization • STC: State Trading Corporation • UNCTAD: United Nations Conference on Trade and Development

E. *Important Dates*
1. *Political*
August 15, 1947: Independence
1951: First General Election
1957: Second General Election
1962: Third General Election, War with China
1964: Nehru's death
1965: War with Pakistan

1966: Mrs. Gandhi becomes Prime Minister
1967: Fourth General Election
1969: Congress Party Split
1971: Fifth General Election, War with Pakistan
2. *Plan Periods*
First Plan: April 1951–March 1956
Second Plan: April 1956–March 1961
Third Plan: April 1961–March 1966
Interim Period: April 1966–March 1969
Fourth Plan: April 1969–March 1974
Fifth Plan: April 1974–March 1979
3. *Other Major Dates*
1948: First Industrial Policy Resolution
1950: Formation of the Planning Commission
1956: Second Industrial Policy Resolution
1958: Formation of the India Consortium
1966: Devaluation
1969: Bank Nationalization

PREFACE

Endurance is surely one of the most applicable words to describe the task of writing a book about India's development. As suggested by the prelude title, India is embarked on an odyssey of which the political, social, and economic bounds are uniquely nebulous, complex, and important. Thus it is not surprising that to establish an understanding of India's course required me to set off on a prolonged and difficult journey of my own.

The most remote source of my interest in India that I can recall was a friendship which I had as a youngster with an accomplished Indian diplomat. Later, as a student in London, my curiosity about South Asia was stimulated not only by a foray into the workings of the Indian credit markets but also by a bridge partner who hailed from Ceylon. An Indian colleague at the Conference Board subsequently added to my interest. Thus in 1968, when the U.S. Treasury asked if I would become its representative in New Delhi, there was little need to think twice before saying yes.

I went to India singularly unequipped to understand that country's economy. Conventional economic theory was of some avail but not really adequate to the task. Likewise, political theory, history and sociology each had insights, but, with rare exceptions, authors who had dealt with South Asia had not related these various strands in a fully meaningful way.

The three elements that most influenced me to write about the Indian economy were the failure of "old-India hands" to deal comprehensively with the various dimensions of development, the ill-founded short-term optimism or pessimism of most observers of the Indian scene, and my own hunch that India was making poor use of its resources and that, without sacrificing democracy, it could achieve greater material progress than in the past. A more precise description of my approach follows in the prelude, and my reactions to the political crisis which overtook India in 1975 are stated in the epilogue. Here I wish to point out that to counterpoise economic development and democracy is to raise a moral dilemma for which there is no satisfactory resolution. As the reader will see from various passages in the book, my view of this dilemma is strongly influenced by a stubborn but genuine conviction that these goals are complementary and that, in practice, there is no need to choose.

I believe that Judd Polk and Wolf Ladejinsky would have shared this view. These two men, who by tragic coincidence passed away in mid-1975, were instrumental in inspiring this book. Moreover, each of them added significantly to the array of analytic tools that I have been able to bring to bear on the subject, as well as to the underlying assumptions of how societies and economic systems operate. It is with great appreciation for their contributions that I regret they will not see the final product.

There is virtually no end to the list of other colleagues and friends who, by commenting on drafts, raising new perspectives, and forwarding difficult-to-obtain documents and in a host of other ways, have aided me in writing this book. At the top of the list are William Diebold, Jr., and William Barnds. Aside from acting as alter egos during the 2½ years that I was privileged to spend as a fellow at the Council on Foreign Relations, they gave critical attention to countless ideas, drafts, and redrafts and were a vital source of sympathy and encouragement.

The Council contributed in many ways. Its Committee on Studies, chaired first by Grayson Kirk and later by Robert V. Roosa, not only approved the India study at an initial stage and later endorsed the manuscript for publication but offered many constructive suggestions. Moreover, in keeping with Council tradition, a group of academics, businessmen, and government officials was constituted to act as a sounding board and a source of pertinent new ideas. This group, composed of "old India hands" and others more generally knowledgeable in development matters, met on five occasions to review working papers. Without implying that responsibility for the final product rests with anyone other than myself, I am pleased to acknowledge my debt to them and to their deft and wise chairman, Phillips Talbot. The members of the group were William Barnds, John Beyer, William Diebold, Jr., Ainslee T. Embree, Marcus Franda, Orville L. Freeman, Robert L. Heilbroner, Amos A. Jordan, Jr., Andrew M. Kamarck, John P. Lewis, Hart Perry, Gustav Ranis, Roger Revelle, John B. Rhodes, Jr., Helena Stalson, Sidney Sober, Ernest Stern, Kenneth W. Thompson, Thomas P. Thornton, Myron Weiner, Abraham Weisblat, Richard W. Wheeler, W. Howard Wriggins.

At the Council on Foreign Relations, May Wu was rarely out of sight for long. As my research assistant and rapporteur for the Council's study group, her wit and wisdom were most helpful. Similarly, I am grateful to Robert Valkenier for his imaginative editorial support; Lorna Brennan, whose staff arranged to have the people and the papers in the right places at the right time; the staff of the Council library, who rose fully to the problems of obtaining obscure documents about India; and a host of others.

I am particularly indebted to friends in India, especially those in Madras, Delhi, Calcutta, Bombay, and Mangalore. Economists, businessmen, humorists, taxi drivers, and even government officials have contributed in various ways to the final vision expressed here. I hesitate to include the last category, of course, as it was in the role of a United States government official that I first visited India. I should add promptly that anyone surveying these pages for indiscreet tales of Indo-American relations is bound to be disappointed: these are largely irrelevant to the story of Indian development.

Last, but hardly least, I thank my wife Nancy and son David for their inspiration and endurance of times when I was physically present but otherwise absent from family life. Without their understanding, I know this book could never have been completed.

New Providence, N.J.
December 1975

INDIA'S
SECOND
REVOLUTION

PRELUDE TO AN ODYSSEY

The future becomes the present, the present the past, and the past turns into ever-
lasting regret if you don't plan for it.

—Tennessee Williams,
The Glass Menagerie

And so these men of Indostan
    Disputed loud and long,
Each in his own opinion
    Exceeding stiff and strong,
Though each was partly in the right,
    And all were in the wrong!

So, oft in theologic wars
    The disputants, I ween,
Rail on in utter ignorance
    Of what each other mean,
And prate about an elephant
    Not one of them has seen!

—John Godfrey Saxe,
"The Blind Men and the Elephant"

Many eminent and experienced observers of the Indian scene have erred in
their predictions of how India would evolve after it obtained Independence in
1947. Whether we turn to the apocalyptic school of famine forecasters and
believers in the inevitability of Indian political disintegration, or to the heady
optimists who foresaw "takeoff," green revolution, and India's rapid emergence
as a modern industrial state, it is startling to see how wrong most pundits—
Indian and foreign—have been. From the record of inaccurate forecasting one
could draw the conclusion that the information for understanding the course of
events is inadequate.

Undoubtedly this is true in some degree, but there is another, more signifi-

cant consideration which, incidentally, justifies this latest contribution to the
already extensive literature on Indian development. Behind the name "India"
stands one-seventh of the world's people, a large proportion of them in health,
nutritional, and material circumstances that are judged inadequate by Indian—
indeed, universal—standards. Looked at from any perspective, the large and
unremitting economic needs of these people add up to an imperative for social
transformation which few can ignore, and which is a cause for high passion on
the part of those intimately concerned with India. Accordingly, two schools of
thought have emerged with respect to India's prospects.

The optimists have interpreted the end of colonial rule and the upsurge of
nationalism in the late 1940s and 1950s as the occasion for economic development. As embodied in the constructive approach of the First and Second
Development Decades and the so-called Revolution of Rising Expectations,
their view has been that the development processes which the West has used to
become affluent could be adapted and applied in the developing countries and
that global uplift could thus be realized.

In contrast, the doomsayers often have regarded Indians and the peoples of
other less-developed nations as incapable of holding their countries together,
much more creating the conditions for economic progress. For various economic, social, and political reasons, and sometimes because of a revulsion
against the backward and rudimentary conditions prevailing in many parts of
India, the pessimists adopted the gloomiest attitudes toward this nation. Their
dire forecasts have been stridently stated and widely circulated in all but the
most encouraging periods in India's recent history.

The consistently wide publicity which the world's media have given to the
Pollyannas and the pessimists, and to India's actual situation, which has fluctuated repeatedly between the extremes of the bleak and the encouraging, is
symptomatic of India's importance in the world. Humanitarian concern may be
the most important aspect of international interests in India because it under-
lies all other interests and because the essence of humanity is inalienable. Even
so, a variety of world economic and political issues, some of them enduring and
others ephemeral, have also heightened concern for India's development. Most
prominent, from an American point of view, have been those which have been
indiscriminately lumped under the label of "communist threat." Because this
can be separated into a concern about the spread of communist ideology and a
more immediate aim to contain Soviet and Chinese expansionism, it is more
complex than is readily apparent. But the simple and not necessarily incorrect
logic applied by United States strategists has been that a strong democratic
India would weigh in the balance against America's cold war adversaries. Other
motives for the United States to support Indian development—a wish to
nurture democracy, the pursuit of commercial relations, and so forth—have
also been genuinely significant, albeit many have regarded them as being of a
lower order of importance in policy formulation.

There is a psychological aspect to the international concern for India which includes but is not limited to India's size, humanitarian concerns, and global realpolitik. India's history distinguishes it as one of the cradles of civilization; in the middle of the third millennium B.C. the peoples of the Indus Valley were among the most socially advanced. Recurrent golden periods in the subcontinent's history have added greatly to man's cultural and scientific heritage. The humanistic influence of Buddhism, for example, has lasted for more than 2,500 years and has had a profound worldwide impact. More recently, the influence of Mahatma Gandhi—his spiritual message, philosophy, and way of life—has been impressive for its intensity and global reach.

Another psychological reason why India has attracted and held the attention of so many foreigners is that it is a frontier nation. I think it belittling to describe Indian efforts to achieve democracy and development as an "experiment," but to say that since 1947 India has labored at a frontier of world society is to grasp the seriousness and the newness of the tasks India has set for itself. The peculiar post-World War II problems of developing backward countries— as contrasted with reconstruction and the long-term evolutionary development in the West—have received enough attention elsewhere to go without elaboration here. Suffice it to say that India's confrontation of modernizing and traditional forces, the clash among socialist, free enterprise and indigenous Indian approaches to society, and the attendant social conflicts are paralleled by the experiences of many developing countries. But India was among the first nations to gain independence after World War II, and because of its size, its diversity, and its sophistication, it has perforce been on the forefront of modern economic and social development. Although India's international significance has declined from the peak it reached in the 1950s, India remains a major actor on the world stage.

To say that India is on a frontier is to imply that in time the Indian polity will improve its capacity to structure its natural environment and social relationships in the interest of the people. Indeed, I believe that, given the current state of man's knowledge about himself and this planet, the question is not whether Indian economic conditions will improve, but when. This position is subject to contradiction, of course, particularly insofar as this book has been written at a time when India is at a low point in its struggle for economic improvement. The failure of India's 1972 and 1974 monsoons and skyrocketing international fuel and fertilizer prices following the 1973 Middle East war seriously hampered India's ability to meet its food needs. Moreover, when foreign grain was available, it generally was so costly as to preclude India's purchasing adequate supplies to supplement its domestic production. For these reasons and because of the unequal distribution of food among regions, between urban and rural areas, and among individuals, India remains vulnerable to problems of malnutrition, inflation, hoarding, unemployment, industrial recession, and, witness the crisis of 1975, social instability.

To predict whether India's situation will grow worse or improve in the near future is as hazardous as predicting the world long-range weather outlook, one of the key factors on which the issue turns.[1] There can be no doubt, however, of the existence of two paramount needs: first, that India mobilize and rationalize its food resources so as to prevent a serious famine in the coming years; second, that India formulate and implement a long-run strategy to make certain that the balance between available food and basic human nutrition needs is never again allowed to tilt toward disaster. Although there is a great deal that the world community can do to help India with its immediate and longer-term problems, there is no escaping the responsibility of Indian people for their own welfare. Thus, next to national security, there is no Indian objective with higher priority for the coming years than that of maintaining minimum standards of caloric intake.

Regrettably, this prescription was just as apropos in 1966 and earlier as it is today. And if Indian public policy during the remainder of the 1970s is not more decisively and consistently attuned to agricultural needs than in the preceeding 10 years, it is certain that there will be another crisis. Will the Indian government learn from its past experiences and now extend its ongoing efforts to produce more food and to slow the population growth rate? Will the World Food Conference sponsored by the Food and Agriculture Organization (FAO) in Rome in November 1974 serve as the focus for an international consciousness-raising, whereby the world community will pattern a new system to tailor global food production to meet global requirements? The answers elude any certain prediction but are central to how the world will evolve. Clearly they set India at stage center in the drama to come.

The Approach

Because this book is about India's economic development, broadly conceived, to proceed without reference to social and political forces—domestic and international—would be meaningless. There is a danger, however, in taking such a holistic approach to Indian development: the number of relevant variables and their interlinkages are so profuse and complex that they defy description, much more analysis. Nonetheless, and with no intention of disparaging the many fine books which have been written about India's economy, I believe the macroscopic approach taken here sheds a new and color-true light on the subject.

It is ironic, therefore, that one of the key determinants in my analysis is the

[1]Concerning the world's weather, an ominous note for the next decade has been sounded by many climatologists who believe that the 0.3°C cooling of the earth's annual average temperature which has been noted in recent years is indicative of a significant worsening of agricultural conditions. This view is summarized in a *Statement of the International Federation of Institutes for Advanced Study* adopted at Bonn, Germany, May 10, 1974.

profound diversity within India. In order to understand India's ethos, it is imperative to take a microscopic approach and pinpoint the parts of which the Indian whole is composed. The resultant regime of moving from the general to the specific requires considerable semantic gymnastics and much selectivity in the choice of illustrative material. In short, the approach of this book is eclectic and, in my eclecticism, I have often had to rely on circumstantial evidence because other testimony is unavailable.

Intellectually, a model would have been a far more satisfying way to describe the economic process in India, but, as well understood by Gunnar Myrdal, the macrodynamics of Indian society defy the simplifications necessary for meaningful model building.[2] Although it has been possible for me to use models to analyze specific questions such as the effect on development of military spending or of foreign private equity investment, even these constructions do not give definitive answers to the questions asked, and they certainly cannot be generalized to the economy at large.

Another characteristic of this book is that it takes an "existential" appraoch to India's economic situation. Existential not only in the sense that it underscores the significance of diversity and the inadequacy of seeking to explain the subject through an abstract model or a particular ideological doctrine, but existential because it recognizes that random events and exogenous influences are among the determining factors. At another level it is existential because it assumes that discontinuities occur; that straight-line projections of the past into the indefinite future are bound to be wrong; and that human beings—mainly Indians—are responsible for the current and future situation in India. Ashoka Mehta, an experienced and venerable economic statesman, has described India's situation in terms which closely parallel my approach.

> At the moment, we are engaged in what may be described as a second revolution. The first revolution was when we freed ourselves from political bondage. In those days we were fortunate to have legendary leaders who could inspire and draw out the noblest and best in us. We are now going through an economic and social revolution, but we do not seem to have the same kind of legendary leaders. Today, it becomes our responsibility to be our own leaders and to generate a greater involvement in the economic and social transformation that is taking place. The nation would have lost its soul, if we had not accepted our responsibility during the freedom movement. So also today let the nation shoulder its responsibilities for development.[3]

Can the book that I am describing by successive approximations have a thesis? Or is it too rooted in the description and analysis of organizations and

[2]See his *Asian Drama: An Inquiry into the Poverty of Nations,* published for the Twentieth Century Fund by Penguin Books (1968), particularly app. 3.

[3]Ashoka Mehta, *Economic Planning in India* (New Delhi: Young India Publications, 1970), p. 101.

institutional relationships to focus on a concrete hypothesis? My view is that through a systematic, if selective, examination and evaluation of the many determinants of India's economy and how they are related, an informed view about the Indian economy emerges. This view may prove difficult for some readers to accept because to emphasize the multiplicity of the variables affecting India's development and the degree to which each of them changes in significance from one period to the next is to eschew simple explanations. Nonetheless, to the extent that conclusions follow from an approach that employs rigorous analysis and has predictive value, they must be regarded as a thesis in the broadest sense of the word.

One additional issue which I should clarify before proceeding is whether this is a book about economic policy. The correct answer is that it is and it is not. Although policy has been a major determinant of India's economic situation, other factors such as history, technology, human skill levels, and availability of economic resources also have been prominent. Policy therefore is only one of many interconnected determinants, albeit there are implications for Indian policy in every chapter. Although I have noted policy implications for the United States as they arise and in the concluding chapter, I have treated this area only at a general level on the grounds that shedding new light on India's objective situation is the first priority of this book and that any extensive effort to prescribe and justify United States policy might detract from the more basic need for analysis.

Finally, a semantic caveat must be entered. Various commonly used words and phrases, because they are imprecise, jargon, euphemistic, or otherwise flawed, are subject to misunderstanding. "Laissez faire," for example, can mean, in the Manchester School sense, a prohibition against official interference in the economy; it is also used more generally to mean that some decisions about production and consumption are left to private persons. In like manner, there are problems raised by such terms as "gross national product" and "balance of payments." Even though concepts underlying these terms are of questionable merit and the published statistics which purport to measure them are often very inaccurate, there is no way to write about development without using them. I shall try to clarify their meaning as they are introduced, but as this book is not about semantics or economic theory, I shall provide only as much explanation as is needed to put them into proper context.

What This Book Is About

The starting point of this study is a comprehensive, if telescoped, analysis of the Indian political economy. The twentieth century has seen an outpouring of new ideas about, and methods for, restructuring society. Governments have responded by becoming activists on such issues as economic growth and income distribution. Thus, my initial task has been to scrutinize the politics of economic development to reveal how social factors such as diversity and unity have operated to shape India's economy and how they, in turn, have been affected by it. Chapter 1 also deals with ideology as a factor in politics and investigates the diverse sources from which political power is derived. In outlining the course of India's development since Independence, it traces roughly a cyclical pattern in which there is a cause-and-effect, reciprocal relationship between doctrinaire socialism and economic stagnation, on the one hand, and liberal pragamatism and relative progress, on the other. A discussion of Center-state relations is included to illustrate how mammoth political problems complicate the making and implementation of economic policy.

Many studies of India's economy begin by analyzing the Five-Year Plans, a convenient starting point, but not necessarily the most revealing. The alternative I have employed in Chapter 2 is a two-stage exposition which first deals with the natural and human resource base and the conditions in which production and consumption occur. This narrative is intended to animate the situation of the Indian people, 80 percent of whom live in rural communities in which traditional social mores, subsistence farming, and barter are common. The stark reality of actual Indian economic conditions stands in marked contrast to the relative sophistication of Five-Year Plan documents. Be that as it may, it is necessary to pursue the analysis at a second stage, a more conventional overview of India's national income, fiscal, monetary, and balance-of-payments circumstances.

International relations have had an important impact on the course of Indian economic development, in the first instance through India's economic transactions with other countries. World politics—notably India's wars with China and Pakistan and the cold war which induced the United States to arm Pakistan—have been equally important, however, as they have repeatedly caused India to commit its domestic economic resources to nondevelopment objectives. Accordingly, Chapters 3 to 6, which address India's international relations with the West, Communist countries, and multinational bodies such as the Aid India Consortium, feature, but are by no means limited to, foreign aid relationships. They deal with the various reasons why outsiders have seen themselves as having a role in India and the ways in which foreigners have exercised their power to influence the course of India's economic development. They also discuss how India has expended its energies in shaping and parrying foreign initiatives and how it has projected its economic interests abroad.

The purpose of Chapters 7 to 10 is to examine how Indian economic policy is made and implemented within the parameters discussed in preceding sections of the book. The emphasis here is on how the combined objectives of growth, social justice, and self-reliance shaped India's choice of economic strategy, how that strategy has been applied to the agricultural, industrial, and banking sectors, and how effective it has been in practice. I have devoted particular attention to India's 1969 bank nationalization because the operations of financial institutions are critical for development and also because government policy toward the banking sector illustrates so many aspects of how India's economy operates.

The concluding chapters draw together the strands of the preceding analysis to weave them into a coherent whole. In addition, they measure India's economic performance by analyzing it in the light of India's past experience, its underlying economic needs, the potential for progress, and what was forecast by the government. The book ends in a sense where it begins, with a brief discussion of broader geopolitical and social issues as well as India's prospects and its place in the world community.

PART I

SOCIAL, POLITICAL, AND ECONOMIC BACKGROUND

CHAPTER 1

THE POLITICS OF ECONOMIC
DEVELOPMENT

The distinction between economics (what is produced and how it is consumed) and politics (who governs and how) is clearer in principle than it is in practice. Moreover, because the exercise of political power is importantly determined by—or aimed at—economic factors, and the setting of the economy's course is partly a function of politics (political and economic power tend to be concentrated in the same hands[1]), an investigation of the Indian political and social systems is essential. It will become apparent that the linkages between economic and political factors are vital, ubiquitous, complex, and in a continuing state of flux.

Continuity and Diversity: Caste,
Community, Region, Class, and History

To devote just a few paragraphs to the subject of how India's social organization is reflected in its economy borders on the arrogant and I beg the indulgence of those social scientists, historians, linguists, and philosophers whose areas of expertise are so grossly neglected in what follows. The rationale for addressing this subject is not merely that social and cultural factors play a critical role in the dynamics of economic and political systems, but that the reality of India's size and diversity—close to 600 million people, fourteen major languages, six important religions, and so forth—has imprinted a special character on its development.

The Hindu religion—or, more properly, social order—is universally recognized as a uniquely Indian approach to metaphysical and worldly affairs. Its

[1]For analysis of the connection between rural economic and political power, see George Rosen, *Democracy and Economic Change in India* (Berkeley: University of California Press, 1966), particularly p. 96.

11

complexity and various inflexibilities have caused many observers to stereotype it as hopelessly backward, rigid, and unchanging. Recent investigation of family, village, caste, and other constituent elements, however, has illuminated the flexibility and diversity that exist within Hinduism, not only hierarchically among various caste groups, but also horizontally between regions and between urban and rural situations.[2]

To the extent that one can generalize, the basic element from which both village and urban societies are formed is the extended family composed of brothers, wives, elderly parents, children, and grandchildren, all of whose members are likely, according to tradition, to live in the same house and exploit common property. Kinship relations are regulated by long-standing norms which accord particular duties and status to each family member, with special emphasis on the intimacy and continuity of relationships among males. Leaving aside non-Hindus and Harijans (individuals so low in the Hindu social system as to be without rank and therefore untouchable) for the moment, each family belongs to one of the many subdivisions (*jati*) of the four Hindu castes. There may be one or a great many different jatis represented in a particular village. Jatis, which may be either localized or distributed throughout the whole country, represent the traditional horizon for finding a spouse, and an individual's jati is, in effect, the outer limit of his traditional peer group.

Castes are related to each other hierarchically according to historical and functional factors. According to the most popular of the caste (*varna*) schemes, Brahmans are reputed to have sprung from the mouth of the god Brahma and therefore occupy the highest place in the social order. Their traditional function is to provide learning and spiritual guidance. Kshatriyas are supposed to have emanated from Brahma's shoulders and are the hereditary rulers and providers of government, order, and military security. Vaishyas, associated with Brahma's thighs, are traditionally farmers and merchants. Sudras, according to Hindu lore, sprang from Brahma's feet and are responsible for such tasks as barbering and carpentry. Omitted from this four-tier Brahmanical structure are casteless people, Harijans and non-Hindus of all kinds.

Villages may include one or several castes, and in practice there may be considerable muddling of function as, for example, when Brahmans engage in farming or lower castes manage some religious events. The rule, however, is that there is little personal mobility among castes and, although there are recorded cases of entire jatis being mobile over extended periods of time, these are rather unusual.[3] The gradual commercialization of Indian society in the

---

[2]On the subject of Hinduism, see, for example, M. N. Srinivas, *Social Change in Modern India* (Berkeley: University of California Press, 1966); David G. Mandelbaum, *Society in India* (Berkeley: University of California Press, 1970); or for a less-detailed presentation, Selig S. Harrison, *India: The Most Dangerous Decades* (Princeton, N.J.: Princeton University Press, 1960).

[3]See reference to M. N. Srinivas in part 5 of Milton Singer, *When a Great Tradition Modernizes: An Anthropological Approach to Indian Civilization* (New York: Praeger, 1972), p. 386.

past several centuries, especially since World War II, has made class—as distinct from caste—more important to the society and has thus increased personal mobility.

The kinship and hereditary relationships which regulate service and patronage within and among families are known as the *jajmani* system and are among the most important ties which bind India's traditional social system together. These are reinforced by the concepts of *dharma* (duty to fulfill the role into which a person is born) and *karma* (promise of "just rewards"), which keep individuals committed to the social system and modulate challenges to the hierarchy in such a way that adaptation is possible without obliteration of the basic structure. Also important in sustaining the system are notions of ritual purity and pollution according to which individuals, families, jatis, and castes regard many contacts (including intracaste contacts) as defiling. Procedurally, ritual and symbolic behavior are found in every society, but in India they are unusually widespread and significant as buttresses of the social order.

In determining just how important caste is to India, it is apparent that there always have been gaps between theory and practice, and that these have been widened in recent years. Rigorous application of the *jajmani* system, for example, implies the need for each village to have a large number of jatis to fulfill all the functions of the system, a situation which conflicts with the size of villages and the number of families of like jati who tend to live together in the same village. Even historically there have been departures from the formal *jajmani* system. And although tradition still grips much of rural Indian society, the meaning of universal adult franchise is that jatis which are numerically dominant within the village now are able to vie with higher-caste families for political power. Nonetheless, although changes in the structure of land tenure, increasing use of wage labor, monetization of rural India, and growing rural-urban mobility have eroded the importance of hereditary and kinship relations in the countryside, the significance of kinship, dependency, and hierarchy remains great. Even outside the village, according to one Indian sociologist, "Considerations of caste, community, and blood relationship persist at all levels and in all spheres of activity, whether it be industry, public service, or politics."[4] That this situation is beginning to change, especially at the highest reaches of government, is evinced by the fact that at the time of its 1971 war with Pakistan India had a Brahman prime minister, a Harijan defense minister, a Muslim agriculture minister, a Parsi army chief of staff, and a Sikh external affairs minister.[5]

Of India's population, roughly 65 percent is caste Hindu, 20 percent is outside the formal caste structure by virtue of belonging to untouchable or tribal groups, 10 percent is Muslim, and the remainder belongs to Sikh, Buddhist, and other religions. Historically, Indians of diverse religions have

[4]See K. Srinivasan, *Productivity and Social Environment* (New York: Asia Publishing House, 1964), pp. 76–78.

[5]See William J. Barnds, "Soviet Influence in India: A Search for the Spoils That Go with Victory," in *Soviet and Chinese Influence in the Third World* (New York: Praeger, 1975).

often not lived in harmony, and religious differences (communalism) continue to pose problems. Ainslie Embree has noted that there are two opposing views about communalism: some observers believe that South Asia's bitterly contested religious quarrels of the past millennium are due to basic religious antagonisms; others feel that "a religious vocabulary" has been used to mask the conflicts stemming from "the realities of social and economic exploitation." Undoubtedly there is merit in both of these arguments. What is important, as Embree notes, is that political leaders, in making India a "secular state" to overcome its religious differences, have justifiably been concerned not only with separating church and state, but also with making the state "religiously neutral."[6] Partition is the outstanding illustration of how religious diversity has critically determined India's path; but repeatedly since 1947, communal conflicts have deeply affected the course of events.

Regional differences, common to most large nations, are especially acute in India. There is a basic ethnic difference between the fair-skinned Aryans of the north and the dark-skinned Dravidians in the south. Moreover, there are 13 indigenous languages spoken by 10 million or more, thus vastly complicating the nation's communication problem. The current link language, English, is regarded by many Indians as unsuitable, not only because it is a foreign tongue and a reminder of the colonial period, but because it is spoken by only about 2 percent of the population. Hindi, which 30 percent speak, is the only contender as the national language, but attempts to substitute it for English have been bitterly opposed by elite groups who are more comfortable with English and by the non-Hindi-speaking peoples of southern India and other regions who regard Hindi as a threat to their unique cultural heritages and their ability to compete for government jobs.[7]

Conflict over language has waxed hot and cold depending on the vigor with which the Hindi proponents pressed their case. It has been violent on occasion, as in 1964 when more than 50 persons lost their lives during anti-Hindi agitation spearheaded by student groups in the state of Tamil Nadu.[8] In response to this conflict, Delhi became more attuned to the wishes of non-Hindi-speaking groups. Its strategy of using English for many important functions while simultaneously and very gradually extending the knowledge of Hindi, embodied in the Official Languages (Amendment) Act of 1967, offers some hope for a very long-term solution of this vexing problem.

Various nonlinguistic regional issues (statewide division of development funds, sharing of river waters, etc.) have traditionally raised acrimonious debates. The case-by-case solutions which they have demanded have been costly

[6]Ainslie T. Embree, "Pluralism and National Integration: The Indian Experience," *Journal of International Affairs*, vol. 27, no. 1, January 1973, pp. 49–50.

[7]W. H. Morris-Jones, *The Government and Politics of India* (New York: Anchor Books, 1967), p. 93.

[8]Robert L. Hardgrave, Jr., *India: Government and Politics in a Developing Nation* (New York: Harcourt, Brace & World, 1970), p. 113.

in terms of the scarce political and economic capital expended. Politically, regionalism is reflected both in interstate rivalry and in friction between the Center and state governments. It has grown as the initial Congress party monopoly of state governments has been broken. For example, after winning power in Tamil Nadu (1967), the regionally based DMK party fought tenaciously to have a large measure of authority for industrial policy taken from Delhi and vested in the state governments.[9] Not surpisingly, the Center's reaction to this idea was thunderous silence.

Overlapping the caste, communal, and regional differences in Indian society are class distinctions. The emergence of class as a factor in Indian society has been hastened by recent developments such as industrialization, constitutional democracy, and national independence. Its implications vary according to its different manifestations: (1) "modern" and "traditional" society, (2) urban and rural populations, (3) elite and nonelite elements of society, as well as (4) the rich and poor.

According to Marx, peasants could not form a class because relations among them are "strictly local—the identity of their interest begets no unity, no natural union, and no political organization."[10] Marx was correct in the sense that the Indian peasantry as a whole has not coalesced into a potent political force, but rural society shows definite class structure, overlaid on caste and other elements. Indeed, well-to-do peasants have demonstrated a keen ability to organize politically, although, true to Marx's hypothesis, Naxalite and other radical peasant movements generally have been notable failures. Nonetheless, rural India is hardly the first area where the class struggle was slow to develop and evidence is accumulating that improving communications, better leadership, and more desperate economic conditions will make the less-well-off peasant class a more powerful political influence in the future.

In urban India, the division into lower, middle, and upper classes is more akin to the structure of Western society, and although the traditional social structure has shown remarkable adaptability,[11] modernization is more apparent than in rural areas.[12] The chaos of city streets, public transportation, and bazaars, and the impersonality of bureaucratic and factory jobs have tended to homogenize individuals' public lives and even to diminish the latitutde for adhering to traditional mores in private. Although urban housing patterns still

---

[9]See the *Report of the Centre-State Relations Inquiry Committee* (P. V. Rajamannar, chairman), (Madras: Government of Tamil Nadu, 1971).

[10]Quoted in Lloyd I, Rudolph and Suzanne H. Rudolph, *The Modernity of Tradition* (Chicago: University of Chicago Press, 1967), p. 18.

[11]Even in the cities, where democratic institutions, schools, courts, and other alternatives to "traditional" sources of authority are at their strongest, sociologists find the caste system able to change fast enough to maintain its relevance. See, for example. Owen M. Lynch, *The Politics of Untouchability: Social Mobility and Social Change in a City of India* (New York: Columbia University Press, 1969), pp. 203–211.

[12]See, for example, M. Singer, *When a Great Tradition Modernizes*, op. cit.

show considerable clustering by caste and religion, such modern influences as class, wealth, and occupation also determine where people live. Generalizations about these issues are difficult because the relative importance of traditional and modern life-styles—the significance of adaptability and radical social change—vary enormously among individuals, and even in each individual's approach to different types of social situations.

Historical, caste, religious, and regional factors diminish the force of what in other countries are natural alliances between classes and parties. In India, for example, a significant proportion of the leftist leadership comes from elite groups. Similarly, the strength of communism from state to state correlates poorly with the level of industrialization.[13] To the extent that there is a connection between class and political affiliation, it is especially important for the Congress and Communist parties. Congress draws proportionately more strength from the relatively well-to-do farmers and urban groups, whereas the Communists appeal to the urban working class and rural poor, particularly in Kerala and West Bengal.[14]

Over an extended period of time the Congress party has struggled mightily to accommodate the interests of all classes, an extraordinary effort that has accomplished much for its continuing dominance of Indian politics. Few problems, however, have proved more intractable for the Congress and the Indian government than obtaining the cooperation of various social groups. Workers' organizations, lobbies of well-to-do farmers, business associations, and the bureaucracy itself have demonstrated increasing militancy in their demands and growing skill in using the Congress and other channels to achieve their objectives.

In addition to the social distinctions noted above, there are cleavages and centrifugal forces arising from ideology, attitudes, and individual personalities.[15] Before addressing these, however, it is necessary to consider the mix of geographic, historical, traditional, and modern factors which have combined to strengthen rather than weaken Delhi's writ. Although India's highly structured social system is an essentially conservative force, it has demonstrated great adaptability. By virtue of these seemingly contradictory characteristics it has been able to survive and provide India with a "social cement" of unusual durability. Consequently, if India's leaders sought to emulate the Chinese government and destroy the existing social order, a great barrier to development would be removed but perhaps only at the cost of national disintegration (social and perhaps even geographic). So long as the system remains in place, however, India's modernizers must contend with hierarchical relationships,

[13]See Paul R. Brass, "Political Parties of the Radical Left in South Asian Politics," in Paul R. Brass and Marcus F. Franda, eds., *Radical Politics in South Asia* (Cambridge, Mass.: M.I.T. Press, 1973), pp. 3–116.

[14]See D. L. Seth, "Profiles of Party Support in 1967," *Economic and Political Weekly*, Annual Number, January 1971.

[15]On the significance of personality, see Rosen, op. cit., pp. 87–90.

the immobility sanctioned by the hereditary role most individuals are born with, disparities of wealth and welfare, and the Hindu value system which, by its doctrine of reincarnation, "tends to lower the level of human aspirations, but places a premium on passive acceptance rather than amelioration of the human situation, whether by hard work or by social reform."[16]

Resistance to change is due in large part to vested interests. Because the political, social, and economic powers normally reinforce one another, mobility emanating from any one of these sources threatens the power balance outstanding among the others and, not unnaturally, is forcefully resisted by those who stand to lose. In addition, India is no different from other countries in that all but the very lowest on the social ladder have something to lose as society evolves. Opposition to change, however, is not merely the result of an anachronistic system struggling for self-preservation, or the effort of an elite to maintain its position. In a nation as poor as India, and as beset with population and resource problems, tolerance for new adversities is low; individuals are inclined to protect themselves against risks, even at the expense of forgoing potential benefits. In view of the search for security by workers,[17] it is not surprising that India and other developing countries have proved to be conservative and resistant to change, and that rhetoric—the halfway house between indifference and action—occupies an important place in Indian society.

It would be a grave error, however, to understate India's adaptability and openness to change. These are most tangibly demonstrated in its new industrial sector, and, as should be evident from the discussion of agriculture in Chapter 8, even the humblest of Indian farmers are not averse to adopting new production techniques when it can be demonstrated that they will increase profits. As phrased by Milton Singer:

> Indian society and culture are not "traditional" in the nineteenth-century stereotype that is dominated by unchanging traditions and immemorial customs. . . . The traditionalism of Indian civilization lies elsewhere—in its capacity to incorporate innovations into an expanding and changing structure of culture and society.[18]

Singer's point is supported by historical evidence. Repeatedly invaded, India has undergone long periods of absorbing foreign customs and Indianizing the invaders. Admittedly, Hindus reject the historical legitimacy of Islamic rule, and Muslims are alien to Hindu customs. Moreover, as noted by Selig Harrison; "Each region can claim its own golden age somewhere in the millennia of Indian history, but one region's golden age was often another's dark age."[19]

[16]H. W. Kapp, *Hindu Culture, Economic Development, and Economic Planning in India* (Bombay: Asia Publishing Co., 1963), p. 16.

[17]Richard Lambert, *Workers, Factories, and Social Change in India* (Princeton, N.J.: Princeton University Press, 1963).

[18]See M. Singer, *When a Great Tradition Modernizes*, op. cit., p. 385.

[19]Harrison, op. cit., p. 13.

Nonetheless, as noted by Robert Frykenberg, the struggle for political legitimacy has been fought at another level, the opposition of local and central forces. Traditionally, "it is clear that, just as district officers undermined central authority, they in turn were undermined by village leaders." India's political structure must be seen as the exercise of power within power; there has been "no bedrock of ultimate loyalty beyond family, caste, and village"; and local forces, through direct opposition to and corruption of the agents of central power, have typically resisted central power.[20] In short, conflict has been institutionalized and has thus been reduced as a threat to the society.

Tolerance and the ability to cope with diversity—even thrive on internal differences—are not just phenomena of India's past quarter century. Their lineage goes back at least to the third century B.C., when the Hindu emperor Ashoka adopted Buddhism and converted many Indians to that religion through peaceful means. Intellectual liberalism was the rule in the reigns of the Hindu ruler Harsha (seventh century) and the Mogul emperor Akbar (sixteenth century), who both were able to instill more than the normal amount of harmony and national integrity in India. Akbar is even alleged to have incorporated the principle of tolerance into his personal life by having Hindu, Muslim, and Christian wives, simultaneously. The strength of geographic and historical continuity follows from the basic Indianness of Indians. Muslims in Bengal, for example, are largely converts from Hinduism and often bear more cultural affinity to other Bengalis than to Muslims from other parts of India.

In explaining India's capacity to abide diversity, the role of the foreigner looms large. The strength of villages, derived from the constant need to counter potential exploitation by outsiders, is paralleled by India's well-developed ability to react to foreign influences with a mixture of adaptation and indifference which preserves the basic Indianness of society. Recurrent invasion of South Asia has not only had the negative effect of making Indians suspicious of foreigners, but also the positive effect of making the country responsive to the dictates of nationalism. Since Independence, the growing cohesiveness of India must be ascribed not only to the integrative forces of better education, improved communications, and so forth, but equally to the existence of external threats such as Pakistan. It is significant that India's two most significant secessionist threats came from areas as diverse as Tamil Nadu and Nagaland, regions geographically remote from Pakistan, and also where Delhi had been insensitive to local issues, including language.

In summary, the pluralism of Indian society is matched by impressive forces of national cohesion. Integrative factors, which have prevailed to various degrees in the course of India's history, received some impetus during the period of Mogul authority and, subsequently, during the colonial period. They

[20]Robert E. Frykenberg, "Traditional Process of Power in South India: An Historical Analysis of Local Influence," in Reinhard Bendix, ed., *State and Society* (Berkeley: University of California Press, 1968), pp. 107–125.

have been most powerful, however, in the post-Independence years when the unifying concept of nationalism combined with improved communications. The prospect is that unless Delhi should be so absentminded as to try to force states to follow nonvital social or economic policies of proved unpalatability (enforcing Hindi, for example), the integrity of India as a nation will not be seriously challenged from within. Nonetheless divisions within India will not disappear and will require sustained and skillful conciliation by India's political leaders if they are to be prevented from undermining the development effort.

Political Ideology: The Force of Democracy

In his *Ethics*, Aristotle distinguished between timocracy (rule by all those who are educated and qualified to wield power) and its degenerate case, democracy (rule by the masses). India's situation does not fit precisely into either category; it is democratic in principle, but in practice it combines rule by the many and the few. Its distinctive feature, which Aristotle can be excused for not forecasting, is that permeating India's elaborate web of social hierarchy there is systemic elitism which contravenes the nation's egalitarian Constitution. The most convincing explanation for departures from democratic practice, one which does not challenge India's acceptance of democracy as a goal, is that India has a history of conquest by local and foreign princes. This heritage, in combination with the rigid structure of Indian society, in which rule from above and obedience from below were the accepted norms, has constituted a major barrier to the introduction of democracy and could not be shed overnight.

The colonial period and the nationalist struggle substantially altered Indian conceptions of how society should be organized. A large number of Indians received some exposure to the relatively egalitarian sociopolitcal system of the British, but because expatriate British often showed disdain for Indians, Western egalitarianism appeared to many as flawed, if not hypocritical. Whether the colonial period delayed India's transition to a more modern society is a moot point, beyond the scope of this book. What is clear is that one of the principal British contributions to India was the idea of constitutional democracy; Gandhi and other leaders have accepted it and made it a basic tenet for the new nation.

India's attachment to democracy has had significant consequences for development insofar as the operations of legislative, administrative, and judicial branches of government have emphasized constitutionality and correct procedure. In practice, of course, application of these legal principles to economic issues has sometimes been inimical to rapid change; it has thus contributed to both social stability and economic stagnation. Less concern for legal procedure would not necessarily lead to economic progress, however, and it would be wrong to assume that India could not develop in spite of its devotion to constitutional principles. The point here is central to the political dilemma which was one element of Prime Minister Indira Gandhi's 1975 crisis: that the functioning of an economy under a democratic regime may call for policies that are somewhat different from those under an authoritarian system. According to a growing number of observers, India's slow development stems from its effort to run a "command economy" with a political system which does not have adequate authority for the task.[21] The basis for this argument is that the practice of democracy assumes more sophistication and education on the part of India's masses than in fact exists. This thesis, however, remains far from proved. Its weaknesses are that it makes no allowance for the difficulties of reconciling representative government with India's traditional social structures, virtually overnight, and that it ignores the subjective question of what alternatives there are to democracy in the short and long run.

Gandhism, Capitalism, and Socialism

In contrast to the readiness with which India was able to agree on democracy as its political goal, there has been an unending and bitter debate over the choice of an economic system. Although the governments of most countries which obtained their political independence after World War II have taken active roles to spur economic modernization (it was only at the close of the 1960s that it became popular to question the desirability of modernization and that thought was given to preserving the "cultural authenticity" of societies), they have enjoyed an element of flexibility in the choice between socialist and capitalist alternatives, and they have often adopted compromises between these two extremes. In the case of India, however, the decision was more complex: not only were advocates of both the right and the left powerful and highly sophisticated, but the philosophical legacy of Gandhi, blending traditional social structure with modern egalitarianism, posed a magnetic third choice.

Mahatma Gandhi's approach to society—a product of his personal experiences, the omnipresence of colonial rule, and India's social heritage—is an extraordinary mixture of prescriptions guiding the choice of social goals and means for their achievement; of specific changes needed in India and general remedies for the world order; and of thinking and action. India's acceptance, in principle, of his emphasis on the need for change (social modernization, elimination of caste, egalitarianism, and so forth) through orderly and peaceful means is among the reasons why John Lewis has described "India's Distinctive Development Process" as one of "radical economic change."[22]

In advocating material and moral equality, Gandhi conceived of a society where injustice would be removed peacefully through moral force and through

---

[21]Baldev Raj Nayar, for example, in applying David Apter's general theoretical frame, reaches the conclusions that a "reconciliation" type of economic strategy is suited to India's political and social system, and that the government has sought to apply a "mobilization" strategy which is inappropriate. See Baldev Raj Nayar, *The Modernization Imperative and Indian Planning* (Delhi: Vikas Publications, 1972), pp. 72–73.

[22]John P. Lewis, *Quiet Crisis in India* (Washington, D.C.: The Brookings Institution, 1962), p. 8.

the transformation of individuals into better members of the community. Because the betterment of society was envisaged as stemming from the improvement of individuals and without coercion, the Gandhian approach proceeds from the people rather than by government fiat. Indeed, it is highly suspicious of centralized power in all forms. The totality of Gandhi's approach is often denoted by the word *sarvodaya,* loosely translated as "welfare for all" or "service to all."[23]

Gandhi rejected class conflict and advocated egalitarian objectives such as voluntary redistribution of wealth, minimum wages, income ceilings, and widespread distribution of employment opportunities. While not opposed to some forms of large-scale industrialization, he was wary of its potential for displacing labor, concentrating wealth, and disrupting the village-based social system which he regarded as ideal. In his view, promotion of traditional methods of production and cottage industries promised to make the village self-sufficient and permit simple decentralized government to assume responsibility for most official functions. The Bhoodan movement of voluntary redistribution of land, begun by Vinoba Bhave and continued by Jayaprakash Narayan, is a characteristic manifestation of Gandhian economic thinking. Although Bhoodan has not fully lived up to the expectations of its leaders, and there are few examples of pure Gandhism applied on a large scale in India, the influence of Gandhi is significant insofar as it combines with other forces and permeates government policy and the larger social system. Indeed, when younger economists such as K. N. Raj and Mahbub ul Haq advocate more attention to administrative decentralization, labor-intensive technology, and other "new" development techniques, they might correctly be described as "neo-Gandhian."

The attitudes of both socialists and capitalists have been in stark contrast to Gandhism on a number of issues. They have been anxious to industrialize India through large investments. They have been more willing to rely on centralization of political and economic power at the expense of local initiative. And they have been more inclined to use foreign resources to accelerate the process of industrialization.

Indian socialism, which owes its popularity to many factors, has been influenced by two quite different movements: democratic Fabianism, as formulated at the London School of Economics, and Soviet Marxism. The appeal of Fabianism is intellectual in the sense that the doctrines of (1) social ownership and social management of the means of production and (2) egalitarian distribution of output were bound to attract Indian leaders who were committed to taking an active role in speeding their nation's development. Socialism had an additional attraction for the Indian people because of a linguistic quirk; in the

[23]Margaret W. Fisher and Joan V. Bondurant, *Indian Approaches to a Socialist Society,* Indian Press Digests, Monograph Series No. 2, Institute of International Studies, University of California at Berkeley, July 1956, p. 35.

1930s "socialism" was incorrectly translated in many Indian languages by a word which implied egalitarianism.[24]

The strength of Marxist socialism was largely practical. Nehru and others admired the speed with which the Soviets had modernized their economy, and some of them believed that the Soviet experience was more relevant for India than the West's more gradual industrialization in the nineteenth century. A third dimension relates to foreign affairs: socialism was a unifying concept and basis of identification for the "nonaligned" countries of which India was a leader. This has remained the case even though nonsocialist nations have since identified themselves with the Third World movement and India's leadership position has been eroded.

Although Jayaprakash Narayan, Acharya Kripalani, and a considerable body of India's intellectual elite were confirmed and active socialists, it was Jawaharlal Nehru who was most responsible for establishing socialism as a leading influence on official policy. According to one of his biographers, Michael Brecher, "Nehru is a convinced socialist but he is not a Communist. . . . He drank deeply of Marxist literature in the thirties but he *never* became intoxicated."[25] Nehru recognized that the practice of socialism in India would have to differ from the pattern elsewhere and, according to L. K. Jha, he "was conscious of the danger in adopting a label which had already been used in a number of countries to describe a variety of socio-economic systems, no one of which was exactly what India wanted."[26] Arun Shourie, in chiding those who aspire to gain influence in India by quoting Nehru, has noted that because many of Nehru's remarks were designed for particular times and audiences, they are contradictory.[27] Nonetheless, on the basis of what Nehru said and what he did, we can be fairly certain that the notion of socialism which he sought to introduce in India had among its principal elements (1) improvement of the position of the poor and socially disadvantaged; (2) rapid industrialization based on investment in heavy industry and expansion of the public sector; (3) central planning and government control over the economy through, in many areas, substitution of administrative controls for market forces of supply and demand; (4) a pragmatic and flexible approach to India's problems; and (5) democracy.

Nehru gave Indian socialism both procedural and objective content. His insight on India's need for a unique brand of socialism was vindicated by the

[24]L. K. Jha, "Democracy and Socialism in India," *India News,* Apr. 6, 1973. In private correspondence Governor Jha has noted that socialism was translated by the Hindi *samyavad—samya* meaning "equality" and *vad* meaning "ism." The correct translation, in his view, would be *samajvad—samaj* meaning "society".

[25]Michael Brecher, *Nehru: A Political Biography,* abridged ed. (Boston: Beacon Press, 1962), p. 233.

[26]Jha, op. cit.

[27]Arun Shourie, "On Citing the Scriptures," *Economic and Political Weekly,* Aug. 25, 1973, pp. 1539–1541.

special character of Indian society and its capacity to absorb socialist doctrine. The business community, for example, had recognized the need for some official effort to spur India's economic development when it produced the so-called Bombay Plan in 1944, but it was strongly opposed to public ownership of industry. Moreover, socialism per se was too intellectual to attract mass support, and its strength therefore came from militants within the Congress and Communist parties.[28] This is illustrated by the experience of India's Socialist party, which has continued in existence, but whose role has been more as the conscience of the nation than as a political power in its own right. It is hardly surprising, therefore, that it was not until December 1954 that the Indian Parliament passed a resolution calling for a "socialist pattern of society," and not until January 1955 that the Congress party, meeting at Avadi, made a similar pledge. Nor is it surprising that Nehru's motive for the timing of this apparent leftward shift is unclear. The only reason cited by Brecher is that during a 1954 visit to China Nehru had gained the impression that China's growth rate was faster than India's and that this endangered India's potential position in Asia.[29]

The recent course of free enterprise in India has proceeded at two quite different levels, rural and urban. The place of the wealthy landowners (frequently known in India as kulaks) was paralleled in the cities and towns by a rising upper-middle-class bourgeoisie. Wealthy families such as the Tatas and Birlas, with industiral empires comparable to those of the Carnegies and Vanderbilts, stand at the apex of Indian capitalism. Because of its importance in both rural and urban structures, Indian capitalism has retained considerable political power, but it has been subject to unremitting attack and has gradually lost some of its authority.

Capitalism's strength lies not only in the political power wielded by private individuals and associations, but also in the economic contribtuion that private capital, management expertise, and initiative offer to Indian development. Nehru recognized this potential and, on occasion, was a most articulate proponent of private enterprise. Chester Bowles, twice United States Ambassador to India, was a strong advocate of Indian private enterprise on grounds that economic risk taking is better done outside government. As seen by Bowles, economic failures of private entrepreneurs are benign compared with failures of public enterprise which, at the extreme, may cause governments to fall. The threat posed by failure of any government-owned enterprise in a democracy puts a heavy premium on public sector managers and their political superiors to

[28]The complexity of socialist penetration of Indian politics is indicated by an analytic piece entitled "Congress, Leftists in Dogfight," by Kewal Varma, in the *Financial Express*, June 21, 1972. Varma notes the fragmentation of socialists *within* the Congress according to whether the individual came from the Communist camp, Praja Socialist party, or smaller leftist parties. He describes the infighting as venomous and "most strange because there is hardly any difference between the groups on major policy objectives."

[29]Brecher, op. cit., p. 203.

act according to rigid SOPs, unimaginatively, and risklessly, whatever the cost—hardly a dynamic prescription for bringing about social and economic development.[30]

While not without means to defend itself, capitalism has not attracted serious intellectual support, albeit there has been a large body of well-to-do farmers who have defended private ownership and the existing income distribution. Capitalism's lack of appeal for the masses derives not only from its insensitivity to equity but its identification with the laissez faire policies and foreign domination of the colonial period. Finally, heavy concentration of the ownership of Indian industry in the hands of a tiny minority and the monopolistic practices of private industry are hardly likely to have endeared capitalists to the Indian people, a point which leftist politicians have advertised widely. In practice, the weight of anticapitalist pressure has been directed against privileged individuals rather than against antisocial commercial practices. This is why capitalism has been defended tooth and nail by those who stood to lose, whereas the antisocial practices of private enterprise have gone relatively untouched and have sometimes become incorporated in the practices of public enterprise. The convergence in the style of operations of public and private sector firms is a subject to which we shall return in Chapter 7.

Ideology in Practice

As seen by David Apter, "Ideology involves more than doctrine." It may link "particular actions and mundane practices with a wider set of meanings, giving social conduct a more honorable and dignified complexion." or it may serve as a "cloak for shabby motives and appearances." Moreover, "ideology is not philosophy. . . . It is in the curious position of being an abstraction that is less abstract than the abstractions contained within it." The importance of ideology to social reformers is that it "is a way of indicating the moral superiority of new ideas."[31] Thus, for example, when Nehru redirected India's effort from large cooperative societies to small ones, his rhetoric emphasized the need to encourage village-level self-reliance. His larger objective, to transfer more of the administrative responsibility for the cooperative movement from the Reserve Bank of India in Bombay to the Delhi bureaucracy, was scarcely mentioned.[32]

What can be said about the practical implications of ideology in India? Gandhian, socialist, and capitalist ideological thinking has rarely been precise but, as in most countries, the doctrines appear crystal clear compared to the melange of policies included in party platforms. Rhetorically, despite their disagreements on private enterprise, both left and right parties in India have

[30]Chester Bowles, "The Developing Nations' Greatest Need," *New York Times Magazine*, Apr. 12, 1964.

[31]David E. Apter, *The Politics of Modernization* (Chicago: University of Chicago Press, 1965), p. 314.

[32]Daniel Thorner, *Agricultural Cooperatives in India: A Field Report* (New York: Asia Publishing House, 1964), pp. 19–20.

extolled the essentially hierarchical virtues of traditional India as well as a more egalitarian and modern pattern of society. Moreover, even on real issues such as bank nationalization (1969) and exchange-rate devaluation (1966) there has been a surprising amount of agreement in the public postures of liberal and conservative forces. This suggests that the Indian political scene is as attuned to the acquisition of power as to the implementation of any particular ideology. This thesis is supported by the variety of ideologies existing within most political parties, with the notable exception of the Communist and Socialist parties. The prime example of mixed ideologies has been the Congress, which has striven to sustain not only left and right factions, but subgroups at both extremes and in the middle. Congress's diversity and its long-standing dominance in Indian politics are largely explained by its pre-Independence heritage. Because of the preeminence of Independence as a political issue, the Congress attracted members with a wide diversity of economic views. It owed its strength to the combination of (1) mass support in rural India; (2) the political and organizing role of its intellectual elite; and (3) the financial contributions of nationalist-inclined industrialists and wealthy landowners. Thus, when the Congress became India's ruling power, its choice of economic policies was affected by commitments to various factions of the party and a strong desire not to alienate any of its supporters.

The conclusion toward which this discussion leads is that, except for democracy, which modern India has never challenged as an objective, there have been so many ideological differences in India as to prevent any one approach from becoming dominant. In practice, for each policy objective (democracy, egalitarianism, nationalism, and centralization) there are one or several counterobjectives (authoritarianism, elitism, internationalism, and decentralization). In principle, the juxtaposition of these conflicting goals should have been an asset to India's development process because it invited the widest possible range of criticism of existing practice and encouraged innovative thinking. In practice, such benefits have been reaped, but Indian pluralism also has been a liability. The recurrent need to compromise has often subverted rational policy by (1) delaying decisions, (2) requiring second-best solutions, (3) leading to the adoption of inconsistent policies, and (4) causing too frequent changes in policy in response to shifting balances of political power.

In testing the constancy of ideology as a determinant of Indian policy, one can identify six inflection points at which critical decisions reversing the direction of economic policy were made. As suggested earlier, the give and take appears to be mainly between socialist and capitalist forces, but Gandhian factors also played a role. Moreover, the actual course of events coincides only roughly with the notion of a cyclical pattern.

¶ 1948: When announced, India's first Industrial Policy Resolution was regarded as a retreat from socialism. Nehru defended it on grounds that the economy was weak and that the achievement of India's economic development required full participation of the private sector.

¶ 1955: In the wake of a generally successful First Five-Year Plan, the Congress pledged itself to a "socialist pattern of society," the Imperial Bank was nationalized, and the decision was made to have a bold Second Plan.

¶ 1957: To quell mounting business anxiety and encourage investment, a de facto compromise was made between left and right forces whereby *both* the public and private sectors would advance swiftly.[33] This compromise, while not reflected in any change of the language of the revised Industrial Policy Resolution (1956), was a real factor, as indicated by the subsequent actions of government and business.

¶ 1966: Owing to a devastating drought, foreign exchange shortage, and industrial bottlenecks, a retreat was made from socialist policies. Greater reliance was placed on the free play of supply and demand, import restrictions were liberalized, and investment decisions were redirected toward productivity at the expense of egalitarianism.

¶ 1969: In response to India's comfortable food position and divisive political situation, Mrs. Gandhi bifurcated the Congress party and shifted toward socialist policies. Banks and other private firms were nationalized and the Planning Commission put new emphasis on social justice rather than growth.

¶ 1974: Agricultural and industrial reverses caused mounting disaffection with leftist sloganeering and led India to deemphasize socialist policies. After a one-year trial, the wheat trade was denationalized and, in many areas, private enterprise was accorded greater scope for its operations. Budget constraints restricted social programs.

This simplified and abbreviated description of critical moments in India's post-Independence experience suggests the existence of (1) an economic cycle which has ranged from stagnation to lively development and (2) a policy cycle which has fluctuated between doctrinaire socialism and a more liberal, pragmatic approach. Evidence to support this observation, along with the further thesis that the two cycles are linked in a relationship of mutual causality, comes from various sources which we shall examine in succeeding chapters. Suffice it here to say that the existence of a policy cycle undermines the criticism often made by Westerners and some Indians to the effect that India's policies are motivated mainly by ideology. Nevertheless, the linkage between economic progress and ideological policies can still be traced according to a rough, circular pattern in which economic growth (such as the record harvests attributable to the green revolution) creates confidence and invites Indian leaders to experiment with socialist economic policies (such as the 1973 nationalization of the wholesale wheat trade). Because many of these policies are unproductive, the economy eventually falls into adversity; this, in turn, causes government to

[33]See Brecher, op. cit., p. 204.

adopt more pragmatic measures (such as denationalization of the wheat markets), and as these are successful, a new turn of the cycle begins.

Ideology's importance to India's development is overrated, perhaps because failures attributable to ideology are more apparent than successes. Indeed, although India in 1975 is a more socialist state than it was in 1947, and political arguments are often couched in socialist rhetoric, Indian economic policy has been less dominated by ideology than its critics charge. At the macroeconomic level, India has been willing to retreat from doctrinaire socialism when the economy was in trouble. At the microeconomic level, many experiments which have not worked have been jettisoned or modified. Moreover, when forced to deal with crisis situations, policy has been extremely pragmatic and effective. Finally, there are a number of economic policy areas (size of money supply, agricultural research and extension, investment in transportation infrastructure, and so forth) where little attention has been paid to ideological considerations.

The explanation for this state of affairs lies partly in the presence in India of nonsocialist ideologies. Socialism may be more significant than its rivals, but there are some issues and some time periods when its proponents are weaker than the opposition. Of still greater significance is the existence of what might be called a "pragmatic threshold"; socialist policies which go beyond this point, by imposing what government regards as excessive short-term costs, are reversed or modified. Thus, one can justify the conclusions that (1) conflict among ideologies is a prominent feature of the Indian political scene, (2) no ideology has a monopoly over policy making, and (3) socialism is more prominent than its rivals. It is only in an authoritarian nation, which India is not, that one would expect to find a monolithic political and economic policy role for ideology.

Sources of Political Power

In 1947, the transfer of power from a colonial to an Indian government was exciting, not only because alien rule had ended but also because of the conditions under which this change took place. World history shows few precedents for the peaceful transfer of sovereignty and, even more novel, the extension of universal adult franchise to a nation of 360 million persons. The large size of India's population, the speed with which the new Indian government extended its writ to an area larger than that controlled by any of India's precolonial rulers, India's geopolitical importance, the significance of Indian Independence for the fast-withering British Empire, and the recently enhanced scope for government to concern itself with economic and social affairs are reasons why Independence was viewed globally as an important event with major implications for the world's future.

The haste with which the British departed the subcontinent made it particularly difficult to predict how independent India would be governed, much more whether its constituent states would cohere as a nation. Except for Partition, however, the possible South Asian disaster scenarios have been more in the minds of foreign observers than in the actions of the Indian people and their leaders. India's political leaders adopted the Western idea of constitutional democracy, and nationalism emerged in the post-World War II years as a greater binding force than many had anticipated. It is not so surprising, therefore, that under Congress party tutelage the administrative and judicial arms of government continued to function after 1947 and that provision was made for a permanent legislature. The sections which follow address the question of political power in India: who holds it, and how it is exercised.

Rural India

In India, as elsewhere, the long-term strength of constitutional democracy is closely related to the state of social justice and the opportunity for participation by members of the society. To what degree, however, can a population which is generally poor, illiterate, inexperienced in national political affairs, and inured to traditional and hierarchical relationships shoulder the responsibilities of democracy just because a constitution has been promulgated?

Not surprisingly, India's peasant class strongly supported the Congress at the polls. The Congress was the party of Independence; it occupied the political center through an array of candidates whose positions ranged from left to right; and it was the party in power, positioned to reward its friends and punish its opponents. But for an individual to vote for a political party does not ensure its responsiveness to his interests. A 1973 report by the Task Force on Agrarian Relations is one among many official findings which show that the poorer peasants are politically unorganized at state and national levels, unable to articulate their just demands, and therefore neglected by government and disadvantaged within the society.[34] India's rural poor have been outbid, so to speak, by the wealthier farmers. Writing in 1970, Rajni Kothari put it this way:

> The newest power group in Indian politics is that of the kulaks, the class of independent owner-cultivators drawn from a variety of social groups, who are making agriculture a thriving business proposition and one that provides them with a base for effective political bargaining at higher level.[35]

Political power in India is derived from, and exercised at, local, state, and national levels. The current situation in India is reminiscent of the historical dualism between village power and central power in which cadres of administrators played an intermediating role. But it is also quite different insofar as the new democracy requires that demands and communications should be transmitted between the governed and the governors, not just in one direction.

[34]*Report of the Task Force on Agrarian Relations* (New Delhi: GOI, Planning Commission, 1973), p. 25.

[35]Rajni Kothari, *Politics in India* (New Delhi: Orient Longmans Ltd., first published by Little, Brown & Co., 1970), p. 354.

Moreover, in contrast to the colonial administration's preoccupations with law and order and revenue collection, India's government now has assumed responsibility for improving the nation's socioeconomic situation.

In 1958, India began to introduce the so-called *panchayati raj* system of local self-government not only for the purpose of gaining more central control in some areas, but to make the voice of the people audible, and to nourish democratic decentralization. The three-tier system now operates at village, block, and district levels within most states, and its officials have acquired varying amounts of administrative and development responsibilities. Its effectiveness in representing the rural masses has been hampered, however, by such factors as (1) the inexperience of most peasants in using such institutions; (2) the ability of local elites (often well-to-do peasants) to control the panchayati raj system and use it for their own purposes; and (3) the competing sources of power which are represented at state and central governments.

It is difficult to generalize about the political situation of poor peasants. In contrast to the well-to-do rural interests which tend to reign supreme at the state government level, the ability of the very poor to exercise power at the village level varies enormously. The interests of poor peasants are usually better represented in Delhi than at the state level. This is because national leaders tend to be less parochial than their counterparts at the various local levels rather than because of any difference in the capacity of the people to make known their needs.

Studies of the social background of Indian parliamentarians reveal a systematic bias in favor of the affluent, educated, and urbanized minorities in which well-to-do rural interests hold a share of central power.[36] These elites maintain their status through various means, including (1) their superior economic position, which also affords them control over the economic destiny of others; (2) their active participation in political party activities; and (3) their holding of party office, elective government office, and bureaucratic positions. As India modernizes, the government is increasingly able to provide valuable allocations of electricity, water, fertilizer, and bank credit. This change has not been lost on India's rural elite who, in pursuit of economic advantage and in contrast to the poorer peasantry, have emerged as a formidable political force.

The Party

Mahatma Gandhi regarded Independence as the primary, if not the only, legitimate political goal of the Congress. He distinguished social service as the party's continuing task and in January 1948, on the eve of his assassination, he urged that the Congress terminate its political role.[37] Gandhi's wish was not followed, however, partly because many Indians believed that a consensus government would be the most effective way to meet India's post-Indepen-

---

[36]See, for example, Satish K. Arora, "Social Background of the Fifth Lok Sabha," *Economic and Political Weekly,* Special Number, August 1973, pp. 1433–1440.

[37]Morris-Jones, op. cit., p. 79.

dence problems, and partly because Congress leaders hesitated to renounce their privileged positions and vie with one another for power. As a consequence, the Congress has continuously dominated the national political scene, even after a massive setback in the 1967 parliamentary elections indicated that other political forces were gaining strength.

The Congress began its life in 1885 as an organization of upper-class, urban Indians who sought greater privileges from the British within the then existing order of colonial rule. The process of expanding its membership, broadening its base to include people from diverse social backgrounds, and increasing its opposition to the British was gradual and did not progress very quickly until Gandhi's return to India after World War I. Gandhi's early efforts to universalize the Congress were thwarted by the alienation of low-caste groups owing to the party's domination by Brahmans, and also by the self-serving pro-British sentiments of India's elites such as the traditional ruling class and many large landholders.

By 1947, however, the political center of gravity of the Congress had shifted from urban to rural and the party was widely acclaimed as the Party of Independence. The common interest of the Congress in broadening its base and of local groups in affiliating themselves with the dominant party had greatly strengthened the Congress, and despite defections by right and left factions, the party has continued to include a wide diversity of political ideologies. Nonetheless, although almost all the diverse interests within the Congress have symbolic representation,[38] real power has generally been kept in the hands of the politically active—the urban petty bourgeoisie and the newly emergent rural upper middle class.

The answer to the question of how the Congress decides on its political platform is found in the party's enormously complex structure.[39] Congress committees, which are responsible for the party's organization, operate at the national, state, and local levels. Because members of each committee are elected by the next smaller territorial committee, a clear link is established between the local level and the All-India Congress Committee (AICC), the apex of the pyramid. The party's executive, the Congress Working Committee (CWC), is partly elected by the AICC and partly appointed by the president of the Congress party, but it is also responsible to special-interest groups such as the trade unions, business associations, and women's groups, and to others with special claim to influence, such as ideologues and party members serving in government.

The relationship between the Congress party and the Congress-controlled

---

[38]See, for example, Norman K. Nicolson, "The Indian Council of Ministers: An Analysis of Legislative and Organizational Careers," paper presented at the 25th Annual Meeting of the Association of Asian Studies, Chicago, April 1973.

[39]For a full unraveling of the structure and analysis of its consequences, see Myron Weiner, *Party Building in a New Nation* (Chicago: University of Chicago Press, 1967).

central and state governments is symbiotic in the sense that party leaders are often prominent in the government and vice versa. Government policy, however, is not a carbon copy of the party platform nor is the reverse true. Indeed, within two months of Independence, when Acharya Kripalani resigned as Congress president, the reason was not just that the job had become less important after Independence but that there was inadequate harmony between party and government. In contrast, during the years 1951–1954, Nehru served simultaneously as prime minister and party president in order to reduce conflict and mobilize support for his program. He did so with misgivings, however, insofar as he personally favored a sharp distinction between the party and the government systems. Nehru is quoted as saying that "normally, a party lays down the broadest lines of executive policy and leaves it to the government to work out."[40] In 1948, however, he went well beyond this formula in ignoring the sentiments of the Congress. The Industrial Policy Resolution, introduced by the government in that year, was a far cry from the socialist objectives which Nehru himself had fought to include in the party platform. In contravening the more leftist recommendation of the Congress Economic Programme Committee, he courted the ire of the party's general secretary, Shankarrao Deo, and many members.[41]

The ambiguous and shifting pattern of party-government relationships suggested above accords with the Congress practice of having minority factions represented at its upper echelons, within Parliament and even at the ministerial level. Through a remarkable reconciliation process Congress members of both Communist and right-wing persuasion have served together at the highest levels. Thus, differences between the Congress and the government, because of the parallel diversities of view within both organizations and the double role which most leaders play, must be interpreted as a third political dimension, and of equal significance, as differences among rival factions within the party or within the government. The critical factor in this dynamic situation has been, beginning with Nehru in 1951 and perhaps excepting the troubled period from 1964 (Nehru's death) to 1969 (Mrs. Gandhi's splitting of the party), that the prime minister has generally held enough power to arbitrate all important disputes and settle them according to his or her wishes.

The strength of the Congress party at the national level is largely the result of the fragmentation of opposition parties which allows it to win large parliamentary majorities while polling less then a majority of the popular vote. Although India has been evolving very gradually toward a multiparty political system, as late as the 1971 parliamentary elections there was no opposition party with all-India geographic strength. The Communist Party: Marxist (CPM) came closer

[40]Unpublished Prasad papers, letter of J. Nehru to J. B. Kripalani, May 2, 1947, in Stanley A. Kochanek, *The Congress Party of India: The Dynamics of One-Party Democracy* (Princeton University Press, 1968), p. 158.
[41]Ibid., pp. 164–165.

to all-India strength than any other minority party, but even the CPM had real power in only two of the Indian states.

The greatest weaknesses of opposition parties are that (1) they are divided and in opposition to each other; (2) they fail to generate mass support because, to differentiate themselves from the Congress, they feel they must avoid the political center of gravity which is occupied by the Congress; (3) the Congress has been flexible and has incorporated opposition party ideas into its own program when such action was justified;[42] and (4) they often are conceived as regional parties or derive strength solely from regional factors. Indeed, despite the presence of minority parties in the Indian Parliament, the process of legislation resembles the process of deciding policy within the Congress. In 1967, the role of the smaller parties increased as the counterpart of the Congress's weak showing in the elections. Congress strength in the Lok Sabha (lower house of Parliament) declined to 283 seats (54.4 percent) from the 361 seats (73.1 percent) it had won in the 1962 election. Moreover, because the Congress lost control in a number of state capitals (in some it participated in coalitions and in others it became the opposition party), the historically important gulf between central and local power was widened and there was some erosion of the continuity and stability of government authority.

The Bureaucracy

India's great legacy from Britain—or nemesis, depending on one's point of view—was the civil service. The administrative machinery developed during the colonial period was made up of three distinct cadres, one to serve the central government, another for the states, and the "all-India services," which was shared between the states and the Center.[43] Included among the all-India category was the Indian Civil Service (ICS), which has gradually been succeeded through attrition by the Indian Administrative Service (IAS). This elite group has had first claim on India's most talented young men and women and, despite its small size, has been the almost exclusive source for staffing senior government positions. Its strength has derived from its high standards of recruitment and training, the extensive experience and responsibility it has given to officers early in their careers, and a tradition of diligence and honesty. Although the strict qualifications for entry into the IAS have made this service a preserve of the children of elite families,[44] efforts to recruit officers from diverse backgrounds have broadened its social composition. Moreover, the policy of sending

[42]For example, when the Praja Socialist party (PSP) put forward a 14-point program in 1953, Nehru followed suit and several months later the Congress announced its own Social and Economic Program, which included several of the PSP points; see Morris-Jones, op. cit., pp. 101–102.

[43]For a more detailed description of the Indian bureaucracy, see Morris-Jones, op. cit.

[44]In a study of the Indian civil services, V. Subramaniam found a positive relationship between the prestige of various services and the class of their members. For all services, he found that more than 80 percent of the members came from the "urban, salaried,

IAS officers outside their native states has made the service perform a national integration function. To talk of India's bureaucrats, however, is not just to talk about the IAS. There are more than 11 million employees of government and quasi-government bodies, with jobs ranging from factory worker, clerk, sweeper, and peon, to schoolteacher and atomic scientist.

A major problem for the IAS and other administrative cadres has been created by the government's assumption of new functions. The proficiency of the Civil Service in its pre-Independence and mundane tasks of collecting taxes and preserving law and order did not fully equip it to deal with the new economic and sociopolitical responsibilities to which it has fallen heir. Operations such as dissemination of the green revolution technology, management of public sector industry, and stewardship of family planning programs have required an expertise and style not commonly found among civil servants, and it has come as a rude shock that even many of the elite generalists of the IAS have had difficulty in these new areas of responsibility.

To some degree, the new orientation has had a retrograde effect on India's administration.

1. An intense and bitter rivalry has evolved between the technocrats and the bureaucrats, both of whom wish to administer public sector enterprise, a management task for which neither is fully qualified.

2. The criteria for judging an official's performance in the new policy areas are less clear-cut than in the old. Moreover, the need for development is so great and the process so complex that acceptable rates of progress are sometimes imperceptible in the short term. These factors reduce the system's ability to make officers accountable for their work.

3. The new responsibilities bureaucrats have acquired have opened new opportunities for patronage. Not all civil servants are able to resist the opportunities for malfeasance when the stakes are very high and the alternative opportunities for living a comfortable life are very limited. (See Chapter 11.)[45]

4. The traditional antagonism between senior bureaucrats and politicians which dates to Independence, when the new Indian government regarded everybody who had worked for the British administration with some degree of skepticism, has been increased by the enlarged role of government. Whereas each group regards itself as superior and heir to a special tradition and responsibility, IAS officers are not positioned to play national political roles and elected officials are unable to do the work of the civil service. Their mutual dependence is a source of conflict, particularly at the state government level, where IAS officers are sometimes regarded as interlopers from the Center.

and professional middle class." See *Social Background of India's Administrators* (New Delhi: GOI, Ministry of Information and Broadcasting, Publications Division, 1971), pp. 124–125.

[45]Because I view the widespread corruption in India more as a consequence of India's style of government than any innate social propensity for extralegal transactions, this subject is treated more fully in Chapter 11.

5. Since the early 1970s there has been an effort to "politicize" the government by giving responsible positions to civil servants who are committed to the sociopolitical goals of the administration. The best-known incident occurred in 1973 when Mrs. Gandhi broke a precedent by choosing the third in line as chief justice of the Indian Supreme Court in preference to other, more senior judges. Her immediate objective was to prevent a repetition of the 1969 situation in which the Supreme Court had ruled against the government on bank nationalization and other matters. Mrs. Gandhi's action did not abrogate the Constitution, but it did rouse fears about the independence of the judiciary and the future of democracy. Other efforts to obtain a committed civil service in the 1970s have exacerbated the malaise of administrators and enhanced the atmosphere of ambiguity which has come to pervade government operations.[46]

The cumulative impact of these factors caused one former Secretary to the Government of India to write an article in 1973, entitled "Crumbling Administration," in which he complained of the decline in discipline, integrity, and public motivation of bureaucrats.[47] That an IAS officer should write so candidly on this subject indicates the extent to which the Delhi atmosphere had become accusatory and demoralized and how difficult it was for even the most skilled and dedicated civil servants to function satisfactorily. It is particularly lamentable that many bureaucrats have come to look after their own interests—self-aggrandizement or self-preservation—as a primary on-the-job concern just at the moment of acquiring important new development responsibilities.

Other Centers

One of the happy features of democracy is the multitude of aspirants to power. But power is not a homogeneous good, and competing claims, which generally add to a large multiple of the amount available, are justified by what one might call the "pluralism of power." The power to say yes and the power to say no are not identical; the power to use rhetoric is not the same as the power to formulate, much less to implement, public policy; and for each of the many diverse functional questions requiring action, there are different groups whose interests are specially affected, and who therefore exercise more power than on other issues.

To judge from the number of daily newspapers (793 in 1973, including 73 published in English), the Indian press leads an active existence, an impression confirmed by its editorial liveliness and acidity. The Indian government appears to be about as sensitive—or as impervious—to press criticism as most other governments, and its efforts to manage the news have generally been mild. In the early 1970s, however, there were signs of a changing relationship; the newspapers became bitterly critical of Mrs. Gandhi and her government's economic policies just at a time when resource scarcities had led the govern-

---

[46]See Arun Shourie, "Controls and the Current Situation: Why Not Let the Hounds Run?" *Economic and Political Weekly,* August 1973, pp. 1467–1488.

[47]K. K. Dass, "Crumbling Administration," *Seminar,* January 1973, pp. 56–59.

ment to reduce the supply of newsprint, thereby exacerbating the recrimina-tions.[48] This dispute was aggravated by other differences, and in 1975 strict censorship was imposed. Nonetheless, because (1) the papers are only one among many influences on the voters and official policy and (2) press freedom is an important ingredient of democracy, during normal times the controversy is likely to persist roughly within the pre-1975 boundaries.

Indian business groups are well organized, adequately financed, and accorded symbolic status, such as the annual ritual of having the prime minister go before the Federation of Indian Chambers of Commerce to explain how businessmen fit into the government's economic plans and to listen to how, from the business point of view, the government should solve the nation's problems. There is little evidence, however, that these public meetings have much more than symbolic meaning. In practice, the situation is that "Individual business houses have been successful in gaining specific, individual, distributive benefits, but business collectively has not been able to influence the broad outline and direction of public policy in India."[49] The place of larger business interests has generally been determined by (1) the ad hoc judgment of the prime minister as to the current economic situation and the potential role of private business and (2) the profusion of on- and off-the-record negotiations between individual businessmen and government officials at elective and bureaucratic levels. The contradiction between the existence of private industry in a socialist society and the ability of private enterprise to contribute to the development process has contributed to an unfortunate ambivalence in policy toward business which, in turn, has had a restraining effect on development. (See Chapter 9.)

India's urban working class has laid claim to political power through the trade union movement and the ties by which the labor groups are associated with political parties. India's trade unions traditionally have had strong political ties. The Congress party, for example, created the Indian National Trade Union Congress (INTUC) in 1948 to rival the Communist party--controlled All-India Trade Union Congress (AITUC), which then represented the bulk of India's organized labor. Other major unions have since been organized, all of them with socialist political connections. The question whether the link between party and trade unions has favored workers or politicans leads to no definitive answer. Parties have used their labor support to demonstrate publicly their political power, and the unions have often resorted to nonpolitical actions to benefit their members. Moreover, workers are sometimes unreliable political agents, as illustrated in 1972 when the Prime Minister asked workers to put their contribution to the nation's economic progress on the same war footing that had defeated Pakistan in the previous year. Her pleas were met with derision and an almost total reluctance to temper wage and other demands, not

[48]*New York Times*, Dec. 17, 1973.
[49]Stanley A. Kochanek, *Business and Politics in India* (Berkeley: University of California Press, 1974), p. 323.

only by unions associated with opposition parties, but by INTUC and workers on the government payroll. This is hardly surprising because the living standards of Indian labor are low, even if they are higher than those in rural India. Data for the period 1951–1969 show that to the extent that it does have political power, labor has not substantially improved its position; wage rates have risen by 138 percent while the consumer price index has increased by 108 percent.[50]

Labor's real power depends less on the formal trade union structure than on its location in urban areas. Its geographic concentration and role in industrial production give it critical mass and make it a potentially explosive element in a society whose demands must be heeded. Economic resources such as food allocated to "fair price" shops (government stores selling essential commodities at subsidized prices) and political capital such as the dissolution of the Gujarat State Assembly in 1974 have been expended in generous quantitites to assuage the demands of the urban workers. Although members of labor unions may have little claim to special privileges within the system as individuals, when they act collectively they frequently hold a veto power over policies which they disapprove.

There are many other important institutions such as caste and religious groups, organizations which follow Gandhian principles, and regional associations. These may influence policy either by direct action or through their connections with individual bureaucrats and politicians, but their power on larger issues is likely to be negligible.

Government Power: An Overview

As in other countries, governments in India not only are the executors of power but are powers unto themselves and to some degree are self-perpetuating. Indian governments are generally the result of neither a one-party nor a fully effective multiparty system. They differ enormously according to level, region, and other factors. Thus, although the next several pages are focused on the exercise of power by the national government, it should be noted that the organization of power differs at state and local levels; the parochial interests grow more important and legislation less important as one descends the geographic ladder.[51] Center-state relations which are critical to the achievement of development goals but complicated by overlapping authority and frequent misunderstanding, are considered on pages 47 to 52.

India employs a conventional parliamentary system which includes the normal panoply of prime minister, cabinet, cabinet committees for political and economic affairs, ministers, interagency committees, ad hoc bodies, a president, and upper and lower houses of Parliament. What is unique about the system—

---

[50]Computed from *Basic Statistics Relating to the Indian Economy* (New Delhi: GOI, Planning Commission, 1971), pp. 1 and 7.

[51]Under the British, officials known as "collectors" were appointed at the district level and given extensive executive, legislative, and judicial authority. The system of collectorates has been continued since Independence in some parts of the country.

and more difficult to analyze than its organization—is the way the legislative and executive interrelate and the interplay within the executive.

The members of the Congress Parliamentary party occupy a special position in the system. They are representative of the diverse factions at the highest level and therefore responsible both to the party and to the faction within the party from which they are drawn. They also are responsible to the Indian people and the Constitution for the legislation they adopt. In practice, by showing disciplined loyalty to the party whip which generally has been controlled by the prime minister, the Congress members of Parliament have diminished the power of the legislative branch within the system. The practice of promulgating new legislation by presidential ordinance and later submitting implementing legislation for the Parliament to debate and rubber-stamp, which began in 1969 with the nationalization of India's 14 largest private commercial banks, has further reduced the significance of Parliament. Thus, the importance of the Congress Parliamentary party has gradually become a matter determined by the stature of individual members and their ability to influence the leadership.

The presence of a Planning Commission within government is hardly unique, but in India it bears special significance both because it was constituted before equivalent bodies in other countries and because of its symbolic value as the agency which was designed to fulfill India's deep commitment to central planning. The timing of the Indian Planning Commission's birth, soon after Independence, reflected the handiwork of Nehru, who regarded its role as so critical that he nominated himself as its chairman and relied on it to lead India's transformation into a wealthy, modern, industrial nation. Indeed, Nehru chose his highest-ranking and strongest associates to serve as members and invested the Planning Commission with so much authority that it was sometimes jealously regarded as a minigovernment in competition with the formal ministerial system.[52]

Since Nehru's death, the Planning Commission's role within the government, which had always been somewhat hampered by other government agencies, has been weakened by its having to share policy-making authority with the functional and finance ministries and by its having little voice in how policies are implemented.[53] This evolution was accelerated when men of lesser political standing were appointed members of the Commission and when it became

[52]See B. Shiva Rao, "The Future of Indian Democracy," *Foreign Affairs*, vol. 39, no. 1, October 1960, p. 136.

[53]The Sept. 28, 1973, edition of the *National Herald* chided that the Planning Commission "has neither the conviction to continue nor the courage to pass away." It lamented the performance of former Vice Chairmen Ashok Mehta and D. R. Gadgil "in reducing the Planning Commission to a zero," and sympathized with the then current vice chairman, D. P. Ahar, who was unable to manage the institution to suit his socialist objectives. The article further noted the impotence of the Commission in dealing with other parts of government, to say nothing of real issues.

clear in India and elsewhere that the benefits from planning which had been idealized in the 1950s could only rarely live up to expectations. This is not to belittle the significance of planning and the potential value to India of revitalizing its Planning Commission from the low state to which it fell in 1974. What is needed is a mix of (1) politicizing the work of the Commission to bring it generally into harmony with current political directions and economic realities; (2) appointing members who not only understand—and are sensitive to—political-economic issues, but have political clout within the government; and (3) better integrating the Commission at the overall policy-making and implementation levels of government.

Conflicts, faulty communication, and imperfect coordination are not peculiar to the Planning Commission's relationships with other official bodies. They are common to the executive branch and operate vertically (from ministers to minor functionaries) and horizontally (not only between independent bodies but within them). In later chapters I shall show how damaging these characteristics are in a country like India, which, because it depends heavily on administrative controls to regulate the economy, requires more than a normal amount of official coordination to run smoothly.

The question this brings us to is, Where does power lie within the government? Indeed, does it exist in any meaningful sense, or are the elements of power counterpoised in such a way as to vitiate one another? The answers return us to the entire range of official and nongovernmental forces that have been discussed. In the first place, the situation in India bears some parallel to the alienation envisioned by Franz Kafka in his "Great Wall of China." Just as the messenger in this short story is unable to deliver a communication from the emperor to a distant citizen because of an infinite number of barriers, the Indian government, despite its de jure power, faces awesome difficulties in extending its writ at the village level. Not only do the geographically, politically, and socially remote masses have trouble in communicating their views to Delhi, but the central government has enormous problems in explaining its strategies, much more enforcing its policies, throughout the country.

At the Center there have been periods when, reflecting India's traditional and hierarchical social order, one person held immense power. By dint of controlling the Congress party that person was also prime minister, leader of the Congress Parliamentary party, and chairman of the Planning Commission. Other important individuals existed, but power tended to migrate among them according to their closeness to the chief.[54] In contrast, during the short periods when India was without strong leadership and power has been more diffused,

[54]In 1973, for example, the Prime Minister sought to learn why the government was procuring less than the targeted amount of food grains. She first bypassed the Agriculture Ministry and asked the Planning Minister to investigate. Later, unsatisfied with his response, she had the Minister for Heavy Industry look into the situation.

rival forces have tended to offset each other and the resultant nonexercise of power has not produced meaningful management of the economy, except when mobilization to meet crises demanded national unity.

Finally, we must ask what orchestrates India's great diversity and what prevents it from becoming a cacophony of national disintegration. The eclectic answer I have been building toward is that what binds India is a mixture of social, historical, ideological, and political forces. One of the most important of these is the Indian capacity to tolerate adversity, a characteristic which has been firmly established over the millennia and is readily observable in all aspects of Indian society. The great limitation of India's assets is that whereas they are adequate to the task of holding the nation together under ordinary circumstances and their negative side effects (mainly inaction) are suppressed in time of crisis, they do not provide enough centrifugal force to assure rapid social change and economic development.

India is served by a complex and dynamic mix of personal, party, bureaucratic, and institutional power which is highly relevant to the process of development. Democratic institutions exist, but under circumstances of illiteracy and economic dependency, their functioning is far from ideal. Political power and the economic power it conveys have ostensibly been transferred to the Indian masses, but in reality these powers are still wielded by an elite minority. But this elite, however undesirable, is more democratic than its predecessors, as measured by caste, community, class, and regional characteristics. Thus, the current situation in India is a reasonably appropriate halfway house, located between traditional Brahmanical elitism and the truly democratic objective to which Gandhi and many other Indians have aspired.

Political Evolution

India's progress has been deeply affected by the interplay of the economy with politics, international affairs, and other forces which will be discussed presently. Various observers have described India's evolution as dominated by the search for national integrity, the escape from poverty, modernization, and so forth. In reality, it is all these and has therefore followed an uneven course.

The Prelude

Although India's political preoccupation before 1947 was Independence, this did not foreclose the opportunity for some Indians to gain direct experience with government while the British were still present. The sense of national unity, compromise, and cooperation which developed before 1947 was a strong asset in subsequent years. Substantively, it was established during the pre-Independence period that India's socioeconomic policy would highlight three interrelated goals: economic growth, social justice, and self-reliance. This became clear as early as the Congress party's resolutions of Lahore (1929) and

Karachi (1931),[55] and the tendency to rely on administrative controls to govern the economy was reinforced by the World War II experience when even the Western governments resorted to their use.

The meaning of growth, equity, and self-reliance and the linkages among them are discussed in Chapter 7. Suffice it here to say that these objectives are subject to varying interpretations and that Indians have held quite diverse conceptions of how they should be implemented. Further, the interpretation of the objectives and the relative emphasis among them have changed over time as domestic and foreign economic and political conditions have evolved.

Consolidation: 1947–1955

India's entire first quarter century of Independence has been a period of consolidation, but the need to set precedents and establish policy directions was particularly acute during the first few years. Early events, such as the assassination of Gandhi, trauma of partition, migration of more than 10 million people, and communal chaos in which 500,000 lost their lives were so severe that they might have shattered even the best-established government. For India, they were just the prelude to a series of internal regional and constitutional challenges. A problem arose in negotiating the acquiescence of princely states to incorporation within the Indian Union, particularly for Hyderabad and Junagadh, where the local rulers resisted yielding their sovereignty to become pensioners of India. The case of Kashmir was more complex, and it was only after a military engagement with Pakistan in 1948 that a truce was reached and this province was partitioned.

The process of constitution writing was eased for India by the existing agreements in principle among its leaders on democracy, egalitarianism, and so forth, which had been forged in earlier years. There remained, nonetheless, important questions of federalism, such as the serious differences of view on the setting of state boundaries. In the course of time these were resolved—at least temporarily—and the new Constitution went into effect on January 26, 1950. When the first general elections were held in 1951–52, the Congress party won control of all the state legislatures and 364 out of 489 seats in the Lok Sabha.

Despite political distractions, economic policy received a fair amount of attention during this period. Leftover World War II controls affecting the distribution and pricing of food grains and other key commodities were removed, and other policies were adopted to increase food production, promote cottage industries, and so forth. The government promulgated its first Industrial Policy Resolution in 1948. The resolution disappointed socialists because of its nondoctrinaire approach to the allocation of industry between the public and private sectors. It also failed to win the confidence of industrialists, and their contribution to development remained below potential until the government finally won their understanding and cooperation almost a decade later.

[55]See *Report of the National Planning Committee* (K. T. Shah, ed.), (Bombay: GOI, 1949).

In a major policy move, the National Planning Commission was established on March 15, 1950, and the First Five-Year Plan began in 1951. Although this Plan has been judged by S. Chakravarty, an economist who has since served as a member of the Planning Commission, as "essentially a collection of several projects" in which "the model was largely an intellectual appendage with little impact on actual Plan formulation,"[56] the Plan's very existence signaled a great victory for the advocates of nationalism over localism, of modernization over traditional village society, and of guided economy over laissez faire.

Nation Building: 1956–1965

No precise date marks the end of India's early consolidation and the beginning of the next period of nation building, but a number of important changes in both foreign and domestic affairs took place in the mid-1950s. For foreign policy the period from 1954 to 1965 was particularly significant. When Nehru met Chou En-lai in 1954, they agreed to base relations between their countries on five principles (the so-called Pancheel Agreement). India was a leading mover in the 1955 Bandung meeting of nonaligned nations. Delhi made repeated efforts to normalize relations with Pakistan, but these were abortive. India went to war with China in 1962 and with Pakistan in 1965. French Pondicherry and the Portuguese holdings, including Goa, were integrated into the Indian Union despite the need to use force in Goa, which was in clear defiance of Gandhi's principles and attracted much criticism in India and abroad. During this period India also strengthened its ties to the United States and the Soviet Union; commercial and aid relationships with both countries were initiated and enlarged (see Chapters 3 to 6).

The strength of India's new democracy was tested repeatedly during this period and was found to be considerably greater than expected. When Nehru died in 1964, he was succeeded through an orderly democratic process by Lal Bahadur Shastri.

More difficult was the problem of integrating India's diverse regions; this recurred dramatically and persistently in such issues as the setting of state boundaries and the choosing of a national language. (See pages 14 to 19.) Although the British and the Congress had been inclined to create states so as to reflect linguistic patterns, in 1948 this was seen as dangerous on grounds that it (1) would support localism at the expense of national unity, (2) would cause a loss of administrative efficiency, and (3) would encourage a tendency to discriminate against the interests of weaker linguistic and caste groups.[57] This view prevailed to only a limited degree, and beginning with the Telegu-speaking

[56]See Jagdish N. Bhagwati and Sukhamoy Chakravarty, "Contributions to Indian Economic Analysis: A Survey," *American Economic Review,* vol. 59, no. 4, part 2 (September 1969).

[57]See Morris-Jones, op. cit., p. 86, and F. G. Bailey, *Politics and Social Change: Orissa in 1959* (Berkeley: University of California Press, 1963). The latter touches on state and local politics in the state of Orissa.

people of Andhra (1952), there have been recurrent agitations in various parts of India for regional autonomy. For example, the States Reorganization Act of 1956 sought to create a single Bombay State, but was superseded in 1960 and Bombay was divided into Gujarat and Maharashtra. Other regional issues have included autonomy for Nagaland (1961) and creation of a predominantly Sikh state in 1966 by carving out Haryana from the Punjab. Regional issues have remained important in the political scene as illustrated by the 1973–74 agitation to bifurcate Andhra Pradesh and such proposals to revise state boundaries on grounds of efficiency as the one which would have divided Uttar Pradesh (population 90 million) into smaller, more manageable administrative units.

Whereas coping and amelioration were the keys to many of India's domestic and external political problems during the period 1956–1965, economic policy provided considerable scope for positive and aggressive initiatives. The Indian economy had not performed well in the first few years after Independence, but this was more the result of bad weather and postwar (World War II and Korea) economic readjustment than of poor policy. In contrast, during India's First Plan (1951–1956) agricultural production fared so well that it was possible to provide ample food and cloth by historical standards. This reinforced the upbeat mood of economists and officials, and it is understandable that the "bold" effort to expand the Indian economy which began in this period had as its guiding principle that no progress that was physically attainable should fail for lack of financial resources.[58]

The government showed its concern for improving the position of the rural poor and mobilizing them as a resource for development by launching a Community Development (CD) program in 1952. The concept of agricultural progress and improved rural communications, sanitation, and education assumed by Community Development was so extraordinary that it moved Arnold Toynbee to speculate: "The practical idealism of the great Indian enterprise may be going to bring about one of the most beneficent revolutions in the peasantry's life that have been known so far in history."[59] The CD program was gradually extended from the 300 villages where it was born as an experiment to the entire country. The CD program, which is discussed in greater detail in Chapter 8, has been significant not only because its economic objectives are critical but because, in seeking to modernize rural India, it has tipped the rural power equation slightly more in favor of the poor. Thus, when in the late 1950s it was realized that the achievements of the CD program were failing to match expectations, Community Development was not abandoned; instead, the panchayati raj system was initiated in 1958 to mobilize local energies for development and to hasten the prerequisite economic and political changes.

The work of the Planning Commission grew progressively more sophisticated and relevant to policy decisions. The analytic underpinning of the Plans

[58]For a discussion of the bold approach of the Third Plan, see J. P. Lewis, *Quiet Crisis*, op. cit., chap. 4.

[59]Quoted in *The New India* (Delhi: GOI, Planning Commission, 1958), p. 175.

became more rigorous; the simple, finance-oriented model on which the First Five-Year Plan was based was replaced in the Second and Third Plans by increasingly more detailed multisectoral models based on physical rather than financial magnitudes.[60] As a leading influence in economic policy, the Planning Commission took primary responsibility for setting India on a course of investment in heavy industry, pioneered Community Development, and innovated other far-ranging policies.

The Industrial Policy Resolution of 1948, which had roughly defined the scope of public and private sector enterprise, had made an important concession to private business by ruling out nationalization as a major policy instrument for the next decade. In fact, those nationalizations which did occur during 1948–1958—Air India (1953), life insurance (1956), and the Imperial Bank (1955)—were justifiable as special cases.[61] Even though it took a benign approach toward nationalization, the government treated investment applications from private firms warily. It sought to fill India's industrial vacuums with public sector enterprise and by 1965 had created an impressive industrial empire. In 1949, Nehru announced a relatively liberal policy toward foreign investors in India which was contrary to a 1945 resolution of the Congress party's National Planning Committee. It was opposed by Indian businessmen who feared competition,[62] but subsequently Indian entrepreneurs became more positive about investment from abroad because they saw joint ventures as one of the few ways to gain government approval for their expansion plans. In contrast, the government never lost its suspicion of foreign firms and excluded many would-be investors.

India gained enough confidence during the early 1950s for Nehru to commit his party and government to a "socialist pattern of society" in the winter of 1954–55. The second Industrial Policy Resolution (1956) greatly resembled its 1948 predecessor and appears to have been promulgated as much to reassure private industry as to implement the new socialism.[63] Be that as it may, the base created by the substantial economic progress which had been made during the First Plan, the decision to adopt a bold economic strategy for the Second Plan, and the efforts to exploit private entrepreneurial resources for the development effort together accelerated India's economic—especially industrial—progress.

There were two persistent problems, however, which eventually required India to reduce its rate of expansion. First was a shortage of foreign exchange.

---

[60]For a more detailed analysis of Indian planning, see Chapter 7.

[61]For instance, the Imperial Bank, which was renamed the State Bank of India, accounted for about one-third of commercial bank deposits and in many areas acted as the government's fiscal agent.

[62]Michael Kidron, *Foreign Investments in India* (London: Oxford University Press, 1965), pp. 71–72.

[63]J. N. Bhagwati and Padma Desai, *India: Planning for Industrialization and Trade Policies since 1951* (London and New York: Oxford University Press, for the OECD, 1970), p. 143.

In part because the private industrial sector invested as much in the first two years of the Second Plan as had been allocated for the full five years, India developed a severe balance-of-payments crisis in 1958. Substantial foreign assistance began to arrive in India at that time, but the demand for imports continued to outpace India's purchasing power and thereby remained a constraint on economic expansion. The second problem, which did not become manifest until the monsoon failures of 1963, 1965, and 1966, was food production. India's need to put a greater share of its development effort into agriculture had been concealed by good weather and the U.S. PL-480 program, but it could no longer be ignored.

In summary, for the decade beginning in the mid-1950s India made exceptional industrial progress but did so at the cost of growing imbalance among industrial sectors, inadequate attention to agriculture, and increasing reliance on foreign assistance, a situation which led to economic dislocation in later years. For a time it appeared as though India had found an approach to its unique development problem, but a combination of ill luck and ill management eventually forced a rethinking of policy and a new period of experimentation.

The Ship Adrift: 1965–1969

The traumatic Sino-Indian war of 1962 led India to double its defense budget, and further increases in military spending were stimulated by the inconclusive 1965 war with Pakistan. In Chapter 3 I shall analyze how these wars diverted scarce economic resources and the attention of India's leaders from development. This factor together with adverse weather and India's own questionable economic strategy contributed to India's deepening economic problem. The government, relying on administrative controls instead of market prices to regulate the economy, lost touch with basic supply and demand factors; prices began to rise; inefficiency engulfed large segments of industry; imbalances and bottlenecks developed among various sectors; completion of industrial projects ran behind schedule; agrarian reform lost its momentum, as did the Community Development program; and, largely related to these disruptions, the rupee's international exchange rate became grossly overvalued. These ills appeared even more serious when release of the 1961 census data showed that India's population was growing faster than had been anticipated, thereby reducing per capita incomes below previous estimates. The coup de grace for the economy came in the form of two successive droughts. Production of food grains fell from its record high of 89 million tons in 1964–65 to 72 million tons the following year and amounted to only 74 million tons in 1966–67. Prices soared, it was necessary to arrange massive relief imports to prevent famine, and industrial production reacted to the shortage of agricultural raw materials and the weakness of consumer demand by going into a tailspin.

The most significant lesson of the 1965–1967 crisis, which to India's later regret it learned only imperfectly, was that measures to spur agricultural production were critically needed not only to raise then current nutrition standards, but to cushion the impact of future monsoon failures. The priority of larger domestic food output was raised by the real danger that in a future drought situation India would be unable to obtain adequate amounts of food from abroad or to unload and transport them to where they would be needed. It was further enhanced by Indian resentment of the United States' policy of doling out relief grain in limited amounts and using these food allocations as leverage for obtaining changes in India's economic policies. (See Chapters 4 and 6.) As the Pearson committee noted of the drought and postdrought period, "This painful experience, though perhaps accelerating the rate of policy change, certainly reinforced India's desire for independence of food-grain imports."[64]

The government's reaction to this situation was to give agriculture more status in the budget and planning process than it had received during the Second and Third Plans; to accelerate the introduction of the green revolution technology; and to concentrate its efforts on short-term growth opportunities at the expense of helping backward regions. In addition, on June 6, 1966, India devalued the rupee by 57.5 percent and instituted various reforms in its fiscal and foreign trade regimes. Paradoxically, the renewed determination to achieve food self-sufficiency and to eliminate foreign assistance conflicted with India's short-term need to maximize the inflow of external aid in order to underwrite its import liberalization and other policies. Thus, India's misunderstanding with the Consortium over the postdevaluation economic policies it would follow and the amount of aid that aid donors would provide greatly heightened India's discomfort in its relations with the West.

The Third Five-Year Plan ended in 1966, and, in view of the difficult economic conditions prevailing at the time, India postponed the beginning of the Fourth Plan until 1969. The purpose of what came to be known as the Plan Holiday was to allow for completion of unfinished projects and a general review of economic policy. In 1967, when Indians went to the polls to vote in the nation's fourth general election, they showed their deep dissatisfaction with the economic situation. The Congress failed to obtain majorities in the legislatures of eight states, and its margin in the Lok Sabha was substantially reduced. The forces eroding one-party dominance in 1967 were born of frustration and manifested themselves, not so much by the electorate's turning to right or left parties, as by increased emphasis on state politics and growing attention to regional personalities and issues. The postelection position within the states was extremely varied, ranging from outright Congress majorities and Congress-led coalitions to the militant states' rights Dravida Munnetra Kazhagam (DMK) government of Tamil Nadu, the right-wing Swatantra-led coalition in Orissa, and the Communist-led United Front government in Kerala. This shift of political power, from the Center to the states and from the Congress to smaller

---

[64]*Partners in Development: Report of the Commission on International Development* (New York: Praeger, 1969), p. 289.

parties, combined with the shaky economic situation and led to a period of agitation and unrest for which no resolution appeared until 1969.

The Move Leftward: 1969–1974

In the summer of 1969,[65] Mrs. Gandhi brought her differences with the right wing of the Congress to a head and, by splitting the party, emerged as the dominant influence in Indian politics. (See Chapter 10.) Bank nationalization and the choice of a Congress candidate for the presidential elections scheduled for later in the year, the two issues which figured most prominently in this drama, reflected the Prime Minister's sense of priorities. With an eye on the parliamentary elections, which were to be held sometime before the spring of 1972 (in reality they took place in 1971), she took advantage of the sense of confidence created by recurrent record-breaking food grain harvests to establish a socialist reputation and to increase her control over the Congress, especially at the national level. Mrs. Gandhi's political strategy succeeded brilliantly, and campaigning on the slogan *garibi hatao* (abolish poverty) in the 1971 parliamentary elections, her wing of the Congress won an impressive victory over its rivals and assumed full control of the national government. Her popularity was fortified by India's success over Pakistan in the December 1971 war for Bangladesh independence, and she led her party to another resounding victory in the local elections held in the spring of 1972.

The 1971 war was especially significant for this period, not only because it moved India further from the United States and closer to the U.S.S.R. (an Indo-Soviet Treaty of Peace, Friendship, and Cooperation was signed near the psychological peak of the crisis), but because it marked a turning point in India's economic fortunes. Although Indian industrial production and investment had never fully recovered from the drought-induced recession of 1965–1967, they had improved considerably and, in response to good monsoons and the spread of the green revolution, agriculture had fared very well. The 1971 war was brief, but the preparations for it, and the costs of feeding and reconstructing Bangladesh in its wake, were significant drains on India's development resources. Thus, India's euphoria in the months immediately following the war was not long-lived, largely because of agricultural reverses. Contrary to expectations, the 1971–72 growing year was not so good as its predecessor. Subsequently, the 1972 monsoon was a disaster, the national food grain stocks and the relief efforts in Maharashtra State were mismanaged, and other problems added to India's growing sense of disillusionment (see Chapter 8) and exacerbated India's inflation, chronic unemployment, and widespread shortages.

Economic problems during this period can be traced in part to the Prime

[65]A fuller account of the period 1969–1974 appears piecemeal in various chapters of this book and in my article, "India's Economic Development and the Force of National Politics: The Four Seasons of Its Discontent," *Asia*, Supplement No. 1, Fall 1974.

Minister's having allocated more of her time to clearing the political field of opponents than to development. This focus on partisan politics, together with economic adversity, created a climate of malaise and political strife throughout much of the country. Although a lengthy agitation to bifurcate Andhra Pradesh failed, the government in Andhra was eventually defeated in the state parliament, and the same fate befell the governments of Gujarat, Bihar, Orissa, and Uttar Pradesh, even though the state leaders had been handpicked by Mrs. Gandhi.

The process of decay without compensating regeneration reached its limit in 1974, when domestic stagnation was accompanied by skyrocketing international prices for petroleum, fertilizer, and food. India's leaders were so alarmed by the prospect of widespread hunger's becoming widespread famine that they decided to import concessionally priced United States grain in spite of their 1972 vows to avoid such imports. During this period social discipline degenerated so badly that some Indian observers speculated that India's first nuclear blast was timed to provide the government with a much-needed dose of prestige and self-respect and to give it enough authority to force India's striking railway workers to a settlement. Charges of corruption and moral bankruptcy were leveled against the government and society with growing intensity, and such prominent leaders as Jayaprakash Narayan and India's president, V. V. Giri, were foremost among the critics.

When the state of economic and political turmoil became acute in 1974, pragmatism became the order of the day. For example, the 1973 nationalization of the wholesale wheat trade was recognized as having failed to increase government control over wheat stocks and it was reversed in 1974. The Fifth Plan was recognized to be nothing more than an outdated collection of phantom numbers, and D. P. Dhar was replaced as vice chairman of the Planning Commission by Mrs. Gandhi's trusted aide P. N. Haksar. And in the summer of 1974, a far-reaching economic program (credit squeeze, forced saving, investment in critical industries, etc.) was adopted. In short, India entered 1975 with its government engaged on many different fronts to extricate the nation from the economic and political morass into which it had fallen. But whereas some of the new policies promised to ameliorate current problems, the long-term efficacy of India's development effort was as uncertain as at any time since Independence.

Center-State Economic Relations

The relevance of the political order to the economy is nowhere more decisive than in the case of Center-state relations. The linkages among semi-independent but vertically and horizontally related governments extend from data collection and joint decisions on basic strategy to the formulation, implementation, and evaluation of policy. And because India relies so heavily on government authority to regulate economic activity, close coordination between state and central governments is more essential to the effective operation of the economy than in most other countries.

The division of responsibilities between the Center and the states is fixed by the Seventh Schedule of the Indian Constitution (Article 246), which explicitly lists their individual and joint areas of responsibility. This federal characteristic of the Constitution is important in practice, but the modalities of Center-state intercourse also are largely influenced, if not dominated, by India's complex social, economic, political, historical, and ideological circumstances. In contrast to such functions as national defense, foreign relations, and the mint, which naturally fell to the central authority, certain other important powers, including the right to tax agricultural income, were allotted to the states. Among the principal reasons why the Constitution gives considerable responsibility to state governments are (1) the strong regional identification of Indians; (2) the quasi-independent status of many of the princely states before Independence; (3) the widespread agreement that Gandhi was correct in his belief that the good society requires local autonomy; and (4) the historical distrust of strong central authority. It was generally recognized that the Center had superior ability to formulate policies, to mobilize resources, and to rationalize India's development according to national needs and resource availabilities. But what Rajni Kothari calls the "politics of scale," the need for decentralization (1) to make maximum use of local energies and talent, (2) to be responsive to local demands, and (3) to carry the Center's writ to the furthest corners of the country, was also regarded as important.[66]

The Indian Administrative Service, an all-India body controlled by the Center but divided into state cadres, has been the important bridge between the national and local levels. Because its officers are shifted among local positions (e.g., from collector to state secretariat) and to positions of national responsibility such as the Delhi ministries, they have been uniquely placed to interpret the Center to local government and vice versa. They have done so, however, with some bias toward Delhi's preeminence, in part because their careers are decided at the Center, and in part because their training leads them to transfer routine matters from lower to higher authority.[67]

In the late 1960s, a study team of India's Administrative Reforms Commission (ARC) lost no time in putting its finger on the extraconstitutional nexus between Center and states. In its first paragraph the *Report* asserts that "Politics and administration are inseparable in the sense that administration is meant to give effect to politically determined programmes."[68] The *Report* shows how the

[66]Rajni Kothari, "Political Reconstruction of Bangladesh," *Economic and Political Weekly*, Apr. 29, 1972, p. 884.

[67]The "hierarchical movement of paper," the unwillingness of bureaucrats to make decisions, is noted in Paul Appleby, *Public Administration in India: Survey of a Report*, (New Delhi: GOI, Cabinet Secretariat, 1953, p. 18.

[68]*Report of the Study Team on Centre-State Relationships*, 3 vols. (New Delhi: GOI, Administrative Reforms Commission, 1968), vol. 1, p. 1.

Congress party's simultaneous control over the Lok Sabha and state parliaments has provided a mechanism for the resolution of issues between local and central governments, and how tensions are heightened when states are ruled by non-Congress governments, an observation that is supported by the experience of Kerala, Tamil Nadu, and West Bengal.

A recurrent complaint among some Indians is that there is an unequal relationship between the central and state governments which is not the intention of India's constitution writers.[69] Proof for this assertion, however, is by no means readily available. Although the clear purpose of Article 246 is to give extensive authority to both central and local governments, other parts of the Constitution appear to favor the Center. For example, Delhi is empowered to impose its will on the states by (1) issuing direct instructions; (2) assuming special authority in time of security, political, or financial peril; and (3) redrawing state boundries. In addition to these extraordinary legislative and administrative powers, which are so severe as to preclude frequent use by Delhi, there is a broad range of economic activities where the Center's position is dominant.

One area where the Center enjoys a special ascendancy of power is finance. In contrast to the limited fiscal options open to the states, Delhi not only is more able to undertake deficit financing, but also has exclusive authority to receive and dispose of foreign assistance funds, a revenue channel which has proved to be much more important than anticipated in 1950. In India it is generally believed that the states have become increasingly dependent on the Center for revenues because they do not have the capacity to raise their own financial resources.[70] The premise for this assertion, that the base for taxation open to the states has grown more slowly than the base from which Delhi obtains its revenues, contains an element of truth. Nonetheless, it is also clear that the rural elite who control the state legislatures have been notoriously unwilling to tax themselves. Consequently, the share of total state spending provided by the central government has been high ever since the First Plan period. (See Table 1-1.)

A second area in which the states have been weaker than Delhi is planning. It was always understood that the central government would control macroeconomic variables affecting aggregate demand and supply, but many planners believed that there was still great scope for the states to plan at the microeconomic and local levels. Only in retrospect has it been recognized how India's chosen style of comprehensive planning with its focus on forward and backward linkages in the production process and its concern for nationwide social justice, heavily concentrates decision making in Delhi. This tendency to centralized planning was augmented by the failure of most of the states to organize local institutions parallel to, and able to work with, the national Planning Commission. Responsibility for this situation rests not only with the initial lack

[69]See, for example, the *Report of the Centre-State Relations Inquiry Committee,* op. cit.
[70]For example, see the *Report of the Study Team on Centre-State Relationships,* op. cit., p. 17.

TABLE 1–1
FINANCIAL DEPENDENCE OF STATE GOVERNMENTS

	First Plan, 1951–1956	Second Plan, 1956–1961	Third Plan, 1961–1966	Interim period, 1966–1969	Fourth* Plan, 1969–1974
State expenditures (billions of rupees)	33.5	58.5	107.2	99.1	275.9
Revenues received by states from Center, net (billions of rupees)	12.1	24.4	46.5	40.7	115.0
Central finance as a share of state spending (percent)	36.0	41.7	43.4	41.7	41.7

* Estimated.

Note: The table does not show that the dependency of some states is much greater than others.

Source: RBI Bulletin, September 1974, p. 1723.

of planning skills at the state level, but also with the state governments, most of which ignored Delhi's repeated efforts to induce them to develop a capacity for planning.

As seen by the Administrative Reforms Commission, the situation was largely due to the central government:

> As a result of planning the three horizontal layers of administration repre-
> sented by lists of central, concurrent and state subjects have been vertically
> partitioned into plan and non-plan sectors and that within the plan world,
> the compulsions and consequences of planning have tended to unite the
> three horizontal pieces into a single near-monolithic chunk controlled from
> the centre.[71]

The ARC recommended a devolution of responsibility to the states, a suggestion which was echoed and amplified by the Rajamannar committee. This body,
appointed by Tamil Nadu, questioned the very constitutionality of the Planning
Commission and was particularly critical of the far-flung powers of Delhi in the
field of industrial licensing. The Rajamannar committee went so far as to call
for a transfer of the Center's powers to the state governments, even in cases
where foreign collaboration was involved.[72] Reflecting its near total dissatisfaction with the national leadership, the Communist-dominated Kerala State

[71]*Report of the Study Team on Centre-State Relationships*, op. cit., p. 95.
[72]*Report of the Centre-State Relations Inquiry Committee*, op. cit., p. 109.

government went even one step further and on one occasion submitted an alternative national plan outline.[73]

The National Development Council (NDC), composed of the prime minister, members of the Planning Commission, and state chief ministers, was founded in 1952. It was to deal with such challenges and to improve the Plan mechanism through better coordination of central and state governments. In practice, however, although the NDC has arbitrated some differences, the infrequency of its meetings and the absence of a substantial supporting staff are indicative of both the limited political purposes for which it has been used and the number of other arenas in which interstate and Center-state economic differences have been resolved.[74]

Beyond financial and formal planning matters, the states are dependent on the will of Delhi for various other critical economic decisions. The choice of where new public sector industry will be established, the interstate allocation of vital agricultural and industrial inputs such as kerosene and fertilizer, and the distribution of food are all prerogatives of the Center. And because many of them involve interstate transfers of commodities, they are bound to remain the responsibility of the central government so long as the direction of the economy is set by administrative controls rather than by a market price mechanism.

The states, for their part, are far from helpless in their dealings with the Center. Ironically, it is in the area of finance that they have been most adept at getting what they want. Quite aside from their success in wresting more money from the Center, thereby saving themselves the strain of raising revenues, some states have aped Delhi's habit of deficit finance and have built up substantial unauthorized overdrafts at the Reserve Bank of India. No amount of Delhi rhetoric and negotiation has been adequate to cause the offending states to mend their ways. In April 1972, for example, the central and state governments finally agreed to limit the states' overdraft facilities, and the Center undertook to provide long-term funding for past debts, but by September 1973, the states had already begun to abuse the new system.[75]

On the expenditure side, the state governments are no less powerful. Although the national government makes law and sets policy on many development and administrative matters, many of these must be implemented through state and local government channels. Consequently, monies appropriated by Delhi are sometimes not used at all or are misspent, albeit there are limitations on the extent to which states can reallocate funds to programs for which they are not intended. The deliberate nonspending—impounding—of funds is symbolic of the broader powers of nonimplementation exercised by the states. The failures of many state authorities to undertake agrarian reform (see

[73]A. H. Hanson and Janet Douglas, *India's Democracy* (New York: W. W. Norton, 1972), p. 175.

[74]See *Interim Report on the Machinery for Planning* (New Delhi: GOI, Administrative Reforms Commission, 1967), p. 22.

[75]*Economic and Political Weekly,* Sept. 8, 1973, pp. 1619–1620.

Chapter 8) or to implement fully the family planning program are typical of their ability and willingness to frustrate the nation's most important programs, even when finance is provided from outside.

The balance of power between Delhi and the states has shifted over time as, for example, when central authority was weakened by the Congress electoral defeat in 1967 or when it was subsequently restored as a result of Mrs. Gandhi's 1971 election victory. Apart from these cycles, however, there does not appear to be any marked trend toward toward greater state or central authority. Perhaps the outstanding feature of Center-state relations is the degree to which these linkages continue to be characterized by extreme tension, distrust, and indiscipline. The states' practice of passing Delhi misinformation about farm output[76] is not atypical of the lack of cooperation between these levels of government, a situation that has become so bad that the states have begun to keep senior officers in Delhi for the primary purpose of expediting the central government's approval of various requests.[77] Such noncooperation and non-coordination promote delays and other forms of governmental inefficiency. For example, when in 1972 Tamil Nadu proposed to nationalize the Madras Aluminum Company, not because of its socialist beliefs, but in order to forestall an anticipated take-over of this firm by Delhi,[78] the result was disastrous. In the confusion which followed, the merits of the case for public ownership of the company were obscured and, not surprisingly, the firm's owners were so dismayed by the debate over its future that they halted new investment and otherwise allowed the value of the company to deteriorate.

In summary, Center-state economic relations are critically important in the way of India's development. As the intermediary between the worlds of abstract planning and village reality, the state governments are strategically placed to abet or retard the development process. But for various reasons, including interstate rivalry, the self-aggrandizing policies of states in their demands on—and insensitivity to requests from—the Center, Delhi's occasional heavy-handedness, and the strength of vested agricultural interests within the state governments, India's development has been slowed. Considerable improvement is possible in communications between state and central governments, and this, together with an improvement in Delhi's policies, would mitigate the situation. In the final analysis, however, India's political pluralism presents the choice of accepting a reduced pace of development and greater social inequity or forfeiting a degree of the democracy which permits local forces to resist the will of the central government.

[76]See *Economic and Political Weekly,* Apr. 28, 1973, p. 780. The underlying problem is that when food production is low, the states maximize relief from the Center by understating their output, and when production is high, they maximize receipts of fertilizer and other inputs for the next crop by overstating production.

[77]*The Overseas Hindustan Times,* Aug. 23, 1973.

[78]Phani Mitra, "India Reverts: The Economic Factors," *South Asian Review,* vol. 6, no. 4, July 1973.

CHAPTER 2
THE ECONOMIC POSITION

An understanding of the Indian economy begins with an appreciation of India's resource base—natural, human, and capital. Some readers may object that the capital stock does not fall within the definition of a resource base insofar as it is the creation of human effort. But, from a practical point of view, the quality, accessibility, and usefulness of human and physical resources—the degree to which they can be mobilized for development—are as fixed at any given moment, and as subject to change over time, as the capital stock. Indeed, changes in the capacity of human and natural resources to contribute to economic development may be the requisite condition for improving the nation's capital stock. The state of India's development is affected also by institutional factors and the process whereby farm, industrial, service, and government sectors of the economy interact. The relationship between resources and the economic institutions through which they are linked is reciprocal in the sense that as development takes place, institutions tend to become more efficient and interdependent.

I have used a mainly subjective approach in dealing with Indian resource and institutional issues, partly because the existing data are not very reliable and partly because narrative reveals more about the *process* of the economy. In the subsequent analysis, I have presented a more conventional statistical outline of the Indian economy. One must be cautious in using these data, however, not only because of inaccuracies, but because they can be very misleading. For instance, they gloss over interregional diversity, an important aspect of the Indian economy which I deal with at the end of the chapter.

India's Millions

The 1971 census recorded India's population at 548 million, slightly larger than that of Africa and South America combined and exceeded only by one other country, China. The 2.2 percent annual average growth rate of population during 1961–1971 was slightly higher than the previous decade, reflecting a small reduction in the birthrate and a somewhat larger decline in the death rate. The dramatic long-term consequence of improved health measures has been to raise the life expectancy of Indians, from 32 years in the period 1941–1950 to 46 years during the decade ending in 1970. If India's population continues to grow at the current rate of a little over 1 million per month, it will reach 1 billion by the year 2000. According to one expert:

> The lowest imaginable population for India 30 years from now [the year 2000] is well above 850 million—and that would be making assumptions about fertility decline that scarcely anyone believes feasible. The World Bank's current projections for India show more than 950 million by the year 2000 with fertility declining fairly rapidly and mortality moderately; with unchanged fertility—a very unlikely possibility—the total would reach 1,250 million.[1]

Social scientists in India and elsewhere have long debated whether there is an "optimum" size for population. Their failure to agree is warning that within limits there is no magic relationship between population numbers and the supporting resource base. Nonetheless, unless one is prepared to ignore (1) economic reality (there are declining returns to scale of fixed factors of production such as land) and (2) the political and technical problems of managing very large numbers of people (what Rajni Kothari calls the "politics of scale"[2]), there is reason to believe that India's current population size and rate of growth are larger than desirable. For example, in 1971 India's population density averaged about 350 persons per kilometer of arable land, about double what it had been only four decades earlier and considerably more than in most countries, excepting Japan, Korea, and a number of European nations. Another facet of the population position, attributable to the rapid growth rate, is the large proportion of Indians below the age of 15, that is, nonworkers. India's "dependency ratio," defined by the number of persons under 15 years of age (42 percent) and over 60 years of age (6 percent), is normal for developing countries, but unfavorably high compared with the approximately one-third of developed-country persons within these age groups. A more comprehensive analysis of how India's demography has affected its economy is included in Chapter 7.

Despite India's slow, long-continued trend toward urbanization, the great majority of the people (80 percent) continue to live in villages, of which there are more than 575,000. Most of these villages have only limited commerce and communication with the outside world and are characterized by the use of rudimentary economic practices, illiteracy, poor health, the absence of social

---

[1] Robert H. Cassen, "Population Growth in India," *Environment and Change,* December 1973, p. 247.

[2] See "Political Reconstruction of Bangladesh," op. cit., p. 884.

amenities, poverty, and wide disparities in social and economic status. Living conditions in the cities are not fundamentally better than in the villages, albeit they are characterized by even greater and more conspicuous contrast between traditional and modern and between rich and poor.

The Search for Employment

In 1974, India's labor force was estimated at 183 million.[3] The prospect that 65 million additional workers will be added to this labor pool in the next 12 years led the Planning Commission to assert that "employment is perhaps going to be the most important challenge to development planning during the perspective period."[4] Unsaid, but not unrecognized by the Plan's authors, is that to a considerable degree unemployment, underemployment, income disparities, and laggard growth rates are all facets of the same phenomenon; it is unlikely that major improvement can be achieved in any of these areas without coincident progress in the others. What is urgent about the need to create new jobs for the next 15 years is that, in contrast to the birthrate and the food supply which will be responsive to policy measures taken in the next few years, forthcoming entrants into the labor market are already born: there is no way to prevent, or even to substantially delay, them from asserting their claims to employment when they come of working age.

Although information about the size of the labor force is notoriously unreliable, certain broad generalizations are possible. Of great importance is that the distribution of the working force among various occupations has remained constant over time (Table 2-1). Indeed, agriculture's share in 1971 was 72.1 percent, precisely what it had been in 1951, India's priority on industrialization notwithstanding. The share of workers engaged in manufacturing rose substantially during the first decade of planning but declined subsequently as the double-edged sword of rising productivity and slower industrial growth cut new job opportunities at a time when the labor force was growing fast.

In contrast to the long-term stability of India's occupational structure, unemployment has mushroomed, in both rural and urban areas. Compared with the Planning Commission's 1969 estimates, which placed the number of unemployed at 9 to 10 million (approximately three-fourths of them rural), a special Committee on Unemployment reported to the Commission that 1972 unemployment stood at 18.7 million (16.1 million rural and 2.6 million urban).[5] As emphasized by Gunnar Myrdal, it is difficult to interpret these figures because,

[3]For 1971 it was estimated at 170 million, of which 138.6 million were rural and 31.4 million urban. See *Draft Fifth Five-Year Plan, 1974–79* (New Delhi: GOI, Planning Commission, 1974), vol. 1, p. 3.

[4]Ibid.

[5]*Economic and Political Weekly,* June 9, 1973, p. 1012.

TABLE 2–1

DISTRIBUTION AMONG OCCUPATIONS IN INDIA (percent)

	1951	1961	1971
Agriculture	72.1	71.8	72.1
Mining and quarrying	0.6	0.5	0.5
Manufacturing	9.0	10.6	9.5
Construction	1.1	1.1	1.2
Trade and commerce	5.2	4.0	5.6
Transport, storage, and communications	1.5	1.6	2.4
Other	10.5	10.4	8.7
TOTAL	100.0	100.0	100.0

Source: India: Pocket Book of Economic Information: 1972 (New Delhi: GOI, Ministry of Finance, 1972).

under conditions of persistent labor surplus, there is a tendency for disappointed job seekers to drop out of the labor force and for workers to be absorbed through institutional changes which reduce the average productivity of labor; i.e., available work is more widely shared.[6] Research by Raj Krishna shows that the combined total of unemployed and underemployed in 1971 amounted to 29.3 million, 26.2 million of them in rural areas.[7]

India's growing underutilization of its work force was not unforeseen. As early as 1959, Professor D. R. Gadgil observed that the expansion of job opportunities in India's cities was not as fast as had been expected and that it was not keeping pace with the labor supply, which was expanding rapidly in response to population growth and immigration from rural areas.[8] The trends Gadgil had identified were sustained, and more than a decade later the prospect for meeting future demand for jobs in India's cities remained poor, according to V. V. Bhatt:

> Total employment in the organized [mainly urban] sector is 17 million and even if it grew at double the rate experienced in the past two decades, that is, about 10 per cent per annum, this sector cannot absorb even half the [expected] addition to the labor force.[9]

[6]See Gunnar Myrdal, Asian Drama: An Inquiry into the Poverty of Nations (Harmondsworth, England: Penguin Books, 1968), vol. 1, chaps. 22 and 23.

[7]Raj Krishna, "Unemployment in India," Presidential Address to the Indian Society of Agricultural Economics, 1972; reprinted by the Agricultural Development Council, New York.

[8]D. R. Gadgil, Planning and Economic Policy in India (New York: Asia Publishing House, 1965), pp. 123–127.

[9]V. V. Bhatt, Two Decades of Development (Bombay: Vora, 1973), p. 38.

Indian economists have long been sensitive to the employment problem, even if they have not known what practical steps should be taken to solve it. Various remedies have been suggested, and of those which have been tried some have yielded expected benefits.

1. For India, the chosen route to development has always been expanding the economy to provide new production and new employment, while also narrowing income disparities. But in many years India has not attained a growth rate sufficient to absorb the growing work force, and the poor have borne the economic brunt of the shortage of new jobs.

2. On repeated occasions and in various ways India has aided labor-intensive sectors of the economy, especially cottage industries and rural works. For example, the authors of the Third Plan proposed a major rural works program, but like most of its successors, it was neither fully nor well implemented. As seen by India's National Council of Applied Economic Research, its defects included faulty planning, organization, and implementation, particularly the government's false "notion that a public works programme should be considered in addition to or outside the normal five-year plans."[10]

3. Although there is no challenging the commonplace that countries like India should prefer labor-intensive technologies, implementing this strategy has not been easy for various reasons. First among these is ignorance: the evaluation of alternative technologies cannot be done until after production begins, and even then the various standards (conventional cost accounting, social cost accounting, etc.) do not always lead to the same conclusion. In practice, there is, in some industries or processes within industries, no substitute for sophisticated technology, and in other areas substituting labor for capital poses intractable management problems or, while technically feasible, is hopelessly inefficient. It is difficult to generalize about technology, other than to say that a labor-intensive but flexible approach is needed. India's experience includes projects where errors have been due to both excessive and insufficient labor intensity.

4. Finally, various crash programs for the endemically unemployed, drought victims, educated unemployed, and so forth, have been launched with varying—usually low—degrees of success.

The preceding discussion of population and employment has done less than full justice to the complexity and diversity of India's situation. Other significant aspects of the problem to which a more detailed analysis would have to turn include differences among the states; the extent to which entire families, or even larger units such as clans, are the appropriate unit for measuring unemployment or, alternatively, the degree to which the traditional joint family system has been weakened, making the nuclear family of father, mother, and children the relevant unit; commercialization of traditional family relation-

[10]"Employment with Growth," National Council of Applied Economic Research Occasional Paper No. 23 (New Delhi, 1971), p. 8.

ships; effects of migration of one or several family members to the city; and the extension of the unemployment phenomenon to the children of elite families as well as the lower classes.

A dimension of India's labor problem closely linked to employment is the issue of "human capital," the motivation, efficiency, and skill levels of workers as affected by their education, nutrition, and social environment. India's labor force has often been maligned as lazy and unsuited to development, a myth which has not yet been fully dispelled. As seen by modern analysts, cultural differences led foreign observers to confuse laziness with idleness caused by ill health, absence of opportunity, and similar factors. Moreover, on the question of skills, India's ability to build modern factories, atom bombs, and econometric models is now as unquestioned as the ingenuity and resourcefulness of the Punjabi mechanic.

In seeking to determine which problems affect the labor force, we must turn to other questions such as whether available skills match the economy's requirements, whether education is providing the requisite social attitudes to transform a "traditional" society into a modern industrial state, and whether the managerial capacity and personal flexibility needed to make labor efficient are evident in India's working population. Taking literacy as a measure of education, the character and dimensions of this issue are very clear. Although literacy has grown, from 16.6 percent in 1951 to 29.4 percent in 1971, the schooling process has not been able to keep up with the growth of the population, and by 1971 the number of illiterates in India also had grown—by more than 80 million.

The message, that government must increase production, improve social services, and upgrade India's human capital simultaneously, is clear, but the methods for doing so, the political will, and the requisite finances are less apparent. In 1973, Mrs. Gandhi told an international gathering in New Delhi that India needed to simultaneously slow the growth of population and accelerate the growth of national production.[11] Nonetheless, just a few months later the Indian government slashed its funding for the family planning program as a part of a general budgetary cutback. By concentrating attention on income disparities and human capital, the Draft Fifth Plan, is a hopeful sign that the government will deal with these issues, a sign which should not be taken as a forecast, however, in light of the established large gap between political promise and policy reality. The Draft Plan cites statistical and conceptual problems to explain why it has avoided publishing estimates of current and future employment and unemployment. The Commission's position on the accuracy of data is justified, but the fact remains that concealing the magnitude of India's labor problem is no substitute for policies to contain it. This issue is certain to become a growing source of political tension in India if the government fails to expand

[11]Text of Prime Minister's address to the "One Asia Assembly," Press Release No. 621, Indian Embassy, Washington, D.C., January 1973.

employment opportunities over a wide range of geographic regions, skill levels, and industrial sectors.

Natural Resources: The Underutilization
of a Fair Endowment

Contrary to the views of many Westerners who believe that India's wealth is limited to the luxuriant foliage and spice gardens of the south and the life-styles of the Mogul emperors and their colonial successors, India has a good endowment of natural resources. This is not to say that natural resources are abundant, but there is little doubt that the diversity and volume of India's endowment is quite adequate to sustain a standard of living much higher than now prevails. Since this assertion, that India is well off with respect to natural resources, is hardly the conventional wisdom, I shall develop the supporting evidence in some detail.

The availability of food and shelter are determined not only by the quantities of water, land, and other factors, but also by the quality of these inputs, the extent to which they combine in favorable mixtures, and the degree to which their spatial and temporal pattern suits the society's economic demands. Thus, climate is an important determinant of economic conditions,[12] as anyone who spends just a few non-air-conditioned days in the heat of an Indian summer can testify. Evidence from archaeological studies indicates that the topography of India has changed substantially and, from a human point of view, for the worse during the past several millennia. Flooding due to large-scale deforestation is regarded as a possible reason for the decline and virtual disappearance of the Indus Valley civilization of Mohenjo-Daro and Harappa about 1500 B.C. More recently, the process of transforming India's forests into deserts has continued as virgin lands have been put to the plow and the goat culture of the sub-Himalayan region and elsewhere has accelerated soil erosion and done untold damage to the terrain.

The Indian climate is erratic and defies generalization. It ranges from the continously icy high Himalayas and the permanently arid Rajasthan desert to the seasonally hot and cold, wet and dry Gangetic plain, to the temperate climate of the hill areas of both northern and southern India, and to the continuously warm, damp climate in parts of southern India. Annual average rainfall ranges from almost none in the desert and 30 to 50 inches in the fertile Ganges Valley (the American Midwest receives roughly 30 inches each year), to over 150 inches in scattered areas. Characteristic of India's rainfall pattern is its concentration in a few months; the monsoons are highly variable and frequently fail to provide adequate water for a large portion of the country.

---

[12]See, for example, Douglas H. K. Lee, *Climate and Economic Development in the Tropics* (New York: Harper and Co. for the Council on Foreign Relations, 1957).

Flooding and drought are common occurrences, but whereas they both attract newspaper attention and cause considerable inconvenience and personal suffering, flooding usually has a positive net effect on agricultural production whereas the effect of drought is invariably negative. Temperatures in India vary considerably among regions and seasons, but the bulk of the land area is either semitropical or tropical and agriculture is practiced throughout the year. India's location close to the equator provides an important advantage in that the minimum amounts of sunlight required for cultivation are available even in midwinter. Thus, rainfall variability and insufficiency, not temperature, are the principal climatic factors that tend to depress India's food output and make it excessively variable.

Because there is no objective way to measure the "goodness" of climate, it is not fruitful to try to compare India's situation with that of other countries. In contrast, the quantity of arable land available to support farming can be measured with some degree of accuracy. As the decade of the 1970s began, India's average of 334 persons per square kilometer compared with the United States' 117, Japan's 2,084, Germany's 790, and Brazil's 343.[13] The usefulness of even this comparison is limited of course, insofar as it does not allow for variations in the fertility of the soil, salinity, land contour, drainage, irrigation potential, and other important factors. It does suggest, however, that India's land resources are adequate to satisfy current and even prospective nutritional needs, a suggestion which is reinforced by the production increases which have been achieved where green revolution techniques have been introduced.

The green revolution, which is easier to describe than to implement, is such a key element in India's development that we shall return to it repeatedly, especially in Chapter 8. Its power stems from the combination of scientifically developed hybrid seed, fertilizer, herbicide, and controlled irrigation which gives it potential for increasing crop yields and the number of crops that can be grown each year on a plot of land by a multiple of the annual production possible under traditional methods of cultivation.

India's vulnerability to the vagaries of the monsoon has led government and farmers alike to place high priority on impounding waters for irrigation, especially the flood of monsoon rain and melting snow which each year flows above and below ground from the Himalayas to the sea. Government estimates show that of the potential 660 million cubic meters of usable annual river flows (surface water), utilization at the end of the Fourth Plan reached 250 million cubic meters, compared to 95 million cubic meters in 1951.[14] Exploitation of the Brahmaputra, the only significant river system in India which remains to be developed, has been delayed, not only by economic constraints, but by the need

[13]*FAO Production Yearbook, 1971* (Rome: FAO, 1972). *UN Statistical Yearbook, 1971* (New York: United Nations, 1972).

[14]*India: 1974* (New Delhi: GOI, Ministry of Information and Broadcasting, 1975), p. 208.

to enlist the cooperation of East Bengal and perhaps also China. Since Independence, India has more than doubled its use of rechargeable groundwater resources, but it still employs only one-third of the potential. Thus, although India has substantially increased the amount of land under major and minor irrigation since 1951 (Table 2-2), and the lengthy gestation period for large-scale projects suggests that a significant amount of new irrigation will be added, India's critical need for additional progress in this area and its large potential indicate that irrigation should continue to command very high priority.

That India is at an early stage of modernization is indicated by the extent to which human labor has not yet been replaced by animal power and animal power by mechanical power. The energy crisis which followed the Middle East war in 1973 highlighted the dependency of economic growth on adequate and cheap power and lends credence to the thesis that North America and Europe developed rapidly because of the ready availability of inexpensive coal in the nineteenth century and petroleum in the twentieth. India's coal resources, which are found mainly in the northeast, are very extensive, albeit they are generally not of the highest quality and they are geologically situated in ways which make mining costly. There are also very extensive and economically workable lignite deposits in Tamil Nadu, Gujarat, and elsewhere. Although India has increased its use of these fossil fuels, production has not grown anywhere near as fast as it might have, largely because of a decision to use petroleum instead of coal and also because management, labor, and other problems have made coal mining one of the least efficient industries in India. Production of coal has been not only inadequate to meet demand (a shortfall which has been exacerbated by transportation problems), but infinitesimal with

TABLE **2–2**
SPREAD OF IRRIGATION IN INDIA (million hectares)

		Under irrigation	
	Potential	*1951*	*1974*
Surface water	72	16.1	27.1
(Major and medium)	(57)	(9.7)	(19.6)
(Minor)	(15)	(6.4)	(7.5)
Groundwater	35	6.5	16.0
TOTAL	107	22.6	43.1

Note: Total arable land (not all of which can be irrigated) is estimated at 175 million hectares. Of this, 142 million hectares were under cultivation in 1974. The potential for irrigation is expected to increase in response to technological innovations.

Source: Draft Fifth Five-Year Plan, 1974–79 (New Delhi: GOI, Planning Commission, 1974), vol. 2, p. 105.

respect to reserves. Production of 76.4 million tons of coal in 1972–73, for example, compares with known reserves in excess of 80 billion tons, an exploitation rate which would stretch the life of known reserves for more than 1,000 years. The government nationalized coking coal mines in 1972 and noncoking coal mines in 1973 as a means to spur production of coal and meet other objectives. Although the intended acceleration of output did not occur immediately, the post-1973 energy crisis gave this nationalization special significance, and the large new investments government made in coal mining promise to increase the use of this resource greatly.

The size of India's petroleum reserves is unknown, but seismographic studies of offshore locations, done largely with Soviet assistance, indicate that they may be very substantial. In 1973, India's domestic production of crude petroleum amounted to 7 million tons, about one-third of its total need. To supplement this production, which comes mainly from Gujarat and Assam, India has belatedly begun exploration in a number of other areas, including the potentially rich deep-sea deposits in the Bay of Cambay (see pages 297 to 298). Although bringing deep-sea petroleum resources into production is bound to be time-consuming and costly, it is possible that at Cambay and other sites there is so much petroleum that India can become self-sufficient, if not a net exporter of energy.[15]

India also is fortunate in its hydroelectric potential, particularly in the north, where reservoirs are renewed each year by rainfall and melting Himalayan snow. Southern India also depends to a considerable degree on water-generated energy but has less room for expanding its use of hydro power; most rivers have already been exploited and the annual inflow of new water to reservoirs is less certain than in the north because monsoon runoff is the only source. Although India has made enormous strides in exploiting its hydro resources, it is anticipated that by the year 1978–79 only 8.8 percent of a 215 billion kilowatt-hour potential will be realized. Among the factors inhibiting higher output are the uneven distribution of potential among regions, the costliness of creating reservoirs and installing hydroelectric facilities, the long gestation periods for hydro investments, the frequency of running facilities at less than 100 percent of capacity, and political problems of sharing water with Nepal and other nations.

India has embarked on a program to use nuclear power stations to meet its growing energy needs. The Tarapur plant near Bombay has been in operation since 1969, three more facilities are under construction, and others are in the planning stage. The thorium and other materials used to fuel nuclear plants are found in India in quantities adequate for domestic use and export.

[15]India's Petroleum and Chemicals Minister, K. D. Malaviya, was reported in the *Indian Express* of Jan. 22, 1975, to have said that he would not be surprised if India attained self-sufficiency in oil by 1980.

In 1972–73 India generated 67 billion kilowatt-hours of electricity. Although this was more than three times the amount produced in 1960–61 and a very large multiple of what was generated in 1947, it was not enough to prevent the Indian economy from suffering an extreme power shortage. The fault did not lie with India's planners, but rather with such factors as (1) the widespread and prolonged delays encountered in the completion of new power generating facilities (see Table 2-3); (2) difficulties in transmission of electricity; and (3) underutilization of installed capacity due to excessive downtime of equipment, erratic weather which reduced the flow of water into reservoirs, and shortages of coal due to the inefficiency of the coal mines and railroads alike. Because domestic use of electricity has developed slowly (consumer purchasing power and transmission systems are two of the most significant hindrances), the principal effect of the power shortages has been to impede and raise the costs of agricultural and industrial production.[16]

India's geological situation has not yet been fully explored, but it is known that the country has a wealth of mineral resources, including roughly 10 percent of the world's known high-grade iron resources. In addition, there are substantial deposits of exploitable bauxite, copper, diamonds, manganese, phosphate, and other minerals. These resources are not always in readily accessible areas nor are they consistently of the highest quality. Nonetheless, when one takes account of India's economic needs and the potential that mining offers for development, one cannot reach any conclusion other than that India has not exploited its mineral wealth at anywhere near full potential.

[16]See *Draft Fifth Five-Year Plan*, op. cit., vol. 2, p. 122.

TABLE **2–3**
INSTALLED CAPACITY FOR POWER GENERATION:
TARGETS AND ACHIEVEMENTS

	Planned additions to capacity		
	Target (mil. KW)	Achievement (mil. KW)	Shortfall (percent)
First Plan, 1951–1956	1.3	1.1	15.4
Second Plan, 1956–1961	3.5	2.2	35.7
Third Plan, 1961–1966	7.0	4.5	35.8
Interim period, 1966–1969	5.4	4.1	24.1
Fourth Plan, 1969–1974	9.3	4.6*	50.0*

*Anticipated.

Source: *Draft Fifth Five-Year Plan, 1974–79* (New Delhi: GOI, Planning Commission, 1974), vol. 2, p. 118.

Illustratively, the life of *known* reserves at 1971 rates of production would be copper (369 years), bauxite (152 years), phosphorite (226 years), and iron ore (302 years). Looked at from another point of view, India's steel industry could have benefited from indigenous raw materials (iron ore, coal, and limestone), inexpensive labor, and foreign assistance to become a source of exports, but, in reality, India has been unable even to meet domestic steel requirements. The reasons for this disappointing situation are discussed in later chapters.

The Process of Economic Activity

India, more than most developing countries, combines modern and traditional institutions and technologies into a diversity that is lost in generalization and statistical averaging. India's communications situation is illustrative. In sophistication, the transportation network ranges from the footpaths that link Himalayan villages to the jet aircraft that connect major cities. The railroad system is impressive for its length, the variety of services offered, and the number of passengers it carries each year. But all of India's transportation modes tend to have more than a fair share of unreliable moments, and the same is true for other communications systems such as mail, telephone, and telegraph. India's most important vehicles for mass communication are the state-owned All-India Radio network, which broadcasts in many languages, and the press, which is privately owned.

A survey of other sectors of India's economy confirms the impression that despite significant development since Independence, the current situation is marked by the coincidence of generally rudimentary facilities and wide diversity between the most advanced and the most primitive. What is less obvious and, because of its complexity and variety defies description—much more analysis—is the urban-rural, agroindustrial, government-private, and other key institutional linkages which define the distinctive character of India's economy. Nonetheless, these and India's many institutions importantly affect the course of India's development.

Agriculture

No analysis of the Indian economy can escape the fact that roughly 80 percent of the population and close to one-half of the gross national product is in the agricultural sector. And, just as farms are cultivated with technologies which range from protohistoric to ultramodern, the organization of rural society is an amalgam of the modern and traditional. In many parts of India, the practice of private ownership of land which the British introduced to replace the earlier system of communal landholding has had a major effect on society; the resultant disparities between landowners and laborers are a phenomenon only of the past several centuries.[17] In practice, whereas there is a vast disparity in where villages fall between the poles of "traditional" and "modern," there are very few villages which are insensitive to tradition or have not sustained some degree of modernization in the past quarter century.[18]

In India's "traditional" farm economy the level of technology is not only rudimentary but also inflexible. Human and animal labor are the basic sources of power. Irrigation, to the extent that it exists, is based mainly on diversion of river water through canals or the lifting of water from shallow wells by Persian wheels and similar methods. There is great dependence on the monsoon and, because the rains are extremely irregular in most parts of India, there is a large element of uncertainty in decisions taken by agriculturists. The bulk of farm production is of essential commodities such as grains (rice, wheat, and coarse grains), pulses, and cotton. There is also production of fruits and vegetables, and in some areas jute and other cash crops are grown. Meat and fowl production are not important for most farmers, although animal husbandry is essential for motive power and the production of milk, eggs, wool, and dung (which is dried and used as fuel).

In most of India it is customary for farmers to cluster in villages and to walk miles to reach the scattered pieces of land they cultivate. The concentration of landownership in the hands of a small rural elite is no guarantee against small and fragmented landholdings, which are common. Tradition-bound farm communities are comparatively isolated: economically, the bulk of production is consumed where grown and little is imported from outside; politically, as villagers have little communication with the seats of power, they make little input into public policy and policy often ignores their interests; even socially, the villages have only limited intercourse with the world outside, except for neighboring communities. In short, the difficulty of transportation in and out of the villages and the scarcity of marketable surpluses which would cause peasants to travel frequently to market are limiting factors just as the traditional social mores passed from one generation to the next narrow the horizons of rural Indians: the physical isolation of villages is buttressed by a psychological isolation. Shortages of food, medicine, shelter, water, and other basic amenities are another, related aspect of traditional village life.

The picture of traditional village life drawn in the preceding paragraphs is much too stark to be applied generally to all Indian villages and at all times. But it is a caricature and, as such, contains an important element of reality. At the opposite extreme is the "modern" village, a community in touch with the outside world and an area where the green revolution has transformed the pattern of life and livelihood. In the modern village traditional crops such as

[17]See Daniel Thorner and Alice Thorner, *Land and Labor in India* (New York: Asia Publishing House, 1962), p. 53.

[18]On peasant society in India, see George Rosen, *Peasant Society in a Changing Economy,* to be published in 1975 by University of Illinois Press.

wheat and rice are grown, but hybrid seeds are used in conjunction with irrigation (often electric or diesel-driven pumps operating in deep wells), chemical fertilizer, insecticide, tractors, and safe storage areas for harvested crops. Because local production exceeds consumer needs, farmers have frequent occasion to visit market centers and have incomes to acquire nonfarm commodities. Modern technology not only leads to higher incomes but, through monetization of income and consumption, to a much more lively link between the village and the nation at large. Communications are relatively good, for roads are needed to move the crops to market and to obtain fertilizer and other farm inputs. Basic amenities are more plentiful because farmers are aware of the "better life" and can afford to pay for it. And even though the income distribution may be uneven as in the traditional village, the poorest sectors of the society tend to be better off than their counterparts in traditional villages. Finally, modern villages attract an agglomeration of tertiary farm and other small-scale commerce and industry.

To what extent is the green revolution transforming the "average" Indian village from traditional to modern? We shall address this question in Chapter 8. Suffice it here to say that the varieties of Indian experience are profuse. The green revolution has started out in India as mainly a wheat revolution, and it has seriously affected the modalities of farm life in only a limited number of regions such as the northwest, the Tanjore District of Tamil Nadu, and the Andhra coast.[19] The effect of the green revolution is further complicated because elements of modernity may appear long before the advent of major change, and "traditional" social and economic relationships may linger long after modernity's arrival. What is clear about the green revolution is that where it has been most fully applied, the social and economic transformation in its wake has been immense. The socioeconomic pace needed to produce two and even three crops per year on land which previously produced only one, and the resulting increase in output, have commercialized and depersonalized relationships and profoundly transformed the structure of rural society, its economic viability, and its dependence on Indian cities and factories.

The place of agriculture in India is predominant not only because farming directly accounts for a large share of the gross national product and satisfies the nation's inescapable need for food, but because of its central position as an employer of mass labor, consumer of factory production, and producer of raw materials for processing in industry. When the value of industrial and commercial activities directly in support of farming (chemicals, fertilizer, power, and transportation) and the value of production by industries which depend on agricultural production for their raw material (notably textiles, but many others) are combined with value-added in agriculture itself, it is quite clear that

---

[19]Rice is the principal crop in Tanjore and Andhra, but the special circumstances which have permitted major increases in production in these two areas have not yet been generalized for application in other regions.

very little development can take place in India without progress in agriculture. But to say that favorable harvests are a precondition for industrial growth is not to say that they are a sufficient condition, as evidenced by the industrial stagnation which occurred in India despite the good harvests of 1967 to 1972. Finally, in judging the relative priority of Indian agriculture, international land/people ratios must be considered. These suggest that although food self-sufficiency may be a correct Indian objective for many years to come, for the long term India should integrate its economy into the world economy in order to trade the manufactures of its labor for the food others produce with their more adequate land resources.

Nonfarm Commerce and Industry

Village and small industry are still an important source of employment, output, and exports in India. In 1968, for example, handicrafts, textiles (hand-loomed material accounted for almost half of total cloth production), and small-scale industries as a whole accounted for nearly 28 percent of total Indian factory output. This was accomplished even though the average amount of fixed capital per employee in the small-scale sector was only Rs. 3,170 compared to over 20,000 in large-scale units.[20]

Indian industry as a whole (including mining) accounts for only about one-sixth of India's gross national product, but because manufacturing sectors (1) produce commodities vital to the rest of the economy and (2) are on the frontier of the development effort, their strategic importance is proportionately greater. The psychological and ideological attractions of petroleum refineries, steel mills, and similar trappings of twentieth-century technology are well understood by Westerners. The intrinsic significance of heavy industry is sometimes belittled by outsiders, however, as they do not recognize the full implications of India's "industrialization imperative": (1) national security is better defended if military weapons are manufactured at home; (2) full participation in the benefits of international trade requires the development of industrial capacities so that manufacturing exports can supplement traditional exports of primary commodities; and (3) full use of the growing number of employables requires extensive industrial expansion. In short, the viability of India as a modern nation is vitally affected by the pace of its industrial progress.

In 1947, although India ranked among the world's leading industrial nations, its industrial capacity was largely confined to infrastructure such as railroads and to light manufacturing for domestic consumption (textiles alone accounted for nearly 50 percent of manufacturing output). The steel plant built by the great Indian entrepreneur Sir Jamshedjee Tata and a few other heavy-industry facilities existed at that time but were exceptional. Following Independence, however, there has been a remarkable diversification and enlargement of Indian industry, and even though India has not grown as quickly as many other

---

[20]*Draft Fifth Five-Year Plan,* op. cit., vol. 2, p. 160.

nations, it has retained its place as one of the world's larger industrial nations. The explanation of why Indian industry grew lies in Nehru's perception that if India was to be strong, it would have to modernize and industrialize: to take advantage of existing managerial and technical skills, the relative freedom with which technology could be imported, the willingness of some foreign investors to establish factories in India, and the availability of foreign official aid funds and technical assistance.

Because Indian industrialization sprang from diverse roots, it has developed in various ways. In its effort to control the "commanding heights" of the economy, government concentrated on what became known as the "core" and "priority" sectors, mainly heavy industries and capital goods manufactures where India had little or no earlier experience. Private businessmen, large and small, engaged in the wide range of sectors where government permitted them to invest, particularly in those catering to consumer demands. Some states (Tamil Nadu, Punjab, and Maharashtra) benefited greatly from industrialization, while others (Bihar) received considerable new public investment but continued to experience less than average per capita income. West Bengal, the pre-Independence industrial heartland, gradually lost place to Madras, Delhi, Bombay, Hyderabad, Poona, Ahmadabad, Bangalore, Kanpur, and other new industrial centers for various reasons: (1) a change in the commodity composition of manufacturing reduced the importance of raw materials accessibility; (2) the central government decided (for equity, political, and defense reasons) to distribute industry more evenly throughout the country; (3) the states competed actively for new investments; and (4) West Bengal suffered from labor-management problems and a deteriorating industrial climate.

The technologies used by Indian manufacturers have depended not only on the range of technical options, which varies among industries, but on when the factory was built and the national origin of the foreign collaborator, if any. Although there are extreme examples of companies using only high or low technologies, many Indian firms use intermediate types, and the mixture of advanced and traditional technologies within a firm—as when raw materials are moved about steel plants by head basket—is both common and economically sound. Because Indian industry is characterized by this continuum and diversity of technologies, the concept of economic dualism is less applicable in India than in other developing countries where there are stark contrasts between the modern and traditional with little in between.[21]

The number of workers in India's so-called organized sector (mainly urban and larger institutions) amounted to more than 17 million in 1971, the majority employed by the central, state, and local governments. (See Table 2-4.) Employees of larger Indian firms (public and private sector) are better organized and better paid than other workers and form an industrial elite. India's trade union

[21]On the significance of dualism, see W. A. Lewis, "Economic Development with Unlimited Supplies of Labor," *Manchester School of Economic and Social Studies,* May 1954.

TABLE 2–4

EMPLOYMENT IN INDIA'S "ORGANIZED" SECTOR,* 1971 (thousands)

Industry	Public sector	Private sector	Total
Plantations, forestry	279	871	1,151
Mining and quarrying	185	402	587
Manufacturing	813	3,779	4,592
Construction	871	129	1,000
Utilities	436	45	482
Trade and commerce	342	291	633
Transport and communication	2,230	93	2,323
Service, including government administration	5,627	996	6,623
All industries	10,784	6,607	17,391

*Excludes establishments employing fewer than 25 workers.

Note: Totals may not add, owing to rounding.

Source: Employment Review (New Delhi: GOI, Ministry of Labor, June 1971).

system, while embracing only a fraction of the total work force, is highly developed. Unions are generally sponsored by, or associated with, particular political parties, and there usually is great interunion rivalry. Strikes and other industrial disputes are frequent and are often caused by jurisdictional, organizational, and political conflicts rather than economic issues.

At the apex of India's industrial hierarchy are a few dozen family-controlled conglomerate empires which are largely the creation of businessmen from particular communities, such as the Parsis from Bombay and the Marwaris from Rajputana. These industrial giants have been preserved and even expanded since 1947 despite India's desire to create a "socialist pattern of society." They owe their power to their ability to (1) parlay established industrial positions into market leadership; (2) attract management, new technology, capital, etc., often through joint ventures with foreign companies; and (3) exercise political influence. The principal question attending their future (see Chapter 9) is whether, because of the management and technical assets of some of them, the government will overlook their antisocialist implications and close connections with the resented foreign capitalists. The answer to this question will depend somewhat on whether the Indian government acknowledges that these large houses operate with divergent amounts of industrial statesmanship and whether it formulates policies which deal with companies according to their merit.

Finally, as Table 2-4 indicated, government is an important employer in India. About three-fourths of government workers are at the state and local levels, and although a substantial portion of this work force is employed in administrative and public service capacities, government does occupy a commanding position in heavy industry and other particular sectors of the economy.

Macroeconomic Sketch

Subjective narrative about the Indian economy not only tells a great deal about the modalities of how the system operates but, to some degree, is more reliable than Indian economic statistics, which at best are only rough indicators of the parameters they purport to measure. The problem stems not only from the gargantuan task of gathering and processing masses of data, but from purposeful distortion of information (for example, the misreporting of farm output described on page 52.

Nonetheless, there is valuable information to be gleaned from official data, and statistical errors, if not offsetting, can be cross-checked to test their plausibility. One last caveat about Indian statistics concerns the large role of agriculture in the Indian economy; because annual variations in rainfall cause large fluctuations in farm production from year to year, annual changes in national accounts data also are large and not necessarily indicative of underlying trends.

National Income

That India is a poor country is undisputed, albeit conventional estimates which show its national income in the Indian fiscal year (IFY) 1971–72 to be the rupee equivalent of $47.7 billion (about $86 per capita) are misleadingly low. Since Independence, India's national income has grown at an average of roughly 3.3 percent per annum (Table 2-5), a big improvement over the 0.7

TABLE 2–5

GROWTH OF NET NATIONAL PRODUCT (average annual percentage change measured in constant prices)

Period	Population	Net national product	Per capita net national product
1951–52 to 1955–56 (First Plan)	1.8	3.4	1.6
1956–57 to 1960–61 (Second Plan)	2.1	4.0	1.6
1961–62 to 1965–66 (Third Plan)	2.2	2.6	0.3
1966–67 to 1968–69 (interplan years)	2.2	4.4	2.1
1969–70 to 1973–74 (Fourth Plan)	2.2	2.8	0.5
1951–52 to 1973–74	2.1	3.3	1.1

Sources: Computed from *Economic Survey*, various issues; *Commerce Economic Studies* X; and Vadilal Dagli, ed., *Twenty-five Years of Independence: A Survey of Indian Economy* (Bombay: Vora, 1973).

percent growth rate estimated for the first half of the twentieth century,[22] and even more impressive in light of the economic stagnation India experienced during the period 1800–1950.[23] In the post-Independence period the annual rate of population increase has accelerated to 2 percent, and consequently income per head has grown at only 1.1 percent per year. This rate is well below Plan targets and is disappointing because it implies that India's strategy of accelerating growth and gradually shifting the economy's center of gravity from agriculture to industry has not yet had the desired effect. Because of bad weather in 1965–66 the growth figures for the Third Plan appear lower than justified and those for the next three years are exaggerated. In subsequent years, however, the slow growth rate is due to a deceleration in the rate of progress rather than to any statistical mirage.

Structure of Net National Product

Because the growth of agricultural production has been marginally less than the increase in total Indian output (goods and services), the significance of agriculture as a share of national income has declined.[24] The "conventional" national product estimates presented in the first part of Table 2-6 cannot be extended beyond IFY 1968–69 because of a change in the Indian government's method of data presentation. This data series shows that during the two decades, IFY 1948–49 to 1968–69, the share of agriculture in net national product slipped from 49.1 percent to 40.0 percent. Owing to drought, it reached a low point in the mid-1960s from which it rebounded in response to several factors, including the industrial recession and the green revolution. Nonetheless, in 1973–74 agriculture's share of national income was close to its all-time low and likely to decline further. An ill omen for the Indian economy is that the reduction in the share of national output of agriculture appears to be balanced more by an increase in the share of public and private services than in the share of mining and manufacturing sectors.

Agriculture

Although agriculture is critical to the Indian economy, its growth has been very uneven. As indicated by Table 2-7, wheat has been the star performer, and pulses (critical because they are the principal source of protein for many Indians) have been the outstanding laggard. (In part, the reason for smaller

[22]Angus Maddison, *Class Structure and Economic Growth: India and Pakistan since the Moghuls* (New York: W. W. Norton, 1971), p. 76.

[23]See V. V. Bhatt, "A Century and a Half of Economic Stagnation in India," *Economic and Political Weekly,* Special Number, July 1973, p. 1229. Bhatt estimates that in the period 1788 to 1929 per capita income declined by 30 percent.

[24]Note that the juxtaposition of agriculture's having maintained its share of a growing employment pool and its decline as a contributor to India's national product implies a reduction in the relative efficiency of farm labor.

TABLE 2-6

ESTIMATES OF NET NATIONAL PRODUCT BY INDUSTRY OF ORIGIN (percentage distribution)

Industry groups	At 1948–49 prices*				At 1960–61 prices†			
	1948–49	1950–51	1955–56	1960–61	1960–61	1965–66	1970–71	1973–74
Agriculture, animal husbandry, and ancillary activities‡	49.1	49.0	47.9	46.4	52.5	44.2	46.2	43.2
Mining, manufacturing, and small enterprises	17.1	16.7	16.8	16.6	19.2	23.6	22.3	22.6
Commerce, transport, and communications	18.5	18.8	18.8	19.2	14.1	16.4	15.8	16.3
Other services¶	15.5	15.7	16.5	18.2	14.7	16.8	16.6	18.8
Net domestic product at factor cost	100.2	100.2	100.0	100.4	100.5	101.0	100.9	100.9
Net factor income from abroad	-0.2	-0.2	0.0	-0.4	-0.5	-1.0	-0.9	-0.9
Net national product at factor cost	100.0	100.0	100.0	100.0	100.0	100.0	100.0	100.0

*Conventional series.

†Revised series.

‡Including forestry and fishery.

¶Comprising professions and liberal arts, government services (administration), domestic service, and house property.

Source: Economic Survey, various issues.

TABLE 2–7
GROWTH OF AGRICULTURAL PRODUCTION* (percent per annum)

	First Plan, 1951–52 to 1955–56	Second Plan, 1956–57 to 1960–61	Third Plan, 1961–62 to 1965–66	Interim, 1966–67 to 1968–69	Fourth Plan, 1969–70 to 1973–74	Total period, 1951–52 to 1973–74
Cereals	5.0	3.8	−2.1	10.0	2.7	3.3
(Wheat)	(5.4)	(4.4)	(−1.1)	(18.9)	(4.8)	(5.4)
(Rice)	(5.4)	(3.8)	(−2.5)	(8.9)	(2.1)	(3.1)
Pulses	5.2	1.7	−5.2	0.8	−1.0	0.2
Oilseeds	2.0	4.3	−1.2	2.0	4.1	2.3
Fibers	6.6	3.3	−1.3	−1.0	5.5	2.9
(Cotton)	(6.8)	(5.6)	(−2.7)	(3.9)	(2.5)	(2.9)
Sugar	1.0	8.9	2.3	0.1	1.8	3.1
TOTAL†	5.2	4.0	−1.3	6.2	2.8	3.1

*Crop year ends June 30.

†Includes other items.

Source: Economic Survey, various issues.

pulse production is that land was more frequently devoted to grains when the prospective profits from such cultivation became greater than from growing pulses.) The impact of the green revolution not only is evident in the growth of wheat production but is reflected in rising output per acre cultivated. As shown by Table 2-8, as India's potential for increasing farm acreage diminished toward the end of the 1950s, productivity gains began to play an increasingly important role in raising output. Improving per acre yields became particularly significant in the late 1960s when the green revolution strategy was stressed, and, by the growing season 1972–73, the cumulative increase in productivity amounted to 41.9 percent compared to a 26.3 percent rise in the amount of land under cultivation. Although India still has some desert which can be irrigated, and some saline areas and wastelands which can be reclaimed, such resources are limited and costly to develop. Thus the main basis for raising future output is expansion of double-cropping, fertilizer use, and other productivity-increasing measures.

Industry

The comparatively rapid increase in India's industrial output (over 6 percent per annum) is readily explained by the small base from which it began its growth and the emphasis government policy placed on this sector. (See Table 2-9.) Just as important to the economy as growth is the degree to which the structure of industrial production has been redirected from consumer items to

TABLE 2-8
INDEX OF AGRICULTURAL PRODUCTION: AREA AND YIELD
(base: 1949-50 to 1951-52 [average] = 100*)

| Year† | Index numbers of | | |
	Area 2	Production 3	Yield per hectare 4
1950-51	100.0	100.0	100.0
1951-52	101.8	100.7	99.0
1952-53	105.6	107.1	101.3
1953-54	109.1	113.7	104.2
1954-55	112.2	118.7	105.9
1955-56	113.8	122.2	107.3
1956-57	114.6	121.8	106.3
1957-58	116.1	127.5	109.8
1958-59	117.7	129.6	110.0
1959-60	119.7	138.5	115.7
1960-61	121.2	142.4	117.5
1961-62	122.4	145.5	119.0
1962-63	123.4	145.9	118.2
1963-64	123.9	150.9	121.7
1964-65	123.3	148.6	120.5
1965-66	122.7	144.7	117.9
1966-67	123.5	145.2	117.5
1967-68	124.5	154.2	123.8
1968-69	126.9	167.7	132.2
1969-70	127.5	174.8	137.1
1970-71	130.6	186.4	142.9
1971-72	125.8	184.5	143.4
1972-73	126.3	184.6	141.9

*Three-year moving averages.

†The agricultural year is July-June.

Source: Economic Survey, various issues.

heavy engineering and capital goods. In the period 1960–1973, for example, the index of industrial production doubled, but growth rates for consumer items did less well than the overall index: food manufacturing grew by 54.6 percent, textiles by 12.2 percent, etc. In contrast, despite the industrial recession which began in the second half of the 1960s, impressive growth was recorded for manufactures of chemicals (+201.8 percent), basic metals (+115.8 percent), and nonelectrical machinery (+355.0 percent). These growth rates notwithstanding, the comparatively fast increase of India's industrial produc-

TABLE 2–9

INDEX OF INDUSTRIAL PRODUCTION: SELECTED YEARS (1960 = 100)

	1951	1956	1961	1966	1969	1973
General index	54.8	78.4	109.5	152.4	172.5	193.4
Mining and quarrying	66.6	78.7	105.4	137.1	147.4	163.6
Manufacturing	54.6	79.6	109.1	150.8	167.2	193.1
Food manufacturing	66.9	79.6	108.6	127.2	137.0	154.6
Beverage and tobacco industries	58.0	71.1	107.0	158.9	164.0	179.3
Textiles (cotton and jute)	79.7	98.0	102.8	108.9	109.5	112.2
Footwear and other textiles	63.5	67.4	115.4	184.2	177.2	151.3
Wood and cork products, except furniture	43.5	46.9	95.5	201.7	256.6	158.4
Paper and paper products	38.5	58.1	105.8	160.0	201.4	238.8
Leather and fur products	72.4	70.6	100.9	120.9	88.9	76.1
Rubber products	56.1	69.6	112.9	160.2	215.5	251.2
Chemicals and chemical products	42.4	63.7	113.4	166.7	217.5	301.8
Petroleum refinery products	11.0	69.6	106.0	195.9	280.0	332.8
Nonmetallic mineral products	39.0	62.0	106.9	149.1	175.2	226.8
Basic metal industries	46.5	56.4	118.7	186.4	209.7	215.8
Metal products, except machinery	30.7	74.6	112.4	209.6	205.1	243.1
Machinery other than electrical machinery	22.2	52.2	121.2	281.8	349.1	455.0
Electrical machinery and appliances	26.3	56.5	110.0	224.9	322.4	436.1
Transport equipment	19.6	102.8	116.7	164.5	135.4	148.7
Electricity generation	35.7	58.5	116.3	207.8	301.1	383.8

Addendum: average annual growth
rate of total output (percent)
1951–1956   7.4
1956–1961   6.9
1961–1966   6.8
1966–1969   4.2
1969–1973   3.8
1951–1973   6.1

Sources: Economic Survey, various issues; Basic Statistics Relating to the Indian Economy: 1950–51 to 1960–61 (New Delhi: GOI, Planning Commission, 1971); and Monthly Abstract of Statistics (New Delhi: GOI, Ministry of Planning), October 1974.

tion index in the face of the slow growth in that sector's employment of labor suggests that mechanization, with its attendant improvement in labor productivity, is an inescapable feature of industrial growth. Thus, this sector must enjoy a still faster rate of expansion if it is to absorb an appreciable amount of India's growing work force.

Commercial Services

Trade, transportation, and communications are not the most popular areas for economic analysis, but they are critical to both the traditional and modernized sectors of the economy. As shown by Table 2-6, they account for roughly one-sixth of India's net national product, and their share of the total has grown by a small amount. If income per person were to rise more rapidly in the future, it is likely that the share of commercial services would increase more than proportionally.

Public Administration and Defense

Although published Indian national accounts data do not facilitate analysis of how public sector spending has changed as a proportion of total net national product, budget data indicate that the importance of public spending has roughly tripled, from 5.6 percent of national product in IFY 1950–51 to 17.8 percent in IFY 1970–71. Included in this figure is defense spending, which increased from 1.8 percent of net national product in IFY 1950–51 to 4.2 percent in IFY 1971–72. (See Table 3-1, page 112.) Most of this increase in defense spending took place during the first half of the 1960s, when India was engaged in conflicts with China and Pakistan. State and central government budget data show that over the course of time an increasing proportion of expenditures is controlled by Delhi. Total outlays by the Indian States and Union Territories in IFY 1968–69 equaled 73 percent of central government spending, compared with 89 percent in IFY 1950–51.[25]

Consumption and Distribution

National accounts data for consumption in countries at India's stage of development are, at best, informed estimates because of the inaccuracies of the sample surveys which must be used to measure how much is consumed at the point of production and never enters the market economy. Because a large proportion of family income in India is devoted to necessities, mainly food (Table 2-10), the secular change in per capita availability (production plus net imports plus net inventory change) of a limited number of items which account for the bulk of consumer spending can be used to measure changes in the welfare of the Indian people. The information presented in Table 2-11 indicates that the availability of such goods has, in most cases, just barely kept pace with the growth of population, and in the case of pulses, it has fallen substantially. Combining (1) the fact that India's per capita net national product has risen by about 25 percent since Independence with (2) these data showing little per capita growth in consumption of basic commodities leads to the suspicion

[25]Computed from data on pp. 124–126 of *Basic Statistics Relating to the Indian Economy*, op. cit.

TABLE **2–10**
PER CAPITA MONTHLY CONSUMPTION: 1964–65 (rupees)

	Rural	Urban	City
Food items	19.3	22.7	32.3
Cereals	11.6	8.7	7.4
Pulses	1.3	1.3	1.4
Milk and products	1.8	3.3	5.5
Edible oil	0.8	1.4	2.2
Other	3.8	8.0	15.8
Nonfood items	7.1	13.3	26.0
Clothing	1.9	2.1	2.8
Fuel and light	1.6	2.1	2.7
Durable goods	0.5	0.7	1.3
Other	3.1	8.4	19.2
Total, all items	26.4	36.0	58.3

Note: Average size of household used in sample: 5.2, rural; 4.6, urban; and 4.0, city.

Source: India: 1971–72 (New Delhi: GOI, Ministry of Information and Broadcasting, 1972), p. 179.

that the fruits of India's growth have been shared unequally; that income disparities between wealthy and poor Indians have remained large and even may have widened.

Economic inequality in India cannot be documented precisely, but sample survey data confirm the existence of vast disparities. This is illustrated by Table 2-12, which divides the Indian population into deciles according to disposable income. According to the table, in the early period (mid-1950s) the poorest 10 percent of the population had only 3 percent of India's total disposable income. In contrast, the wealthiest 10 percent enjoyed a 34 percent share. The table also shows that the distribution of disposable income is more equal in rural India than in the urban areas and that for the period considered there was no major shift in the basic pattern of distribution from the mid-1950s to the early 1960s. More recent work on this subject by Dandekar and Rath[26] and others supports the conclusions of India's Income Distribution Committee (P. C. Mahalanobis, chairman) that there has been "no significant change in the distribution of incomes although they do indicate a slight probable increase in inequality in the urban sector and some reduction in inequality in the rural sector."[27]

[26]V. M. Dandekar and N. Rath, "Poverty in India: Dimensions and Trends," *Economic and Political Weekly,* Jan. 2, 1971.

[27]*Report of the Committee on Distribution of Income and Levels of Living* (P. C. Mahalanobis, chairman), (New Delhi: GOI, Planning Commission, 1964), part 1, p. 23.

TABLE 2–11
PER CAPITA AVAILABILITY OF IMPORTANT CONSUMER ITEMS

Year	Cereals (grams/day)	Pulses (grams/day)	Edible*† oil (kg/year)	Sugar† (kg/year)	Cloth (meters/year)	Electricity†‡ (kwh/year)
1950	NA¶	NA	3.3	3.0	11.0	1.6
1951	333	60	NA	NA	NA	NA
1952	325	59	NA	NA	NA	NA
1953	349	63	NA	NA	NA	NA
1954	387	69	NA	NA	NA	NA
1955	372	71	3.2	5.0	14.4	2.4
1956	360	70	NA	NA	NA	NA
1957	374	72	NA	NA	NA	NA
1958	349	58	NA	NA	NA	NA
1959	393	75	NA	NA	NA	NA
1960	382	65	4.0	4.7	15.0	3.4
1961	400	69	3.9	5.8	16.0	3.8
1962	399	62	3.9	5.4	15.6	4.2
1963	384	60	3.5	4.9	15.9	4.4
1964	401	51	4.4	5.1	16.8	4.7
1965	419	62	3.4	5.7	16.4	4.8
1966	360	48	3.2	5.1	15.7	5.2
1967	362	40	4.0	4.3	15.3	5.7
1968	404	56	3.3	5.0	16.3	6.0
1969	398	47	3.7	6.1	15.4	6.5
1970	403	52	4.3	7.3	15.3	7.0
1971	418	51	4.0	6.7	14.1	7.3
1972	420	47	3.1	6.1	14.8	7.5
1973	383	41	3.8	6.0	13.6	NA
1974	408	40	NA	NA	NA	NA

*Includes vanaspati.

†Fiscal year April–March.

‡Domestic use only.

¶N.A. = not available.

Note: The table includes net domestic production and imports.

Source: Economic Survey, various issues.

The disparities in disposable income can be illustrated by the so-called Lorenz curve technique (Figure 1). In the Lorenz diagram population deciles are measured on the horizontal axis; income and other indicators are measured on the vertical axis. A hypothetical, perfectly egalitarian distribution in which each decile of population accounted for 10 percent of income is shown by the 45-degree diagonal. The greater the departure from this line, the greater the inequality of income or whatever else is being measured. The value of the

TABLE 2–12
DISTRIBUTION OF DISPOSABLE INCOME IN INDIA (percent)

Income-group decile	Early period*			Late period†		
	Rural	Urban	All-India	Rural	Urban	All-India
First	4	3	3	3	2	3
Second	4	4	4	4	4	4
Third	5	4	5	6	4	6
Fourth	5	5	5	7	5	6
Fifth	8	5	5	8	6	7
Sixth	8	8	9	9	7	7
Seventh	10	8	8	9	7	9
Eighth	12	11	11	12	10	11
Ninth	15	15	16	18	12	12
Tenth	29	37	34	24	43	35
TOTAL	100	100	100	100	100	100

*1953–54 and 1954–55.

†1961–62 and 1963–64.

Source: V. V. Bhatt, *Two Decades of Development: The Indian Experiment* (Bombay: Vora, 1973), p. 50.

Lorenz curve is that it underscores how in India disparities in disposable income are greater than disparities in grain consumption, but much smaller than disparities in family wealth (as measured by landownership). It would be incorrect to interpret the comparatively more egalitarian distribution of grain consumption, noted by the Mahalanobis committee, as an indication that the data on disposable income exaggerated disparities. The difference between grain and income disparities is a function of the distress situation of the poor, who, in contrast to the rich, must devote the major portion of their incomes to buying grain. Moreover, the slight improvement in the distribution of cereal consumption which Mahalanobis detected may have been merely a statistical mirage or a shift in the consumption pattern of the poor toward inferior grain varieties.[28]

India's large income and grain consumption disparities are a function of an even more inegalitarian distribution of wealth (also illustrated in Figure 1). Information about wealth disparities in India is conspicuously unreliable, but the general pattern is indicated by the distribution of land among rural families

[28]B. S. Minhas, "Rural Poverty, Land Redistribution, and Development Strategy," paper presented to the Seminar on Employment and Income Distribution, New Delhi, 1970 (mimeograph), p. 6.

FIGURE 1

Illustrative Lorenz Curve for Cereal Consumption, Disposable Income, and Wealth

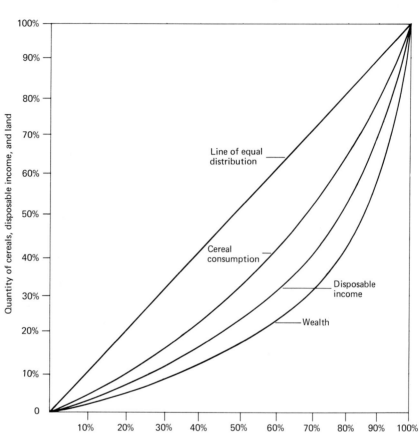

Note: Land ownership is used as the measure of wealth.

Source: P. C. Mahalanobis, *Talks on Planning* (New York: Asia Publishing House for the Indian Statistical Institute, 1961.

(Table 2-13). More than 10 percent of India's rural families are landless and the next poorest fourth own less than half an acre. By comparison, the 437,000 families comprised in the richest 0.6 percent of landholders own more than 11 percent of the total acreage. The distribution of dividends and other indicators of *nonfarm wealth* suggest that the rural pattern of enormous disparities is repeated for India's urban population.[29]

[29]For example, the top 10 percent of households earning dividends account for more than 50 percent of such payments. See *Report of the Committee on Distribution of Income,* op. cit., appendix, table 7.

TABLE 2-13
DISTRIBUTION OF LANDOWNERSHIP IN RURAL INDIA: 1960–61

Size of land-holding (acres)	Households		Area owned	
	Number (thousands)	Percent of total	Acres (thousands)	Percent of total
0–0.005	8,464	11.7	NA*	NA
0.005– 0.49	19,005	26.2	1,732	0.5
0.50– 0.99	4,574	6.3	3,330	1.0
1.00– 2.49	11,484	15.8	19,064	6.0
2.50– 4.99	10,984	15.2	39,401	12.4
5.00– 7.49	6,007	8.3	36,783	11.6
7.50– 9.99	3,310	4.6	28,517	9.0
10.00–12.49	2,310	3.2	25,551	8.0
12.50–14.99	1,375	1.9	18,852	5.9
15.00–19.99	1,793	2.5	30,708	6.7
20.00–24.99	1,094	1.5	24,152	7.6
25.00–29.99	622	0.8	16,932	5.3
30.00–49.99	1,005	1.4	37,460	11.8
50.00 and above	437	0.6	35,379	11.1
TOTAL	72,464	100.00	317,861	100.00

*NA = not available.

Source: Compiled from Indian Statistical Institute, National Sample Survey, Seventeenth Round, Report Nos. 140 (1966) and 176 (1967), New Delhi.

Although many Indians regard as deplorable the unequal distribution of income and the government's failure to change this to better reflect the leadership's socialist objectives, India's situation is considerably more egalitarian than that of many other nations. According to one study based on a sample of 44 developing countries, India's poorest 20 percent earned 8 percent of national income. This compared to 5.6 percent for the sample as a whole. Moreover, the study showed that India's richest 20 percent had a 42 percent share of its income, compared to 56 percent for the sample as a whole.[30]

Savings, Investment, and Productivity

From various not altogether consistent sources it is possible to gather a rough impression of how India's savings and investment processes have evolved. Since

[30]I. Adelman and C. T. Morris, Economic Growth and Social Equity in Developing Countries (Stanford, Calif.: Stanford University Press, 1973).

the early 1950s, the Planning Commission and the Ministry of Finance together have spearheaded a drive to increase the share of domestic savings in national income. In response to their development policies the savings rate, which stood at barely over 5 percent in the years just following Independence, has been increased substantially. It peaked in 1965–66 at 11.1 percent, however, and in the subsequent period of economic adversity it has been slow to recover lost ground. (See Table 2-14.)

According to official statistics, Indian households, including unincorporated economic units, account for between two-thirds and three-fourths of total domestic savings. Information about this sector is elusive, however, and it is likely the savings capacity of households is substantially understated.[31] Illustratively, statisticians encounter difficulties when they estimate nonfinancial savings, as in the case of a farmer who uses part of his income to invest in a new

[31]See K. N. Raj, "Some Issues Concerning Investment and Savings in the Indian Economy," in E. A. G. Robinson and M. Kidron, eds., *Economic Development in South Asia* (New York: St. Martin's Press 1970), pp. 278–298.

TABLE **2–14**
SAVINGS AND INVESTMENT (as a percentage of net domestic product)

	Domestic savings	plus	Foreign capital inflow	equals	Investment
1950–51*	5.5		. . .		5.5
1955–56*	7.0		1.0		8.0
1960–61*	8.5		2.5		11.0
1960–61	8.9		3.1		12.0
1961–62	8.6		2.2		10.8
1962–63	9.6		2.4		12.0
1963–64	10.7		2.0		12.7
1964–65	9.8		2.2		12.0
1965–66	11.1		2.3		13.4
1966–67	9.0		3.2		12.2
1967–68	7.9		2.7		10.6
1968–69	8.4		1.1		9.5
1969–70	8.4		0.8		9.2
1970–71	8.3		1.3		9.6
1970–71*	10.1		1.2		11.3
1971–72*	11.4		1.5		12.9
1972–73*	11.0		0.8		11.8
1973–74*	10.0		0.8		10.8

*As a percentage of net national product.

Sources: *Fourth Plan Mid-term Appraisal* (New Delhi: GOI, Planning Commission, 1971), vol I, pp. 38 and 40; *Second Five-Year Plan* (New Delhi: GOI, Planning Commission, 1956), p. 8; *India: Pocket Book of Economic Information: 1972* (New Delhi: GOI, Ministry of Finance), p. 271; and RBI, *Report on Currency and Finance: 1973–74*, p. 11.

piece of machinery. Moreover, many financial and other transactions go unre-
ported owing to income tax evasion. Nonetheless, in contrast to people with
subsistence incomes who by definition are unable to save, India's poor have
shown a remarkable ability to refrain from consumption when it is in their
interest and the institutional machinery is present. This explains why, in
response to the increase in Indian national income since 1947 (perhaps supplemented by a more unequal income distribution), Indians have increased the
proportion of their total incomes devoted to saving. For example, the percentage of household income invested in financial instruments has grown from 0.2
percent in 1950–51 to 4.8 percent in 1971–72. The positive investor response
to improved real and financial investment opportunities suggests that if India
were to experiment with the high interest rate policies which have been so
successful in Taiwan, South Korea, and other developing countries, it might
further increase savings.

Private Indian corporations have saved as much as 0.8 percent of national
income in prosperous years, but their ability to save has declined to near zero
during periods of general economic adversity. Corporate savings as a percentage of national income have shown no tendency to increase over time, a
situation which is consistent with the Indian government's policy of gradually
reducing the importance of large private enterprise but not necessarily with
national growth objectives. In contrast to corporations, the government sector
has substantially increased its savings ratio since the First Plan years, when
savings averaged about 1 percent of national income. The savings rate reached
almost 3 percent during the Third Plan but fell back to less than 2 percent
during the late 1960s and early 1970s. To finance its increased savings, the
government has greatly expanded its revenues; it has roughly doubled its tax
collections to about 15 percent of net national product.

Foreign capital flows to India—from official and private sources—have
supplemented domestic savings and added to the amount of funds available for
investment. Inflows of such foreign financial resources, which were negligible
until 1957, grew to roughly 3 percent of national income within a very few
years. By the end of the 1960s, however, they had declined to about 1 percent
and, barring a major change in the prospect for foreign assistance, they are
unlikely to become much larger.

India is no exception to the rule that investment, which by definition equals
the sum of household, corporate, government, and foreign savings, is function-
ally linked to the savings capacity. Just as the effort of savers to meet their
targets affects the volume of resources available for investment, the aggressive-
ness of investors affects the amount that is saved. India's net capital formation
increased from about 5 percent of net national income in the early post-
Independence years to almost 12 percent during the Third Plan: it sustained a
more than tenfold increase in public sector investment, and private net capital
formation increased fourfold. To finance public investment, the government
has increasingly gone beyond its own savings and co-opted savings of the private

sector, a practice which at least partially explains why the differential growth of public and private investment is so great. In 1970–71, for example, public savings covered less than one-fifth of the government's investment program; the remainder was financed with savings of the private domestic and foreign sectors.

To concentrate investment so heavily in the public sector, the Indian government not only has had to maintain high tax rates and heavy borrowing from the capital markets, but has had to restrict private investment through a complex network of administrative controls, the subject of Chapters 9 and 11. Suffice it here to say that policy may have posed a greater constraint on investment than officials realized at the time policies were adopted; the government discouraged investment not only by the large private "monopoly" firms but by many smaller private interests. For example, farmers reacted to ill-considered land reform legislation by failing to install irrigation equipment or even destroying existing pumps in order to retain title to larger amounts of land. The curbing of private investment is particularly disquieting because of the government's tendency to respond to rising budgetary deficits by reducing its own rate of investment.

Although India has managed to increase its rate of investment, the joy that should attend this change is diluted by the declining productivity of investment expenditures. According to P. R. Brahmananda, the failure of the national income growth rate of 3.4 percent per annum to keep pace with the 4.2 percent per annum growth rate of the capital stock during the period 1950–51 to 1968–69 reflects a reduction in the productivity of Indian capital (for this period the capital/output ratio increased from 2.1:1 to 2.8:1).[32] To some degree, the extended industrial recession which began in the mid-1960s and the decline in the productivity of Indian investment are aspects of the same problem.[33] By concentrating its investment effort on heavy industry, India created a structural imbalance in the economy: this policy made national economic growth heavily dependent on the demand for output of the heavy industrial sector and the availability of the raw materials used by it. Thus, when short supplies of domestic raw materials, which could not be remedied by imports owing to foreign exchange shortages, combined with domestic recession, they forced Indian industry into a vicious circle of stagnation. Not only did the consumer goods sector operate inefficiently and at levels well below capacity, but the excess capacity in this area caused a reduction in the demand for new investment which left the capital goods industries working at only a small fraction of their rated capacities. Be that as it may, it would be preposterous to conclude that because India has encountered diminishing returns on investment, it

[32]See Brahmananda, "The Secular Behavior of the Indian Economy," in Vadilal Dagli, ed., *Twenty-five Years of Independence: A Survey of Indian Economy*, (Bombay: Vora, 1973), pp. 25–53. The capital/output ratio measures the rupee value of the investment capital required to produce a rupee's worth of goods.
[33]Ibid.

ought to cut back its investment program. The correct prescription to reduce the capital/output ratio is more careful attention to the investments chosen, to the technology used, and especially to the efficiency with which investments are managed. Economic growth based on higher capacity utilization of existing plant and equipment would go a long way to making the growth of national income equal or exceed the growth of capital formation.

Fiscal and Monetary Systems and Inflation Experience

The Indian government inherited a sophisticated financial system from the British, and although it has encountered the same kinds of constraints on financial policy as other developing countries, India has used this system to influence its macroeconomy as well as individual sectors. A principal handicap for financial policy in developing countires is that the volume of petty transactions and the low incomes characteristic of the economy mean that to levy taxes is often either impractical for bureaucratic reasons or regressive in the sense that the burden falls on those who can least affort it. Moreover, a diminishing but still significant amount of economic activity occurs beyond government's reach. For India, it is estimated that in 1964–65, monetary (cash and credit-financed) transactions accounted for only about three-quarters of the gross national product,[34] i.e., that the level of "monetization" of the economy amounted to 75 percent. Nonmonetary activity (barter and direct consumption of goods by producing households) was especially important in rural areas and in less-developed states such as Bihar and Madhya Pradesh. Factors affecting the pace of monetization include (1) the speed with which increasing farm productivity produces agricultural surpluses for sale in the market and farm demand for industrial output; (2) the progress of social modernization, particularly the substitution of wages and lump sum payments for barter and subsistence farming; (3) the availability of output-increasing inputs such as electricity and fertilizer; and (4) the availability of money itself, both in the form of cash and as bank facilities.

Analysis of India's fiscal system is complicated by the concurrent existence of three different budgets at the central government level—cash, development, and Plan—and the absence of published information which would permit full interpolation among them. Moreover, for political, bureaucratic, and historical reasons, expenditures are sometimes reclassified or classified according to arbitrary distinctions, thereby further impeding budget analysis. Nonetheless, on the basis of what is known about the revenue and expenditure of the central

[34]Kamita Prasad, *Role of Money Supply in a Developing Economy* (Bombay: Allied Publishers, 1969), p. 21.

and state governments (summarized in Table 2-15), certain general statements are possible.

1. Despite the limited possibilities for raising revenue in a poor country, India's government has increased the ratio of total outlays (central and local governments) to national income from less than 10 percent in 1950–51 to 25 percent in 1970–71.

2. The principal means for expanding revenues has been increases in taxes collected by the central government. Higher tax rates have often been introduced during periods of national emergency and have not been withdrawn once the emergency was over.

3. In India's federal form of government, the Center has been constitutionally barred from levying income taxes on agriculturists, and the state governments have been politically unwilling to levy them; the upshot has been that this sector has been lightly taxed, and the public treasury has suffered accordingly. Moreover, there has been discrimination in favor of middle- and high-income agriculturists over their industrial counterparts, and efforts to redress the situation by imposing excises on farm inputs have favored wealthy farmers rather than the poor and, more generally, have discouraged production. (See

TABLE 2–15

BUDGETARY TRANSACTIONS OF THE CENTRAL AND STATE GOVERNMENTS
AND UNION TERRITORIES (billions of rupees)

	1950–51	1960–61	1970–71
Total outlay*	8,998	26,314	78,427
Development	3,263	12,507	35,373
Nondevelopment	5,440	10,336	36,924
(Defense)	(1,683)	(2,810)	(11,993)
Current revenue	7,865	17,307	58,606
Tax revenue	6,267	13,504	47,524
(Personal and corporate			
income)	(1,732)	(2,784)	(8,437)
(Customs)	(1,572)	(1,700)	(5,240)
(Other indirect taxes)	(2,963)	(9,020)	(33,847)
Nontax revenue	1,598	3,803	11,082
Capital receipts	1,188	9,552	15,585
Internal (net)	1,156	6,066	12,148
External (net)	32	3,486	3,437
Budget deficit (−) or surplus (+)	+55	+545	−4,236

*Total outlays do not equal total of development and nondevelopment categories owing to small amount of unclassified transfers.
Source: India: Pocket Book of Economic Information: 1972 (New Delhi: GOI, Ministry of Finance), pp. 195–202.

page 249, Chapter 8.) Another consequence of inadequate farm taxation has been to place an excessive tax burden on urban incomes and other nonfarm revenue sources. Because personal income tax rates have been very high—at times just a few percentage points below 100 percent—there has been a strong inducement for the rich to conceal their wealth, thereby reducing the tax base and encouraging the spread of black markets. Consequently, middle-income and other salaried workers who are unable to conceal their earnings bear an unreasonably heavy tax burden.

4. India's potential for increasing its tax revenues therefore lies in a combination of its co-opting a share of rising national income, increased taxation of agricultural income, and a more effective effort to capture vagrant taxes. There is very little scope for raising tax rates; indeed, India's 1974–75 budget lowered personal income tax rates on the higher income brackets with the hope that this would reduce the incentive for evasion.

5. Reliance on foreign aid as a source of budget support was not significant until the late 1950s. It reached a peak a decade later and has since declined. Gross aid flows may increase again, but debt service payments on past aid also will grow, thereby substantially reducing the likelihood that net foreign assistance will enter as a major determinant of India's fiscal situation.

6. Although the share of government spending in national income has risen, its development impact has been diluted in recent years by a rising share of nondevelopment spending out of the total outlays. Development expenditures rose from 36.2 percent of total government spending in 1950–51 to 47.6 percent in 1960–61 but fell back to 45.1 percent in 1970–71. Still more significant, gross capital formation financed by the central government fell from 49.9 percent of total central government spending in the Second Plan to only 33.1 percent in the Fourth Plan. (See Table 2-16.)

TABLE **2–16**
CAPITAL FORMATION AND THE CENTRAL GOVERNMENT BUDGET

	Total expenditures of the central government (billions of rupees)	Gross capital formation financed by central government (billions of rupees)	Capital formation as a share of central government spending (percent)
First Plan	37.5	16.0	42.7
Second Plan	78.2	39.0	49.9
Third Plan	152.6	71.5	47.5
Three-year plan holiday	134.8	51.3	38.0
Fourth Plan*	331.6	109.8	33.1

*Estimated.

Source: Computed from *Economic Survey,* various issues.

TABLE 2–17
FINANCIAL TRANSFERS BETWEEN CENTER AND STATES (billions of rupees)

	1950–51	1960–61	1970–71
States' share in central taxes	0.53	1.79	7.55
Grants to states	0.34	2.24	5.70
Loans to states (gross)	0.61	3.28	10.18
Loan repayments by states	−0.12	−0.95	−6.65
Interest payments by states	−0.03	−0.58	−2.59
Net transfer	1.33	5.78	14.19

Source: RBI Bulletin, June 1973.

7. If in America the "power to tax is the power to destroy," in India the emphasis is that the power to spend is the power to procreate and nourish. As shown in Table 2-17, substantial amounts are transferred each year by the Center to state governments. In some cases, the formulas for determining how much should be transferred and how it should be divided among the states are set by "Finance Commissions" which are periodically constituted. In other cases, and in the case of direct central government spending, Delhi has considerable discretion and, as in many other countries, the process is highly politicized and sometimes without sensitivity to economic rationality.

India's resistance to inflation has been greater than that of most developing, and even many developed, countries. Its finance ministers have been prevailingly conservative, and until the 1970s government deficits were held within moderate—according to many analyists, excessively moderate—bounds. As a result, there has been only limited pressure on India's central monetary authority, the Reserve Bank of India (RBI), to create more money than was needed to keep pace with economic growth, and with the exception of years when the monsoon failed, India has had little inflation. The average annual increase in the index of wholesale prices has been only 3.8 percent for the period 1950–51 to 1970–71. For 1970–71 to 1973–74, however, the rate of inflation averaged roughly 12 percent per annum. We shall turn later to the food shortage, budgetary deficits, high oil prices, and other factors which caused this departure from normal.

Financial institutions in India range in sophistication from international commercial banks to indigenous moneylenders; they are fraught with imperfections but are infinitely better than those found in many other developing countries. The power of the rural moneylender, his contribution to the society, and his relationship to the organized sector are dramatically portrayed in R. K. Narian's novel The Financial Expert. Because of the importance of finance to development, I have devoted Chapter 10 to the political economy of India's 1969 bank nationalization.

Balance of Payments and Transactions Abroad

India's international economic situation is more similar to that of the United States than is commonly recognized. Because both countries are large in land area and population and have diversified natural resources, they are relatively self-sufficient, and if forced to do so by extraordinary circumstances, the Indian and American governments both could choose the costly option of operating their own economies with little reference to foreign demand or supply. Like America, India's ratio of imports to gross national product is less than 5 percent, compared to more than 20 percent in many rich and poor countries of smaller size.

Although India emerged from the Second World War with a comfortable backlog of international monetary reserves, these were eroded by the combination of (1) pressure to supplement the meager supply of goods available for

FIGURE 2

India's Foreign Exchange Reserves in Relation to Annual Imports

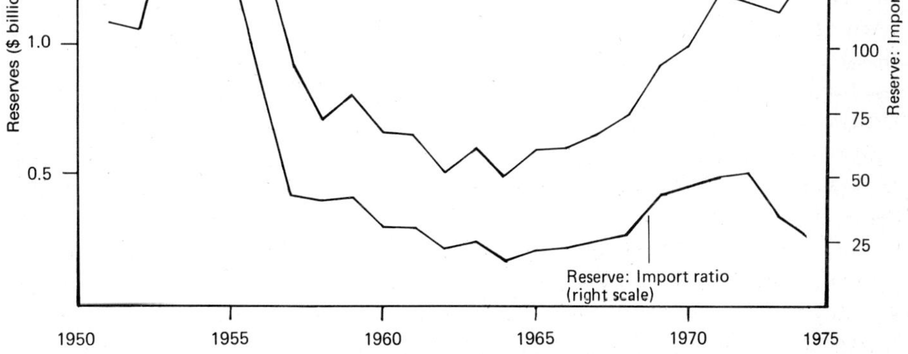

Source: IMF, International Financial Statistics, various issues.

domestic consumption, (2) additional demands for imports attributable to the development effort, and (3) stagnation of export earnings owing in the early 1950s to laggard international demand for "traditional" exports and lower international prices for primary commodities such as jute and tea. In the mid-1950s India suffered the first of what became a chronic series of foreign exchange crises. Figure 2, which shows annual changes in the level of reserves and the relationship of reserves to imports, illustrates the near exhaustion of usable reserves associated with the droughts of the mid-1960s and the subsequent rebuilding of reserves, which was sharply reversed in 1973 as a consequence of the need to import food on commercial terms and the skyrocketing cost of petroleum and other commodities. To dwell on India's reserve position or its balance-of-payments experience, however, is to risk missing an important point. These variables are at best indicative of relative changes in the health of India's external position, but they do not begin to suggest the absolute shortage of international purchasing power. More specifically, these data do not tell the story of how, since the mid-1950s, India has been slow to increase its foreign exchange earnings from trade and aid, and how the resulting unrequited demand for imports has constrained economic development.

Partly because of falling international prices and stagnant demand for its traditional exports and partly because of the government's decision to emphasize import substitution rather than export promotion (see Chapter 9), Indian exports scarcely grew during the period from Independence through 1960–61 (Table 2-18). In the subsequent decade the average annual rate of export growth was accelerated to 4.3 percent, largely as a result of the recovery of primary commodity prices and India's entry into nontraditional export markets such as hand tools and other basic engineering products. Rapid export growth in the period 1972–1974 occurred because of international price inflation and the opening of Bangladesh as an export market. Insofar as the first of these factors was offset by spiraling import prices and the second required large, compensating capital exports, India's long-term export health will require product diversification and a deeper penetration of world markets.

Although India has diversified its exports, it continues to rely on a limited number of traditional and primary commodities for the bulk of its foreign exchange earnings (Table 2-19). For example, of the 1970–71 total, major contributions were made by jute (12 percent), tea (10 percent), iron ore and concentrates (7 percent), and cotton manufactures (6 percent). The destination of India's exports also is heavily concentrated; about 50 percent of them goes to the United States, Britain, Japan, and the U.S.S.R. The proportion of Indian exports sent to Britain and even the absolute amount have fallen as the relative size of Britain's economy in the world system and the importance of the Commonwealth have declined. The Soviet share has risen gradually and steadily since the mid-1950s, when Moscow began to take a more serious interest in India.

The commodity composition of Indian imports (Table 2-19) reflects India's

TABLE 2–18
INDIA'S FOREIGN TRADE (millions of dollars)

	Exports	Imports
1950	1,146	1,165
1951	1,611	1,793
1952	1,295	1,696
1953	1,116	1,208
1954	1,182	1,297
1955	1,276	1,413
1956	1,300	1,725
1957	1,379	2,243
1958	1,221	1,843
1959	1,308	1,986
1960	1,331	2,327
1961	1,387	2,277
1962	1,403	2,361
1963	1,631	2,477
1964	1,749	2,876
1965	1,687	2,924
1966	1,577	2,731
1967	1,612	2,807
1968	1,760	2,509
1969	1,835	2,213
1970	2,026	2,125
1971	2,034	2,421
1972	2,459	2,249
1973	2,943	3,238
1974	3,906	5,064

Source: IMF, International Financial Statistics, various issues.

overall economic situation and its policies. Imports of most consumer items have been virtually eliminated in favor of capital goods, fuel, fertilizer, industrial raw materials needed for development, and food to supplement deficient domestic production. India's import policies are discussed in the context of its larger industrialization strategy in Chapter 9. Suffice it here to say that in 1973 roughly 40 percent of India's imports were food, fuel, and fertilizer, all items for which it had, and still has, enormous potential for increasing domestic production.

Changes in the provenance of Indian imports have been determined by a number of factors, including (1) the amount of "tied" aid received from various countries, (2) the commodity composition which varies from year to year, (3) continuing efforts to increase trade with the Eastern bloc countries, and (4) changes in the structure of the world economy and the competitive positions of various countries. Thus, changes in the structure of imports have tended to parallel changes in exports; the Soviet Union relationship has grown gradually and significantly while imports from Britain have declined.

Other international economic issues which must be noted here but cannot be fully analyzed until later are the style of India's foreign trade policy and the attitude toward allowing foreign equity investments in India. In brief, India has chosen to negotiate its balance-of-payments position through government fiat rather than market forces of supply and demand. It has maintained an overvalued exchange rate and, with the exception of 1948 and 1966, avoided devalua-

TABLE 2-19
DETAILS OF INDIA'S FOREIGN TRADE (millions of dollars)

	1950–51	1970–71
Exports, total	1,261.3	2,046.4
By destination:		
U.S.S.R.	2.9	279.7
United States	243.4	276.3
Japan	21.6	271.3
United Kingdom	293.6	227.1
Egypt	12.4	75.2
Sudan	8.8	51.1
Germany (Federal Republic)	. . .	43.1
Ceylon	41.4	42.4
Czechoslovakia	21.2	39.5
Canada	29.0	37.3
Australia	62.4	32.7
Other	674.3	1,343.0
By commodity:		
Jute manufactures	236.9	252.2
Tea	167.8	197.6
Iron ore and concentrates	0.4	136.4
Cotton manufactures	250.7	130.0
Iron and steel	6.1	120.8
Leather	54.2	95.4
Fresh fruits and nuts	22.9	72.5
Textile yarn and thread	53.8	46.0
Crude vegetable materials	28.6	45.3
Tobacco, unmanufactured	29.6	41.9
Sugar	0.4	39.1
Other	851.0	1,158.1

* NA = not available.

Note: Columns may not total, owing to rounding.

Source: India: 1973 (New Delhi: GOI, Ministry of Information and Broadcasting), pp. 309, 311, 314, and 315.

tion. This "command" strategy has been implemented through a highly complex system of import and export controls; a policy of gradually "canalizing" foreign trade through state agencies; and a reorientation of trade toward countries willing to substitute bilateral trading for international competition. At the time of Independence the bulk of foreign equity investment in India was by British firms, largely in traditional areas such as plantations and cotton textiles. To the extent that new foreign investments have been made in the past quarter century, they have been concentrated in modern industries such as petroleum, chemicals, and manufacturing, and have come from various sources, including

	1950–51	1970–71
Imports, total	1,365.4	2,178.4
By provenance:		
United States	250.3	594.8
United Kingdom	284.1	168.0
Canada	46.0	156.4
Germany (Federal Republic)	. . .	142.5
U.S.S.R.	0.4	139.6
Iran	77.77	122.1
Japan	21.2	111.0
Egypt	69.1	53.1
Australia	70.1	48.8
Other	748.8	1,487.5
By commodity:		
Machinery, nonelectric	140.3	342.5
Wheat, unmilled	208.2	231.1
Iron and steel	30.0	196.1
Petroleum, crude and partly refined	NA*	141.2
Raw cotton	210.2	131.7
Electrical machinery	46.0	92.4
Chemicals	19.3	90.6
Copper	17.9	80.3
Transport equipment	73.3	77.7
Fresh fruits and nuts	20.0	47.7
Other	745.2	1,383.6

TABLE 2-20
FOREIGN ASSISTANCE AND THE INDIAN ECONOMY

	Up to end of First Plan 1951–1956	Second Plan 1956–1961	Third Plan 1961–1966	Interim period 1966–1969	Fourth Plan 1969–1974
Gross aid (millions of dollars)	423.6	3,003.6	6,022.2	4,306.1	5,329.7
Debt service (millions of dollars)	49.4	250.7	1,139.5	1,310.0	3,260.0
Net aid (millions of dollars)	374.2	2,752.9	4,882.7	2,996.1	2,069.7
National income (millions of dollars)	81.6	129.2	181.4	107.6	256.1
Population (millions)*	382.9	423.3	472.1	515.4	550.8
Gross aid/national income (percent)	0.5	2.3	3.3	4.0	2.1
Net aid/national income (percent)	0.4	1.9	2.6	2.8	0.8
Gross aid/person (dollars)	1.11	7.10	12.75	8.36	9.67
Net aid/person (dollars)	0.97	6.01	10.33	5.81	3.76

* For 1954, 1959, 1964, 1968, and 1971, respectively.

Note: Rupees converted to dollars using Rs. 4.7619 = $1.00 through the Third Plan and Rs. 7.5 = $1.00 thereafter.

Source: Economic Survey, various issues.

the United States. Although the amount of foreign equity investments in India is not unduly large (the 1968 book value was a little over $2 billion), and because it is concentrated in certain key industries such as pharmaceuticals, rubber, petroleum, and a few other sectors, the status of foreign companies in India is a highly controversial issue.

Foreign assistance is a principal focus of Chapters 3 to 6. As shown by Table 2-20, gross aid inflows were insignificant during the First Plan period, but became more important in subsequent years. During the Fourth Plan, however, debt service (payment of interest and repayment of past loans) grew faster than new inflows, thereby reducing the net importance of foreign capital to the Indian economy. The inherent danger of this situation is that it evolved long before India developed its own resources to bear the burden of accelerating economic progress. Moreover, it has happened even though India has taken a major share of international economic assistance to developing countries and even though the growth rate of India's large population has been lower than that of many other poor countries.

Linkages, Causality, Interdependence, and Diversity

The picture of India's political economy which emerges from the foregoing analysis is striking and, because of India's size, unique. Poverty, "unmodernized" technical and social modes, undeveloped natural and human resources, heavy dependency on a fickle climate, a predominantly agricultural orientation, and laggard growth rate are among its outstanding features. What is important about this picture, however, is not the individual elements but the dynamics of how they fit together to form a coherent, albeit not very reassuring, whole. The pervasive linkages among variables affecting development reflect direct and indirect interdependency rather than one-way causality. Moreover, in addition to the ubiquitous array of chain relationships that determine the progress of the Indian economy, there are significant factors, such as the monsoon, which are beyond the immediate control of the Indian government. Of course, the longer the time period considered, the greater the extent of human responsibility. For example, even if weather modification is not feasible, over time the building of irrigation systems offers a means for reducing reliance on the climate. Nonetheless, exogenous events such as drought and war must be accorded real importance as factors determining the pace and character of India's development.

Time is a significant factor in the picture. Since Independence the structure of the Indian economy has become increasingly interdependent. This change can be observed in the relationships among industrial sectors, and between industry and agriculture, production and finance, and domestic and foreign transactions. The new links are common to most developing economies and are the consequence of such factors as growing specialization in production,

TABLE 2–21
SELECTED COMPARISONS FOR MAJOR INDIAN STATES

	Population (millions)*	Population density (people/sq. km.)*	Literacy (percent)*
Andhra Pradesh	43.5	157	24.6
Assam	14.6	186	28.1
Bihar	56.4	324	19.9
Gujarat	26.7	136	35.8
Kerala	21.3	549	60.4
Madhya Pradesh	41.7	94	22.1
Maharashtra	50.4	164	39.2
Mysore	29.3	153	31.6
Orissa	21.9	141	26.2
Punjab	13.6	269	33.7
Rajasthan	25.8	75	19.1
Tamil Nadu	41.2	317	39.5
Uttar Pradesh	88.3	300	21.7
West Bengal	44.3	504	33.2
All-India	547.9	178	29.4

Sources:

*India: 1974 (New Delhi: GOI, 1975).

†Report of the Finance Commission: 1969 (New Delhi: GOI, Manager of Publications, 1969), p. 124.

‡Draft Fifth Five-Year Plan, 1974–79 (New Delhi: GOI, Planning Commission, 1974).

§India: Pocket Book of Economic Information: 1972 (New Delhi: GOI, Ministry of Finance).

¶Report of the All-India Rural Credit Review Committee (Bombay: RBI, 1969), p. 120.

exploitation of economies of scale, and introduction of technological and managerial improvements. But whereas domestic economic interdependence offers the eventual and inevitable path to long-run development, on occasion it has been very troublesome. Economic bottlenecks which have emerged in some areas have been costly, especially when they have initiated vicious circles in which the original bottleneck is further narrowed because of its downstream impact. The development policy implication of this situation is that in designing and implementing programs, officials must be circumspect with respect to the possibilities for breakdown that they introduce into the system. Thus, to postulate that the insufficiently experienced government of an immense nation should formulate circumspect plans—the task the Indian government has defined for itself—is eminently wise at one level, but at another level it is asking for the superhuman.

Another dimension of India's economic situation is the enormous economic

Urban population as percentage of total state population, 1961 †	Estimated amount of land irrigated (percent of potential)‡	Per capita income, 1964–65 (rupees)§	Factory workers in total population (percent)§	Population per commercial/coopera- tive bank branch (thousands)¶
17.4	40.5	438	0.61	79
7.7	3.9	441	0.50	134
8.4	21.7	229	0.51	196
25.8	33.6	523	1.69	33
15.1	40.0	393	0.99	61
14.3	17.7	373	0.56	74
28.2	39.2	526	2.05	32
22.3	46.3	420	0.91	35
6.3	36.8	347	0.35	194
23.1	72.3	575	0.89	43
16.3	36.8	356	0.33	73
26.7	70.0	434	1.05	46
12.9	36.6	374	0.48	128
24.5	60.2	498	1.94	106
18.0	37.7	418	0.93	65

diversity among and within the Indian states. These differences are regional, such as those between politically distinct jurisdictions, and locational, as in the case of urban and rural interests. They are also functional and social insofar as they involve occupational, class, caste, religious, and other differences.

By comparing selected social and economic variables among states, Table 2-21 illustrates not only the major differences among Indian states, but the degree to which states which are progressive tend to excel in all areas and vice versa. Broadly speaking, an imaginary belt running east-west through the middle of India and including most of Rajasthan, Madhya Pradesh, eastern Uttar Pradesh, Bihar, Orissa, the northeast, and West Bengal, encompasses the poorest and slowest-growing part of the nation. Both statistically and to the casual observer, economic conditions generally appear better in most areas to the north and south of this belt. Moreover, the pace of development appears faster in those areas which are already most advanced. Although the evidence to support this sweeping generalization is anything but precise, the interstate differences are so great, and the political and economic consequences of the disparities so important, that they cannot be ignored.

There is no simple explanation for why some of India's social groups and regions have developed faster than others. Historical, cultural, natural resource endowment, and political factors are all of importance and promise to remain significant for the future. The importance of the disparities is that by posing a "real world" which is so complex as almost to defy human analytic—much more management—capacities, they compound the problems of economic planners. Moreover, the interregional disparities are important for the political tensions they generate and for their causing more second-best compromises than would be the case in a less disparate nation. On the other side of the ledger, India is so diverse that no faction has ever been able to monopolize political power or to gain complete control over the economy, a situation which may have abetted Indian national unity. In the chapters that follow I shall try to give proper weight to the significance of diversities among the various sectors of the Indian economy, but only the most important of these can be examined.

PART II
INTERNATIONAL RELATIONS AND INDIA'S ECONOMY

CHAPTER 3
ECONOMIC DEVELOPMENT
AND FOREIGN RELATIONS

How does a country which for many years devoted its political strength to achieving independence arrange its external relations after it has won freedom? What relationship does India's domestic economic position bear to its foreign policy? Why should a book about development pay attention to the broader aspects of foreign policy together with the more obvious subjects of foreign trade and aid? There are no quick answers, but just as development and domestic politics are closely interrelated, so the significance of foreign relations for India's economic progress goes well beyond the immediate effects of international commerce and foreign aid. External considerations, ranging from subjective attitudes and ideology to the clash between development and strategic goals, have been highly relevant to India's economic experience.

At the outset, I must admit to a special reason for diverting pages from more conventional economic analysis. Just as Western perceptions of India frequently have been inaccurate and dim, so Indian perceptions of the West have been faulty. Although this generalization does not apply to all Indians and Americans at all times, I think it fairly characterizes enough political leaders and bureaucrats in both societies to explain why both the substance and the style of Indo-American relations have generally been so disappointing to the two sides.[1] In part, this problem arises because, despite unfamiliarity with each other's ways and a frequent inability to communicate, the new world order of interdependence makes it inevitable that we each take decisions which affect the other.

In Washington, India has usually been assigned a political priority which, if not low, does not measure up to what Indians regard as their full international importance. In misinterpreting this low coefficient of concern to mean that the United States has no real interests in India, some American policy makers have been prone to take decisions causing frequent and unnecessary diplomatic

[1]See William J. Barnds, "India and America at Odds," *International Affairs* (London), vol. 49, no. 3, July 1973.

failures. In New Delhi, the Indian government is subject to a parallel set of misperceptions and has tended to overdiscount the impact of its actions on the United States and the reactions of American officials. As a result, there is a persisting gap between the Delhi and Washington views of India's global importance. Americans have regarded India as pretentious, overbearing, and seeking influence disproportionate to its international position; Indians have deeply resented what they regard as American overconcern about poverty and inattention to their legitimate strategic interests. Moreover, a related misunderstanding has occurred with respect to how Delhi and Washington appraise the world role of the United States.

Another major reason for discussing larger aspects of India's foreign policy is closely related to the problems of mutual misunderstanding: the abiding need to explain why India is relevant to the United States. Why should Americans study, much less worry, about a country which is 10,000 miles away, accounts for less than 2 percent of United States exports and less than 1 percent of United States imports, is culturally very different, and is historically closer to Britain? Much of the answer is revealed by disregarding rhetoric and concentrating attention on experience, a great deal of which relates to the economic sphere. For those who agree with Chester Bowles's thesis that "policy is not made but accumulated," the revealed preferences and priorities derived from what has actually happened in Indo-American relations are the best guides to understanding public policy.

Finally, as will become clear, the impact of foreign factors on India's development has come not only through bilateral channels but also through multilateral political and economic relationships. India has not only been affected by the international system, but because of its size, experience, and competence at articulation, has affected the modalities of international development relations and has sometimes served as a model for other poor countries. And, in designing its political and economic policies with an eye to assuming a leadership role among Third World countries, India has imparted a special character to its own development.

India's ambition to shape the international order should not be overemphasized, however, as there has been considerable opposition in India to foreign involvement. Moreover, to the extent that some foreign countries have actively sought to affect the course of Indian development—be it for economic or political reasons—India has found it necessary to spend much energy in parrying foreign initiatives. This situation has combined with India's poverty and reduced India's ability to affect the course of international affairs, even in Asia. This is not to deny that its Third World initiatives have often led to action, only to underscore that the disparity between India's international power and its ambition is largely attributable to domestic economic weakness.

Whether India should be regarded as a model has been a lively question both in India and abroad. India's apparent qualifications are its size, need for development, and commitment to democratic planning, characteristics which sometimes epitomize and sometimes stand in stark contrast to other developing countries. Since the early 1950s one of the more fashionable and less rewarding activities of scholars, journalists, and others has been to compare India's situation with China's more egalitarian and totalitarian society. Even though too much was made of such comparisons and they are now more generally recognized as misleading, Indians and Westerners alike continue to make them. Fortunately, however, there is a countertendency to regard India as *sui generis*.[2] This is a healthier state of affairs insofar as it requires that India and other developing countries be seen as individual entities rather than as an amorphous mass of homogeneous poverty. It also relieves India of responsibility for acting according to any preconceived pattern appropriate for a model country, but not necessarily for disregarding its immediate policy needs. Nonetheless, the use of India as a model has some logic if in generalizing about development it is understood that models may provide insights but are not substitutes for specialized knowledge of individual countries. Moreover, to say that India can be regarded as a model only within limits is not to deny that in particular areas its experience has been repeated by other countries. As will be discussed in Chapter 6, for example, the consortium technique of coordinating aid for a recipient country was developed for India and later applied elsewhere.

One last caveat. Within any country communications tend to be limited to narrow channels; politicians talk to politicians, businessmen speak among themselves but not with outsiders, and economists, scientists, and others do the same. Similarly, at the international level, there are (1) cadres of economists who are expert in formulating five-year plans but know relatively little about the decision-making processes used in industry; (2) associations of businessmen who discourse on domestic and international commerce but, because they have little feeling for the development impact of their actions, are more concerned with resisting the political environment than with seeking to restructure their own operations to enrich company and country; and (3) civil servants and others who convey information among countries but also have their limitations. The reason for this digression on communications is to note that ideas are transmitted by a complex process and to underscore that an enormous opportunity for greater cross-fertilization exists at both domestic and international levels.

Foreign Affairs as a Reflection of Domestic Affairs

One way to understand India's foreign relations is by extension; because external policy is directed to many of the same goals and shaped by the same forces which influence domestic policy, its content and style are roughly parallel. There are three principal and related objectives which have implications for both internal and international policy: (1) territorial integrity, security, inde-

---

[2]The very pessimistic prospects for India as stated in Gunnar Myrdal's *Asian Drama* (published in 1968; op. cit.) helped in this change of outlook.

pendence, and prestige; (2) economic development; and (3) the organization of society so as to reflect social justice.

On territorial matters, Delhi's insistence on maintaining national integration and domestic order is paralleled by its decision to include Goa and other border areas in the Indian Union and its resistance to the Chinese incursion in Ladakh. In international forums India generally has supported national territorial integrity, although Indian leaders viewed the 1971 emergence of Bangladesh as an anticolonial event rather than an abridgment of sovereignty. As in its domestic posture on social issues, India supports development and social justice with respect to ordering relations within other sovereign countries and among nations. India has voiced strong objections to aspects of the international trade, aid, and payments systems. This opposition to what it regards as "neocolonialism" and "economic imperialism" clearly parallels the theme of antiexploitation which appears so often in Indian domestic politics.

The ordering of priorities, whether between domestic and international objectives or within each sphere, is difficult. Priorities are related; they both conflict with and complement one another; and there is an inescapable subjectivity in the ordering process which leads different men to give different weights to the same objective. The competition between economic investment and military spending is the classic example of how difficult it is to allocate scarce resources. No doubt, a strong and diversified economy is the prerequisite for a strong armed force; development requires domestic and international security.

One way to resolve such conflicts is to assert "national independence" as the overriding national objective. Thus, according to Baldev Raj Nayar, India's "basic impulse for industrialization has been national power in general, and military strength in particular."[3] Nayar correctly criticizes foreign economic advisers for paying inadequate attention to national power and prestige as Indian objectives, but he overstates his case by categorizing mass welfare and internal social goals as being of secondary importance.[4] In reality, India seeks a multiplicity of objectives; these are interrelated, they have shifted over time, and only during the most profound crises has there been anything that approaches a unanimity of Indian opinion.

What is unique about nationalism as a motivating spirit in India and other countries is that it focuses not on one or several modes of national achievement, power, and prestige but embraces them in combination. From this characteristic it derives its great strength. Nonetheless, the tangible and specific goals subsumed under the heading of nationalism have volatile priorities which change in response to current circumstances. Just as drought inevitably brings economic goals to the fore, so the threat of war necessarily reallocates national effort toward military objectives. For these reasons, in the long run, the threat

[3]Nayar, op. cit., p. 53.
[4]Ibid., pp. 152–154.

to India's national integrity and well-being posed by economic scarcity must be regarded as equally important as the threat of foreign invasion.

Ideology, Attitudes, and Foreign Affairs

India, among the first of the colonial fiefdoms to regain independence and a darling of international liberal opinion, not surprisingly has felt a strong need to project its world view actively and in a variety of ways. India's credentials and competence for this role were enhanced by its size, the universalism of Gandhi, the popular appeal of the positions it advocated, and the intelligence and rhetorical abilities of its spokesmen. But India's large size and cultural uniqueness have sometimes operated to impair its influence abroad. India's experience in world politics, while hardly inactive, has been somewhat limited, partly because during colonial and more recent years foreign affairs have been the preserve of small elite groups and partly because, historically, the balance of foreign influence has been predominantly on the side of the penetration of India by outsiders rather than Indian initiatives outside South Asia. Although not nearly as inward-looking as imperial China, India has suffered more from culture-imposed limitations than most countries.[5] Moreover, India has been subject to a provincialism which affects other large countries, including the United States and China; and even when it has overcome the inclination to ignore what is beyond its geographic boundaries, it has tended to interpret the larger world according to Indian values rather than to seek, in the style of a smaller country, to understand foreign values.

Nehru and his colleagues found it easy to transform the nonviolence of Gandhi into a foreign policy of "nonalignment" and "peaceful coexistence." Similarly, India's commitment to domestic democracy was easily projected at the international level into the position that the correct relationship among sovereign bodies is one country, one vote (not a vote weighted by economic or military power or by population numbers). Other important Indian objectives with economic content—egalitarianism, socialism, growth and modernization— are viewed as goals to be met among, as well as within, nations. Finally, at the procedural level, the importance which the Indian government attaches to its active management of domestic society is paralleled internationally by strong support in principle, and usually in practice, of supranational organizations such as the United Nations and the World Bank.

More than most governments, India has couched its foreign policy in moral and ideological terms, a practice which has not always proved to be in its best

---

[5] A dramatic, if dated, historical illustration is the behavior of Brahman sepoys in the nineteenth century. One reason for the 1857 Mutiny was fear among them that some of their members were being converted to Christianity and that this would result in sepoy units being sent abroad, a violation of Hindu religious belief. See Hardgrave, op. cit.

interests. For example, the domestic perceptions and mood generated by its own foreign policy left India less prepared for the Chinese invasion in 1962 than might otherwise have been the case. Motivated by its moral and ideological concerns, India has often expressed itself in a style irritating to other countries. India's use of the pejorative phraseology "exploitation" in economic discussions with OECD countries, for example, has not inclined these potential aid donors to be more generous. Finally, there have been occasions when India has appeared insincere: in contrast to the high principles which it has expounded, it has ignored morality when its national self-interest was at stake.

Since the 1950s the importance of ideology in India's foreign policy has declined perceptibly. One reason is that India has learned, particularly after 1962, that strategies based on ideological positions are not always the most effective and sometimes involve conflicts of interest. Moreover, India has failed to meet various of its domestic and international economic and political objectives, and as rival and more convincing voices have been raised, India's influence in the Third World and the world at large has declined. The leaders who came to power in the post-Nehru era have not been of the same stature as their predecessors so that even when they spoke on world issues, others were not as prepared to listen as in the 1950s. Finally, in the 1970s, the winding down of the cold war and the growing cooperation among the superpowers have deprived India of a forum and an issue. This is not to say that new issues have not arisen or that India's voice has disappeared. A comparison of Nehru's speeches on the international order with Prime Minister Gandhi's addresses to the UN General Assembly (1968) and the United Nations' environmental conference in Stockholm (1972) shows no shrinkage in India's concern for moral and ideological issues or of its leadership ambitions.[6] The comparison does show, however, that a new strain of pragmatism has entered into India's foreign policy.

Somewhere below ideology on the intellectual's scale of human endeavor lie attitudes. Although the inspiration for human attitudes may sometimes be base, they are often expressed in the same elegant language as ideology and play a key role in social relations. Attitudes can be distinguished from ideology by their having something less than a philosophical base but, in practice, ideology and attitudes may overlap to the extent of being practically indistinguishable. Although attitudes are amorphous, and although there is such a diversity of views in India, the importance of attitudes to foreign affairs and development requires comment.

India's approach to international self-reliance, one of the three primary goals of economic policy, illustrates how attitudes penetrate the economy. Depending on how self-reliance is interpreted with respect to trade, aid, and investment, and what costs and benefits follow from these various interpretations, self-

---

[6]See address by Mrs. Gandhi to the Plenary Meeting of the General Assembly (1693d meeting) Oct. 14, 1968, 23d Session, and address to the UN Conference on the Human Environment as reported in the *Los Angeles Times,* June 15, 1972.

reliance may be a rational or foolish objective. In principle, the official approach has been liberal and, at least in theory, compatible with a large amount of international interdependence; indeed, it has been almost technical in nature. As formulated in the Third Plan and restated in the Fourth and Fifth Plans:

(1) Self-reliance means elimination of special forms of external assistance.
(2) Self-reliance cannot be achieved forthwith and has to be phased over time.
(3) The justification for external assistance during the intervening period must be that it helps to build up the growth potential of the economy to the level where it can support an adequate level of investment from its own production and savings.[7]

In practice, however, agencies of the government, including the Planning Commission, have been less liberal and more dogmatic in their pursuit of self-reliance than might be expected from this statement. This is demonstrated by India's emphasis on maximizing national autonomy in defense and food production and in the draconian rules which prohibit the import of any product available in India regardless of comparative cost, delivery date, or similar factor. (See Chapter 9, pages 285 to 287.) This stands in sharp contrast with the policy statements of many Indian leaders which repeatedly maintain that increased foreign commerce can be helpful in solving domestic resource and international balance-of-payments problems.

The autarkic approach to self-reliance is by no means disreputable and many Indians subscribe to it. For instance, Dr. Subramanian Swamy, an economist who has worked for some time in the not too radical offices of the IBRD (International Bank for Reconstruction and Development) and taught at Nehru University in Delhi, is an articulate advocate of Indian autarky. According to Dr. Swamy, India's development would proceed at a faster pace—at 10 percent per annum—if planners would abandon their efforts in the areas of foreign trade and investment and concentrate on accelerating purely domestic growth. He recommends a faster population growth rate on grounds that this could act as a demand pull factor in raising production and providing the work force for future growth.[8] In 1972, Dr. Swamy's ideas were considered and rejected as unrealistic by an unprecedented special meeting of the senior economic secretaries to the Indian government. But the very fact that the secretaries had to deal seriously with a supporter of autarky is indicative of how attractive this attitude is to many Indians, including some political leaders. Even a random selection of official speeches and documents reveals plentiful evidence of a deep-seated feeling that India should realize greater self-reliance, and this attitude would surface as a still greater force in public policy if India's international economic or political relations were to become less favorable.

[7]*Draft Fifth Five-Year Plan,* op. cit., vol. 1, p. 3.
[8]Subramanian Swamy, *Indian Economic Planning: An Alternate Approach* (New Delhi: Vikas Publications, 1971).

Related to self-reliance is a pair of contradictory attitudes which have had a real but unmeasurable impact on policy and hence development. First, India has sometimes been accused of xenophobia because of the determination with which it practiced its nationalism, for instance, the sentiment that foreigners should not be allowed to benefit from the exploitation of Indian natural resources. In contrast, many Indians go to extremes in denigrating their national capacities and achievements while expressing effusive admiration for all things foreign. The underlying attitude of inferiority, however mistaken, has consequences for political and economic policy. For example, when Indian companies from both the public and private sectors need industrial licenses, they frequently search out foreign collaborators because the licensing authorities distrust the competence of local engineers to develop appropriate technology and thus are more likely to approve applications which call for help from abroad.[9] This conflict of attitude over the relative merits of foreign and domestic ideas and products has led to inconsistencies in policy and instances where one or the other view prevailed more on the basis of its bureaucratic and political clout than on the merits of the case.

Indian attitudes and style have sometimes proved incomprehensible, if not annoying, to foreigners. Illustrative is an essay which I. G. Patel wrote while still finance secretary in the government and one of its most influential policy makers. In this remarkable comment on the Report of the Pearson Commission, Patel abstracted himself from his then current role as an advocate for aid and participant in the foreign assistance relationship. He denounced Western liberals and cold warriors alike for their selfish motivation and inept management of foreign assistance, for their "strident style of performance-oriented aid diplomacy," and for their insensitivity to the economic and political problems of developing countries. In groping toward a new aid relationship, Patel argued that "the style that is most likely to suit the decade of the seventies is not one of [donor country] intervention or even involvement but of duty done without too much fuss or subsequent direct bother."[10] Patel's critical evaluation of Western motives and methods of aid giving was not only indiscreet but, by ignoring historical sequences, misleading.

Unquestionably, he was correct in identifying the cold war as a principal reason why some Westerners supported economic aid programs and in deploring the occasional, frenetic, and excessive intervention of donors. But he understated the noteworthy humanitarian motives which buttressed foreign assistance throughout the period and were primarily responsible for the announcement of Point Four before the onset of the cold war. Moreover, to

---

[9]See Mark Frankena, "The Industrial and Trade Control Regime and Product Designs in India," *Economic Development and Cultural Change*, vol. 22, no. 2, January 1974.
[10]I. G. Patel, "Aid Relationship for the Seventies," in Barbara Ward, ed., *The Widening Gap: Development in the 1970s* (New York: Columbia University Press, 1971) pp. 295–311.

anyone familiar with the U.S. Congress (the world's largest aid-appropriating legislative body), Patel's formula for "slipping a check under the door and not asking any further questions" was almost totally romantic and impractical. His attitude toward aid relations is disturbing because it reveals a deep communications problem between the United States and India.

In the spirit of Mark Twain's dictum that one should never blame oneself until one has exhuasted all other possibilities, it is hardly surprising that some Indians have blamed their country's economic problems not only on domestic demons but on "foreign devils," be they oil companies which were thought to have pushed up the price of petroleum (India learned how complex the issue of oil pricing is when, in the early 1970s, it became a direct purchaser in the market); a demonic American government which has been indicted for unloading its surplus grain in order to make India dependent on imports of United States wheat (most economists feel that insufficient investment in Indian agriculture, low grain prices, and the vagaries of the monsoon are more relevant in explaining why India imported food); or the CIA, which has been accused (but not convicted) of committing multiple sins, ranging from abetting industrial unrest to diverting the monsoon. This kind of scapegoatism harmed political and economic relations with the United States and hence India's economic development.

Just as the principle of decentralized village-level organization that Gandhi favored was overwhelmed by the penchant for central authority and planning, so at the international level India has shown a strong preference for official intervention. For example, it has "canalized" its foreign trade through state trading agencies and negotiated to balance its exports and imports with each trading partner through bilateral trading arrangements. In 1974, India had operational trade agreements with 23 countries. There is only scant evidence as to how valuable these agreements have been to India, although the discussion of Indo-Soviet trade in Chapter 5 suggests that if bilateral trading has worked to India's advantage, it has not done so to the extent advertised by the government. Skepticism about bilateral trading arises not only because of the suspected wiliness of foreigners who are thought to have exacted economic payment from India in return for political support, but because the practice of substituting bureaucratic command for the free play of market forces is thought to be economically inefficient. (See Chapter 11.)

The foregoing suggests that India has infused its foreign relations with a mix of ideological and stylistic idiosyncrasies, and I now propose to explore how this has affected India's development. Suffice it here to say that Western concern for India's welfare, while correlated with cold war diplomacy, was motivated still more forcefully by other factors. Even though there was competition in aid giving between the East and the West at certain times, and although Western umbrage at India's foreign policy did adversely affect the assistance made available, the relationship between aid and foreign policy is too complex to explain on the basis of only one or several factors.

The Political Preoccupation and Defense
Burden

To put aside for the moment the direct relationship between Indian foreign policy and economic development, there can be no doubt about the significant reciprocal ties between national security and development.[11] India's defense budget rose markedly after its 1962 war with China, but the burden of maintaining national security cannot be measured by money alone; I regard India's continuing confrontation with Pakistan to be an even more critical international variable affecting its development. The China episode, however costly, was of limited duration. Moreover, although it did cause India to lose a small piece of territory which was almost valueless except for China's transportation system, it did not genuinely threaten India's national integrity. In short, it was an aberration, unlikely to be repeated and, therefore, of less consequence than the repeated wars with Pakistan, where vital economic and political issues were at stake.

India's conflict with Pakistan touched on a particularly sensitive nerve. The Congress party had resisted partition of the subcontinent from the outset on grounds that the religious distinction between Hindus and Muslims was less important than the shared historical and cultural identity which these communities had from living in the same land for centuries. Many Indians regarded the sectarian and political reasons for establishing a separate Pakistan as irrational and false. Consequently, there has been a lingering hope that an eventual reunion of the now sovreign nations will be achieved. This sentiment has grown weaker with time, and the tone of a relevant All-India Congress Committee (AICC) resolution seems very remote from the current reality:

> Geography and the mountains and seas fashioned India as she is, and no human agency can change that shape or come in the way of her final destiny. Economic circumstances and the insistent demands of international affairs make the unity of India still more necessary. . . . The AICC earnestly trusts that when the present passions have subsided, India's problems will be viewed in their proper perspective and the false doctrine of two nations in India will be discredited and discarded by all.[12]

In practice, the situation between India and Pakistan has been one of noncooperation in the economic sphere, omnipresent political tension, and more than occasional warfare. Conflicting claims over Kashmir generally have served as the focal point, but East Bengal became paramount in 1971. The

[11] For a comment on the interdependence of economic and security issues, see Charles L. Schultze, "The Economic Content of National Security Policy," *Foreign Affairs*, vol. 51, no. 3, April 1973.

[12] Quoted in V. P. Menon, *The Transfer of Power in India* (Princeton, N.J.: Princeton University Press, 1957), p. 384.

consequent emergence of Bangladesh as an independent nation has so substantially reduced Pakistan as a credible military threat to India that it may now be possible for Indo-Pakistani relations to assume a more favorable balance of cooperation over conflict. Nonetheless, India will be loath to relax its vigilance on its western border, and its post-Independence support of Bangladesh is certain to claim some Indian resources which it might otherwise use for domestic development.

The economic consequences of India's continuing confrontation with Pakistan (and China) are apparent in India's budget and balance of payments, but the true magnitude of economic costs and economic opportunities lost is only partially revealed by these data. India's deliberate measures to conceal the full extent of military expenditures are part of the problem of ascribing costs. In addition, there has never been a time when India felt immune from attack and, therefore, there is no truly peacetime budget for comparison. Nonetheless, the budget figures shown in Table 3-1 correctly indicate that Indian defense spending rose substantially as a consequence of the Pakistan and China wars.

One way to determine the impact of military spending on the Indian economy is by building a model, an approach which is not as meaningful as its reliance on quantitative methods would suggest. Assume, for example, that in the absence of its conflict with Pakistan and China, India could have held its defense spending to 1 percent of its net national income. This compares with an actual average spending rate of 3.5 percent for the decade IFY 1960–61 to 1969–70. Coincidentally, India's military spending in IFY 1969–70 also amounted to 3.5 percent of the national income. According to the assumption that only 1 percent of GNP would have been directed to military spending in a nonconflict situation, India's actual demand for defense preparedness reduced what would otherwise have been available for consumption or investment in IFY 1960–70 by 2.5 percent.

But this is not all. If military spending in previous years had been held to 1 percent of national income, and if the amounts saved could have been devoted entirely to productive investment, the Indian capital stock could have been increased by a cumulative total of roughly Rs. 55 billion during the decade. Applying the conservative capital/output ratio of 4:1 to this amount[13] indicates that net national income at the end of the period (IFY 1969–70) could have been increased by close to Rs. 14 billion, equivalent to more than 4 percent of net national product. When this 4-plus percent is added to the 2.5 percent derived in the previous paragraph, it shows that if India had enjoyed a less threatening international environment, the amount of national income available for nonmilitary purposes would have been 7 percent larger in IFY 1969–70, a more than trivial amount. Moreover, if this model were extended for a longer period of time, the benefits of nonconflict would grow commensurately larger.

Are there so many assumptions in this model as to render it inapplicable?

[13]The capital/output ratio indicates the amount of new investment required to bring forth an additional amount of production.

TABLE 3–1
ANALYSIS OF DEFENSE SPENDING

Year	Defense expenditure (Rs. crores)	Total GOI expenditure (Rs. crores)	Defense as portion of total GOI spending (%)	Net national product (Rs. crores)	Defense as a portion of net national product (%)
1950–51	168	531	31.6	9,530	1.8
1951–52	181	566	31.9	9,970	1.8
1952–53	185	520	35.6	9,820	1.9
1953–54	196	595	33.0	10,480	1.9
1954–55	195	789	24.7	9,610	2.0
1955–56	190	919	20.7	9,980	1.9
1956–57	212	1,098	19.3	11,310	1.9
1957–58	280	1,481	18.9	11,390	2.4
1958–59	279	1,506	18.6	12,600	2.2
1959–60	267	1,714	15.6	12,950	2.1
1960–61	281	1,856	15.1	13,279	2.1
1961–62	313	2,149	14.5	13,993	2.2
1962–63	474	2,795	17.0	14,796	3.2
1963–64	816	3,453	23.6	16,973	4.8
1964–65	806	3,955	20.4	19,997	4.0
1965–66	885	4,223	21.0	20,624	4.3
1966–67	909	5,304	17.1	23,771	3.8
1967–68	968	5,075	19.1	28,134	3.4
1968–69	1,033	5,023	20.6	28,808	3.6
1969–70	1,101	5,581	19.7	31,778	3.5
1970–71	1,199	6,102	19.7	34,279	3.5
1971–72	1,525	7,547*	20.1	36,070	4.2
1972–73	1,600	7,313†	21.9	38,573	4.1

*Revised budget estimate.

†Budget estimate.

Sources: Economic Survey, various issues; Data on the Indian Economy: 1951 to 1969 (New Delhi: Ford Foundation, 1970); India (New Delhi: Ministry of Information and Broadcasting), various issues.

This is a fair question insofar as the analysis takes no account of a variety of relevant factors. Those which would tend to increase the IFY 1969–70 benefits to India of lower defense spending include (1) extra investments which could have been made if defense spending had been lower in years prior to IFY 1960–61, (2) the possibility for depressing the ratio of defense to net national product even lower than 1 percent, (3) the compound interest effect of reinvesting some of the additions to net national income which would have been achieved in earlier years, and (4) the understatement of the real value of prior years' investments (made at preinflation prices) and the corresponding understatement of the larger output which would have been possible in the terminal year.

There also are unstated assumptions which, if taken into account, would reduce the potential economic benefit of lower defense spending. For instance, it is unlikely that all the resources saved from defense would have been invested. Undoubtedly some would have been consumed. Moreover, there would have been some loss insofar as the Indian economy would not have performed as well in peacetime as during war periods. The splendid efficiency with which the otherwise moribund West Bengal economy coped with an influx of nearly 10 million refugees from East Bengal in 1971 is evidence of the degree to which India's performance in time of crisis cannot be projected into everyday affairs.

Despite all these positive and negative qualifications, the model has some validity. Even if its estimates are off by a substantial margin (high or low), the amount of extra consumption and investment available to the Indian economy if defense spending had been lower is at least modest, and possibly quite substantial. Emile Benoit has used a much more complex model, different assumptions, and a different time period to estimate that with reduced military spending the growth of India's GNP could have been raised by roughly 0.23 percent per annum. He regards this as only a marginal improvement.[14] Leaving aside my own belief that the potential for economic benefit is considerably larger, I think Benoit is too quick to dismiss the 0.23 percent as insignificant. When translated into per capita terms, it represents an increment of 20 percent above the rate of increase actually experienced in India's national income.

Undoubtedly the most important qualification to any model is that the impact of military preparations extends to many areas beyond the government's budget. For example, the foreign exchange costs of warfare and maintaining military preparedness may be very great. Regrettably, our knowledge here is skimpy for various reasons: India, like many other countries, conceals the amount of weapons imported by misclassifying these purchases under other import categories such as machinery; imports of supporting equipment and supplies such as petroleum are indistinguishable in trade data from civilian-related imports; and exports lost because of the diversion of domestic Indian production to meet defense needs do not even appear in the foreign trade statistics. In 1963, it was estimated that the foreign exchange component of India's arms budget was 38 percent,[15] a figure which has declined as India has grown more self-sufficient. Nonetheless, from what is known about the sophistication of the equipment used and the costs of fielding combat troops, there can be no question that India has channeled sizable amounts of foreign exchange into defense, enough to have had a significant effect on its development effort.

[14]Emile Benoit, *Defense and Economic Growth in Developing Countries* (Lexington, Mass.: D. C. Heath & Co., 1973), pp. 166–168.

[15]B. N. Ganguli, "Defense Production and Defense Expenditure," *Economic Weekly*, Annual Number, February 1963, p. 152.

Another obvious economic cost to Indian development associated with its estrangement from Pakistan involves the disintegration of the subcontinent's economic unity after the British departure. The most prominent loss was the mutually beneficial trade in which Indian coal and manufactures were exchanged for Pakistani fish and farm products. Indian exports to Pakistan, which amounted to $231.7 million in 1948, declined rapidly and eventually reached the zero level. Since the 1971 war there has been a rapid—and sometimes illicit—revival of trade on India's eastern border. Although political reasons will make it more difficult to restore India's trade with West Pakistan, its revival would be equally if not more valuable to India, and at the 1972 Simla meeting Prime Minister Gandhi and President Bhutto took tentative steps in this direction.

In addition to the internal diversion of financial resources to the military and the balance-of-payments costs, the continuing state of tension with Pakistan and China has affected the Indian economy adversely by diverting scarce managerial talent and political capital from development. India has courted Muslim leaders in the Middle East in order to show its nonsectarian character and to neutralize Pakistani diplomacy. This strategy has neither been particularly costly to India nor yielded great political or economic benefits. In 1974, for example, India was unable to obtain a concessional price for its petroleum imports but was able to negotiate special financing arrangements. Indeed, it was ironic that in seeking to solve its oil payments crisis, India was able to strike a deal with Iran, a Muslim country to which it had devoted less attention than to others, and one which it had strongly criticized for aiding Pakistan.[16] What is interesting about the 1974 Indo-Iranian deal is that the Shah, by making special economic provision for India while simultaneously giving military support to Pakistan, adopted a foreign policy framework for his relations with South Asia similar to that used by the United States in an earlier period.

By disrupting the flow and discouraging foreign contributions of economic assistance, India's military conflicts have adversely affected development. The U.S. Congress and executive, for example, have had a long-standing concern that resources not be diverted from development to military purposes. This interest, which reached its zenith during the Kennedy and Johnson presidencies, is reflected in aid legislation such as Section 620 of the Foreign Assistance Act of 1961, which requires the president to "take into account before furnishing development loans":

(A) The percentage of the recipient or purchasing country's budget which is devoted to military purposes;
(B) The degree to which the recipient or purchasing country is using its foreign exchange resources to acquire military equipment; and

[16]See the *New York Times,* Feb. 23, 1974.

(C) The amount spent by the recipient or purchasing country for the purchase of sophisticated weapons systems, such as missile systems and jet aircraft for military purposes, from any country.[17]

Actually very little United States economic assistance was withheld from India because of these provisions, but it does not follow that aid to India did not suffer because of the military situation. When, at the time of the 1965 war, the United States suspended aid to India, the effect was unsettling. In 1971, when aid was again suspended and not resumed, the effect was costly. A broader argument, which is difficult to evaluate because of its global character and because the rhetoric and real intentions of the U.S. Congress are not identical, is that if India and other developing countries had been less concerned with military matters, the U.S. Congress would have appropriated larger amounts for foreign economic assistance.

A Capsule *Tour d'Horizon* of India's Foreign Affairs

A description of India's aid, trade, and investment relations with the super-powers follows in the next two chapters. Suffice it here to say that India's attitude toward the United States and the Soviet Union has been conditioned in part by the dilemma of choosing between socialist-totalitarianism on the one hand and capitalist-democracy on the other. In practice, the choice has been made easier—but no more pleasant—for India by the rather consistent United States policy of providing Pakistan with military, economic, and political support. Although United States policy was motivated mainly by cold war and developmental objectives, it had the ancillary effect of strengthening Islamabad's determination and ability to take positions on Kashmir and East Bengal which were costly to India. Consequently, Delhi has usually regarded United States policy as anti-Indian, notwithstanding the United States order of priorities which accorded India more bilateral economic assistance than any other developing country.[18]

Because of its size, economic assets, and potential for self-reliance (which gave it the capacity to support all but the very most advanced military technology using indigenous resources), India preferred that there be no Great Power involvement in the subcontinent if it meant support for its adversary, Pakistan. Insofar as it proved impossible to isolate South Asia from the Great Powers,

[17]Committee on Foreign Relations of the U.S. Senate and House, *Legislation on Foreign Relations* (Washington, D.C.: Government Printing Office, 1973), p. 69.

[18]For a full exposition of Great Power activities in South Asia, see William J. Barnds, *India, Pakistan, and the Great Powers* (New York: Praeger Books for the Council on Foreign Relations, 1972).

Delhi felt that its second-best policy was to seek through diplomatic means to minimize the amount of assistance (particularly military aid) going to Pakistan and to maximize its own receipts of foreign assistance. This strategy bore some fruit during the interwar period 1965–1971 but, following the dismemberment of Pakistan in 1971 and the attendant reduced military threat from this quarter, it became less relevant.

Many observers have regarded India's ability to play off the West and the Soviet Union against each other and thereby to gain economic advantages as significant. Undoubtedly, the cold war inclined the Great Powers to take a greater interest in India than might otherwise have been the case, and to some degree this caused them to respond more positively to Indian initiatives for more and different kinds of economic assistance. Their interest, however, did not always take the form of economic aid to India. Indeed, to the extent that the very costly Indo-Pakistani and Indo-Chinese conflicts were by-products of the cold war—or were exacerbated by Great Power conflicts—it would appear that on balance India was disadvantaged by Soviet-American tensions.

A similar series of questions arise with respect to how Sino-American rivalry has affected Indo-American relations. Hans Morgenthau has correctly pointed to the fallacy in "looking at the relations between the United States on the one hand, and China and India on the other, in terms of a competition between China and India."[19] Nonetheless, America's relations with India have been conditioned by the fear of direct Sino-Indian military confrontation and also by a more ambiguous social and political competition between these Asian giants. If China had emerged as a decisive winner in any of these competitions or had threatened Indian democracy, this would not have been a matter of indifference to the United States.

India's ideology, culture, size, and geopolitical position are reflected in its policy toward the smaller neighboring states of Nepal, Sri Lanka, and Afghanistan. Contacts with these nations, which have been conditioned by India's goal of countering Pakistan and China, have also reflected a degree of paternalism parallel in some respects to the Great Powers' relationships with India. The assumption of some Indians that Nepal is an anomaly of history which should have become an integral part of the Indian Union also affects policy. On economic issues, India has been torn between generosity toward its less fortunate neighbors and concern for its own standard of living. In Nepal, for example, India has been forthcoming, but it has provided mainly projects tied to Indian exports of specific commodities. This policy is not surprising given the scarcity of Indian resources, but it does stand in ironic contrast to India's position vis-à-vis the Consortium where India has contended that international assistance should be free of all economic conditions. In political matters India has followed the United States practice of reacting to local crises by asking few questions and imposing few conditions on the aid it has extended. Thus, in

[19]See Selig Harrison, ed., *India and the United States* (New York: Macmillan, 1961), p. 52.

assisting a beleaguered Sri Lanka during that country's 1971 insurrection, India acted to exclude foreign influence and to forestall any change in the subcontinent's balance of power.[20] Similarly, India lost little time in providing the equivalent of $225 million for relief and reconstruction in Bangladesh following the 1971 war.[21]

Anglo-Indian relations are a curious amalgam of resentments originating in the former colonial relationship, common interests, nostalgia, and close personal ties. These were bound to make Britons and Indians important to one another, but the United Kingdom emerged from the Second World War so weak that its capacity to play an active role in India was small. Britain's relatively modest role in the Colombo Plan is indicative of how, despite good intentions and moral commitment, it has been unable to support its former colonies with real and financial resources. Thus, as India has developed new relationships, the British have been declining in significance; both political and economic ties have become less important and Britain's absorption into the European Economic Community (EEC) was merely another in a series of events which lessened Indo-British ties.

There is considerable economic complementarity between India and the EEC, but, even so, diplomacy has not overcome reservations on both sides, and economic relationships have been slow to develop. A principal problem for India has been its suspicion of the EEC as a neocolonialist organization which, if given the chance, would exploit Indian economic resources without making commensurate payment. Moreover, for historical, political, and pecuniary reasons the European Economic Community has devoted more attention to Africa than to other developing areas.[22] In light of the difficulties Britain experienced in negotiating entry into the EEC, it is hardly surprising that Britain has encountered obstacles in representing Indian interests in EEC external policy. This was especially evident in the frustrating Indo-EEC arrangement following Britain's entry into the EEC,[23] and in the nebulous nature of the cooperation agreement finally reached in late 1973.

Relations with Japan have been largely economic owing, in no small part, to Japan's aggressive economic and timid political policies in the postwar period and to India's focus on global, Great Power, and strictly local problems rather than on regional Asian affairs. The current positions of the two countries in the world order stand in sharp contrast. Japan has developed the economic power which, in Delhi's hands, would raise India's foreign policy position to the level its leaders desire. Japan, in contrast, has played down the consequences of its

[20]Denzil Peiris, "Pride and Prejudice," *Far Eastern Economic Review,* May 21, 1973.

[21]*Explanatory Memorandum on the Budget of the Central Government for 1973–74* (New Delhi: Government of India, 1973).

[22]Michael Lipton and Peter Tulloch, "India and the Enlarged European Community," *Journal of International Affairs,* vol. 50, no. 1, January 1974.

[23]See Malcolm Subhan, "An 'Empty Shell' for India," *Far Eastern Economic Review,* Apr. 30, 1973.

own development and generally eschewed the political role which its economic strength invites. In their bilateral relations, India has sought with some success to develop its exports to, and elicit official assistance from, Japan. Japan has emphasized the development potential of direct equity investments in India and has been somewhat disappointed that several promising opportunities have not evolved according to expectations. Japanese firms, while continuing to explore new investment opportunities, have become wary of economic relations with India because of the difficulties encountered in the past.

International Economic Policy

Relations with other developing countries are played out in the context of India's economic and political position in the Third World. (There are also special issues in Asia and Africa due to the existence of Indian emigrants, but these are less important to overall Indian policy.) India is a member of the principal international economic institutions, such as the IMF, GATT, and the IBRD. Reflecting both Indian national views and broader developing country positions, India has often been very critical of both the procedural style and substantive content of these Bretton Woods institutions.[24]

Indian officials have objected repeatedly that the rules for the world economic system are often decided without regard to the needs, wishes, or counsel of the Third World, even in matters such as economic assistance, which directly affect the special interests of the developing countries. It is not without considerable justification, and even occasional American support, that Indian officials advocate more use of the international institutions and a greater role for developing countries within the organizations. Moreover, even if the system devised by the world's economic powers is beneficial to developing countries—a judgment with which Indians often disagree—Indians are critical of weighted voting and other practices whereby the system is not managed according to democratic principles.[25] Despite, or perhaps because of, its economic weakness, India has made significant contributions to the international scene. For example, India has been instrumental in the founding of the International Development Association (IDA) and the United Nations Conference on Trade and Development (UNCTAD).

[24]The importance India attaches to its role in institutional arrangements is illustrated by its reluctance in 1972 to accept the loss of its right to nominate one executive director to the board of the IMF and IBRD, a right for which it had worked hard in the pre-Bretton Woods negotiations. See C. D. Deshmukh, *Economic Developments in India; 1946–1956: A Personal Retrospect* (Bombay: Asia Publishing House, 1957), pp. 119–120. More broadly, India's dissatisfaction has been expressed by former Finance Minister Y. B. Chavan; see *Seminar on World Partnership in the Second Development Decade, 3–4 December 1971* (New Delhi: Indian Investment Centre, 1972).

[25]See my article "Development and the International Monetary System," *International Development Review*, vol. 16, no. 3, 1974.

India's dissatisfaction with the international economic system has been expressed on many occasions, most notably when India has rallied in support of the interests of developing countries. In the 1974 special session of the UN General Assembly, for example, India sided with the raw-materials-producing countries even though the fourfold jump in the international price of petroleum was largely responsible for an acute economic crisis. The cynical but unrealistic explanation for this posture was that India delighted in the discomfort that the higher oil prices caused the United States. More solid reasons were that Delhi supported OPEC publicly in hopes that this would enable India to negotiate a special arrangement with OPEC privately and that supporting Middle East countries is part of India's standard strategy to balance Pakistani diplomacy. Another reason, perhaps no less significant, was that India genuinely supported the social justice implications of greater resource transfers from rich to poor nations.

Indian foreign trade policies, discussed in Chapter 9, are characteristic of many developing countries in featuring import substitution, enhanced access to the markets of developed countries, and better terms of trade.[26] In pressing developed countries to grant trade preferences for the exports of poor countries by reducing tariff and nontariff barriers, India has been more motivated by equity concerns than by a wish to use the world's economic resources efficiently by eliminating trade barriers. Consistent with this policy of elevating development above other economic objectives, India has advocated a balance-of-payments adjustment system which would permit developing countries freely to use various import barriers and export incentives while requiring OECD nations to place greater reliance on domestic demand management and monetary policy. Hence, India was among the more strident critics of the United States 10 percent import surcharge imposed temporarily in August 1971.

Regarding the reverse trade preferences which some developing countries extended to the rich in return for preferred access to developed country markets, India has been relatively silent. This is owing to a combination of economic and political factors such as India's felt need (1) to cultivate African governments in order to hold its leadership position within the developing countries' "Group of 77" and (2) to prevent Pakistani diplomacy from aligning Muslim countries against it. Indian leaders, in character with their activist approach to domestic economic management, have supported the establishment of special international trade arrangements such as agreements to stabilize the supply and price of basic commodities and have negotiated an extensive network of bilateral trading arrangements.

India's international monetary policy has favored the maintenance of fixed exchange rates and world policies to prevent inflation while expanding com-

---

[26]There is no lack of references which show the content of India's foreign economic policy. One good example is a speech by L. N. Mishia, India's Foreign Trade Minister to the Plenary Session of UNCTAD, Apr. 15, 1972, at Santiago, Chile.

merce. With respect to the future of gold in the world monetary order, India, while not prepared to abolish the monetary function of gold, was disappointed when the dollar price of gold was increased by $3 per ounce in December 1971. This change appeared to Indian leaders to hold out the possibility for further revisions in the gold price and to perpetuate an international monetary system which was crisis-ridden and beyond the management capacity of governments. Reflecting its feeling that the international system requires active management, India supported the creation of Special Drawing Rights (SDRs) and, not surprisingly, proposals to distribute SDRs in a way preferential to the developing countries (the so-called link system).

As the world's largest recipient of foreign economic aid, India has actively helped to shape the modalities of international assistance to poor nations. It has consistently sought to make foreign aid more advantageous to developing countries by (1) encouraging grant (or near grant) terms rather than loans; (2) increasing the volume (in accordance with the United Nations target that rich countries transfer 1 percent of their annual GNP to the poor); (3) obtaining multiyear rather than annual aid commitments in order to facilitate forward planning; and (4) convincing donor countries to untie aid with respect to (a) the country where commodity procurement can occur, (b) the commodities for which aid can be used, and (c) the party which uses it in the developing country (public versus private sector). India also has taken the position that, whereas the terms of aid have improved somewhat in recent years, past foreign assistance often was given on harsh terms, thereby saddling developing countries with excessive debt burdens which should be reduced by debt relief. Finally, India has given international expression to its egalitarian outlook by supporting both the UNCTAD III (Santiago, 1972) resolution calling for particularly concessional treatment for the "least-developed" countries (a group in which it is not included) and World Bank President Robert McNamara's advocacy of more aid to the disadvantaged *within* developing countries.

In India, there is a tendency to distrust all large corporations, and as discussed in Chapter 9, foreign equity investments have been regarded as especially threatening. Foreign companies have been held at arm's length not only because they have been linked in Indian thinking with the colonial period, but also because of fear that they would exercise monopoly powers and control over patents to India's detriment, resentments based on their having substituted synthetics for natural raw materials in some areas, and concern that they would engage in intracompany and intercountry pricing practices disadvantageous to India. Despite these reservations, India has sanctioned some new foreign private investments (particularly in industrial areas where it needed to import technology) and has generally supported the right of companies to repatriate profits and to be compensated in foreign exchange in case of nationalization.

Although it has been highly critical of the international economic system, India generally has not tried or has been unable to develop multicountry subsystems where the rules and procedures would be more to its liking. One organization which India has sought to mold is the United Nations Economic Commission for Asia and the Far East (ECAFE). Largely owing to Delhi's persistence, regional monetary and trade cooperation were discussed by ECAFE over a period of years, and the talents of such internationally renowned economists as Robert Triffin were employed in an effort to draw the economies of ECAFE nations into a closer relationship. Although far-reaching proposals by India have not been judged by other countries as compatible with their national interests, this Indian effort has yielded some results such as the Asian Payments Union, which was established in 1974.[27]

The economic impact on India of the overseas Indian communities in East Asia and Africa has been small. Indian companies wishing to do business abroad have been confronted by a variety of Indian and foreign government restrictions which have tended to dampen their enthusiasm and ability to invest. Thus, India has obtained little foreign exchange by way of remitted profits and private remittances, although some sizable illicit foreign exchange transactions are thought to originate in this area.

In summary, India has obtained mixed results from its efforts to improve the responsiveness of the international system to its development needs. In foreign aid matters, the formation of IDA, UNCTAD, and the India Consortium were victories for Indian policy. But on trade, investment, and monetary matters India's initiatives have thus far yielded meager results. It is possible, of course, that India's day in these areas has not yet arrived. Reform of the international trade and monetary institutions has proved to be incredibly elusive, and there has been a noteworthy change of sentiment to increase the participation of developing countries in these negotiations. Thus, it may be that when the disorderly international economic system of the early 1970s is replaced, India will reap handsome dividends from its past efforts.

In Conclusion

In describing India's external relations I have identified four major determinants which together have shaped an Indian foreign policy that bears considerable resemblance to that of other developing countries but is also unique. These factors are:

1. India's pressing concern about its national security which was dominated by its relations with Pakistan and, to a lesser extent, China
2. India's more general external environment, which featured relations with the Great Powers on the one hand, and the Third World on the other

[27]See *IMF Survey,* Annual Report Issue, Sept. 10, 1973, p. 270.

3. India's imperative to proceed concurrently with economic development, social justice, and national integration of its diverse peoples
4. A distinctive Indian attitude toward social organization—domestic and foreign—featuring democracy, equity, antiexploitation, government planning, and universalism

Even though India's foreign posture was a logical extension of its domestic policy, there were bound to be some conflicts among external objectives and between domestic and foreign policies. Their resolution, especially the conflict between military preparedness and development, required that economic resources and political capital be directed to nondevelopmental objectives. Although this loss was offset to some degree by an inflow of resources from abroad and by India's ability to manage its affairs with more than the normal amount of efficiency at times of crisis, on balance, India's conflicts with its neighbors have been very costly to its development.

This chapter has concentrated on India's perceptions about its international situation; in particular, on how it has formulated an economic role for itself in the international community. In turning to a closer examination of India's economic relations with the United States, the Soviet Union, and multilateral institutions, the next three chapters will shift the emphasis somewhat toward the subject of how India is viewed from abroad and how the application of foreign economic power to India's domestic economy has affected its development.

CHAPTER 4

BILATERAL ECONOMIC
RELATIONS WITH THE
UNITED STATES

Political Background

Both in Indo-American and in Indo-Soviet relations, the political observer sees a confusing patchwork of ties motivated by short-term responses as much as by long-run policy. The Great Powers have conditioned their relationships with Delhi on their larger cold war strategies, relations with China, and more direct interests in South Asia. India, for its part, has been reluctant to leave the nonaligned camp in which it has been a leader. Thus, so long as there was Great Power rivalry over India, the most that either the United States or the Soviet Union could hope to achieve was to keep India distant from the opposition camp and to moderate India's criticism of its own policies—their fear that India might align itself with East or West was more of their own making than real, given Indian policy. The cold war, however, was not irrelevant to Indo-American relations. The inclusion of Pakistan in CENTO and SEATO obligated the United States to India's enemy, reduced American credibility in relations with India, and, at times, led American officials to overcompensate in their efforts to convince India's leaders that the United States policy in South Asia was neither malign nor indifferent but supportive of India's own interests. But, regardless of the pronouncements of American officials on the motivation for United States policies in South Asia, the effect of their actions was adverse and very much as feared by India.

American interest in India in the postwar years was also generated by a variety of bilateral and international forces unrelated to the cold war. The intangible sense of international responsibility which has colored so many American policies since 1945 was perhaps the most significant. The United States wished to create the Wilsonian world it had once rejected. To do so, however, America needed prestige and power that would be recognized everywhere, especially by a country as large as India. This reason coincided with a desire to support democracy and to further humanitarian objectives, as exemplified in the Point Four and subsequent foreign assistance programs.

It would be misleading, of course, to suggest that the United States interest in India commenced suddenly at the end of the Second World War. Indo-American links even predate the American Revolution; and in the course of two centuries Americans (limited in number, to be sure) have had serious commercial, missionary, cultural, and intellectual interests in India. Among these, commerce, American food relief provided during the famines of 1896–1900, and the interest of American journalists, especially in the freedom movement, figured prominently.[1] Nevertheless, the importance of these links should not be overemphasized; Indian culture and commerce were remote to most Americans, and few had any understanding of India's problems. Consequently, the United States in 1945 was psychologically unprepared for the role it was to play in India—to say nothing of the world at large.

There was no precedent to guide America in formulating policies toward India and the other newly independent nations, but a coalescence of political, charitable, social, and commercial motivations by the early 1950s added up to enough votes in the Congress to launch the United States on a modest (by Marshall Plan standards), aid-oriented foreign policy. Subsequent to the start of the Point Four program, the Berlin blockade, Communist takeover of China, Korean invasion, and the French experience in Indochina all reinforced American fear of communism and inspired the counterpolicy of building the military and economic strength of those nations which were prepared to remain independent of Moscow and Peking. In their moral fervor, however, some anti-Communists could muster little sympathy for intellectual ambiguity in the form of neutralism and went so far as to equate neutrals with Communists. Consequently, American policy generally disapproved of the Indian position which had led to the Bandung Conference and the Pancheel. Because United States policy toward India was suspicious and begrudging, it was less effective than it could have been. Indeed, the reservations were explicit and highly visible as early as 1951, when the first substantial assistance for India was debated in the U.S. Congress.[2]

Although foreign policy in the 1950s was not phrased in the language of "interdependence," "transnational relations," and "world order," examination of the period shows that American leaders were thinking in these terms. For instance, according to one interesting, if inconclusive, review of American public documents from 1951 to 1967, United States officials cited "anticommunism" as the reason for United States aid to India less often than humanitarian or development motives.[3] Because there was no historical precedent for

---

[1]W. Norman Brown, *The United States and India and Pakistan,* rev. ed. (Cambridge, Mass.: Harvard University Press, 1963), pp. 362–366.

[2]See *India Emergency Assistance Act, 1951,* Hearings before the Committee on Foreign Relations, House of Representatives, 82nd Congress, 1st Session, Feb. 20–23, 1951 (Washington, D.C.: Government Printing Office, 1951).

[3]Joanne F. Loomba, "U.S. Aid to India, 1951–1967: A Study in Decision Making," *India Quarterly Journal of International Affairs,* vol. 28, no. 4, October–December 1972.

United States policy in the postcolonial period and because the course development would take in the newly independent countries was not expected to parallel either nineteenth-century capitalism or twentieth-century communism, much ambiguity surrounded the question of what economic policies countries like India would adopt. Keynesian economic theory, by showing the benefits of official intervention in the economy, supported Roosevelt's social policies and removed some of the stigma from planning per se, but there was still a considerable body of American opinion which thought of India's economic development in free enterprise terms and regarded commercial reasons as the primary motivation for assisting India. To American businessmen, in particular, the alleviation of poverty in India was seen as in the United States interest because it would provide new export markets.

In the late 1950s and early 1960s, a succession of major events—India's foreign exchange crisis, the accession of John Kennedy to the American presidency, India's opposition to the Soviet-proposed *troika* for governing the United Nations, and the Sino-Indian war—overshadowed the prickly impressions which India's defense minister, Krishna Menon, had made on American officials and Washington's disappointment with India's equivocating attitude toward the Soviet invasion of Hungary in 1956. But the improved Indo-American relationship did not last long. India was angered by the United States suspension of aid during the 1965 Indo-Pakistani war and by Western pressure for devaluation in 1966. Its displeasure was tempered by the pressing need for food grain imports during the 1965–1967 drought and for foreign exchange support in the following years, but the idealistic element in the Indo-American relationship, which had been most prominent in 1947 and after the Kennedy election, had been all but extinguished by the end of the 1960s.

Relations between India and the United States were far from ideal during the late 1960s, in no small part because of disagreement over Vietnam. The nadir was reached in 1971 when, during the war for Bangladesh independence, American diplomacy in South Asia was extremely clumsy. For reasons never fully revealed to the public, the United States took a pro-Pakistan position in the dispute and when, toward the end of the war, the U.S. aircraft carrier *Enterprise* sailed into the Bay of Bengal, official relations were so deeply impaired that Ambassadors Jha and Keating were unable to fulfill their normal functions. Even the United States economic assistance program in India, the mainstay which had weathered all previous fallings out between the governments, fell victim to the Indo-American rift in 1971.

Initially India had had reasons for adopting a pro-American foreign policy. Americans had advocated independence for India in the 1940s and earlier. In addition, the commitment to constitutional democracy which Indians and Americans shared created a reservoir of good feeling and a sensed common interest. These positive factors have endured in some measure, but as serious differences on world issues developed between the two countries, Indian attitudes toward the United States have become more mixed with negative feelings and thus more ambiguous. Indian and United States policies have diverged on a great number of international political and defense questions, specifically on issues related to Pakistan and Kashmir.[4] One important factor in Indo-American dissension was that agreement on goals was not tantamount to agreement on means.

India showed little restraint in publicizing its disagreements with the United States and, on occasion, appeared to use them as opportunities to assert the independence of its foreign policy. This tendency had implications for development insofar as Nehru was sensitive to assertions that, because of its economic ties to the West, India was unable to adopt a fully independent foreign policy. Nehru's perception of potential conflicts between India's general foreign policy, its international economic strategy, and domestic development was apparent at an early date.

According to Nehru:

> We would rather delay our development, industrial or other, than submit to any kind of economic domination by any country. (1948)

> Indian capital needs to be supplemented by foreign capital not only because our national savings will not be enough for our rapid development, but also because in many cases, scientific, technical and industrial knowledge and equipment can best be secured along with foreign capital. (1949)[5]

The tactic Nehru and his government adopted to deal with these conflicts was to mix the acceptance of foreign assistance with an attitude of disdain for aid, ingratitude to the donors, and a posture which put responsibility for initiating aid agreements on the donors in order for India to avoid the appearance of asking for help.[6] Not surprisingly, this tactic was harmful to India's relations with the West—so much so that Asoka Mehta, a left-of-center political leader, was moved to lament: "A little more restraint on our language and a little more manners as far as our foreign policy is concerned would help the country get adequate foreign assistance to the Plan."[7] Whether Mehta was instrumental in changing the style of Indian foreign policy is doubtful, although the formation of the India Consortium in 1958 (see Chapter 6) and United States support for India during the 1962 war with China did show the wisdom of avoiding unnecessary antagonism of the West and did coincide with a change in the style of Indian policy. The absence of a strong political leadership immediately after Nehru's death was an additional but temporary reason why India's criticism of the West was toned down. Nonetheless, because there have always been members of the Indian government, bureaucracy, and public who were not recon-

[4]See Phillips Talbot and S. L. Poplai, *India and America: A Study of Their Relations* (New York: Harper and Brothers for the Council on Foreign Relations, 1958), pp. 68–94.

[5]Quoted in R. K. Hazari and S. D. Mehta, "Public International Development Financing in India," Report No. 9, Public International Development Financing Research Project, Columbia University School of Law, New York, July 1964, pp. 34–35.

[6]See P. J. Eldridge, *The Politics of Foreign Aid in India* (New York: Schocken Books, 1969, chap. 5, and Hazari and Mehta, op. cit.

[7]Quoted in Hazari and Mehta, op. cit., p. 38.

ciled to good relations with the West, there have been strains in the relationship even in the best of times.

Since the late 1960s, the occasions when India has actively and publicly disagreed with the United States have become more frequent. America's South Asian policy in 1971 led to the most virulent Indian attack on the United States, but the governments have differed on a number of other specific bilateral issues, not the least of which was the United States plan to build a naval base on the Indian Ocean island of Diego Garcia. Multilaterally, relations between the United States and India have been strained by their contrary positions in the growing confrontation between rich and poor nations and on related fundamental and complex issues affecting environment, ecology, use of the world's resources, and the existence of international and intranational income disparities. Thus, although Indo-American relations have improved since the 1971 trough, continued friction in the future appears inevitable.

The Framework for Economic Relations

In fostering development and commerce, and in conducting trade, investment, and aid relationships, three important economic features have conditioned Indo-American relations:

¶ The disparities of wealth and income have cast a donor-recipient aspect on all bilateral policy discussions. In tariff negotiations, for example, it has been assumed that the United States can ask for equitable treatment vis-à-vis India's other trade partners, but little consideration has been given to the possibility of reciprocal tariff reductions by India to match those of the United States.[8]

¶ It follows from the disparities and relative size of the two economies that there is a large difference in their economic importance to one another. In merchandise trade, for example, Indian exports to and imports from the United States account for about 20 percent of India's total foreign trade. This same stream of commerce amounts to merely 1 to 2 percent of United States foreign trade. Similarly, the book value of United States private direct investment in India amounts to about one-quarter of total foreign equity investment in India but does not represent even 1 percent of total United States foreign investment.

¶ An ideological difference over the roles of public and private sectors has also been of consequence. In contrast to India's bias toward the public sector, the United States has shown a strong preference for steering bilateral and multilateral aid toward private enterprise.[9]

[8]See Lewis, *Quiet Crisis*, op. cit., p. 244.
[9]See David A. Baldwin, *Economic Development and American Foreign Policy: 1943–62* (Chicago: University of Chicago Press, 1966), and Edward S. Mason and Robert E. Asher, *The World Bank since Bretton Woods* (Washington, D.C.: The Brookings Institution, 1973).

Given this economic incongruence and these political differences, it is no wonder that Indo-American economic relations have been anything but smooth and have not realized potential benefits. The conflict between commercial and developmental objectives, while partly responsible for this situation, should not be overestimated. Mercantilism requires some development as a precondition for commercial exploitation. Indeed, there are historical and theoretical grounds for believing that exploitation and development are not mutually exclusive. In particular, unless autarky is adopted as an economic goal for political reasons, it is inconceivable that a development strategy would exclude foreign trade.[10] But even if commerce and development are largely complementary, there are still conflicts between economic partners and between private and social net benefits from economic activity. One cannot easily overlook the widespread American view that the real payoff from development comes in the form of increased commerce (i.e., the businessman's vision of China and India as vast consumer markets) or the motivation of many Indians who stand to benefit from increased commerce and who are concerned with development only to the extent that it serves their own private aims.

Because economic objectives are interrelated, and for other reasons, economic policy instruments also are closely interlinked. This is illustrated by the commonplace that "trade not aid" is the better means for obtaining development as well as by the equally ill-considered practice of overstating the commercial and developmental advantages of aid giving to donors and recipients, respectively. In reality, the profusion of possible interrelations among trade, investment, and aid belie simplistic formulations. The long-standing debate as to whether, by providing poor countries with public capital, foreign aid donors have reduced the incentive for developing countries to accept private equity investment, is indicative of the possibility for linkages between commercial and aid relationships.[11]

Indo-American Trade Relations

With his title "Trade Policy Is Foreign Policy,"[12] Richard Cooper has reminded us of an important linkage which applies in the Indian context. Moreover, his words invite embellishment: trade policy is investment policy is

[10]The long-standing importance India attached to foreign trade as an instrument for development is illustrated by its position during the debate on the proposed International Trade Organization (ITO) when India played a leading role in opposing any limitations on foreign trade policy which could conceivably stand in the way of its industrialization. See Clair Wilcox, *A Charter for World Trade* (New York: Macmillan, 1949), pp. 31 and 45.

[11]See Baldwin, op. cit., p. 68.

[12]Richard N. Cooper, "Trade Policy Is Foreign Policy," *Foreign Policy*, Winter 1972–73.

aid policy is foreign policy is domestic policy is economic policy; it is not easy to say where the linkage stops—if it stops at all.

The guiding principles behind United States trade policy are embodied in large measure in the Bretton Woods institutions, especially the GATT and the IMF, where "most favored nation" and nondiscrimination are prominent concepts. Thus, although the United States has participated in some international commodity agreements, it generally has avoided these as well as bilateral trading arrangements. Furthermore, with few exceptions, United States legislation provides no way to single out India or any other country for trade assistance of the sort which the Soviet bloc provides. This is not to discount the discriminatory character of some exceptional American trade policies (American sugar policy, for example, is of great value to Latin America), but generally the United States has adhered to liberal and open trading principles. Consequently, to the extent that there has been special United States support for India's trade, it has come through such means as (1) favorable treatment by the United States Export-Import Bank, (2) the large United States technical assistance program to help identify Indian export possibilities and to educate Indian officials and businessmen on how to exploit them, and (3) lenient application of United States laws requiring countervailing duties in cases where foreign governments subsidize their exports.

The growing gulf between rich and poor countries has been interpreted by some as a sign that the United States has been negligent in not making more active use of trade policy to spur economic development abroad. Regardless of whether or not one subscribes to this view, however, there is little question that United States trade policy toward India has generally been as fair as toward other developing countries. Indeed, the even-handed treatment which the United States government gave to Indian textile exports during 1972—at a time when India was seeking to "punish" the United States by diverting import licenses from American suppliers to others in retaliation for the United States aid suspension—came as a surprise to Indian officials because they were accustomed to thinking of trade policy as an active instrument in bilateral relations. The American action in 1972 gave some Indians second thoughts about whether the United States government was hostile toward India, albeit it was not known whether the White House had explicitly approved this position or whether it represented a lapse in the President's negative attitude toward India.

In the GATT, India and the United States have had a common interest in opposing the European Economic Community's use of discriminatory policies, especially reverse preferences. But, as noted in the preceding chapter, India has had a somewhat estranged relationship with the Europeans and has taken pains to have good relations with the Africans. Thus, even though the continental Europeans have been loath to compensate India for the loss of Commonwealth perference, India has shied away from joining the United States in condemnation of the EEC. A double standard for rich and poor nations has evolved in the GATT, based on the assumptions that (1) countries in balance-of-payments crisis should sometimes be permitted to deviate from ideal trading practices and (2) many developing countries are in a perpetual state of balance-of-payments crisis. Thus, the United States has generally supported India in the GATT, regardless of bilateral differences. In 1972, for instance, it did not oppose India's request for a waiver to legitimize the import surcharge levied during and after the 1971 war. In contrast, India was one of the most vocal critics of the import surcharge which the United States imposed on August 15, 1971, although it appeared that India was more motivated to obtain an exemption from the United States surcharge for developing country exports than to remove the surcharge altogether.

The adoption of tariff and other trade preferences by rich nations for exports of developing countries is an issue which has deeply involved India and the United States, both bilaterally and through international institutions. The slogan "trade not aid" was featured at the first meeting of the UNCTAD in 1964, and trade preferences were recognized as an obvious means toward this end. It is debatable whether the developing countries had more to gain by obtaining preferential tariffs than through the removal of quotas and nontariff barriers. Similarly, it is not clear whether they would have elicited faster action from the developed countries if they had concentrated their fire on removing discrimination instead of instituting preferences. In any case, the course chosen by the developing countries was resisted by the rich and, initially, was opposed by the United States. The administration did not reverse it's position and accept the principle of preferences until President Johnson's speech at Punta del Este in April 1967. The United States continued to be the laggard on this issue among developed countries and never fully agreed with the EEC on the modalities of how a general perference scheme would operate. As of early 1975, only limited action had been taken in this area by most countries: the EEC had implemented a niggardly preference scheme, and the United States trade bill which was enacted in 1974 provided for what may be even more inconsequential trade preferences.[13]

Discussion of the thus far inconclusive and unrewarding battle over preferences is relevant not only because of the intrinsic importance of the issue, but also because the United States and India played such outstanding and contrary roles. India, more than most developing countries, has the industrial capacity to use preferences as an effective spur to its overall growth, and its involvement in the debate, therefore, combines solid economic as as well as doctrinaire political reasons. Illustratively, when the United States untied its foreign assistance program to the extent of allowing recipients to undertake commodity procurement in other developing countries, India was a major beneficiary. Many of the other trade policy questions arising between India and the United States are directly concerned with aid policies, to which we now turn.

[13]For background, see Harald B. Malmgren, *Trade for Development* (Washington, D.C.: Overseas Development Council, 1971).

Development of the Bilateral Aid Relationship

As a subclass of the international political economy, foreign aid can usefully be interpreted as one of several appropriate responses by the wealthy West to a variety of political and economic concerns. Point Four, limited as it was to technical assistance, was something of a footnote to the costly Marshall Plan. Few Americans at the time had the foresight to see that United States assistance to less-developed nations would extend as far into the future and occupy as prominent a position in American foreign policy as it has. The shrinkage of United States economic assistance from 1.3 percent of American GNP in 1950 to only 0.2 percent in 1970 is partly explained by the failure to recognize the full magnitude of the global development problem and the limits on American willingness to accept responsibility for improving living standards abroad. Illustrative of the degree to which policy was overtaken by events is the Agricultural Trade Development and Assistance Act of 1954 (PL-480), later known as the Food for Peace Program, which was never intended to fill the temporary food needs of a sizable proportion of the world's population as it did during India's 1965–1967 drought. The far-reaching political and economic problems caused by the need to dispose of the billions of dollars' worth of inconvertible rupees which accumulated over the course of this program are analyzed in the appendix to this chapter.

As suggested by the absence of the United States from the first Colombo Plan meeting in January 1950, America was slow to involve itself in the Indian development issue. India's needs for assistance were not fully recognized until later in the 1950s, in part because it had accumulated a sizable sterling balance during the war when its foreign trade experience was one of unrequited exports. Moreover, for historical reasons, there was some expectation that the United Kingdom and other Commonwealth countries would take primary responsibility for filling India's assistance needs.[14] Nonetheless, Truman and Nehru did discuss aid during Nehru's visit to the United States in 1949,[15] and an agreement for technical cooperation in the Point Four mold was signed by the governments in December 1950. Also, unexpectedly and prophetically the United States provided significant commodity assistance to India as early as 1951, a $190 million Wheat Loan. Of symbolic importance because it heralded an enormous United States assistance program in India, this loan also raised domestic and international political problems in both countries, which grew more intense with the passage of time. As seen by Ambassador Bowles, the United States began its food assistance to India with a diplomatic defeat.

[14]Charles Wolf, Jr., *Foreign Aid: Theory and Practice in Southern Asia* (Princeton, N.J.: Princeton University Press, 1960), pp. 84–85.

[15]C. D. Deshmukh, *Economic Developments in India, 1945–56: A Personal Retrospect* (Bombay: Asia Publishing House, 1957).

> The day-to-day [Congressional] debates with many irritable speeches had
> been thoroughly reported in the Indian press. Many Indians had become
> convinced that we wanted to take political advantage of their suffering. . . .
> While our Congress was delaying on the wheat-to-India bill, the Kremlin
> announced that it was sending 50,000 tons of wheat to India at once. It was
> announced that the grain would be loaded onto ships at Black Sea ports and
> that Russia would not stop to haggle about money while the Indian people
> were starving. . . . Even the later arrival from America of forty times the
> amount of wheat sent by Russia did not erase the public memory of this
> quick, dramatic act of the Kremlin. . . . The price which the Russians later
> demanded was outrageous, and far above that which we charged and which
> we had covered by a loan on generous terms. But this fact received far less
> publicity than the original Soviet offer.[16]

The evolution of Indo-American aid relations in subsequent years followed a
twisting course and was subject to a variety of conflicting forces, such as
Ambassador Bowles's aggressive efforts to convince Washington to broaden the
assistance program to include capital as well as technical assistance; American
fears that the Communist party, which had emerged as the Congress party's
principal opposition in 1952 and had taken control of the Kerala State government in 1957, would eventually rule in Delhi; the competitive facet provided by
the first major Indo-Soviet aid agreement in 1955; and the perceived United
States diplomatic need to offset military shipments to Pakistan with economic
aid to India. But when the foreign exchange crisis of 1956–1958 threatened to
halt development and prompted Indian leaders to relent from their policy of
stating external economic needs rather than making specific requests for aid,
the United States response was relatively prompt and forthcoming. Indo-
American political differences were overlooked, and the United States took the
lead in increasing its bilateral assistance and pioneering an India Consortium
under the auspices of the World Bank. For India, the long-standing conflict
between (1) the useful purposes to which external resources could be put and
(2) the concern that requesting foreign aid was unnecessary and would rob
India of its political independence was at least temporarily resolved in favor of
seeking substantial long-term help from abroad.[17]

For almost a decade the forces favoring a substantial United States aid
program in India were ascendant. These included (in addition to the political
considerations already noted) the development of a pro-Indian lobby, which
numbered among its more prominent members Chester Bowles, John Sher-
man Cooper, John Galbraith, President Kennedy, and Senators Kefauver,
Humphrey, Mansfield, and Fulbright; the momentum attributable to the formation of the India Consortium and the appointment in 1964 of John P. Lewis
as Director of the USAID mission in New Delhi; the salubrious effect on aid to

---

[16]Chester Bowles, *Ambassador's Report* (New York: Harper and Brothers, 1954), p. 7.

[17]See I. G. Patel, *Foreign Aid* (Bombay: Allied Publishers for the Institute of Public
Enterprise, 1968), p. 13.

India of President Kennedy's global liberalism; a temporary decline in ideological fervor in both nations; continuing United States agricultural surpluses; and India's obvious requirement for outside support, especially during the 1965–1967 drought.[18]

The era of improved aid relations did not endure, however, as factors opposing foreign aid grew manifold and eventually affected policy. In addition to the constant irritation arising from Indo-American differences on major world political issues, the United States became increasingly restive with India's economic performance and skeptical about its development strategy. In response to this concern, which was shared by other donors, Delhi acquiesced in 1964 to have the World Bank undertake a comprehensive review of India's economic situation. The 10-volume, confidential report of the special Bank Mission led by Bernard Bell "found many things wrong" and laid the basis for discussions which culminated in the Indian devaluation of 1966.[19] Needless to say, the Bell report was not well received by the Indians. On another front, when the issue of American aid for the proposed billion-dollar, public sector steel plant at Bokaro drew opposition in the U.S. Congress, Nehru withdrew his request for American assistance and enlisted support in Moscow. Ironically, the doctrinaire United States attitude toward development issues (as embodied in the report of the Clay committee[20]) caused Nehru to draw closer to the Soviet Union. Finally, the Indo-American aid relationship suffered considerably when the United States was tardy in restoring the aid which it had suspended during the 1965 Indo-Pakistani war and when President Johnson instituted a "short tether" policy of not sanctioning food shipments to drought-struck India until Delhi showed evidence of its willingness to implement economic policy reforms to improve India's agricultural situation.

In short, the years 1965 to 1967 were marked by a level of crisis and tension which was unsustainable. India, overwhelmed by domestic adversity, deeply resented its need to rely on outsiders to feed its people, to say nothing of American and other foreign demands for domestic economic policy reforms. For the United States, the cost of helping India and the strain in its relationships with Delhi seemed to many to be out of proportion or place, given the remoteness of the two countries.

In 1966, however, the mutual displeasure of Indians and Americans was still less significant than what Dean Rusk had earlier regarded as the fundamental basis for the relationship:

---

[18]For a more detailed description of the positive and negative factors during this period, see Eldridge, op. cit., pp. 31–37.

[19]See Mason and Asher, op. cit., pp. 196–197.

[20]"The Scope and Distribution of United States Military and Economic Assistance Programs," Report to the President of the United States from the Committee to Strengthen the Security of the Free World (Clay Committee Report), (Washington, D.C.: Department of State, 1963).

> The basic fact is there is a country of 450 million people which is the largest constitutional democracy in the world. . . . India is not a satellite of ours and we are not a satellite of India. . . . We will have our differences, but we will also have great common commitments.[21]

Although the trauma of India's 1966 devaluation and Western pressure to move the Indian government to this policy action created great friction, the actual rupture of bilateral relations did not occur until 1971. In the interim, the failures (1) of the Consortium countries to provide as much postdevaluation support as India believed it had been promised and (2) of India to undertake all the economic reforms which the Consortium thought had been agreed upon, further strained the patience and tolerance of both sides. The saving grace during these difficult years was a general sentiment to ameliorate India's economic problems; an awareness on the part of Indian and American officials that aid leverage had not been misused insofar as it had been applied to economic rather than political issues; and recognition that foreign pressure, right or wrong, was motivated by good intentions rather than narrow self-interest.

America's bilateral assistance to India peaked in 1966–67 and, with the exception of food aid, which was bound to decline from the lofty levels achieved during the Indian drought, stayed at a plateau until 1971. The question of whether bilateral aid would continue was raised in the most immediate way by the series of events associated with Bangladesh independence. Delhi's anger over what it viewed as blatant use of "aid leverage" to influence its foreign policy was met in Washington by a mixture of resentment, ennui, and resignation. During the uncomfortably many months which elapsed between the departure of Ambassador Keating in the summer of 1972 and the announcement that Daniel Patrick Moynihan would be the new United States envoy in Delhi, most American aid, with the notable exceptions of humanitarian food shipments[22] and debt rescheduling, was terminated. Coincidentally, the USAID establishment in Delhi was dismantled and an understanding was reached that resumption of United States economic assistance would have to follow an improvement in Indo-American relations rather than be its vanguard.

The Quantity and Quality of United States Bilateral Assistance

Because aid issues do not arise in strictly bilateral or multilateral contexts, there is bound to be some overlap between the materials covered here and in Chapter 6. An understanding of Indo-American aid relations is further complicated by the intrusion of certain domestic and international factors subsidiary to

---

[21]Quoted in *Commerce,* July 14, 1962, p. 52.
[22]Food gifts sanctioned under PL-480, Title II.

our main subject. The persistent United States balance-of-payments deficit, for example, constrained both the quantity and quality of United States aid. Similarly, the Indian commitment to central planning conditioned the kind of foreign assistance that India could or would accept.

As shown in Table 4-1, when United States aid to India began in earnest in the late 1950s, it was largely owing to India's need for commodity assistance. American aid was maintained through the thick and thin of bilateral political squabbles during the 1960s and declined during the 1970s when the global United States economic aid program was under pressure. The critical question this rise-and-fall pattern invites is, What would have happened to the flow of United States assistance to India if bilateral political relations had been better? Or, at a more ambiguous level, would global United States aid to developing countries (including what was earmarked for India) have been substantially higher if (1) the Indo-American political imbroglio had not persisted and (2) specifically American problems such as balance-of-payments deficits and the scarcity of resources to carry out both domestic poverty programs and the Vietnam war had not proved so intractable?

These questions notwithstanding, the almost $10 billion of assistance which the United States has provided was more than a trivial amount. Indeed, India received roughly 15 percent of total United States foreign economic aid, excluding postwar loans and grants to developed nations. From India's viewpoint, the inflow of assistance from the United States has amounted to more than one-third of its total aid receipts, and considerably more if America is credited with that part of its contributions to the World Bank and IDA which subsequently was routed to India. The volume of foreign assistance which India

TABLE **4–1**
UNITED STATES AID TO INDIA: AUTHORIZATIONS (millions of dollars)

	Loans	Grants	PL-480/PL-665 commodity aid	Total
First Plan (1951–1956)	220.4	180.9	. . . .	401.3
Second Plan (1956–1961)	710.0	92.6	2,410.1	3,212.7
Third Plan (1961–1966)	1,754.6	35.7	946.3	2,736.7
Interim period (1966–1969)	1,040.4	8.1	1,095.3	2,143.9
Fourth Plan (1969–1974)	535.3	20.9	406.9	963.3
TOTAL	4,260.7	338.2	4,858.6	9,457.9

Note: Data may not total, owing to rounding. Statistics on the utilization of aid—issued by both Indian and American governments—are not only slow in arriving, but are notoriously inconsistent and plagued with discrepancies due to differences in timing, definition, treatment of exchange-rate changes, and so forth. Thus, as my purpose is not to reconstruct the fine points of aid flows, all I claim for the numbers in the next pages is that they came from reputable sources and reflect the actual situation reasonably well.

Sources: External Assistance, 1970–71 (New Delhi: GOI, Ministry of Finance); and *Economic Survey, 1974–75.*

has received appears less impressive when translated into per capita terms, but, as noted in Chapter 11, India's aid situation compared to other developing countries has not been as disadvantageous as is often asserted.

How aid flows are related to India's ability to use external assistance is another matter. To leave aside the domestic and international political problems which a higher level of foreign aid would surely have generated, few economists doubt that as early as the First Plan India had the infrastructure and administrative capacity to manage a much larger inflow of foreign assistance and that this capacity has expanded greatly. This appears to be the judgement of the Indian government; Indians have not disguised their sense of having been shortchanged by the United States and other aid donors. Thus the question of whether the United States has been generous to India in the area of economic assistance can be answered in at least two different ways, depending on one's perspective.

Types of external assistance can be categorized in several ways, all of which are misleading to some degree. One such classification distinguishes among (1) emergency relief, (2) aid to improve everyday consumption standards, and (3) investment assistance to improve productive capacity. But analyses which equate these forms of assistance with the international transfer of (1) food, (2) consumer goods, and (3) capital goods, respectively, are simplistic. Proper management of Indian emergency food relief, for instance, has resulted in higher investment when the grain was distributed as compensation in food-for-work investment projects and when the Indian government sold the grain and used the rupee proceeds to make investments. Or, to the extent that the import of capital equipment has merely displaced Indian production of capital goods and permitted resources to be redirected to consumption, capital goods assistance has made no difference to the total level of Indian investment. Thus, the failure of political leaders and even many economists to understand the logic that "resources are resources" has caused unjustifiable friction over domestic and international programs which are of intrinsic value to Indian development. The PL-480 program is an exemplary case of how badly policy makers can confuse issues.

The commodity composition of aid is even more relevant and controversial than is indicated above. PL-480 food shipments, for example, have allowed India to depress grain prices and to meet the food needs of its urban population. But, as shown in Chapter 8, importing foreign grain supplies also discouraged Indian farmers from increasing their production to levels where imports could be foregone. How should the output-depressing impact of PL-480 be weighed against the improved nutrition that imported food made possible? Would it have been possible to devise a policy to increase Indian food production faster while using grain imports as a temporary support? Because more than half of United States aid to India has been agricultural commodities (see Table 4-2), these are not idle questions, and it is no wonder that they have been considered by both governments as having political as well as economic content.

TABLE 4-2

COMPOSITION OF UNITED STATES AID TO INDIA: COMMITMENTS THROUGH
MARCH 31, 1971 (millions of dollars)

Technical cooperation*	606.2
Wheat Loan of 1951	189.7
PL-480 Title I	4,637.0
(Repayable in rupees)	(4,324.8)
(Repayable in dollars)	(312.2)
PL-480 Title II	555.8
Development loans†	3,122.3
(Repayable in rupees)	(506.0)
(Repayable in dollars)	(2,616.3)
Export–Import Bank	511.7
TOTAL	9,622.7

*Includes some capital assistance.

†Of which $2,151.9 million was nonproject.

Note: See footnote to Table 4-1. The amount of United States aid to India shown in this table is greater than what is shown in Table 4-1 owing to the inclusion of various items, principally agricultural assistance transferred under Titles I and II of PL-480.

Source: External Assistance, 1970–71 (New Delhi: GOI, Ministry of Finance, 1972), pp. 114–128.

The "quality" of foreign aid is determined by the degree to which funds are as freely usable as cash and the ease of the repayment burden. It is significant, therefore, that about two-thirds of United States development loans to India have been of the "nonproject" variety and thereby available for general balance-of-payments support. Although more than half of total development loans was earmarked for use by India's private sector, the fungibility of money effectively precluded this condition from having any significant effect on the allocation of total Indian imports between the public and private sectors. The restriction was not totally benign, however, insofar as by causing extra paperwork it was an irritant to the Indian government and a cause of some economic inefficiency. In addition, the Communist party publicized this and other aid restrictions to disparage United States intentions toward India in general and United States economic assistance in particular. Americans were particularly frustrated in dealing with this situation because, despite repeated private assurances from Indian officials that nonproject assistance was what India wanted, there was scant public acknowledgment in India that it was the United States and not other countries which was being responsive to India's wishes. Moreover, the American Congress preferred project rather than nonproject lending, and, because most congressmen were unable to identify any concrete aspect of India's progress with American generosity, they have tended to dwell on the negative aspects of the Indian economy and gradually have become more niggardly in voting funds for bilateral aid programs.

For a dynamic economy the terms on which external resources are obtained are often less important than the amount. But the priorities tend to be reversed for systems which are growing slowly; if the productivity of investments is low, it is more difficult to generate foreign exchange resources to cover the repayment obligation. Thus, for India, which has barely been able to keep its GNP growing at a rate faster than population, the high grant element in the American aid extended during the First Plan period (see Table 4-1) was particularly appropriate. But Congress did not favor retaining this degree of generosity, and the terms of United States assistance have become less favorable to all recipients, including India. Current American loan terms—40-year repayment with 10 years' grace and interest at 2 percent during the grace period and 3 percent thereafter—are generous compared to most bilateral lenders but are considerably harsher than at the outset of the aid program. And the diplomacy of introducing retrograde assistance terms has hardly had a salubrious effect on aid relations. Nonetheless, frustrating as it was for Indian officials to to see increases in the volume of aid receipts matched by a growing debt service burden, United States interest rates were never so high as to become a political problem.[23]

Another way in which the terms of United States assistance became more onerous in the course of the 1960s was the transition from the practice of permitting India to repay loans in inconvertible rupees to the requirement of dollar repayment. By agreeing to accept local currency repayments on many nonagricultural loans until the early 1960s and on PL-480 until a decade later, the United States had sought to reduce the burden of foreign assistance on India and other poor countries. But when this practice resulted in the accumulation of a huge United States holding of unusable foreign currencies, most notably Indian rupees, it blossomed into a political problem which appeared to some Americans as even larger than the economic problem that would have resulted if the United States had required hard currency repayments.[24]

In the late 1950s and early 1960s continuing United States balance-of-payments deficits became an increasing source of international concern, and the U.S. Treasury sought with mounting fervor to reduce the outflow of dollars from the United States. Partly because of its weak domestic constituency, the United States foreign aid program proved to be particularly vulnerable to the Treasury's new policies. Beginning with the tying of American assistance funds to commodity procurement in the United States (1959), the Treasury progressively required the Agency for International Development (AID) to institute procedures which, at the expense of economic efficiency, were intended to

---

[23]The subject of India's international debt is reserved for Chapter 6, which deals with India's multinational aid relations.

[24]The appendix to this chapter details the multibillion-dollar story of how the United States came to hold an immense rupee hoard, the negative impact this had on Indo-American relations, and the political, legal, and administrative barriers existing in both countries which for many years frustrated all efforts to resolve the problem.

reduce the balance-of-payments costs of American aid. As the largest recipient of United States bilateral economic assistance, India was an obvious choice for experimenting with new financing techniques.

The development costs of requiring India to spend its aid dollars in the United States are difficult to assess. For wheat and other American commodities which were competitive in world markets, the United States restrictions were of no consequence, although the PL-480 requirement that at least half the commodities be shipped in United States bottoms did raise the cost of India's imports over what it would have been in a strictly commercial transaction. In contrast, until the exchange-rate changes of the early 1970s the United States was not competitive in many of the commodities India needed. Consequently, the requirement that United States assistance be used for onshore American procurement made the real value of United States aid substantially less than the nominal dollar amounts.[25]

As pressures continued to build against America's balance of payments, the Treasury spared no effort to reorganize the United States foreign assistance program in ways designed to ensure that AID's activities would result in no foreign exchange leakages. The high point of the Treasury effort was the so-called additionality program, begun in 1967 and intended to prevent recipients of United States assistance from using these funds to buy commodities which they otherwise would have purchased from the United States through normal channels. America's search for additionality almost guaranteed that India would have to use its aid to buy products which were not competitive in world markets; it thereby unequivocally reduced the value and increased the administrative burden of the United States aid program. It was not long, however, before India and other developing countries became profoundly dissatisfied with this program, and the depth of the American payments deficit became more apparent. A United States government assessment of the economic and political costs of seeking additionality in light of the program's value to the amelioration of the larger payments problem yielded no consensus. Nonetheless and after much debate, the White House accepted the Agency for International Development position, overruled the Treasury, and additionality was

---

[25]The best literature on the effects of aid tying in India includes J. Bhagwati, "The Tying of Aid," UNCTAD Secretariat TD/7/Supplement 4; Agenda Item 126 (ii) of the Second UNCTAD Conference held in New Delhi, February 1968; J. Lewis, *Quiet Crisis*, op. cit.; R. M. Honavar, "Industrial Efficiency and Aid Tying," Economic Development Institute, IBRD mimeo, 1967; and Deepak Lal, "The Costs of Aid Tying: A Study of India's Chemical Industry," UNCTAD Secretariat, Geneva, 1968. Studies for Pakistan and Colombia which, without being too precise, demonstrate the considerable cost of tying are: Mahbub ul Haq, "Tied Credits: A Quantitative Analysis," and Thomas L. Hutcheson and Richard C. Porter, "The Cost of Tying Aid: A Method and Some Colombian Estimates," Princeton Studies in International Finance, No. 30 (Princeton University Press, 1972).

scuttled in 1969. This was none too soon, for even though additionality was only a passing phase, the harm it caused to aid relations and United States credibility in the economic development field was great and not easily repaired.

Aid tying has been disadvantageous to development, not only because it has often raised the cost of commodity imports, but also because it has discouraged industrial development in the Third World by discriminating against export trade among developing nations. In addition, aid tying has required developing countries to implement complicated bureaucratic procedures to allocate import licenses, a cause for delays and an opportunity for corruption. As a result, it has long been recognized that "a common approach by all, if not by most, donor countries" to untying "would be extremely valuable,"[26] and India has been among the more outspoken advocates. President Nixon decided in 1969 to untie United States aid to Latin America for purchases within the region and, in 1970, extended this arrangement to all developing countries. This liberalization gave India greater leeway in filling its import needs and, more important, gave it the opportunity to sell to other developing countries and thereby earn United States aid dollars. The United States administration also sought to reach agreement for general untying by developed countries. This possibility was discussed at OECD and India Consortium meetings but was stillborn as a result of America's "New Economic Policy" of August 15, 1971.

The Sovereignty Question

The mere existence of foreign assistance as a class of international transactions is adequate proof that both donor and recipient countries perceive it as in their national interest, but the relationship is asymmetrical in the sense that each partner has its own objectives, and each evaluates the benefits and costs by different criteria. Indeed, the notion that one country is "giving" and the other "receiving" suggests that, unlike trade relations where both partners benefit more or less equally and in the same way, foreign economic assistance imposes an obligation on the part of the recipient and that there is a quid pro quo which must be met through some other action.

Sorting out the extent to which United States assistance to India or any other country has been used as "leverage" to make the recipient change its policies—domestic or foreign, economic or political—is not easy, for several reasons. Intervention based on aid leverage is bound to arouse strong antagonistic and nationalistic reactions in the aid recipient and be politically damaging to any government which acknowledges that it has acquiesced to pressure from abroad. Thus, the use of aid leverage is generally concealed from the public. Moreover, in the normal course of diplomacy, countries make representations to one another and otherwise seek to change each other's policies by using or threatening to use various carrots and sticks. Consequently, aid leverage is not

[26]Malmgren, op. cit., p. 62.

always easy to distinguish from normal diplomatic maneuver. Finally, the rhetoric of intervention which government and private individuals in both donor and recipient countries resort to is sometimes very strident but quite unrelated to official policy.

The issues of how much the United States has been involved in Indian policy making, and the degree to which its intervention has been predicated on using its aid as leverage, are therefore of considerable importance. It would be naïve to think that an aid-giving nation would indulge in the international transfer of purchasing power without some assurance that the aid would be used in a way the donor regarded as in its own best interests. Thus, the rhetoric of thoughtless individuals in developing countries and the new left social scientists in the West notwithstanding, it is quite unlikely that foreign aid should be given without some minimal understanding of how it will be used. But aid conditions come in many forms: donors may (1) predicate future economic assistance on the performance of the aid recipient, either on the recipient's specific use of past funds or, more generally, on GNP performance; (2) require the recipient to change its domestic economic, social, or other policies for the purpose of improving the development process; or (3) demand quid pro quos in policy areas such as foreign affairs, which are not directly related to development.

With respect to the last of these, I think William Barnds is correct in saying:

> There is growing awareness and agreement that requiring recipient countries to meet direct military or political conditions which have no clear relationship to economic development (such as joining an alliance, or pursuing a pro-Western foreign policy) in return for economic aid is not only counterproductive but unnecessary.[27]

But how applicable are these words to the conduct of Indo-American relations, given the direct linking of foreign assistance and politics inherent in the United States suspension of aid to India in 1965 and again in 1971? The answer to this question turns on whether, in suspending aid, the United States thought it was (1) acting for the unselfish purpose of preserving peace in South Asia and promoting development by averting war or (2) acting in its narrow self-interests, perhaps paying off a debt to Pakistan for facilitating Henry Kissinger's first secret trip to China. Revelations stemming from news leaks to columnist Jack Anderson strongly suggest that the United States was motivated to suspend aid for both reasons.[28]

Some observers would conclude from the abysmal state of Indo-American relations in the post-1971 period that the United States should never again allow its foreign assistance program to become entangled with other political issues. The worthiness of this sentiment notwithstanding, I suspect it is a pipe dream which, if pursued too far, would exacerbate rather than relieve tensions

[27]Barnds, *India, Pakistan and the Great Powers,* op. cit., p. 301.
[28]Jack Anderson, *The Anderson Papers* (New York: Randon House, 1973), pp. 205–70.

in United States foreign affairs.[29] Nonetheless, the difference between intervention to bring India's policies more in accord with the donor's foreign policy and intervention to force India to pursue an objective which it has publicly proclaimed as in its own interest should not be ignored. Even the Soviet Union has recognized this distinction and has tempered its use of aid leverage for political purposes. In 1973, for example, Moscow agreed to a number of economic treaties favorable to India, even though Delhi steadfastly refused to endorse the Soviet-proposed Asian security pact.

In addressing the question of how far foreigners should go in pressing for economic reforms in developing countries, there clearly is a desirable middle ground between the extremes of (1) placing aid money in countries where the donor believes it will be wasted and (2) seeking to usurp the political responsibilities of recipient governments in the sphere of economic policy. The search for a balanced approach is reflected in actual policy where, for instance, the United States has found it possible to advocate liberalization of India's industrial licensing procedures but has not dared to press for the slaughter of that portion of the bovine population which is costly and unproductive. Economic rapprochement between India and Pakistan stands somewhere between these extremes insofar as outside pressure for settlement of the Indus waters dispute was tolerated but foreign pressure for an open economic border between India and Pakistan would for many years have been rejected out of hand by both governments.

As seen by Escott Reid, aid diplomacy, as distinct from the substance of aid relations, has suffered from a dearth of historical experience on the part of both donors and recipients. Consequently intermittent excesses of nationalism, arrogance, and impatience on the part of senior and junior officials representing both donor and recipient sometimes have unnecessarily complicated relations.[30] In short, there have been too frequent departures from the balanced perspective expressed by Charles Lindblom:

> The United States and other lenders would be mistaken if they tried to buy the policies they like in India by making aid contingent on India's accepting their advice, at the same time they will do well to make clear that the attractiveness of lending to India—the prospect that it will pay off either to India or to the lender—depends on Indian policy. India can be expected to understand that no prudent lender ignores the size of the payoff in calculating what it is willing to put into the growth process. Even on extreme assumptions about altruism in foreign lending, governments—especially democratic governments—cannot lend and give without tailoring what they do to fit their estimates of the contribution it will make to Indian growth.[31]

[29]The dilemma of formulating a United States policy toward Uganda in 1972, given the antisocial acts of President Idi Amin, illustrates the impossibility of isolating aid from other aspects of international relationships.

[30]Escott Reid, *Strengthening the World Bank* (Chicago: Adlai Stevenson Institute of International Affairs, 1973), chap. 11.

[31]Charles E. Lindblom, "Has India an Economic Future?" *Foreign Affairs*, vol. 44, no. 2, January 1966, p. 250.

In examining the reality of how far Western and Soviet intervention may have influenced India's development strategy, there is a heavy underbrush of charges and counterchanges. Depending on an observer's personal convictions, he could argue either that India's policy mix has been weighted against socialist and Gandhian measures by Western interference, or that free enterprise has not been allowed to play its full role because of Soviet meddling. The historical facts suggest that both views are wrong; that Soviet and Western aid flowed to India for various reasons and, with few exceptions, had little direct effect on Indian policy. This is not to deny that India adopted foreign ideologies as part of its development approach, but to recognize that the transfer of ideas occurred with no compulsion and is unrelated to leverage.

The reason why charges of foreign pressure are repeated so often has to do, in part, with the normal political propensity to blame outsiders for domestic ills and unpopular policies. Equally important, Indian leaders have been widely exposed to foreign ideas through their education at home and travel abroad. Mahalanobis and many of his associates, for example, were exposed to Soviet and Western economic theory. They embraced this learning for its rationality and, in turn, they were embraced by India's political leaders and charged with formulating development plans. Thus it is hardly surprising that India's economic policies reflect foreign values and attitudes. Moreover, given the paucity of the world's knowledge of the development process in the postwar years when economic strategies were being chosen, and India's political need to reconcile conflicting economic strategies rather than to elevate any one of them in a doctrinaire way, Indian policy was bound to remain ambiguous and controversial, and foreigners were certain to attract some blame for economic disappointments.

At a tactical level, there is no evidence to suggest that most differences between Indian and American economists were over anything more than how to achieve goals that had been agreed upon. In shifting priorities, from industry to agriculture in the mid-1960s, and from growth to equity in the early 1970s, there has been considerable identity of view among Western and Indian policy makers. Nonetheless, it is easy to see why the wealth and income disparities between the United States and India have led to a psychology of dependence and exploitation, and to a sensitivity to real or perceived threats to the aid recipient's sovereignty and nationalism. It is an irony that the more the United States and other countries responded to Indian requests that they involve themselves in India's development, the more their counsel was bound to be resisted.

To distinguish when foreign advice is merely coincidental with an aid recipient's new economic policies and when it plays a critical role is not easy. In the mid-1960s, for example, India drastically revised its agricultural policy by sanctioning some new foreign-financed fertilizer plants in the private sector even though the Industrial Policy Resolution of 1956 had reserved this function for the public sector. In addition, India liberalized its import licensing system and made other changes to encourage the introduction of the new green revolution technology. These policy alterations, which would have been unthinkable but for the economic crisis conditions prevailing at the time, were motivated by Prime Minister Shastri's government. Nonetheless, when India's finance minister, T. T. Krishnamachari, resigned in December 1965, the inference was that he had lost in his opposition to foreign pressure. Thus, it was not possible to specify with any precision the relative significance of domestic forces and foreign factors in determining the content and timing of India's new economic policies.[32] What is clear is that, as a result of pressure for agricultural and exchange-rate reform, the United States reaped a harvest of Indian wrath which endured for more than a decade.

To some extent the United States doomed itself to a grating international style of aid relations by choosing to provide program (nonproject) assistance. Whereas project aid is a more straightforward way to ensure that funds will be used in ways which the donor approves and is more amenable to evaluation, it has disadvantages in the sense that it is less flexible. Thus, in recognizing India's critical need for maintenance imports to support its general economy, the United States opted to provide much of its assistance through nonproject loans. These could be judged only by the progress of India's macroeconomy and thereby served as an invitation for the United States to involve itself deeply in the larger issues confronting India's economic policy makers. The strain on aid relations of this involvement was very great, albeit it cannot be judged in isolation from the friction due to the declining United States bilateral aid program and the deteriorating bilateral political situation.

The issue was resolved to some degree in 1973 when the last USAID economist departed from Delhi (ironically, for Islamabad). Symbolically, the mantle of foreign economic adviser was shifted to the multilateral shoulders of the World Bank, where it may prove to fit better. Indeed, events since 1971 suggest that although United States bilateral aid to India may be resumed some day in response to political and developmental objectives, the future shape of Indo-American economic relations—aid, trade, and investment—is destined to be determined more in a multilateral context than during past decades.

A Postscript on External Assistance

What difference has foreign aid—Western or Soviet—made to India's development? This is the irresistible question to which economists can give only the most tentative of answers. Common sense tells us that United States and other foreign aid, by adding to the total resources in India, should have facilitated investment and development. The effect should be substantial, as illustrated by the Third Plan period, when the amount of external aid amounted to more than one-fifth of India's net investment. There is no lack of simple and complex input-output, econometric, and other models which have been designed to describe the macro-Indian economy. But even though almost all these yield

[32]Eldridge, op. cit., pp. 35–36.

coefficients that support the thesis that foreign assistance has had a beneficial effect on development, the models are all deficient in one way or another, particularly in their inability to ascribe causality and in their behavioral assumptions. We simply do not know whether foreign assistance has improved or hurt India's terms of trade; whether it has caused domestic savings to rise or fall; whether it has made investments more or less efficient as measured by the changing capital/output ratio; what its effect has been on the distribution of income; how much of it has been absorbed by corruption; and how it has affected many other critical relationships.[33] Moreover, we have only the most tentative qualitative criteria for judging the net costs of phenomena such as the mélange of intra- and interindustry plant technology and equipment owing to the use of tied aid from a variety of nations.

In seeking a firm rationale for foreign aid, there is some comfort in looking at how various loans are deployed. The effect of aid in relieving bottlenecks is such that a project is intended to release an amount of production far in excess of the amount of the instrumental loan. For example, World Bank President George Woods once calculated that a $2 billion to $3 billion investment in Indian fertilizer plants would contribute a $30 billion increase in grain output in the subsequent decade.[34] It is the countless examples of how foreign aid affects particular sectors that make it possible to draw a stronger conclusion about the positive benefits of foreign assistance.

To measure the benefits of aid with precision, however, is well beyond the capacity of the social scientists' analytic tools and promises to remain there for the foreseeable future. The best that can be done in justifying the transfer of resources from rich to poor countries is to recognize the priority and awesomeness of the task which developers seek to achieve; to note the logic of why aid should help and the specific instances where it has achieved an important objective. When seen in the light of Indian poverty, India's capacity to absorb more investment, historical ties, a shared belief in the open society and constitutional democracy, and the uses to which the wealthy might otherwise put monies appropriated for external aid, the case for continuing and improving the practice of foreign assistance is very strong, if not unassailable.

[33]Paul L. Streeten, *The Frontiers of Development Studies* (New York: John Wiley & Sons, 1972), p. 448.

[34]"Address to the Economic and Social Council of the United Nations," Nov. 13, 1967, p. 6.

APPENDIX TO CHAPTER 4

THE ECONOMIC AND
POLITICAL RAMIFICATIONS
OF LOCAL CURRENCY
(RUPEE) FINANCE

Since 1951, when it began to assist Indian development, the United States has disbursed more than $10 billion in official grants and loans. To ease the repayment burden on India, America made many of the loans, especially those used to finance Indian imports of agricultural commodities under the United States Food for Peace Program (PL-480), repayable in local currency rather than dollars. As a result, by the end of 1973 the United States held rupee claims which, depending on assumptions about rates of exchange, schedules of loan repayments, and expected rates of usage, would have been worth the equivalent of $2 billion to $6 billion by the year 2012.

The political friction which the size of this hoard of American-owned Indian currency generated is undoubtedly the most important ingredient of what came to be known as the "rupee problem." The other major factor which defined the problem was the multitude of administrative and other barriers on both Indian and American sides which, for many years, frustrated all efforts to liquidate the United States rupee claims. From the viewpoint of United States interest, the rupee holdings involved four major questions, all of them intimately tied to broader issues of domestic and foreign policy, both political and economic.

1. There was a conflict between the normal scrutiny which Congress gave appropriation requests and the desirability of giving equal attention to expenditures of excess foreign currency (rupees) which, unlike other spending, had no immediate or important effect on the United States economy or the United States balance of payments. The questions here were (1) whether the rigorous tests applied to the substance of official programs should be relaxed for those endeavors which caused no balance-of-payments or real resource loss and (2)

whether excess currency programs, which are approved by the Congress in substance, should be subjected to the same fiscal scrutiny and criteria as activities requiring the expenditure of dollars.[1]

2. To the extent that foreign currencies owned by the United States could be used instead of dollars, their acquisition represented a potential balance-of-payments benefit. But such benefits could be achieved only at the expense of the PL-480 recipient country which, presumably, obtained agricultural commodities on concessional terms because it was short of hard currency. In short, policies to improve the American balance of payments were not fully compatible with the United States goal of assisting poorer countries. Regrettably, administration spokesmen, beginning with Secretary of State Dulles in 1957, were less than candid in explaining to the U.S. Congress that foreign currencies had limited use.[2]

3. In some instances (most importantly India), the amount of local currency owned by the United States was so great that large expenditures in any one year would have had an adverse impact on the economy of the host country, quite the opposite of what was intended by United States policy. Furthermore, political considerations, namely, invidious questions stemming from the size of United States rupee holdings and expenditures, were a recurring problem in Indo-American relations.[3] Indians have been particularly concerned that the United States might misuse its rupees and abridge Indian sovereignty by interfering in their internal policies and politics as well as their foreign policy. Moreover, India was not only concerned with the level of foreign government expenditure. The Ministry of Finance, for example, wished to limit the flow of American-owned rupees into the Indian branches of United States banks as such flows provided these branches with a competitive advantage over their Indian counterparts. This concern was particularly apparent after India's 1969 bank nationalization.

4. There also existed a very basic contradiction between PL-480 goals; whereas for many years it was of great commercial and political importance to United States agriculture and balance of payments to dispose of large amounts of farm products abroad, progress toward economic viability for the less-developed country often was reliant on the achievement of agricultural self-sufficiency, and the immediate United States balance-of-payments need was for cash, not credit sales. Since 1954, PL-480 language has been amended to reflect greater emphasis on development even though the long-run impact of PL-480 may be to reduce United States exports of agricultural products to developing

[1]See *Testimony of Bureau of the Budget Director Kermit Gordon before the Subcommittee of the Committee on Appropriations, House of Representatives, 89th Congress, Final Session* (Washington, D.C.: Government Printing Office, 1965).

[2]David A Baldwin, op. cit., pp. 162–163 and 226–231.

[3]Comptroller-General of the United States, "Opportunities for Better Use of the United States-owned Excess Foreign Currency in India," January 1971, p. 102.

countries. If, as now apperars possible, developed-country demand for United States farm output grows rapidly, this whole issue may become less important because of declining congressional interest in PL-480.

The discussion which follows is divided into two parts. The first describes the position of United States rupee holdings, anticipated inflows of new rupees, and the principal rules governing expenditures of these funds, as of early 1974. Following, there is a discussion of how United States policies have evolved, the principal concerns of the Indian government as it viewed the United States rupee holdings and the status, substance, and implications of the 1974 rupee agreement signed by India and the United States to end the rupee problem.

Sources and Uses of American-Owned Indian Rupees

In the late 1960s and early 1970s, the United States government typically held liquid rupee balances equivalent in value to about $1 billion (10 percent of India's total money supply). This represented only about a third of total United States rupee assets (the remainder was in long-term development loans to the GOI), but it was the portion which attracted the most critical attention, even though these funds were managed in such a way as to avoid their having an adverse or destabilizing effect on the Indian economy. According to an arrangement with the Ministry of Finance, the United States maintained only small balances with Indian and American commercial banks, and a special account had been established in the Reserve Bank of India (RBI). Deposits in the RBI special account were reinvested in special Indian government securities and thereby had no effect on the Indian money supply.[4]

Each new PL-480 agreement had specified how rupee proceeds were to be apportioned among major uses. On average, 87 percent of the dollar value of receipts had been earmarked for so-called country uses (63.1 percent for loans to India, 17.6 percent for grants to India, and 6.3 percent for so-called Cooley loans to American business interests in India). The remaining 12.9 percent had been allocated for so-called U.S. uses.[5] At any given time, the United States rupee balances were composed of three major categories:

1. *PL-480 country use:* These funds constituted the bulk of rupee receipts from PL-480-financed exports of agricultural commodities. Most of the receipts were either loaned or granted to India to support development and social programs. Country-use rupees were not generally available to support programs of United States government agencies, although they were utilized to fund

---

[4]*Explanatory Memorandum on the Budget of the Central Government for 1973–74*, op. cit., p. 60.

[5]Ministry of Finance, *External Assistance, 1970–71* (New Delhi: GOI, 1971), p. 130.

a USAID Trust Fund for India. The Trust Fund, established on the principle that aid recipients should assume the local costs of the United States program, was used to meet all of USAID's expenditures in India for local administrative and operating costs, including housing, local and international transportation, salaries of local employees, and office supplies. As this funding technique removed control over outlays one step beyond the normal fiscal mechanisms of both governments, it was criticized by both and it did not survive the political abrasions following 1971.

Owing to a change in the PL-480 legislation in 1966 which gradually shifted repayments on new agreements from local currency to dollar obligations, country-use rupees were no longer routinely generated. This is because (a) repayments of loans made from country-use funds were treated as U.S.-use funds and (b) the gradual transition from sales for local currency to sales for dollars under PL-480, which began in 1966, was completed in 1971. Thus, the only source of country-use rupees remaining at the outset of 1974 was through the reallocation of funds from the U.S.-use category, as discussed below. This was significant because, as will become evident, only a small fraction of U.S.-use rupees could be spent each year.

The principal barrier to the disbursement of country-use funds was that expenditures required approval by both the United States and Indian governments. From the Indian side, the expenditure of these monies was a financial transaction involving no addition to the amount of real resources available for economic development; i.e., the only incentive for using United States funds rather than normal budgetary resources was that it reduced the local currency debt to the United States. In the minds of Indian leaders this advantage was often outweighed by the domestic political costs of permitting the United States to receive credit for development programs. From the American side, there was considerable resistance to financing of development activities which were not, in some sense, additional to what India would otherwise have done. In reconciling these positions, it is not surprising that American efforts to influence the course of India's development program without supplying additional real resources was a cause for mutual dissatisfaction and friction.

2. *PL-480 U.S. use:* The source for these funds changed in the early 1970s from new PL-480 agreements to repayments of interest and principal on loans made from the proceeds of past agreements. U.S.-use rupees were available to United States government agencies which obtained them against regular dollar appropriations or Special Foreign Currency Appropriations usable only for the purchase of American-held foreign currencies determined to be in excess by the Treasury. A wide range of United States programs were financed out of rupee holdings: not only routine operations in India but also sales of rupees for dollars to American tourists and organizations, the bulk of the cost of the USAID program in Nepal, and foreign exchange conversions which were negotiated with the aim of reducing the balance-of-payments cost to the United States of worldwide programs of educational exchange and agricultural market

development. Because of the existence of U.S.-use rupees, there has been virtually no balance-of-payments cost to the United States of its Mission in India and the cost to the United States economy has been substantially reduced.

Generally, U.S.-use rupees could not be used to purchase goods for export from India. The exceptions to this rule included aid for friendly third countries (for which India's concurrence was required), and an agreement between India and the United States that permitted the export each year of up to $120,000 worth of furniture, furnishings, and live birds. The United States often expressed interest in raising the level of the export authorization and broadening the list of approved commodities, but it had little to offer to obtain India's agreement.

The expenditure of U.S.-use rupees was circumscribed by a variety of factors including law, international agreement, the general Indo-American political relationship, and economic policy. These restraints arose on both the Indian and United States sides:

¶ Section 104 of PL-480, the foreign assistance acts, appropriation bills, etc., specified various dos and don'ts for excess currency funds.[6]

¶ Indian laws and regulations governing foreign exchange transactions, international trade, and allocation of scarce commodities were applicable to United States operations in India unless special exemption was obtained from the Indian government.

¶ PL-480 agreements were bilaterally negotiated between the two governments and established rules governing the use of rupee proceeds.

¶ Although there usually was no legal requirement for the United States to consult India before spending U.S.-use rupees, as a matter of policy Indian agreement was sought for programs outside the Embassy's normal operating and administrative expenditures.

¶ And finally, as a matter of policy, the United States government generally tried to use rupees so as not to divert a significant amount of scarce Indian resources from the task of economic development.

Although U.S.-use rupees were generally not available for United States government programs unless there was a congressional appropriation, there were several exceptions to this rule. A major portion of the cost of the USAID program in Nepal has been financed by U.S.-use rupees obtained by way of a Special Foreign Currency Authorization (more than $80 million[7]). When India took exception to this particular use, it was phased out, but not without causing

---

[6]In the PL-480 act, published in *Legislation on Foreign Relations* (Joint Committee Report), 93rd Congress, 1st Session, pp. 264–269, one can find a long but incomplete compendium of the structure from the American side.

[7]Ministry of Finance, *External Assistance, 1970–71,* op. cit., p. 143.

some friction between Nepal and India[8] and, consequently, between India and the United States.

It was possible for U.S.-use rupees generated by the PL-480 program to be reallocated to country use (Mondale-Poage Amendment). But before funds could be reallocated and used, approval of the Indian government, responsible Washington agencies, including the Office of Management and Budget and the Senate and House Committees on Agriculture, was required. Although some use was made of this procedure, it was cumbersome and clearly an inadequate route to the expenditure of additional rupee funds.

3. *Non-PL-480 rupees:* The debt service (interest and principal payments) on United States Development Loan Fund (DLF) and Mutual Security Agency (MSA) loans was an additional sources of rupees. These funds differed from U.S.-use PL-480 rupees to the extent that they could not be used under any circumstances in the absence of congressional appropriations. And this money was used to meet only a very limited variety of United States expenses because of a technicality in the United States law. When PL-480 rupees were purchased, a receipt was recorded for the budget of the Commodity Credit Corporation (CCC). In contrast, when non-PL-480 rupees were purchased, this was recorded as a miscellaneous Treasury receipt. Thus, by obviating the need for obtaining appropriations for the CCC, there was a technical budgetary advantage in using PL-480 rather than non-PL-480 funds.

Genesis and Development of the Rupee Problem

Foreign currency holdings of the United States were small and posed no problem until after the Second World War, when foreign assistance programs greatly increased the amount of such funds. Initially, they were controlled by the separate federal agencies administering the assistance programs and generally they were not subject to the same fiscal and budgetary controls which governed the expenditure of dollars; i.e., the regular appropriation process was bypassed.

Section 1415 of the Supplemental Appropriation Act of 1953 (known as the Robaut Amendment) recognized the growing importance of foreign currency holdings and required that, effective with the fiscal year 1954, all uses of such funds be subject to appropriation. The Agricultural Trade Development and Assistance Act of 1954 (PL-480), however, relaxed this requirement for several categories of expenditure, particularly the country-use portion of PL-480 receipts. In 1959, concern about the burgeoning amounts of foreign currency

[8]India was much annoyed when Nepal raised this bilateral subject during an ECAFE meeting.

accruing under PL-480, and increasing demands by United States agencies on the Bureau of the Budget for the allocation of large sums of currency on a "free" (nonappropriated) basis, caused the administration to accept the Budget Bureau's recommendation that appropriations be required for the expenditure of all U.S.-use currencies. In connection with this change, the USFY 1961 budget introduced the Special Foreign Currency Program for obtaining dollar appropriations usable only for the purchase of currencies designated by the Treasury as being in excess.[9]

Beginning with FY 1961, in order to further ensure that the budgetary process would not be circumvented in the case of spending of excess foreign currencies, the Congress approved the House Appropriations Committee's writing of agency appropriations in such a way as to preclude the use of appropriated dollar funds by State, Commerce, and USIA for any programs which were financed in whole or in part with nonappropriated excess currencies.

These developments were occurring at the same time as Edward Mason and his fellow consultants, appointed by Undersecretary of State Douglas Dillon, were reporting on how dangerous the global acquisition of local currencies had become for the United States. According to Mason and his colleagues, there was widespread misunderstanding of the amounts of foreign currency holdings and the conditions attending their use. They expressed particular alarm that the United States was "adopting measures and pursuing methods which seem destined inevitably to undermine the real political and security objectives of foreign assistance."[10]

By 1964, it was becoming clear that one major effect of close congressional control over expenditures of excess currencies was reflected in the skyrocketing of United States holdings of these funds, particularly Indian rupees. Although the Congress was more generous in giving its approval for Special Foreign Currency Appropriations than for regular dollar appropriations, a desire to streamline government operations and a reluctance to allow second priority programs to enter the government's operations tended to deter the development of any brave new program to raise the rate of such expenditures; inflows of additional excess currencies continued to exceed spending authority.

To meet this problem, the Budget Bureau included in the FY 1966 budget a new procedure, the Excess Foreign Currency Authorization which, if approved, would have permitted the President to use 5 percent of available excess currencies for purposes deemed beneficial to the United States under existing laws. The Congress, unwilling to abdicate its fiscal responsibility, disap-

[9]See "Foreign Currency Availabilities and Uses," in *The Budget of the U.S. Government for Fiscal Year Ending June 30, 1961* (Washington, D.C.: Government Printing Office, 1960), pp. 928 ff.

[10]Report of Edward S. Mason et al. to Undersecretary of State Douglas Dillon, Apr. 4, 1960.

proved on grounds that the proposed uses of the funds would have to be spelled out before such authority could be given.[11] Subsequently, detailed programs for the spending of additional excess currencies were gathered from the field by the State Department under guidelines provided by the Budget Bureau. They were presented separately by each agency as requests for Excess Foreign Currency Authorizations. Despite the great emphasis placed on the fact that foreign currencies, not dollars, were being requested, only some of the programs were approved, and appropriations were obtained to fund them. In principle, Congress disapproved of the "authorization" approach. From the agency viewpoint, congressional resistance to "augmentation of budgets" represented an amber light for foreign currency appropriations requests because of the agencies' fear that these might be approved at the expense of higher priority dollar programs.

In 1966, the Mondale-Poage Amendment to PL-480 was passed; it gave limited authority for use of nonappropriated excess currencies (either by loan or grant). Even though it specifically cited only the Foreign Buildings Program and agricultural self-help activities, AID interpreted the amendment as applying to a wide range of activities. Nonetheless, because of (1) hesitancy on the part of the Bureau of the Budget to approve Mondale-Poage uses of funds, (2) continuing congressional interest that the appropriation process be used, and (3) the provision in their annual appropriation which effectively prevents the State and Commerce Departments and USIA from using nonappropriated currencies, only limited use was made of the amendment. Beginning in 1967, there was a growing trend toward belt tightening in all government operations and, therefore, little scope for additional foreign currency programs. In effect the U.S. Congress, because of its innate conservatism and skepticism about the executive, prevented the United States from using its rupee holdings in ways which would impose an undue burden on India.

The record with regard to spending of American-owned rupees for Indian development activities is somewhat different. An early effort to use $300

---

[11]In the Report (No. 427) of the Committee on Appropriations to accompany H.R. 8639 (89th Congress, 1st Session), submitted on May 27, 1965, Committee Chairman John J. Rooney stated under the section "General Provisions": "The proposed special foreign currency authorization as set forth . . . in the budget for fiscal year 1966, to allow the Executive Branch of the Government to use up to 5 per cent of foreign currencies available for the United States uses in each excess currency country during the fiscal year 1966 has not been approved. This proposal would in effect have the Congress give up its authority to decide what these excess currencies (the equivalent of $82,400,000) are to be used for and turn that authority over to the Bureau of the Budget." The proposal of the Bureau of the Budget only mentioned "special programs which are in the national interest and will contribute to the more effective, efficient and economical conduct of U.S. programs." And at the hearings, Kermit Gordon, Director of the Bureau of the Budget, was not able to specify what would be done with the $82-odd million if it were made available.

million equivalent of excess rupees to create an Indo-American Educational Foundation floundered in 1966 on the rock of domestic Indian politics and the charge of "academic imperialism."[12] In contrast, in mid-1969 all the procedural hurdles were cleared and the United States used Mondale-Poage authority to grant the equivalent of nearly $150 million for a rural electrification program.

From the Indian point of view, there was concern about both the size of United States holdings and the uses to which these rupees are put. The PL-480 program was more than sporadically attacked in the Parliament and press[13] as having had an inflationary effect on the Indian economy. The Indian government recognized the importance of rejecting this charge and appointed a special group of experts in 1968 to review the economic issue. The experts found the situation benign,[14] but this did not stop its being used as the basis for Communist-inspired attacks against the United States.

According to the Indian view, the original PL-480 legislation had not envisaged the size to which the program would grow and the massive debt which India would incur as a result of its large grain imports. Indians often regarded United States rupee holdings as "funny money," not representing a claim on real resources. This approach was a valid negotiating position and evinced considerable sympathy with some knowledgeable Americans, but it did not accord with the United States government view as seen by Treasury and Agriculture. The vast majority of expenditures for running the United States Mission in India (including the international air transportation of employees and other official travelers to India) were met with rupees, not dollars.

Other United States government expenses, such as the USAID programs in Nepal, were financed with Indian rupees. AID's loans and grants sometimes served a useful purpose in accelerating Indian adoption of important development programs such as rural electrification. Thus, in direct opposition to America's political interest in getting rid of its rupees, there was a clear United States economic interest in continuing to use available rupees to finance United States programs in India, importantly including Indian economic development.

Nonetheless, the political pressure for an accommodation grew, and the benefits from rationalizing the holding and use of American-owned rupees became so great that in 1970–71 even the ultraconservative U.S. General Accounting Office (GAO) was moved to prepare a report on the rupee problem, which recommended:

---

[12]Its death was speeded by simultaneous disclosures of sub rosa CIA support for American universities. See the *New York Times,* Apr. 26, May 7 and 23, 1966, and the *Washington Post,* May 23, 1966.

[13]B. R. Shenoy, "Monetary Impact of PL-480 Finance," *Eastern Economist,* July 26, 1968, pp. 151–155.

[14]*Report of Expert Group on PL-480 Transactions* (New Delhi: GOI, 1969).

1. That the Budget Bureau encourage the submission to Congress of requests for excess currency funds projects deemed worthy by Government agencies;

2. That consideration of these projects, both within the Administration and Congress, proceed without regard to the various agencies' overall ceilings;

3. That the Budget Bureau explore with the appropriate Congressional Committees the possibility of direct appropriations of foreign currency (as contrasted with the practice of appropriating dollars which could only be used for the purchase of excess currency); and

4. That the Secretary of the Treasury establish more flexible procedures for valuing U.S.-owned Indian rupees in dollars so as to maximize the use of excess currency in India without compromising Congressional control over the use of these funds. This was intended to enhance local currency procurement without penalizing the budgets of the U.S. agencies involved and was to be achieved by establishing a rate of exchange for internal U.S.G. accounting more favorable to the United States than the official rate of Rs. 7.5 per dollar.[15]

In 1970 Secretary of State Rogers appointed Dr. Raymond J. Saulnier to investigate the rupee problem in India and asked him to make recommendations for its solution. After an intensive analysis, including a visit to India and meetings with senior Indian officials, Dr. Saulnier submitted a report which not only ran into formidable United States bureaucratic and political obstacles, but was overtaken by deteriorating Indo-American relations. In 1971, the Administration proposed to Congress legislation to make Mondale-Poage grant procedures applicable to non-PL-480 rupees, a step which would not have provided a full solution to the rupee problem, but would have represented an enormous step in this direction. When the amendment containing the administration's proposal was dropped from the bill to which it had been attached on a procedural question, the administration fixed no timetable for resubmission and the rupee problem continued to be an outstanding source of conflict in Indo-American relations.

The Final Stretch

For Indians politically unsympathetic to the United States, the rupee problem was an ideal issue for launching frequent and vitriolic attacks about America's malign objectives in South Asia. But other Indians, more favorably disposed toward America, were also bothered by our rupee holdings. While acknowledging that the assets had been managed so as to make their impact on the Indian economy and society minimal, they were concerned that, because the accumulation of United States assets continued to outpace expenditures,

[15]Comptroller-General of the United States, op. cit.

the problem could be perpetuated indefinitely unless action was taken to resolve it.

It was not surprising, therefore, that in seeking actions to improve Indo-American relations from the low point reached in 1971–72, the United States administration lighted on the rupee problem. Dissolving this long-standing irritant appeared as a meaningful gesture which would not prove excessively costly or embarrassing to the administration, and would not be subject to misinterpretation by the Indian government. The new United States Ambassador, Daniel P. Moynihan, proved to be an articulate and forceful influence and, in a remarkable series of negotiations, he eventually convinced the United States executive, key congressmen, and the Indian government to agree on a compromise solution.

Moynihan negotiated an agreement which drew on the earlier work of the GAO, Dr. Saulnier, and others. To reduce the size of current and prospective United States rupee holdings, about two-thirds of the American-owned assets ($2.2 billion) were granted to India for use in development programs during the Fifth Plan. The remaining rupees were retained in non-interest-bearing accounts for use by the American government in its programs in India.[16]

In solving the rupee problem, the United States and India removed a serious and long-standing direct impediment to closer relations. One cost of this step, however, may prove considerably larger than anticipated. In obtaining a congressional no-objection to the rupee agreement, Ambassador Moynihan and the administration persuaded a limited number of representatives and senators that this action was not an outrageous bear raid on the U.S. Treasury. It is much more problematic whether they can convince other congressmen that the Indian agreement should not be interpreted as a default, and that developing countries will continue to honor other bilateral and multilateral aid repayment obligations. It is no coincidence that when the House of Representatives voted in early 1974 to deny new funds to the International Development Association, the rupee agreement was one issue in the debate. (India probably would have received about 40 percent or more than $2 billion of these hard currency loans over a three-year period.) Thus, although this congressional action was subsequently reversed, it would be a deep and sad irony of history if, in the process of applying cosmetics to the politically troublesome but economically manageable rupee problem, India and America had cast a still deeper shadow over the future of real foreign assistance.

---

[16]United States Congress, House of Representatives, 93d Congress, 2d Session, *Indian Rupee Settlement Agreement*, Testimony of Ambassador Daniel P. Moynihan before the Subcommittee on Near East and South Asia of the Committee on Foreign Relations, Jan. 29, 1974 (Washington, D.C.: Government Printing Office, 1974).

CHAPTER 5
ECONOMIC RELATIONS WITH
THE SOVIET UNION

India's principal relationships with East Europe—economic and political—have been with the Soviet Union. Merchandise trade agreements with other Communist nations have been long-standing and substantial (India signed its first bilateral trade agreement with Yugoslavia in 1948, five years before its first agreement with the U.S.S.R.), but because these have been less important than ties with the Soviets and have tended to follow patterns established by Delhi in its intercourse with Moscow, I shall generally disregard them in this chapter. Similarly, as the balance-of-payments mechanism used to govern Indo-Soviet economic transactions is generally valid for Indo–East European finance, and as more than three-fourths of the aid India has received from the U.S.S.R. and East European countries has come from Moscow, I shall concentrate on the Indo-Soviet pattern and mention only the most important variations from it.

Indo-Soviet Political Relations

The transformation of the Indo-Soviet relationship since Independence has been as far-reaching as it has been gradual. Soviet reappraisals of how its national interests would be served are largely responsible for why the number of economic contacts and degree of political identification between these nations have grown remarkably. But increased relations are also a function of changes in Indian thinking, in no small part related to hostile Indian reactions to Washington's support of Pakistan.

When Nehru, the principal architect of India's foreign and domestic policy, visited Moscow in 1927, he was deeply impressed by socialism as contrasted with

157

the fascism which later became important in Germany and Italy.[1] His foreign policy of nonalignment, world peace, anti-imperialism, and racial equality was significantly different from Soviet foreign policy but was not incompatible with substantive relations with the U.S.S.R., and the two countries found no difficulty in opening diplomatic relations in 1947.[2] The most important differences between Nehru and Soviet leaders, which were to become less important in the course of time, concerned (1) the posture of the Indian Communist party, whether it would act peacefully within the framework of domestic Indian politics or operate as a revolutionary force, and (2) attitudes toward the legitimacy of Soviet domestic authoritarianism and international assertiveness.

It is hardly surprising that, in 1947, Soviet views of India were less influenced by the nineteenth-century experience of Franco-Russian alliances to drive the British out of India than by the Communist "two camps" thesis in which—à la Dulles—Moscow saw the world as divided into opposing groups, with all those not aligned with the Soviet Union regarded as hostile. With some reason, Moscow was wary of the prospects for socialism in India and, with less justification, it was concerned about whether India's independence from Britain would prove to be genuine. In practice, this led Soviet leaders to support the Communist party of India in its radical opposition to the national government in Delhi. This policy was not moderated until 1950, when the Cominform, hoping to stem the declining popularity of the Communist party in India, decided on a more moderate policy stance which was more easily reconciled with Indian nationalism.[3]

The beginnings of a change in Soviet attitudes toward the Third World were discernible to some observers as early as 1949. In that year the U.S.S.R. voted for a UN program of expanded technical assistance to developing nations, albeit it made no financial contribution until after Stalin died in 1953.[4]

The strategy Soviet leaders formulated to offset United States power—and, to an unknown degree, that of China—called for a general opening to the developing countries, particularly toward India because of its large size and strategic location. Thus, in 1953 Indira Gandhi visited the U.S.S.R., and later that year the first Indo-Soviet trade agreement was signed.[5] From that time onwards the Soviets can be said to have adopted a "showcase" psychology toward India. To support their claim that, contrary to the neocolonialist motives of the West, they acted merely in the name of socialist solidarity, they

[1]Mahalanobis, op. cit., p. 1.

[2]Asha L. Datar, *India's Economic Relations with the U.S.S.R. and Eastern Europe, 1953 to 1969* (Cambridge: Cambridge University Press, 1972), p. 26

[3]See Geoffrey Jukes, *The Soviet Union in Asia* (Berkeley: University of California Press, 1973), pp. 99–104.

[4]K. T. Merchant, "Soviet Aid for Economic Development," in Vadilal Dagli, ed., *Indo-Soviet Economic Relations: A Survey* (Bombay: Vora, 1971), p. 19.

[5]For a more complete description of the Soviet change of attitude, see Joseph S. Berliner, *Soviet Economic Aid* (New York: Praeger Books for the Council on Foreign Relations, 1958), chaps. 2 and 5.

sought to put their aid on a business rather than charitable basis. Moreover, they carefully chose aid projects which could be supported as helpful to India's industrial progress and which would appear to demonstrate the superiority of communism over capitalism.

Détente between the Soviets and Indians was hastened by the events of the following year, which featured an exchange of visits by Nehru and Chou En-lai, the signing of the Pancheel, and the Sino-Indian agreement on Tibet. Early in 1955, Moscow agreed to provide its first major economic aid to India, credits for construction of a steel mill at Bhilai in Madhya Pradesh. State visits exchanged by Nehru, Bulganin, and Khrushchev later in the year were regarded as highly successful,[6] and during the remainder of the 1950s additional Soviet assistance agreements were negotiated to help strategic sectors of Indian industry. The first of these, a 1956 grant to establish a mechanized farm at Suratgarh, Rajasthan, was followed by loans in such critical sectors as machine building, coal mining, thermal power, and drug manufacture.[7]

The newly animated Indo-Soviet relationship was pursued despite reservations on both sides. Nehru was fully aware of the continuing link between the Communist party of India and Moscow, and he disfavored various abrasive aspects of the Soviets' domestic and foreign policies. Moscow, for its part, was displeased by the bourgeois influence in Indian policy, the income disparities between India's rich and poor, and Delhi's ties to the West and China. Thus the growing durability of Indo-Soviet relations in this and later periods must be regarded as a triumph of political expediency over ideological dogmatism. The relationship also delivered substantial and immediate political benefit for both sides as, for example, Moscow's support of India's position on Kashmir and Goa and Delhi's restraint in not criticizing the Soviets for brutally ending the 1956 Hungarian revolution. Moreover, they also served the Soviets' objective of obtaining influence and eventually radicalizing the politics of developing countries.[8]

Beginning in 1959, in part because of China's deteriorating relations with both the Soviet Union and India, Delhi's relations with Moscow became more critical and complex. Soviet support for India not only became a symbol of Soviet disagreement with China, but also served to fortify a nation with potential for helping the U.S.S.R. in its conflict with China. Although India's policies toward China remained largely independent of the altered Soviet posture, Moscow accelerated its aid for Delhi and expanded it to include aircraft, helicopters, and other sophisticated weapons.[9] The Soviets undoubtedly perceived their increasingly close ties with India as the result of, rather than the cause for, their deteriorating relations with Peking. At the time, however, the

[6]Charles B. McLane, *Soviet-Asian Relations* (New York: Central Asian Research Center and Columbia University Press, 1974), p. 55.

[7]Ministry of Finance, *External Assistance, 1970–71*, op. cit., pp. 109–110.

[8]Barnds, *India, Pakistan, and the Great Powers*, op. cit., p. 116.

[9]Jukes, op. cit., pp. 118–119.

extent of Sino-Soviet hostility was not generally known and the reasons for the new Soviet policy toward India were not apparent. Moreover, in the limited 1959 clashes, which eventually led to the Sino-Indian war in 1962, the Soviet Union reacted with caution, a sign that its own troubled relations with the Chinese had not yet led to despair.

The Soviets' increasing patronage of India was also intended to offset the possibility of India's turning to the West at the expense of Indo-Soviet ties. After the policy of antipathy to the Indian government, which marked the late 1940s, had been fully abandoned, a continuing aid program and rhetorical neutrality were a reasonable price for the Soviets to pay in order to maintain their link with India during the decade of the 1950s. In 1962 and thereafter, Moscow became still more supportive of the Indian position by (1) increasing arms shipments; (2) establishing a factory in India to manufacture MIG fighters, a step which was particularly welcomed by the Indians because it appeared to move them a step closer to self-reliance; and (3) identifying Soviet policy more closely with Delhi's foreign goals.

Nonetheless, to the extent that Moscow wished to nurture its friendly relationship with India and, simultaneously, to "expand its ties with Pakistan, both to take advantage of Pakistan's alienation from the United States and to limit Chinese influence in that country,"[10] it was in a predicament. Soviet leaders resolved the conflict by adopting a policy of strict political neutrality between India and Pakistan (including on the Kashmir issue). Under their auspices the settlement ending the 1965 Indo-Pakistani war was reached at Tashkent. But to show their support for Indian economic development, they agreed to aid a number of investments including construction of a mammoth steel mill at Bokaro, which the United States Congress had been loath to finance.

The period 1966–1970 was not an easy one for Indo-Soviet relations. Hindu leaders, in particular, were incensed by Moscow's new position on Kashmir and its 1968 agreement to sell arms to Pakistan. India had other causes for dissatisfaction, expecially insofar as Soviet maps of the Sino-Indian border did not accord with Indian territorial claims, Soviet trade policies did not benefit India to the extent that the rhetoric of trade agreements suggested, and tensions had developed in the aid relationship. The U.S.S.R. met Delhi's complaints mainly with diplomacy. But the Soviets also expressed a muted but genuine dismay with the progress of India's economic development, with the weakness of Indian socialism in general, and with the poor performance of Soviet-aided projects in particular.[11] Soviet concern that India would take a turn toward the capitalist right, which reached its apex in 1968, was not heavily publicized but did make for reticence in Moscow's attitude toward Delhi. To a significant degree Soviet doubts about the competence and the socialist orientation of Mrs. Gandhi's government were soon resolved, and the Soviet diplomatic stoicism was rewarded by a series of events which caused India to move into a closer relationship with the U.S.S.R. Campaigning on the slogan *garibi hatao* ("abolish

[10]Barnds, *India, Pakistan, and the Great Powers,* op. cit., p. 206.
[11]McLane, op. cit., pp. 56–57 and 59.

poverty"), Mrs. Gandhi won an impressive victory in India's 1971 parliamentary election. This confirmed that her 1969 split with the conservative wing of the Congress party and her ascendancy over other political leaders were accomplished facts and allayed Soviet fears that under Mrs. Gandhi's stewardship India would take a bourgeois tack.[12]

Indo-Soviet ties were further strengthened by the concern of both countries' leaders about the Sino-American-Pakistani alliance in South Asia which appeared to be the natural consequence of the emerging Sino-American détente and the international politics of the Bangladesh independence movement, among other factors. Although Mrs. Gandhi had consistently withheld support from the Asian collective security pact proposed by Brezhnev in 1969 on grounds of nonalignment (India was more inclined to support a loosely worded cooperation agreement), the events of 1971 caused India to move with dispatch to negotiate a bilateral Treaty of Peace, Friendship, and Cooperation with Moscow, which was signed during a hastily arranged visit to Delhi by Foreign Minister Gromyko in August 1971. In the wake of the treaty, Indian and Soviet leaders arranged for an itensified series of bilateral visits by political and technical personnel which culminated in November 1973 in the official appearance of Leonid Brezhnev in Delhi. The fruits of the Brezhnev visit, while meager in light of the Soviets' still frustrated desire for an Asian security pact and the Indians' barely fulfilled wish for substantial new Soviet economic assistance (including debt relief), were real, particularly insofar as Moscow agreed to help India by selling it critical commodities and by aiding key industrial sectors such as coal mining. I shall have more to say about this in the pages which follow insofar as they deal with the overall framework within which Indo-Soviet economic relations were pursued as well as the specifics of the trade and aid relationships.

The Framework for Economic Relations

It is noteworthy that in formulating economic policies which would be responsive to political-economic considerations, Soviet leaders have been no more prone to consult the writings of Marx than Americans to refer to Jefferson or Locke. But even if ideology has not dictated immediate objectives and inflexibly bound the Soviets to a particular posture, it has had some influence over the choice of policy goals and the instruments for achieving them. (Indeed, it is hardly surprising that the title of the Richard Cooper article mentioned in Chapter 4, "Trade Policy Is Foreign Policy," is but a variation of a doctrine stated in the *Great Soviet Encyclopedia:* "The foreign trade policy of the U.S.S.R. is part of the over-all foreign policy of the U.S.S.R."[13]) It would be an

---

[12]Bhàbani Sen Gupta, "Moscow, Peking, and the Indian Political Scene after Nehru," *Orbis,* vol. 12, no. 2, Summer 1968.

[13]Quoted from Berliner, op. cit., p. 8.

error, however, to assume that economic considerations are always subservient to political expediency. Moreover, although Moscow may be motivated to engage in commerce with India primarily by political factors, this hardly rules out the potential for economic benefits for both nations. In reality, the gains from international division of labor and foreign trade formulated by Ricardo do obtain in Indo-Soviet exchange, and the Soviet Union and India have obtained important mutual benefits from their bilateral economic relations.

In relating to India on economic matters, Moscow has had two important advantages over the West. At the ideological level, socialism is inherently more attractive to the intellectuals and masses in a country which suffers from poverty, large income disparities, and exploitation by the wealthy. In practice, moreover, because of its monolithic character, the Soviet government often could act with greater flexibility than Western governments. Not only could Moscow arrange to put the best possible public relations face on economic arrangements, but it was able to interrelate economic and political issues and also to take advantage of linkages among aid, trade, and other economic relationships. Beyond the most elementary of such linkages—merchandise trade tied to capital assistance—the Soviet Union was able to offer to (1) substitute barter for normal commercial exchange, (2) partially interrelate its five-year plan with India's, and (3) provide aid for projects which would (*a*) create demand for the output of factories it had assisted India to build in the past or (*b*) create future production that could be exported to the U.S.S.R.[14] In short, a great part of Moscow's success in dealing with India stemmed from its ability to implement an integrated foreign policy.

A survey of the various economic relationships which have developed between India and the Soviet Union reveals five outstanding characteristics of Moscow's approach which, in particular instances, have been complementary or conflicting among themselves.

1. *Economic viability:* Soviet leaders may have been more daring than the West in choosing to support investments such as the Bokaro steel mill and the Aswan dam, but in both trade and aid dealings the U.S.S.R. is also known for its "business is business" attitude. Symptomatic of this concern is the attention Moscow gave to aiding basic industries. Even though the output of these investments will almost certainly be demanded by the Indian economy in future years, they have not always been chosen wisely or implemented efficiently. Thus, through ignorance of Indian conditions and a desire to accommodate Indian wishes, the Soviets have involved themselves in more than an occasional inefficient project. The Soviet-aided antibiotics plants at Rishikesh and the Surgical Instruments Plant in Madras are examples of investments which have not lived up to expectations; the steel mill at Bhilai and the Barauni Oil Refinery are cases of relative success.

2. *Political appeal:* The Soviet Union has endeavored to design its economic

[14]See UNCTAD, "Case Study Prepared by the UNCTAD Secretariat on Trade and Economic Relations between India and the Socialist Countries of Eastern Europe," TD/B/129, July 21, 1967.

programs with India and other developing countries so as to make them appear more politically and economically desirable to the Thrid World and to contrast with the "exploitative" and "neocolonial" programs of the capitalist countries. Moscow claimed that it did not aim to perpetuate the dependence of poor countries and therefore sought to arrange its aid and trade so as to help developing countries escape from their traditional status as unindustrialized exporters of primary commodities. This rhetoric was matched to a considerable degree by actions, albeit Moscow's programs were not ensured of having a high development impact. What is significant here is that Soviet sensitivity to the Indian goals of self-reliance, industrialization, and heavy industry earned Moscow high political marks in its overall relations with India.

3. *Public appeal:* Compared to the United States, Moscow has attracted a far more favorable public reaction to its economic programs in India (particularly as measured by media response) than is justified by the amount and quality of the trade and capital assistance it has provided. In merchandise trade, for example, Moscow has had great success in publicizing the advantages to India of barter arrangements which, by providing an automatic mechanism for equating imports and exports, ostensibly do not deplete scarce foreign exchange reserves of either country. (In fact, for reasons I shall give presently, barter has been costly to India's foreign exchange position.) In aid matters, there has been a tendency to concentrate effort on a limited number of large, symbolic, and obvious projects, particularly schemes which for one reason or another were rejected by Western aid donors.

4. *Ideology:* The Soviets have gone to pains to describe their economic relations with India as qualitatively different from Indo-Western relations and very much in the common interest as conceived within the framework of an international socialist society. Accordingly, Moscow emphasized in the early days of its loan program that its practice of making "low-cost" loans was less demeaning to India and more businesslike than the grant-making practice of Western donors. Historically, although Moscow's first aid to India (the sale of equipment on deferred payment terms to the Hindustan Gas Company[15]), was to a privately owned enterprise, this was an ironic anomaly: subsequent assistance has been concentrated on the public sector. With regard to the extent of Soviet encouragement of Indian socialism, there has been a gradual change. For instance, there is disagreement about the degree to which Moscow pressed India to establish a State Trading Corporation (STC) to manage its foreign trade, but no doubt "that the Soviet trade relationship had a causal impact in establishing the STC" in 1956.[16] Since the early 1960s, the contribution of ideological concerns to Soviet policy appears to have declined and to have been replaced by a pragmatism which emphasizes economic performance.[17] Indeed,

[15]Kidron, op. cit., p. 114.

[16]Stephen Clarkson, "Non-Impact of Soviet Writing on Indian Thinking and Policy," *Economic and Political Weekly*, Apr. 14, 1973, p. 721.

[17]Ibid. and Elizabeth Kridl Valkenier, "New Trends in Soviet Economic Relations with the Third World," *World Politics*, vol. 22, no. 3, April 1970.

there even have been occasions in recent years when the Soviets pressured the Indian government to support private industry.[18]

5. *Low cost:* Whether one examines the commodity compostion and price of goods traded between India and the Soviet Union, or the quantity and quality of capital assistance, the conclusion emerges that Moscow has not always been generous in its economic relations with India. Examples of Soviet niggardliness include the arrangement whereby India prepaid loans received for construction of the Bhilai steel mill and the Soviet-suggested reduction in the amount of capital goods imports for Bokaro which also had the effect of reducing the amount of Soviet aid to the project.

Despite the largely political motivation for the Soviets to widen their economic contacts with India, on balance the results of the relationship appear to be not only in line with India's proclaimed political goals but neutral to—or outright supportive of—India's basic development objectives. Moscow's emphasis on public sector investment in heavy industry was regarded by Indian leaders as especially valuable both because the capital and technical aid received for Bhilai, Barauni, and other plants was needed and because these projects led Western donors to become more amenable to using their own funds for public sector lending. Khrushchev is reported to have said to Nehru that two Western-financed steel plants "Rourkela and Durgapur should also be put in our account."[19] More generally, Moscow's aid to public sector heavy industry permitted India to follow more socialistic policies than might otherwise have been the case.

In light of Nehru's respect for Soviet economic achievements and India's Soviet-inspired commitment to planning, it would not have been unreasonable to expect a heavy Indian reliance on Soviet economic and technical expertise. In practice, however, there was relatively scant contact between India's economic planners and their counterparts in the U.S.S.R. The Indian Statistical Institute in Calcutta, under the stewardship of P. C. Mahalanobis, invited a number of socialist and Communist economists to India. Nonetheless, M. I. Rubinstein, the most effective of the Soviet technicians, is reported to have been less influential than such eminent economists as Oscar Lange of Poland, Charles Bettelheim of France, and Joan Robinson from the United Kingdom. Stephen Clarkson has concluded that

> rather than pushing the Indians into radical action, Soviet influence on the Indian planning system was first to popularize the general idea of planning among Nehru's colleagues, second to restrain Indian policy planners from over-enthusiasm, and third to provide both internal political support through their private conversations with Indian leaders and external ideological assistance through their public writings in the Soviet press.[20].

[18]An example is Soviet resistance to the proposed nationalization of the Delhi company which was distributing Soviet tractors; cited in Clarkson, op. cit., p. 721.

[19]Quoted from *Economic Weekly*, Apr. 25, 1962, by Kidron, op. cit., p. 166.

[20]Clarkson, op. cit., p. 722.

In short, Soviet economists—as contrasted with political leaders—have had only limited impact owing to the Western orientation of most Indian intellectuals and the inflexibilities the Soviets found in applying Marxist-Leninist doctrine to the enormously different Indian society. Consequently, the outlook of Indian intellectuals is often characterized by a "pattern of little knowledge, low credibility, and poor personal contact with Soviet intellectual sources."[21]

In many ways the advantages to India of increased economic ties with the Soviet Union were seen as embodied in the so-called Rupee Payments System. According to the first Indo-Soviet five-year economic agreement (1953), payments—current and capital—were to be made in Indian rupees. It was further provided that settlement of the balance outstanding at the end of the period (usually year-end) could be made in sterling of a fixed gold content.[22] There is no evidence that the Soviet Union ever exercised its option to demand hard currency, but this provision was invoked by some of India's other East European economic partners.[23] In the 1958 Indo-Soviet bilateral trade and payments agreement, the currency settlement provisions were renegotiated so as to reduce the threat to India of foreign exchange loss. Specifically, Moscow and Delhi decided that balances outstanding on termination of the agreement should "be used during the ensuing six months for the purchase of Indian or Soviet goods, as the case may be, or will be settled in such other way as may be agreed upon between the two Parties."[24] Insofar as the Indian government could always argue for using a Soviet credit balance to accelerate its exports to the U.S.S.R. or to increase its aid receipts, this language effectively elevated the question of hard currency conversion to the political level and thereby reduced the likelihood that the Soviets would insist on this kind of settlement.

Even though the Rupee Payments System had little substantive effect on the terms of Indo-Soviet economic exchange and long-term obligation of either side, it was popular for ideological reasons and greatly facilitated the growth of bilateral trade. In contrast, institutional arrangements for changing the underlying determinants of Indo-Soviet trade, the repeated Soviet suggestion for partial integration of the two countries' five-year plans, for example, have been resisted by Delhi. Indian leaders have preferred to keep their future economic options open rather than to commit themselves to long-term purchase and sales agreements which would be the natural consequence of interrelating the two nations' investment programs. Nonetheless, following the 1971 treaty, the Indians did go so far as to agree to creation of a Joint Commission on Economic, Scientific, and Technical Cooperation (1972) which was to "dovetail" the nations' five-year plans. Speculation at the time that this was a step toward Indian membership in COMECON aroused sharp debate in India. The

[21]Ibid., p. 719.

[22]UNCTAD TD/B/129, op. cit., p. 22.

[23]P. N. Arya, "A Study of India's Bilateral Trade and Payments Arrangements, 1951–1968," mimeographed (New Delhi: USAID, Nov. 12, 1968), p. 35.

[24]UNCTAD TD/B/129, op. cit., p. 22.

COMECON link was emphatically opposed by many Indians on the grounds that even if it did lead to economic advance—a questionable assumption—it would fly in the face of two of India's most sacred principles, nonalignment and self-reliance. Eventually Prime Minister Gandhi denied the possibility for a COMECON relationship, but it is not publicly known how seriously such a linkage was considered at the time.[25]

Bilateral Trade Relations

The volume of India's trade with the Soviet Union, which was less than 1 percent of India's global imports and exports in the early 1950s, began to grow in 1956–57 in response to political and economic stimuli, notably owing to the shipment of capital goods for Bhilai. Subsequently, Indo-Soviet merchandise trade grew steadily, from about 5 percent of India's trade following the 1962 war with China, to over 10 percent in the mid-1960s (following the war with Pakistan). India's exports to the U.S.S.R. reached about 15 percent of its total sales abroad in IFY 1970–71 when the U.S.S.R. emerged as the single largest foreign buyer of Indian goods. According to published Indian statistics, imports from the U.S.S.R. have not grown at an equivalent rate, but comparison of these sources with data on Soviet exports to India show a discrepancy which is generally regarded as attributable to Indian imports of military goods which never found their way into the Indian data for security reasons.[26] Military items, notably aircraft and vessels, are especially likely to be overlooked in Indian import statistics insofar as these often do not pass through normal customs channels. A possible explanation for why they appear in Soviet statistics is that Moscow did not want its trade balance to suggest that the Soviets were taking real resources from India.

In judging the economic—much more the political—value of Indo-Soviet trade, there are a number of relevant considerations which, because they are complex and obscure, are difficult to discuss. For instance, the first jump in Indian imports from the U.S.S.R. was largely attributable to the Bhilai steel mill. Thus, without a careful economic evaluation of Bhilai, alternative means whereby India could have increased its steel output, and the worth of investment in steel compared with other industries, it is not possible to be very precise about how beneficial to India Bhilai-generated trade has been. The case of imports for the Bokaro steel plant is clearer in the sense that to a greater degree than with Bhilai there was no practical alternative to Soviet financing and technology. Nonetheless, the skyrocketing costs of Bokaro and the multiple delays in its implementation are reasons for questioning the intrinsic value of this project. As problems of Bokaro construction stem from difficulties of obtaining the proper imports of heavy equipment from the Soviet Union and

[25]See R. V. R. Chandra Sekara Rao, "Indo-Soviet Economic Relations," *Asian Survey*, vol. 13, no. 8, August 1973, pp. 796–798.

[26]See Datar, op. cit., pp. 94–95.

also from the Indian effort to substitute indigenously produced equipment for imports, blame for its costliness should not be ascribed solely to the Soviets.

In India, one of the the advantages claimed for trade conducted under bilateral agreements is that it is more reliable, an argument which is not fully supported by a comparison of trade agreements with actual imports and exports during the relevant periods. As noted by Joseph Berliner, participants have often regarded the trade agreements as "hunting licenses" which "merely signify intentions" with "no assurance that the trade will actually reach the specified level."[27] A not untypical example of the frustrations which have occurred in the area of merchandise trade is the pattern of events which followed a Soviet agreement in principle to buy 54,000 railway wagons from India. Although India had expertise in the production of railway wagons and its industry desperately needed orders to relieve high unemployment rates, the sale bogged down when the Soviets offered to pay only Rs. 60,000 per wagon instead of the Indian offering price of Rs. 98,000 per wagon.[28] The negotiations dragged on for a long time, and the number of wagons for which actual contracts were signed was far below the figure first mentioned. The wagon issue assumed political life in India because senior officials of both governments made repeated assurances that the full order would be completed and raised expectations in India which turned out to be unjustified.

The evolving commodity compostion of Indian exports shows that Moscow has been a valuable trade partner. The Soviets have purchased increasing quantities of Indian engineering goods and other nontraditional commodities, thereby helping to make India less reliant on exports of raw materials and basic commodities.[29] Between 1968 and 1970, for example, India sold 600,000 tons of Bhilai steel to the Soviets. Too much credit for this shift to nontraditional exports should not be given to trade agreements, however, as demonstrated by India's having also increased its foreign sales of such items to Western countries. Indeed, there is evidence that India has not been able to capitalize fully on either Soviet or Western markets because of its inability to increase its output and poor quality control which deterred potential foreign buyers in the East and West alike. Nonetheless, by publicizing the potential for Indian sales to the U.S.S.R., the Rupee Payments System doubtless has had a marginally positive value to India as an export promotion device.

The pattern of Indian imports from the Soviet Union has evolved in accordance with the growing political relationship and with the changing requirements of the Indian economy. Initial growth was spurred by shipments of heavy equipment to be used in Soviet-aided projects. In the course of the 1960s, however, a reduced flow of such products, due in part to India's rising domestic production capacity for such goods and the growing Indian requirements for raw materials and components, changed the composition of India's import demand. Consequently, if the principle of trade balancing was to be preserved,

[27]Berliner, op. cit., p. 81.
[28]*Indian Recorder and Digest*, February 1969, pp. 15–16.
[29]B. R. Bhagot, "Indo-Soviet Trade," in Dagli, ed., op. cit., p. 61.

Soviet leaders were required to choose between diversifying their exports to India in order to maintain the volume or reducing their imports from India. Not surprisingly, Moscow decided to pursue the former, more dynamic course, and this choice was reflected in the five-year Indo-Soviet trade agreement of 1965. Trade data, however, show that the transformation has been slower than expected.[30] The Soviet preference has remained "to export huge quantities of whatever product happens to be in surplus under their own planning system at the time"[31] and to sell scarce products in world markets for free foreign exchange. Nonetheless, the series of announcements in 1973 that the U.S.S.R. would sell larger quantities and a greater variety of the commodities needed by India (petroleum, newsprint, nonferrous metals, and so forth) is evidence that the Soviets intend to accommodate some Indian needs and that the composition of their exports will continue to change.[32]

An important criticism of India's bilateral trade arrangements is that they cause India to be underpaid for its exports and overcharged for its imports, i.e., that the Indian terms of trade with East Europe are less favorable than with other countries. Evidence to corroborate this criticism is elusive because the parties to contracts generally have no incentive to reveal the terms. Moreover, analysis of official trade statistics can be highly misleading because unit costs conceal quality, terms of payment, and other critical differences. Even the theory of why India should be disadvantaged in bilateral trading is less than definitive.[33] Nonetheless, because bilateral trading is such an important feature of India's foreign trade relations, it is necessary to make the best possible evaluation of how it effects development.

Empirical studies as to whether the terms of trade are comparatively worse for India in its commerce with the Soviets have been made by Carter, Datar, and Arya. These all reveal considerable differences for various products (no doubt a reflection of the varying quality and other product differences in items traded with the U.S.S.R. and others).[34] For India's *exports,* the range of conclusions is broad: no net price disadvantage to India (Datar), frequent but unquantified disadvantage (Arya), and a 10 to 15 percent disadvantage (Carter). For India's *imports* both Datar and Carter found that machinery and equipment (generally financed by Soviet aid) were significantly overpriced by international

[30]Datar, op. cit., p. 262.

[31]*Economist* (London), Aug. 11, 1973, p. 72.

[32]See *Economic and Political Weekly*, Dec. 8, 1973.

[33]For a review of the theory, see James Richard Carter, *The Net Cost of Soviet Foreign Aid* (New York: Praeger, 1969), pp. 33–35. To say that the Soviets will benefit because they are the more powerful is to ignore countervailing political reasons why the Soviets would wish to—and could afford to—provide a generous arrangement for a developing country. Moreover, to assert that the Soviets will pay less because the barter price is determined on the assumption that their demand is not reflected in total world demand is to (1) ignore the way bilateral agreements work (e.g., the Soviets bid for tea in the open Calcutta market) and (2) overlook that if some supply is directed toward the U.S.S.R., India may then have the option of raising its prices on free world markets.

[34]Carter, op. cit., pp. 35–41; Datar, op. cit., pp. 167, 182; and Arya, op. cit., pp. 57–70.

market standards—by a minimum of 15 percent and perhaps considerably more. Datar found that other Indian imports from the U.S.S.R. are generally at world prices. That this conclusion conflicts with Carter's analysis to the effect that they are higher-priced may be explained by Datar's having concentrated on Indian data whereas Carter used Soviet statistics.

One strand of circumstantial evidence supporting the thesis that India receives lower prices for its exports to the Soviet bloc than to foreign-exchange-paying countries is the existence of a "switch trade." In practice, some East European countries—but generally not the Soviet Union—have found it profitable to buy commodities from India under rupee trade agreements and resell the merchandise in the West for hard currencies, sometimes at steep discounts from the prices quoted by India itself.[35] According to one press report, in 1967 (a typical year) the Indian government estimated that 5 to 10 percent of its exports to the Soviet bloc were being switch-traded and that important commodities such as tobacco, coir, pepper, oil cakes, tea, and coffee were involved.[36] Moreover, instances of "reverse switch trade" (Western commodities marketed at high prices in India by East European countries) have also been reported. The mechanism used, quoting the value of the Indian rupee at a steep discount from par, strongly suggests that India's terms of trade on these transactions are less favorable than on trade with the West.[37] The existence of the switch trade is indicative of the costliness to India of bilateral trading. But, to the extent that switch trading is a limited phenomenon and an escape valve whereby India acquires highly desired imports which from a political standpoint could not qualify for allocation of scarce foreign exchange, it serves some important functions and may be tolerable.

The rupee area trading arrangements also are disadvantageous to India's balance of payments. First, to the extent that the commodities India exports for rupee payment contain significant amounts of raw materials or imported components that were bought by India with free foreign exchange, there is a pass-through effect insofar as India loses hard currency. Raw cashews, for example, are imported by India from East Africa, shelled, roasted, and exported. Since more than 50 percent of the total revenue from exports of cashews to East Europe is offset by import costs, India's free foreign exchange cost (import payments for cashews to be processed and reexported) of exporting cashews to East Europe in 1972–73 was roughly $16 million.[38] The true foreign exchange cost has been even larger as some of the goods with high import content (e.g., cashews) have been switch-traded.[39]

The second potential avenue for foreign exchange loss is through export diversion, the sale to the Soviet Union and others of commodities which could

---

[35]Arya, op. cit., pp. 55–57.

[36]*Financial Express* (Bombay), Oct. 17, 1967.

[37]*Economist* (London), Jan. 14, 1967. p. 143.

[38]*RBI Bulletin,* March 1974, p. 422.

[39]Some evidence that this was the actual situation in the early 1960s, is cited by Marshall I. Goldman, *Soviet Foreign Aid* (New York: Praeger, 1967), p. 110.

otherwise have been sold in world markets for hard cash. Products involved in the switch trade obviously qualify as a variety of this kind of transaction, but the phenomenon is more widespread. Although it is often asserted that the shoes and other low-quality commodities India sells to the Soviet bloc have no sales potential in world markets, this is blatantly false. Not only are there other international buyers for such goods, but the East Europeans themselves might offer hard currencies for these Indian exports if they were not available on rupee terms. Indeed, in the early 1970s Yugoslavia instituted negotiations to transform its trade with India from rupee payments to free foreign exchange. Moreover, the commodity composition of Indian exports shows substantial evidence that there has been trade diversion to the rupee payment area of tea, pepper, jute, goatskins, and other goods for which there are established world markets.[40] Thus, in judging the impact of bilateral trading, it becomes very important to know about comparative pricing. But this is the point where we started, and it would appear wise therefore to proceed to Soviet aid and postpone the tricky question of evaluation.

Soviet Aid to India

The U.S.S.R. has had various motivations for extending aid to India: as a means to support one of China's rivals; as part of its cold war strategy against the West; because the Soviets themselves have obtained economic benefits; and, to some extent, because foreign assistance was regarded as a means to strengthen international communism. India's reasons for accepting Soviet assistance included the dual premise that accepting help from both East and West would promote nonalignment and also assist development by enhancing the investment program. As the balance of these forces and the character of India's economy shifted over time, there was a progressive increase in Soviet assistance, from near zero during the First Five-Year Plan to a high of $76.4 million in IFY 1968–69. For the post-Independence period as a whole, Soviet aid has amounted to about 5 percent of toal aid received by India. The addition of other East European assistance still leaves the figure well under 10 percent of India's total aid receipts.[41]

Soviet aid characteristically has not been given for general balance-of-payments support purposes: it has been tied to specific projects, mainly public sector investments in heavy industry such as steel, petroleum, and pharmaceuticals. It has been further tied to procurement in the U.S.S.R. Repayment terms, which compare unfavorably with American assistance but less so with Western aid as a whole, generally have called for a 2½ percent rate of interest with the principal to be repaid within thirteen years of the delivery of the commodities, the first payment beginning one year after delivery. As noted by Berliner, Soviet leaders preferred low-interest loans rather than grants not only because

[40]Arya, op. cit., p. 70.
[41]*Economic Survey: 1973–74*, p. 105.

this permitted Moscow to maintain that it was generous, businesslike, and without selfish political interests in the recipient country, but because loans created a dependency relationship owing to the recipient's need to finance repayments.[42]

Soviet economic aid attracted favorable public attention, but by the early 1970s, the standard Soviet aid package had become less useful to India. This is indicated by the increasing lag in the use of authorized credits. For example, although the backlog of Soviet credits stood at $468 million on April 1, 1971, India's use of this asset averaged less than $14 million in each of the subsequent three fiscal years.[43] At this rate drawdowns were not large enough to cover interest on past aid, much less the sum of interest and capital repayment, which amounted to almost $75 million in IFY 1973–74.[44] Inadvertently, the U.S.S.R. contribution to Indian development had become "trade not aid." The decline in Indian use of Soviet aid and the transformation of India's positive balance of payments on aid account to a negative balance were financial indicators not only of a technical mismatch of the kinds of aid India needed and what the Soviets were accustomed to providing, but of a growing tension in Indo-Soviet aid relations which reached a critical level as early as 1968. During a visit to India at that time, Kosygin was so disturbed "by the poor performance of the Soviet-aided projects in the public sector" that he initiated an unprecedented series of visits by Soviet experts which eventually led to the reallocation of some Soviet loans so as to overcome shortcomings of past projects.[45]

The mammoth ($1.5 billion) Bokaro steel project is illustrative of many of the features of Soviet aid and thereby merits attention. The Soviets had scored a previous success in the Indian steel industry with Bhilai, and Bokaro appeared to have equal or greater potential.[46] It was economically viable in the sense that India has plentiful reserves of both iron ore and coal and that there was demand for Bokaro's output insofar as flat-steel products were produced only at the Rourkela mill. A bonus for Moscow was that the otherwise underutilized heavy machine factory which it had helped build at Ranchi could be used to produce some of the equipment for Bokaro. The United States Congress had debated for several years whether America should sponsor this fourth Indian steel mill at Bokaro, and India had withdrawn its request for U.S. assistance when such aid did not appear to be a likely prospect. The grounds for American skepticism—the project was too grandiose, it was to be in the public sector, and so forth—were exactly those which made Bokaro attractive to Moscow.

[42]Berliner, op. cit., pp. 145–152.

[43]*Explanatory Memorandum on the Budget of the Central Government for 1974–75*, op. cit., p. 130.

[44]*Ibid.*, pp. 34 and 142.

[45]Valkenier, op. cit., p. 427.

[46]For an account of the extraordinary effort made by Moscow in assigning its best technical people, speeding construction, and otherwise making Bhilai excel over the sister plants at Rourkela (German-aided) and Durgapur (U.K.-aided), see Goldman, op. cit., pp. 85–90.

The first flow of Bokaro production in 1972 came not unduly long after the Soviet's 1964 offer to assist with the project, but it was well behind the date originally contemplated when the loan agreement was signed in January 1965. Delays in design and construction led to a steep escalation of the project's cost and a major loss in the sense that India found it necessary to import steel during the interim period which it should have been able to produce at Bokaro. One immediate cause for the delay was the effort to incorporate a maximum amount of indigenous Indian materials and equipment in the construction. This objective satisfied (1) the Indian desire for pursuing self-reliance and import substitution[47] and (2) the Soviet interest in rationalizing the white elephant heavy engineering plant at Ranchi[48] and in reducing the cost of Bokaro to Moscow by minimizing requirements for capital equipment exports.

The Indians warmly welcomed Soviet assistance in Bokaro, but Moscow's public relations coup on this score was offset to some degree by its decision to override Delhi's protests and to treat Bokaro as a "turn-key" investment. By excluding the prestigious Indian consulting firm M. N. Dastur from the major role it had been scheduled to play in constructing Bokaro, the Soviets offended Indian sensitivities and probably also raised the economic cost of the project by a significant amount. Many Indians were vexed by the Soviet unwillingness to take account of the recommendations in Dastur's Cost Reduction Study[49] and by charges that Moscow was providing "second-best technology for the steel melting shops and the slabbing mill."[50] Owing to these factors, major delays, and cost escalations, Bokaro became a major source of political tension between Moscow and Delhi. Padma Desai has described Bokaro as a "Greek tragedy" insofar as the conflicts which dogged this titanic undertaking were inevitable, given the initial Indian and Soviet policies. She is especially distressed that the unequal negotiating strength of the partners, which followed from India's decision to seek foreign capital assistance rather than use its own foreign exchange, caused India to "sacrifice . . . important national objectives such as technological self-reliance."[51]

For the Soviets, the difficulties illustrated by Bokaro are of no small consequence. The increasing sophistication of the Indian economy had made their old style of foreign aid increasingly less relevant and less welcome. But it would not be easy for them to adjust to India's changing needs because India's new requirements were more costly to the Soviet economy, less visible from a political and public relations viewpoint and, according to the Soviet view, less likely to be used effectively than past aid. Under these circumstances the temptation for Moscow to follow the American example and to reduce the flow

[47]See editorial in the *Indian Express*, Oct. 5, 1972.

[48]Goldman, op. cit., p. 94.

[49]Padma Desai, *The Bokaro Steel Plant: A Study of Soviet Economic Assistance* (London and Amsterdam: North-Holland Publishing Co., 1972), p. 2.

[50]Ibid., p. 86.

[51]Ibid., p. 87.

of assistance must have been strong. But the Soviet interest in continuing the trend toward closer political relations was also a powerful factor. Thus, when Mrs. Gandhi used the political power she assumed in 1969 for socialist purposes, and when Indo-Soviet diplomacy on various political matters grew closer, it was almost inevitable that the Soviet disposition to adjust to the commodity-oriented aid and trade relationship desired by Delhi would be increased.

Evaluating the Economic Relationship

To construct an economic profit and loss statement which would capture precisely all the costs and benefits of the Indo-Soviet relationship is a task which lies beyond the space and analytic tools of this chapter. I shall conclude, nonetheless, by evaluating some of the factors which would enter into this kind of calculation.

One of the general lessons for Indian development of the Bokaro experience is that excessive reliance on only one aid donor is dangerous insofar as it may create a dependency relationship which will ill serve the Indian economy. It is in this context that the evolution of a major Indo-Soviet commercial relationship parallel to India's economic linkages with the West appears to be beneficial. By diversifying its export markets and sources for imports, technology, and foreign assistance, India has increased its options and taken a step toward greater national integrity.

At another level, the evolution of Indo-Soviet relations has played a featured role in the casual chain which led from the cold war conflict to an increased American willingness to offer foreign aid, to the Soviet aid program, and, finally, to an increase in the amount of—and liberalization of the terms of—Western economic assistance. This improvement in the quantity and quality of foreign assistance to India is one of the few beneficial features of the great power conflict which, otherwise, has been very costly to the development effort. But in the final analysis, it would be naïve to think that economic programs designed to satisfy political objectives would lead to optimum decisions with respect to development.

The United States and the U.S.S.R. were alike in regarding their foreign assistance as investments which would produce economic and political dividends. But there was a difference in emphasis insofar as Moscow was more likely to interpret development as a means of achieving its political goals in India than as an ultimate objective. Thus, it is not surprising that in its economic relations with Delhi Moscow put heavy emphasis on actions which the Indians wanted but was reluctant to undertake programs which would heavily tax the Soviet economy. Nevertheless, from India's point of view, because Soviet assistance was provided for public sector heavy industry and other critical areas for which Western aid was not forthcoming, it was regarded as valuable beyond the nominal cash price.

Assessing the true value to India's development of its economic relations with the U.S.S.R. is complicated by the institutional and procedural arrangements which are routinely instituted by nations which deal with one another according to government fiat rather than through open markets. Since the Rupee Payments System, bilateral trade arrangements, and the Soviet aid program all combine political with economic factors, empirical analysis is but one incomplete way for measuring their value. With respect to merchandise trade with the Eastern bloc, even if a major portion of the rewards have been obtained by India's trading partners, it is still likely that India has received some net economic benefits. Moreover, if the Soviets continue to expand the amounts of fertilizer, petroleum products, and other key raw materials they are willing to export to India, the value of the bilateral trade relationship will shift substantially in India's favor.

On balance, therefore, the value to India of Moscow's foreign economic assistance program can be characterized as microeconomic and tactical, as contrasted with the macroeconomic and strategic objectives the West has tried to achieve with its assistance. Another way of saying this is that although the quantity and financial quality of U.S.S.R. aid were poor by American standards, the Soviets nonetheless achieved some remarkable successes by relieving troublesome bottlenecks in the Indian economy, facilitating public sector ownership of key industries, and moving India closer to the kind of socialism and national independence which its leaders desired. Soviet aid was of only limited value, however: it scarcely affected the overall Indian economy and it imposed a costly repayment obligation on India.

This experience suggests that future Indo-Soviet economic relations will be more a function of political linkages between the two nations than basic economic forces. The extent to which Delhi remains committed to socialism is important in this equation but less significant than whether the Indian economy grows or stagnates. Indo-Soviet merchandise trade is likely to continue its growth in response to the Soviets' growing willingness to supply the commodities India needs for its economy and the Indians' preference for bilateral trading. To the extent that India is able to increase its rate of industrial growth, its trade with the Eastern bloc may increase even faster because of the need for more imports and exports. With respect to aid relations, the future is clouded by the impasse reached when the U.S.S.R. could no longer supply heavy equipment because of India's emergent capacity to produce its own. Nonetheless, the Soviets will be under heavy pressure from India and others to avoid taking real resources from India. They are likely to respond positively by rescheduling debt, by increasing the size of the military aid program, by liberalizing their economic assistance, or by some combination of these. Thus assuming that the Indo-Soviet political alliance remains in force, Moscow can be expected to adopt flexible policies in order to supplement its military aid with assistance for economic development. To be consistent in this approach, if India should encounter another famine or other disaster, the Soviets would seek to be helpful but, unless Soviet granaries were overflowing, Moscow would doubtless limit the size of its contribution to Indian relief.

CHAPTER 6

DEVELOPMENT: THE
MULTILATERAL CONTEXT

   The major concern of this chapter is foreign assistance, the reaction of the international community to India's development needs. The loans and technical assistance which India has received directly from the World Bank Group is only a small part of the story, however, insofar as the IBRD also has served as the focal point for the India Consortium and thereby added a fundamentally new dimension to Indian aid relations. Moreover, through the World Bank connection and otherwise, the pattern of India's relationships with aid donors has had a far-reaching effect on the evolution of aid ties between all rich and poor countries. Thus, after an introductory survey of the parameters within which World Bank relations with India have influenced a broad spectrum of international aid relations and, in turn, have been affected by them, the remainder of this chapter is devoted to the intricate and critical issues raised in the context of the India Consortium.

World Bank Operations in India and
Indian Influence on the World Bank

   India's difficult economic circumstances and its determination to progress within the framework of an open democratic society have consistently dramatized the need for development in the Third World. During the 1950s and early 1960s growing understanding of India's situation undoubtedly made more resources available for dealing with world poverty than might otherwise have been the case. But this was not the only reason for the burgeoning of international aid, and it is difficult therefore to evaluate the degree to which the growing "aid weariness" of the late 1960s and early 1970s was attributable to the disappointing Indian experience or other factors.

   The story of IBRD lending to India began quite early in the Bank's history, albeit after the Marshall Plan had co-opted responsibility for European reconstruction. The Bank's first loan to India, in 1949, was also the first loan it extended in Asia.[1] In the subsequent quarter century, many of the Bank's operations in India were the first of a kind. These related to (1) lending policies affecting public versus private sectors, projects versus programs, and economic versus social investments; (2) institutional changes such as formation of the India Consortium, which was later emulated by various countries including Pakistan, Colombia, and Nigeria; and (3) a variety of technical experiments affecting different aspects of the economy.

In the early days of both the World Bank and United States bilateral assistance programs, lenders preferred to give credits for specific projects rather than provide nonproject (program) lending. In addition, they preferred the private sector to public enterprise. These preferences were at odds with those of India and many other aid recipients, and, in the course of time, both IBRD and United States officials revised their policies. World Bank President George Woods began program lending to India when he became convinced that India's production versatility was so great that the chief bottleneck for development was foreign exchange to buy needed raw materials, components, and specialized equipment. The Bank also was swayed by the argument that not all India's needs could be packaged as projects without substantially reducing the usefulness of loans.

Woods acted to increase the Bank's lending to public sector enterprise for somewhat different reasons: first, he recognized the sovereign right of India and other nations to prefer socialist policies and, second, he found it almost an economic necessity, as in Africa and elsewhere there was a near absence of acceptable private sector borrowers. India's contribution to liberalizing the IBRD's outlook on these two important development policies—due to its own economic situation which seemed to require such changes and to its influence on Bank policy—is indicative of the larger role India has played in shaping international aid relations.

Similarly, India was instrumental in the events leading to the formation of the International Development Association (IDA) and, subsequently, in the management of this new agency and as a recipient of its lending. Beginning in 1949, with the report of V. K. R. V. Rao, chairman of the UN Subcommission on Economic Development, Indians pressed with unrelenting zeal for an institution which could grant or otherwise transfer purchasing power to poor countries on extremely concessional terms. India, because of its enormous need for external assistance and lack of credit-worthiness for the size of the foreign loan program it required, was the impeccable example of why IDA was needed. Thus, when IDA was formed in 1960, it was largely because of Indian initiatives, and since then, a major portion of its funds have been allocated to India.[2]

Despite these and other important contributions to World Bank policy and structure, there have been significant differences between India and the IBRD.

---

[1]IBRD, *Fourth Annual Report of the Bank* (Washington, D.C., 1948–49, p. 16.

[2]Currently, India's share of IDA funds is limited to 40 percent, but in early years it was as high as 52 percent. See Mason and Asher, op. cit., pp. 382–419.

These have arisen not just because the Bank reflects the views of its members as channeled through its executive directors, but because of disagreements between IBRD and Indian officials over important questions of Bank procedure, development policy, and performance evaluation. Although these conflicts have occasionally proved disagreeable, they have been muted by such factors as (1) the growing realization of how much more difficult the development process is than postwar reconstruction, (2) the formation of IDA, and (3) President McNamara's emphasis on reaching the most disadvantaged nations and people through programs affecting education, agriculture, and population. Thus, if the conventional wisdoms—that friction must be generated to hasten development and that friction is an inevitable by-product of development—are correct, the relevant question is not how disagreements between the Bank and LDCs can be eliminated, but how conflict can be managed so as to be constructive for the development program. The slow rate of disbursement of some of the Bank's agricultural loans to India is an example of how, by choosing to aid sensitive areas of the economy, the Bank has entered fields where local political differences and differences between the state and central governments have traditionally retarded progress. And thus far, although the Bank's rural initiatives have generated new tensions, these remain well within acceptable limits. It remains to be seen, however, whether this is because the new policies have not been pushed to the point of effecting substantial acceleration in the pace of development, or whether the Bank has developed a new strategy which can deal effectively with the barriers to change.

The question, "What have we learned about development from our experience in India that has been applied in other poor countries?" does not lead to as positive a response as might be expected in light of the great attention that has been devoted to India. If efforts to generalize about experiences within India are plagued by intertemporal and interregional disparities, international comparisons encounter even greater problems. Better education, health, investment, and so forth are fundamental to development, but to advance general statements about these objectives as development theory is rarely anything more than tautology. Some insights have been achieved through technical analytic innovations such as two-gap models and input-output tables, but all too often these have been only tangentially useful because the data for applying them have not existed, or because the policies they suggested were already known to be desirable or were in conflict with political expediency and therefore unlikely to be adopted or implemented. Similarly, technological innovations have only sometimes been transmitted among developing countries. As measured by the frequency with which ill-fated experiments have been repeated or successful ideas forgotten and reinvented, it is remarkable how short bureaucratic memory has been, even within one country.

In summary, although India has been on the frontier of a great number of innovations and experiments relating to financial, institutional, and technical aspects of development policy, even when these have proved succesful, they have not always been applied in other countries. To take a different type of example, India is the only country for which the IBRD has participated directly in a debt relief package by adjusting the schedule of service payments on its own obligations. Moreover, in many cases where IBRD policies that succeeded in India have been tried elsewhere, they have yielded different, often less satisfactory, results.

Looked at from the opposite point of view, techniques developed outside of India appear to have had only limited application in India. The rice hybrids which have greatly increased production in many parts of Southeast Asia, for instance, proved effective in only a limited number of India's rice-growing regions. Another example of nontransferability is the "graduated response" doctrine according to which the IBRD explicitly conditioned the amount of foreign aid available to Latin American countries on their domestic economic policies.[3] The graduated response approach was not applied in India for various reasons: it was unprecedented in the World Bank's Asian operations, there were internal IBRD differences on whether leverage should be used in this way, and it had little likelihood of success given the particular sensitivities of Indians.

The India Consortium

Both crises and triumphs often look pale in retrospect, and thus it is to the press reports of 1958 that one must turn to capture the sense of crisis and urgency which India's faltering economic situation has generated and the extent to which it was regarded as a challenge not only for India but also for the West.[4] The events of this period occasioned changes of attitude which were dramatic and profound; led to a major, if temporary, buttressing of India's orientation and exposure to the West; deepened the West's commitment to India's continuing democracy and progressive development; and pioneered various responses which the West has since applied to troublesome problems elsewhere in the world.

In a sense, the organization of the India Consortium in 1958 was a logical and spontaneous outcropping of the Bretton Woods spirit and the already well-rooted Indo-Western bilateral aid relationships. But it was also very different: it entailed neither the hegemonic multilateralism of the Marshall Plan, under which there was only one aid donor and many recipients, nor the broader

---

[3]Ibid., p. 425.

[4]B. R. Shenoy, a conservative Indian economist, has suggested that the sense of crisis was generated by alarm at the IBRD that its largest debtor might become insolvent, but the absence of substantiating evidence and the World Bank's willingness to accelerate its loans to India rather than retrench makes this view appear wrong, if nothing less than cynical. See B. R. Shenoy, "Aid to India from the World Bank Group," *Il Politico*, (University of Pavia) vol. 36, no. 3, 1971.

multilateralism associated with most IBRD activities.[5] The Consortium was known in its early years as the Aid India Group; it acquired its new name when a number of European countries joined in the collective effort to assist India. The inclusion of these nations was not only a measure of the progress Europe had made as a result of the Marshall Plan, but an omen of the shifting world balance of economic power which eventually reduced the dollar's role in the world financial and monetary systems and America's leadership on international aid matters. The ironic aspect of the Consortium's formation stems from the contrast between the Indian preference for long-term comprehensive planning and the "rescue India" attitude which led to this important event.

The earliest action portending formation of the Aid India Group was an informal consultation on the Second Plan which took place among the United States, Britain, and Canada in December 1955. The immediate result of this meeting was nothing because "India made no official approach for assistance and had no foreign exchange budget worth the name."[6] Subsequently, however, India's Second Plan was jeopardized by a cumulation of large foreign exchange losses, hostile domestic reactions to tax increases proposed for fiscal year 1957–58, food shortages in northern India, alternating droughts and floods in 1957, and other adverse economic developments. Nehru changed his mind about requesting assistance, and on September 5, 1957, he declared India's readiness to welcome a United States loan of $500 million to $600 million and announced that India's finance minister, T. T. Krishnamachari, would explore the possibilities for such support during a visit to the United States later in the month.[7]

The initial contacts leading toward a major United States commitment to Indian development were difficult. Between the time of Nehru's statement and Krishnamachari's arrival in the United States, the United States International Cooperation Administration's outgoing head, John B. Hollister issued, in what some observers regarded as a "meaningful coincidence," a directive which appeared to limit the United States willingness to help India by ruling out major United States assistance for public sector projects.[8] Later, Krishnamachari received only limited encouragement from Secretary of State Dulles, ostensibly because of congressional opposition to aid appropriations.[9] This chilly reception notwithstanding, in the ensuing months some of America's outstanding leaders raised their voices in support of India in various ways, including a flood of letters to the editor of the *New York Times*. India's supporters made a

[5]Dissatisfaction with institutions such as the India Consortium, which peaked in 1965 and slowed the proliferation of consortia and consultative groups, is described by John White, *Pledged to Development* (London: Overseas Development Institute, 1967), pp. 43–56.

[6]Hazari and Mehta, op. cit., pp. 48–49.

[7]*New York Times,* Sept. 6, 1957.

[8]*Christian Science Monitor,* Oct. 1, 1957.

[9]*New Republic,* Dec. 2, 1957.

powerful case for the political, economic, and humanitarian reasons why the
United States should help India fulfill its Second Plan. In addition, they used
the most dramatic—albeit sometimes misleading—terms to warn of how India's
failure would adversely affect the United States. According to Senator John
Kennedy:

> If the Second Five-Year Plan collapses, so may India. If India collapses, so
> may all of Asia. If all of Asia collapses, so does the security of the United
> States of America. However sharply one may reject the concept of American
> ideals impelling us to help others in need, however blind one may be to the
> dependence of our own economic well-being upon our closing the prosper-
> ity gap between ourselves and the "have-not" nations, no thoughtful citizen
> can fail to see our direct stake in the survival of free government in India.[10]

By January of 1958 the administration had become convinced of the need to
help India, and it announced its willingness to consider loans for India of up to
$225 million from the Export-Import Bank and the Development Loan Fund.
The Indian reaction was positive as evidenced by Krishnamachari's warm letter
of thanks to United States Ambassador Ellsworth Bunker[11] but was marred by
press reports suggesting that the United States had in some way sought to use
its aid as a lever for turning India away from its neutralist foreign policy. The
New York Times reported Nehru as saying, "I want to tell the whole world that
India will not change her policy under any threat or pressure or temptation of
aid."[12] Although the amount of aid proferred by the United States was clearly
inadequate to the need, Indian officials were loath to complain in public. But
Senator Kennedy had no such inhibition and, in a Senate speech asking support
for a resolution he had jointly proposed with Senator Cooper, he asked that the
United States adopt a Marshall Plan type of approach to India. Kennedy went
on to advocate a number of bilateral steps for the United States, and in the
broader context of world poverty, he urged that "we develop international
consortia in which potential creditor nations bring to bear the full armory of
their loan and technical assistance instruments around the development program of the recipient country in question."[13]

India responded with some enthusiasm to this proposed multilateral
approach. B. K. Nehru, a senior civil servant, explored it during visits to the
United States, Britain, and Germany in the summer of 1958, and in late August
representatives of these countries met in Washington with officials of Japan,
Canada, and the World Bank to discuss how the floundering Second Plan could
be rescued. In 1958, the limit of what could be accomplished was amelioration
of India's immediate economic problems. And although the Indian officials

---

[10]John F. Kennedy, "If India Fails," *The Progressive,* January 1958.
[11]Department of State Press Release No. 39, Jan. 29, l958.
[12]*New York Times,* Jan. 23, 1958.
[13]U.S. Congress, Senate, *Congressional Record,* 85th Congress, 2d Session, Mar. 25,
1958, vol. 104, part 4, 5246–5255.

involved were not slow to recognize that the costly liabilities they had assumed to bail out the Second Plan would come back to haunt them in the early years of the Third Plan, the need of the moment was so great and their expectations of future success so high that they welcomed the new aid program. More generous aid terms were not available at the time partly because the United States had suffered a recession in 1958 and was preparing for a presidential election in 1960, and partly because most Western countries were still conservative in financial matters. Thus, India's crisis was eased temporarily but not resolved.[14]

For the United States, the period 1958–1960 was marked by little action and a lively domestic debate about how much and on what terms foreign assistance should be made available to developing countries. Concurrently, American officials had allied themselves with the IBRD in pressuring other Western donors to expand their contributions and to improve the quality of their aid by liberalizing terms. This peculiar situation was more or less resolved—and only temporarily—in favor of global generosity in 1960 with the establishment of the International Development Association (IDA) and the Democratic victory in the United States presidential election.

Prompted by India's continuing need for large amounts of external assistance, in February–March of 1960 World Bank President Eugene Black sent three distinguished international bankers—the "wise men"—on a special fact-finding mission to India and Pakistan. The mission was criticized at the time for its loose terms of reference,[15] but its report, in the form of a letter to Black, played an important role in mobilizing international support for aid to South Asia. The "wise men" concluded that South Asian leaders would not repeat their past mistakes because they had learned much about the development process; that there was a need for anti-inflationary monetary and fiscal policy; and that accelerated growth was within the realm of the possible in India and Pakistan.[16] The key to success, in their view, was a serious multiyear development commitment by India and aid donors.

By choosing the distinguished Dr. Hermann Abs of West Germany, Sir Oliver Franks of Great Britain, and Alan Sproul of the United States, the IBRD managed to dramatize and legitimatize the aid relationship and to enhance the donor countries' sense of responsibility for global development. Moreover, because the mission's report called for coordination among aid donors, it lubricated the consultative process whereby donors would increase their aid commitments and improve their terms in tandem. Thus, at least partially as a result of the bankers' mission, when India and donor nations met in Paris in September 1960, the major topic for consideration was the Third Five-Year Plan, which was to begin in April 1961: the Aid India Group had matured into

[14]See Hazari and Mehta, op. cit., p. 49.

[15]*London Times*, Feb. 29, 1960.

[16]"India's Economic Development and Balance of Payments," published as a pamphlet by the World Bank and reprinted in the *Monthly Review* of the Federal Reserve Bank of New York, April 1961.

the India Consortium.[17] At subsequent meetings in April and May 1961, reviewing the Plan again took precedence over emergency relief. India, for its part, took the unprecedented step of formulating its Third Plan on the assumption that donors would meet foreign exchange needs to the extent that these could not be covered by export and other foreign exchange receipts.[18] The Kennedy administration also took an unprecendented step when it offered to provide a generous $1 billion for the first two years of the Plan, contingent upon matching contributions by other donors. The United States Executive's gamble, that this initiative would goad other donors into making larger loans, was made not only to increase the amount of aid to India but to appease those congressmen who were critical of the amount and multiyear nature of the United States commitment. It was largely justified by the positive response of other donors and the actions of the United States Congress.[19]

In 1962, the outlook for Indian development again became clouded and India found it necessary to begin drawing foreign exchange from the IMF. Consortium donors and the IBRD were increasingly critical of the Third Plan, which was suffering from many of the same ills as its predecessor. In particular, Germany and others felt that their aid was not being used effectively, and America was annoyed with the politics of Nehru and Krishna Menon.[20] Strained aid relationships were saved from further deterioration, however, by India's brief but economically costly military conflict with China. This event evoked the conventional wisdom that with a stronger economy India would be better able to defend itself against the Communist threat, and, accordingly, the flow of Western economic assistance was maintained.

By 1964, however, the combined effect of nascent "aid weariness" on the part of donors and another of India's recurrent food shortages spurred a reexamination of India's development effort and the role of external assistance. Delhi agreed only grudgingly to receive the special IBRD mission led by Bernard Bell. Although the contents of the Bell report have been kept confidential to a remarkable degree, it is presumed that India was advised to (1) retreat from its policy of promoting heavy industry which was leading at the time to considerable industrial imbalance; (2) permit private enterprise to play a more active role in the economy; (3) reduce bureaucratic controls and substitute price-sensitive markets for administrative decision; (4) devalue the rupee; and (5) assign a higher priority to agriculture. When Bell and André de Lattre carried the World Bank's views to Delhi in 1965, "they intimated that without substantial changes in balance-of-payments and import policies no increase in assistance for the Fourth Plan could be expected, and possibly a reduction should be anticipated.[21]

[17]Mason and Asher, op. cit., p. 515.
[18]I. G. Patel, *Foreign Aid,* op. cit., p. 14.
[19]IBRD Press Release No. 690, June 2, 1961.
[20]*London Times,* July 3, 1962.
[21]Mason and Asher, op. cit., p. 196.

Despite the high quality of the Bell Mission's report, great difficulties came in the way of objective analysis. On the Indian side, the acute short-term problems posed by the 1965–1967 drought and the 1965 war with Pakistan transfixed the government's attention. The United States suspended aid following the Indo-Pakistani war and in subsequent months was unwilling to make anything but short-term assistance commitments, even after Tashkent. This policy, intended to (1) coerce the Indians to revise their economic policies and (2) pressure the Soviet Union and other donors to share more of the relief burden, did not promote an atmosphere conducive to objective analysis. Rather, it created an air of frustration, recrimination, mistrust, and, ironically, mutual dependence.

The issues between India and the Consortium were further complicated by the inevitable involvement of domestic politics. In India, the impending 1967 parliamentary elections put a special edge on the government's defense of its policies and its resistance to foreign advice and pressure. The position of the new prime minister, Indira Gandhi, however, was anything but secure within the Congress party power structure. Thus, it was especially painful when, in replying to her critics during a campaign speech, Mrs. Gandhi was pressed to admit that the United States had asked India to refrain from sending arms to Cuba. She went on to rationalize India's accepting aid from America on grounds that "It was thought that the conditions put by the U.S. did not affect our position or honor any way . . . so we decided to take the much needed food from them."[22]

In the United States, where a parallel debate took place, congressmen with isolationist and fiscally conservative views were teamed against an India lobby composed largely of humanitarian liberals and farm interests. President Johnson, who appeared to be somewhat less well-disposed toward India than his predecessor, did not ignore the sentiments expressed in these debates but usually followed his own personal instincts in exercising the balance of power in the formulation of United States policy. As a reaction to his displeasure with India's economic and political policies and with the stinginess of other donors, Johnson practiced an eleventh-hour generosity which exacerbated what was already a troubled economic and diplomatic situation.[23]

By late 1965, India's economic and negotiating positions were nearly desperate. The changes in agricultural policy advocated by the IBRD and the United States accorded fairly well with what many Indians perceived as the needed action, but the pressure to devalue the rupee was not welcome. Thus, when the

[22]*Washington Post,* Jan. 24, 1967.

[23]See article by J. Anthony Lukas in the Jan. 26, 1967, issue of the *New York Times.* Johnson's attitude was clearly expressed in his Feb. 2, 1967, Message to Congress in which he (1) demanded an international effort and multinational planning, (2) emphasized self-help, (3) called for more rapid development and application of modern technology in agriculture, (4) made agricultural development the primary objective in the AID program, (5) encouraged a greater role for private industry, and (6) announced that an additional 2 million tons of United States grain would be made available to India.

international value of the rupee was reduced by 58 percent on June 6, 1966, the decision was taken under duress and despite strong and widespread Indian sentiment that this was a mistaken policy. Devaluation provoked a political storm in India which was deeply exacerbated when the Consortium later failed to sustain the level of nonproject lending to India which the president of the IBRD had committed himself to seek and which Indian officials had assumed as assured.[24] It made little difference that India's pique with the Consortium's failure to provide resources needed to make the devaluation a success was matched by donor annoyance that India had squandered the potential benefits of devaluation by implementing export taxes and similar policy measures which tended to reduce devaluation's economic impact. (See Chapter 9.)

International political tensions notwithstanding, through devaluation and other policy measures India and its supporters had prevented a critical agricultural situation from becoming a famine, and India's record grain harvest in 1967–68 marked the beginning of a brief respite from food shortage. Indian industry, however, did not recover quickly from the drought. Moreover, by 1973, poor weather and other factors combined to confront India again with the specter of widespread hunger. India's aid relationships also fell victim to the mid-1960s drought: the bitterness, which began with the report of the Bell Mission and peaked with the politically distasteful and not fully successful devaluation, endured despite efforts to improve the climate for aid relations.

A new question was posed for the Consortium by India's rising debt service and its growing inability to both fund this obligation and finance critically needed imports. The villain of this piece, although readily identified as the stagnancy of exports, was not easy to deal with because it was intrinsically tied to a combination of managerial and macroeconomic policies central to India's chosen economic system. India's annual debt service had grown after the acceleration of aid flows in 1958, from $250 million in the Second Five-Year Plan period (1956–1961) to $1.1 billion in the Third Plan (1961–1966). But even though India raised the debt problem with the World Bank in its capacity as chairman of the Consortium in 1964 and the subject was discussed at the 1965 Consortium meeting, it was not until 1966 that an active effort was initiated to arrange for debt relief.[25] Even then, because India was the first major foreign assistance recipient for which the Consortium type of debt refinancing was proposed, negotiations progressed slowly. Some Consortium members did act to reduce their share of the debt burden in 1966, but the consultations for a larger joint effort continued through 1967 and agreement was delayed until February 1968.

The IBRD took the leading role in the rescheduling negotiations. With the agreement of other Consortium members, it arranged for an eminent French banker, Guillaume Guindey, to analyze the Indian debt problem from all angles and to shepherd approval for the rescue operations through the national

[24]Mason and Asher, op. cit., p. 197.
[25]*London Times*, Feb. 23, 1966.

governments. The first critical problem M. Guindey faced was to obtain agreement in principle that the escalation of India's debt service obligation to roughly 30 percent of export earnings was cause for a debt relief exercise. In conjunction with the Bank, he proposed and won some support for the criterion that the cost of India's debt servicing should not exceed 20 percent of its export earnings. The next, and more difficult, problem was to find a burden-sharing formula which would be acceptable to all donors. The United States, beset by balance-of-payments problems and annoyed by the hard commercialism of Italy and some other donors, was anxious to have the Consortium members who had given loans on hard terms assume the brunt of the relief. This position was countered by the so-called hard lenders, who held that the value of aid is determined by more than the repayment terms and that the cost of aid to donor economies must be evaluated with respect to a number of considerations including capacity to lend as measured by aid/GNP ratios. Eventually M. Guindey negotiated a mutually acceptable settlement which called for debt relief of $100 million per year for three years.

M. Guindey was flexible on the techniques for providing relief insofar as he recognized the futility of trying to propose a specific rescheduling formula in view of the disparate legislation of the various creditor nations. He recommended that each country provide a quantity of relief roughly equal to postponement for 10 years without interest. This could be achieved through rescheduling payments due, debt cancelation, fresh untied loans, or other means and was calculated to provide a minimum concessional effect of 60 percent using the Development Assistance Committee (DAC) procedure of calculating present discounted value of the relief, and assuming a 10 percent discounted cash flow. These terms were more generous than what some Consortium members were prepared to offer but, on balance, the exercise was regarded as successful. All Consortium members participated to some extent, and in addition to providing some extra capital support for India and retroactively easing the aid terms of a number of countries (particularly Japan and Germany), the principle of using debt relief as an aid vehicle was strengthened.

Throughout the Consortium's consideration of debt relief, the question of conditions was of great importance. Some donors merely wanted assurance that the funds would be put to good use in India's development program; others that India would pay less attention to ideological concerns and reconsider the advantages of private domestic and foreign investment; and others were concerned that India should limit its use of costly suppliers' credits. India's economic relations with the Soviet bloc also were a problem because some donors apprehended that their aid to India was allowing Delhi to repay its debt to Moscow. This issue became acute in later years; I shall turn to it presently.

Debt relief again assumed major importance in 1972. For want of agreement on any alternative, the Guindey solution used in 1968–1970 had been extended for 1971. But the Bank and others regarded this as only an interim solution because the quantity and quality of debt relief under the Guindey formula were viewed as inadequate to justify the special effort needed to obtain donor concurrence. For some donor countries debt relief more or less substituted for other forms of aid and thus provided India relatively little extra benefit. Moreover, debt relief had become a divisive and irritating issue among donors because some were unable (unwilling) to meet the quantity and quality targets recommended by the Bank and generally accepted at Consortium meetings.

India, meanwhile, faced special strains as a result of the 1971 Bangladesh crisis. When the World Bank, assisted at this time by a former governor of Australia's Central Bank, H. C. Coombs, proposed that the amount of debt relief should be increased, most donors were unenthusiastic but nonetheless willing to entertain the possibility. The United States, however, was opposed, and without its participation there could be no debt relief exercise. The American position was based on the political logic of not rescheduling debt during a period when it had suspended most of its aid to India. In additon, the U.S. Treasury was opposed in principle to using debt rescheduling as an aid instrument on grounds that debt relief should be reserved for situations where imminent financial failure threatened. To the United States the IBRD's 1972 proposal to go beyond a second ad hoc extension of the Guindey formula appeared to be mischievous in view of the larger diplomatic issues then current. Thus, the face-saving compromise which eventuated—a Guindey-type, one-year agreement for somewhat more than $100 million—did not satisfactorily resolve either the broad policy issues of whether debt relief should be accepted as a legitimate foreign aid instrument or the practical question of how India would obtain the large amounts of foreign exchange it needed to make its annual debt service payments and development expenditures.

Consortium Operations: The Quantity and Quality of Foreign Assistance

The word "consortium" is misleading insofar as it implies a far more coordinated and businesslike relationship among donors, and between donors and India, than has ever existed in fact. The consortium mechanism has been used for a variety of purposes, most notably to change the burden-sharing relationships among donors and to improve the quantity and quality of the foreign assistance proffered to India. But, in the final analysis, aid relations have remained essentially bilateral: India has signed agreements with sovereign nations and the IBRD. The World Bank Group has played a critical part in determining the modalities for these bilateral negotiations, in providing information about the Indian economy, and so forth, but this pattern does not conform to what is ordinarily described as a consortium.

This departure from the joint action implied by the word "consortium" is not surprising, given the basic differences of attitude and domestic situation of the donor nations. At one extreme, ultraliberals such as Canada, the Scandinavians, and IDA committed themselves to provide grants or very long-term loans at zero or nominal rates of interest. Not too far removed from them in word or deed were what might be called the "establishment liberals" (the United States and Britain) who regarded the mainstream of aid as very concessional loans and technical support. These countries also provided grants and suppliers' credits. Germany, which gave most of its aid on slightly harder terms and was therefore one step removed from the liberal position, distinguished itself as one of the foremost advocates of direct private investment as the path to development. As the Consortium matured, Japan did more to liberalize its foreign assistance than any other major donor. On the basis of its own experience, Japan began with the position that development should be promoted through export growth and that the donor role in this process was to buy commodities that India could export at competitive world prices. But by the early 1970s Japan had moved to a stance similar to that of Germany. Italy has consistently been the least liberal of the Consortium countries. Its officials have maintained that the price of Italian products was so far below world commodity prices that allowing India to buy them on supplier credit terms was a generous act and sufficient justification for Italy to decline in most instances to meet the quantity and quality standards for Consortium aid. Needless to say, this diversity of national views limited the possibilities for the Consortium to act as a unified body.

The value of foreign capital assistance is measurable by two related criteria, the volume and quality of aid flows. Less needs to be said about the first of these because it is more objective. Nonetheless, a problem does arise in drawing the line between ordinary commercial credits—credits used to boost exports and available to both rich and poor countries—and true concessionary development finance. According to Indian statistics (Table 6-1) which follow the OECD Development Assistance Committee's practice of including grants, loans, and commodity assistance as aid, the gross flow of Consortium funds to India did not become significant until the late 1950s, when help was extended for the troubled Second Plan. Gross aid disbursements grew to a peak of $1.6 billion in IFY 1967–68 but subsequently declined, to less than $1 billion in the fiscal years ending in 1973 and 1974. Although the otherwise "informed public" in the West has been slow to recognize this declining trend of international assistance to India, the situation has been alarmingly clear to the Indian government and a few concerned officials in the World Bank and aid-giving agencies of donor countries. The decline is explained in large part by the shrinkage to near zero of American assistance, an irony insofar as it happened at a time when other Consortium donors were gradually responding to long-standing American efforts to get them to increase their aid to India. The danger that the Indo-American altercation poses is that other donors will follow the United States example and reduce their bilateral assistance so fast that, even with increased IDA lending, India's position will deteriorate further.

India's situation with respect to *net* aid (i.e., gross disbursements less debt service) is even less encouraging insofar as it shows that by the early 1970s India was receiving little new help from other countries. Consortium aid disburse-

TABLE 6-1
SOURCES OF EXTERNAL ASSISTANCE—UTILIZATION (millions of dollars)

	Up to end of First Plan	Second Plan, 1956–1961	Third Plan, 1961–1966	Interim period, 1966–1969	Fourth Plan, 1969–1974	Grand total
I. Consortium members	410.5	2,818.2	5,473.9	3,979.5	5,032.5	17,714.6
(U.S.)	(298.2)	(1,646.4)	(3,527.2)	(2,114.7)	(1,504.8)	(9,091.3)
(IBRD)	(71.0)	(67.9)	(259.1)	(120.4)	(219.5)	(1,137.9)
(IDA)	(. . . .)	(. . . .)	(481.3)	(472.8)	(780.0)	(1,734.1)
II. U.S.S.R. and East Europe	. . . .	159.8	514.5	271.9	258.9	1,205.1
(U.S.S.R.)	(. . . .)	(159.8)	(443.1)	(189.2)	(165.8)	(957.9)
III. Other	13.0	25.6	33.8	58.9	38.0	169.3
TOTAL	423.6	3,003.6	6,022.2	4,310.3	5,329.4	19,089.0

Note: Totals may not add, owing to rounding. (For conversion from rupees to dollars, $1.00 = Rs. 4.7619 for the period through the Third Plan and $1.00 = Rs. 7.5 for the subsequent period.)

Source: Economic Survey, 1969–70 and 1974–75.

ments have declined and have been progressively offset by growing interest and service payments. Price inflation has further reduced the real purchasing power of new foreign assistance, albeit inflation has also decreased the burden of earning foreign exchange to pay interest and amortize outstanding debts. All factors considered, India's net aid peaked in IFY 1967–68 at $1.2 billion and declined to $338 million in IFY 1973–74. This troublesome situation not only indicates that the foreign effort on India's behalf is much reduced from former times, but accentuates the importance of the terms on which aid is provided and raises a question about India's future international solvency.

Returning to the impact of aid tying and related practices that reduce the value of foreign assistance (see Chapter 4), what remains to be said is that since the late 1950s, contrary to the United States' example of hardening aid terms, there has been a steady improvement in the conditions on which other donors have extended assistance. The changing pattern of World Bank Group lending is an outstanding example. Since the early 1960s, when it was recognized that India's financial position would remain weak, regular World Bank loans to India have been limited each year to an amount approximately equal to the debt service on previous Bank loans. In place of regular loans the IBRD has allocated more than 40 percent of the annual amounts available for IDA credits to India. These supersoft loans require repayment over a 50-year period, allow for a 10-year grace period, and carry a three-quarters of 1 percent service charge in lieu of interest.

The scolding, cajoling, and educational exercises mounted in the Consortium context also led most member countries to be more generous. The principal exception to this rule was the United States, which practically terminated its grant program by the end of the Third Plan, increased the interest rate on new loans, substituted dollar for local currency financing, and otherwise reduced the quality of its aid. Moreover, after 1967–68 the quantity of American assistance also fell. As a result, and because India's rising debt burden was not matched by commensurate growth of export earnings (see Table 6-2) or gross aid inflows from non-American sources, the case for debt relief was increased.

But World Bank officials and others who promoted this instrument did not anticipate various difficulties which reduced its attractiveness. Some Consortium members, notably Japan, regarded debt rescheduling as tantamount to insolvency and thus became quite uneasy when it was used. Other donors viewed it as evidence that India had not made good use of past loans and, therefore, were dubious about the value of providing further aid. Still other countries regarded debt rescheduling as a devious means for India to evade normal aid-tying procedures. But even though the cumulative strength of these objections deterred Indian officials from pressing for debt relief, India's foreign exchange position was sufficiently precarious that the Bank took the initiative and carefully orchestrated the modest debt rescheduling exercise described above. The cost of this action to improve the terms of past aid ex post facto was not inconsiderable, however, especially as discussion of financial issues did divert some attention from the substance of India's development.

TABLE 6-2
INDIA'S EXPORTS AND DEBT SERVICE

TABLE 6-2
INDIA'S EXPORTS AND DEBT SERVICE

	Merchandise exports (billions of rupees) (1)	Debt service (billions of rupees) (2)	Debt burden (%) (2)÷(1) (3)
First Plan, 1951–1956	30.4	0.2	0.8
Second Plan, 1956–1961	30.7	1.2	3.9
Third Plan, 1961–1966	44.7	5.4	12.1
Interim period, 1966–1969	37.1	9.8	26.4
Fourth Plan, 1969–1974	90.1	24.4	27.1

Sources: *Economic Survey, 1974–75; Third Five-Year Plan* (New Delhi: GOI, Planning Commission, 1960), p. 135; and *Fourth Five-Year Plan* (New Delhi: GOI, Planning Commission, 1969), p. 95.

Consortium Debt Relief and the Indo-Soviet Connection

The debt relief issue became particularly divisive among donors, and between India and the Consortium, when some of the donors became concerned that their aid permitted India to pay the Soviet Union for political and military support. The Consortium countries' long-standing concern about the Indo-Soviet economic relationship was motivated not only by cold war thinking, but by a suspicion that the total package of aid-trade relations did not fully serve India's development interests as advertised by Moscow and Delhi. Not wholly by chance, India's declining ability to service its external debts in the latter half of the 1960s coincided with a reduction in India's utilization of Soviet assistance and a reversal in the flow of real resources that put India in the position of exporting more to the Soviets than it received in return. It was not surprising, therefore, that when the Consortium asked India to justify its economic relations with the Soviet Union, it was not satisfied with the explanation and it advised India to seek debt relief and other forms of economic assistance from Moscow which would make aid from the Eastern bloc more generous.

This Consortium initiative was predestined to be frustrated by several factors, including (1) the special dependence of India on the Soviet Union for military supplies according to which India would almost certainly choose Moscow if the issue were pushed to a confrontation; (2) the absence of reliable Indian or Soviet trade and payments statistics on which the West could base its case; (3) Western misunderstanding of how the "rupee area," bilateral trade, and other

Indo-Soviet economic relations operated; and (4) conflict among such Western objectives as promoting Indian development, preventing Delhi from developing too close a relationship with Moscow, and mundane commercial goals.

The dilemma which the Consortium faced is illustrated by the debate over India's merchandise trade pattern. Consortium countries argued that for India to benefit from its economic relations with the Soviet Union, there must be a net flow of real resources into India. Concurrently, they urged India to improve its balance-of-payments position by increasing its exports to all countries, including the Soviet Union. Although there was no logical inconsistency in India's having a positive inflow of resources from the U.S.S.R. and increasing its exports to the Soviet Union, to do so required India to increase its imports of Soviet goods. But some donors regarded increased Indian imports from the U.S.S.R. as undesirable on both commercial and political grounds: first, because India would become more dependent on the Soviet Union and, second, because Western exports to India might be displaced. These motives were especially apparent in the early 1970s when rival commercial aircraft manufacturers were competing furiously to meet India's need for a medium-range jet fleet. When the Boeing 737 was chosen in preference to British and Soviet contenders, India's choice reflected economic rationality, but it was not made in a political vacuum insofar as the national governments of all contending manufacturers took active part in the sales negotiations.

The question of how the Consortium should react to Indo-Soviet economic relations and how it could resolve its internal differences proved especially intractable, in large part because India's dependence on Moscow meant that the Indo-Soviet relationship was not subject to radical change by the Consortium. To the extent that India tried to defend its relationship on economic rather than military-political grounds, however, it had a credibility gap with the Consortium which caused some members to keep the issue active. Moreover, there was a tendency for some aid donors to believe that by talking tough on Indo-Soviet economic relations, they would strengthen the Indian negotiating hand and embarrass Moscow into being more generous. But even if rhetoric was a legitimate instrument for pursuing this interest, it was not very effective. The more powerful instrument which was proposed—conditioning debt relief on some change in the Indo-Soviet relationship—was rejected, not only because some donors felt that it would be inappropriate or inadequate to the task, but also because some were unwilling to allow debt relief to become a major part of the aid effort under any circumstances. In short, only if India's debt situation were to become as acute as that experienced by Indonesia in 1970 would it be reasonable to assume that the West would withhold debt relief until Moscow agreed to take some roughly parallel action.

What is particularly pertinent about the issue of Indian debt relief is its close connection with broader issues of domestic and international relations. It bridges time periods, from the years when loans were extended, to future years when they were scheduled to be repaid. It has economic content insofar as debt relief can promote development, and the negotiations to obtain it have affected

India's external economic trade and aid relations with both the East and the West. It also has political overtones for relations between India and donor countries, and among India, the Consortium, and the Soviet Union. Because debt relief—essentially a development instrument—has such highly complex and important ramifications, it is a good illustration of why the United States and other countries often find it difficult to become constructively related to the problems of developing nations.

Why a Consortium?

The fundamental question raised by the concept of a consortium is whether a joint effort by donors is more likely to achieve development goals than unrelated individual efforts. At a technical level, it is easy to justify making the IBRD responsible for analysis of the Indian economy on grounds that this avoids duplication of effort. But this falls far short of the Consortium's primary role of increasing the quanity of aid, improving its terms, and making it more efficient. It is in these areas that the Consortium has sometimes conflicted with national legislatures and executives, which generally are reluctant to transfer the fiscal and political authority vested in them by their citizens to any multinational decision-making mechanism.

In view of this inevitable conflict, the intractability of poverty, and the newness of the multilateral approach to development, it is easy to understand why the potential role of the Consortium has been only partially realized. Indeed, the modest achievements of the Consortium technique in improving the quantity and quality of aid and in redistributing the burden of aid among donors appear noteworthy when examined on a case-by-case basis. During the early 1970s, for example, other donors continued the process of improving their contributions even though the United States was not pledging new aid. And in 1972 the momentum of established Consortium relationships caused the United States to participate in debt relief even though such action was contrary to its then current general policy toward India. The precedent for group action to improve the performance of individual donor countries beyond what they might have done if acting on their own was well established during the mid-1960s drought period when the Consortium's joint pledging procedures are credited with having greatly improved the response to India's critical needs.[26]

[26]According to I. P. M. Cargill, vice president of the IBRD and formerly chairman of the India Consortium, "I have no doubt at all that in the United Kingdom, perhaps in the United States, certainly in Germany, France and the smaller Consortium countries, the ability of the administration to obtain support of legislators and the general public for development assistance to India has been facilitated by the fact that they can point to a concerted international effort to help economic development in India." See I. P. M. Cargill, "Efforts to Influence Recipient Performance: Case Study of India," in John P. Lewis and Ishan Kapur, eds., *The World Bank Group, Multilateral Aid, and the 1970s* (Lexington, Mass.: D. C. Heath and Co., 1973), p. 95.

Participants in the India Consortium welcomed the opportunity for group action, for many of them regarded India's problems as so large as to defy piecemeal action. But although donors entered into the Consortium mode with the impression that this was the only way they could hope to bring pressure to improve Indian economic policies, there was very little "ganging up" against India, and the bulk of policy changes due to the Consortium consisted of aid liberalizations by donors. At the operational level, it was hoped that the Consortium would justify its existence by reducing the amount of scarce Indian bureaucratic machinery required to manage the various bilateral aid relationships. In practice, however, the Consortium has tended to supplement rather than replace bilateral relations, and even in the matter of day-to-day operations, there has been little simplification other than to occasionally associate a national donor with the IBRD in the joint financing of a project.

On the key question of influence (aid leverage), there can be little doubt that the Consortium has sought to affect Indian economic policy.[27] There is an enormous difference, however, between the conceptions of the Consortium "as a forum for getting our (Indian) plans endorsed by the donor countries,"[28] and as a vehicle for "serious efforts . . . to influence economic performance in India" in "balance-of-payments policies, controls over imports, and the relative stress to be put on agricultural output."[29] Clearly, the line between reasonable and excessive influence is ambiguous and there is no consensus as to where it falls. But assuming that there is some agreement on the boundaries within which this line falls, have these been trespassed on occasion? For what purposes has leverage been applied? Has foreign influence caused India to adopt good policy? The semantics of diplomacy and the hypothetic nature of assessing what might have happened if alternative policies had been followed conspire to prevent any clear answers. There is merit, nonetheless, in the L. K. Jha conception of the Consortium's exercise of influence as "leaning against open doors."[30] In most cases when the Consortium exerted pressure, donor country thinking was roughly in harmony with Indian thinking. Thus it is hardly surprising that there is no consensus as to whether the use of leverage in particular instances such as India's 1966 devaluation substantially affected Indian policies, much less whether the development impact was good or evil. Illustratively, the most sensible comment that can be made about the devaluation experience (see Chapter 9) is that, but for the large amounts of assistance donors made available, India would not have dared to experiment with import liberalization and other policy changes.[31]

[27]See such divergent but knowledgeable sources as *Partners in Development,* op. cit., p. 300; Mason and Asher, op. cit., pp. 428–437; Reid, op. cit., pp. 82–83; Patel in Barbara Ward, op. cit., pp. 295–311; and Jha, "Comment: Leaning against Open Doors," op. cit., and Cargill in Lewis and Kapur, op. cit., pp. 89–101.

[28]Patel, *Foreign Aid,* op. cit., p. 13.

[29]Mason and Asher, op. cit., p. 455.

[30]Jha, "Comment: Leaning against Open Doors," op. cit.

[31]Mason and Asher, op. cit., p. 679.

The rather limited scope for economic leverage reflects both the tendency for India's leaders to make pragmatic decisions when there is a crisis and the intensity and emotional political resistance to any foreign intrusion into the economic policy arena. India has been as immune to Western efforts to wean it from socialism, emphasis on heavy industry, and aid from Moscow as its leaders were quick to emphasize agriculture in the years immediately following the disastrous drought of 1965–1967. Individual cases where leverage can be cited as having changed Indian policy (IBRD loans to India which required the states to raise their electricity rates,[32] for example) are relatively trivial in the larger scheme of aid relations. It is notable, however, that even the imposition of these technical conditions which could serve no other donor interest than Indian development has been criticized as "unnecessary internal interference."[33] In reality, because foreign influence has such political overtones, there has been far more discussion of the leverage issue than it merits.

Although the conventional wisdom says that multinational assistance is superior to bilateral because it inhibits extraneous conflicts between donors and recipients from affecting aid relations, the World Bank and Consortium have occasionally used economic leverage in the area of political affairs. Escott Reid had described one instance; the uncomfortable role of the IBRD and other donors during the South Asian crisis of 1971 and, in particular, the visit Consortium Chairman I. P. M. Cargill made to East and West Pakistan in June 1971. According to Reid, because of Cargill "the President of Pakistan and most of his advisors in Islamabad" were better informed "of what was happening in East Pakistan and of the reaction in the outside world." Moreover, at that time "the Consortium subjected Pakistan to a form of economic sanctions" which was not extended to India.[34] An earlier case of foreign intervention, the protracted and eventually successful efforts of the World Bank and aid donors in arbitrating between India and Pakistan in the Indus waters dispute is an especially good example of how leverage can be used to achieve political and economic benefits. Arbitration of this dispute was facilitated by the promise of substantial funds to exploit the water resources once agreement was reached.[35] Thus, because the scope for this intervention was defined by the reality that the Indus settlement was in the interests of, and politically acceptable to, both countries, it was quite unlike the 1971 experience and was welcomed by all concerned.

Development assistance purists have advocated the strict separation of aid relations from other foreign affairs. They have been less than totally convincing, but have demonstrated that too close a link between foreign aid and other policies—particularly in the short term—can ill serve both over the course of time. Thus, the belief that multilateral institutions were a good way to insulate

---

[32]Ibid., p. 437.
[33]Jha, "Comment: Leaning against Open Doors," op. cit., p. 100.
[34]Reid, op. cit., p. 168.
[35]Mason and Asher, op. cit., pp. 610–627.

aid relationships from other tensions explains why, by IFY 1973–74, India obtained about 40 percent of its aid from the World Bank and IDA. The issue of substituting multilateral for bilateral aid merits reconsideration, however, in light of (1) the tendency to replay bad bilateral relations in the Consortium forum and thereby complicate the recipient's relations with all donors and (2) evidence that the onus of external pressure cannot be multilateralized.

The first of these issues was dramatically posed by the Consortium's position following the United States aid suspension in 1971. For many months it was uncertain whether the United States would effectively end the debt rescheduling exercise by refusing to participate. But even when America was pressured into rescheduling, the amounts involved had to be drastically scaled down in order to obtain its concurrence. In short, Indo-American differences had come much too close to destroying India's broader aid relations for the issue of multilateralization to be decided without careful examination.

With respect to the second issue, a reading of the Indian press shows that much of the blame for pressuring India into its 1966 devaluation was placed on the United States, even though the IBRD, IMF, and Consortium countries all played a role. When this outcome is contrasted with the repercussions of the more bilateral United States efforts to have India change its farm policies, President Johnson's "short tether," self-help reports, and so forth, the choice for the United States between bilateral and multilateral aid is far from obvious, and attention to considerations such as congressional views about multinational institutions is clearly desirable.

From India's point of view the issue is not merely bilateral versus multilateral aid. As I. G. Patel has noted, even in the absence of foreign aid India would "still have to reckon with the currents and crosscurrents of international power politics," and therefore the really important issue for an aid recipient is "defining the extent to which it is safe for a country to depend on outside help."[36] In this context the Indian government welcomed the Consortium at first as a means to obtain emergency relief and second as a channel for external assistance which would not make India dependent or subject to foreign meddling in its policies. More recently, as the amount of net outside assistance has dwindled and the tendency for donors to provide gratuitous advice has grown more pronounced, there has been less Indian enthusiasm for foreign aid. Indeed the sluggish recovery of the economy in the postdevaluation period should be interpreted as the direct consequence of Delhi's determination to rebuild foreign exchange reserves so as to reduce India's vulnerability to foreign pressure. This notwithstanding, the Consortium has maintained its popularity in Delhi largely because it has appeared as a more rational and statesmanlike means for India to enlist donor support for its development than any foreseeable alternative.

[36]Patel, *Foreign Aid,* op. cit., pp. 26–27.

PART III
THE MANAGEMENT OF ECONOMIC POLICY

CHAPTER 7
DEVELOPMENT OBJECTIVES, STRATEGY, AND POLICY

It would be misleading to suggest that India adopted a consistent set of economic goals in 1947 or 1951 and pursued them without deviation to the present time. Nonetheless, whether one looks at official rhetoric or at policy, it is clear that India's concern for growth, equity, and self-reliance is long-standing and, allowing for periodic changes in their relative priorities, this interest has been consistently pursued.

India's development strategy—as distinct from goals—has been shaped by a variety of factors: economic resources, intellectual predispositions, technology, and so forth. Strategy has been more subject to change than objectives, but in many respects, it too has included consistent elements. For example, even though India adopted a flexible response to the relative priorities of the agricultural and the industrial sectors, it pursued central planning and social control of the economy's "commanding heights" continuously, albeit with varying success from one year to the next.

Policies, not surprisingly, are still more subject to revision than goals or strategy. But although India's policies have frequently—perhaps too frequently—been changed to adjust to the evolving economic situation, there are some measures, such as those designed to achieve monetary stability and import substitution, which have prevailed more or less throughout the period. To the extent that India's objectives, strategy, and policies have changed but also show considerable consistency over time, they justify an analysis which does not dwell on chronology.

The Aims of Economic Policy

The economic objectives of growth, social justice, and self-reliance are hardly unique to any nation. But in India, their current and historical significance demands discussion. Not only is there constant debate about their relative priorities, but the Indian government has varied its emphasis among them over time in order to accommodate its actual policies to current circumstance. Meanwhile, international attitudes toward the content of development and the means to achieve it have also been changing.

In most years since Independence, growth has been India's preeminent economic objective. The logic for this choice was that, with some guidance from the government, the achievement of growth would more or less automatically eliminate poverty and reduce India's reliance on imports. The primacy of growth in the early post-Independence years is reflected in Nehru's reply in the Constituent Assembly (1948) to a proposed motion which called for a socialist economy and nationalization. According to Nehru, "Production comes first and I am prepared to say that everything we should do be judged from the point of view of production."[1] That Nehru, India's foremost political leader, made such a categorical statement (one which, incidentally, was not followed in practice) indicates what weight Indians have attached to enlarging output. In reality, India's development experience resembles that of many other developing countries in that targeted growth rates have not been achieved and increased production has not always "trickled down"to the poor.[2] As a consequence, since the late 1960s policy makers have paid increasing attention to questions of equity.

Like growth, social justice is well rooted as an economic objective in the pre-Independence thinking of the Congress party. But although to achieve social justice under Indian conditions required rapid economic growth as well as more equitable distribution of production, the Indian debate on which of these aspects should be emphasized in policy has been vitriolic and interminable. A prominent shift in emphasis toward the distributive aspect of social justice and away from growth began in 1969 and peaked in 1971 with the adoption of Mrs. Gandhi's popular election slogan, *garibi hatao* ("abolish poverty"). It was embodied in the Planning Commission's document *Towards an Approach to the Fifth Five-Year Plan* (published in the spring of 1972, when C. Subramaniam was vice chairman of the Commission), but a later Planning Commission document, *Approach to the Fifth Five-Year Plan* (published in the autumn of 1972 after D. P. Dhar had succeeded Subramaniam at the Commission), suggested that there had been some return to the growth-oriented approach. The language of the Draft Fifth Five-Year Plan (1973) was sufficiently ambiguous to imply that although there had been some retreat from the 1971 emphasis on equity, this goal would continue to be a major determinant of policy. Among the multitude of difficult policy issues raised by equity are (1) whether equity should be equated with egalitarianism or whether merely establishing a floor under

[1]See Dorothy Norman, ed., *Nehru: The First Sixty Years* (New York: John Day Co., 1965), vol. 2, pp. 379–380.

[2]See James P. Grant, "Development: The End of Trickle Down," *Foreign Policy,* no. 12, Fall 1973, pp. 43–65.

incomes would satisfy the social good; (2) how improving equity is related to the distribution of (*a*) economic income, (*b*) economic assets, and (*c*) political power; and (3) whether it would be more economic to seek social justice by establishing more equitable wage and income patterns, by using a package of tax and transfer payments to narrow consumption disparities, or other means.

India's third objective, self-reliance, has been stressed at times of national crisis such as at Independence, during periods of food scarcity, and when India was engaged in international conflicts. Self-reliance is intimately linked to India's other major economic goals, and its roots can be discerned in the *swadeshi* movement, begun early in the twentieth century, and the Gandhian idea that village-level self-sufficiency produces national strength and personal virtue. India's dissatisfaction with its growth rate and the unyielding nature of income disparities have resulted in greater pressure for policy to follow an autarkic course. Although Delhi has resisted this pressure, Indians have continued to ask questions about autarky: whether they should seek self-sufficiency generally or only in selective areas such as defense production; whether self-reliance requires import substitution and the phasing-out of imports, or merely that India export enough to pay for its imports and eliminate the need for foreign assistance. The diversity and scope of these issues reflect the multiplicity of views on India's choice to be an outward-looking nation or to withdraw from what some Indians regard as inequitable world economic and political systems. Thus far, India has not taken the narrow view on economic self-reliance. Its focus has been on "aid to end aid"[3] and on import substitution to (1) spur domestic development, (2) meet particular production needs, and (3) relieve balance-of-payments pressures.

The attraction for India of growth, equity, and self-reliance as primary economic objectives is that they have broad appeal and can be interpreted to include many other goals. Moreover, they are complementary.

¶ Growth is hastened to the extent that unemployed Indians are provided with income-producing jobs that raise the productivity of the national work force (equity). It is also stimulated by substituting domestic production for imports (self-reliance).

¶ Equity requires economic growth: to the extent that it is politically difficult to reduce the absolute income of well-to-do members of the society, the redistribution of relative income shares has rapid economic growth as a quid pro quo. In contrast, as demonstrated by the wide attention given since the mid-1060s to the dependence of developing countries on the industrialized nations, self-reliance is not as significant a factor for domestic equity as it is internationally.

¶ Self-reliance is a direct consequence of growth in the narrow sense that without growth India would have remained dependent on imports. More

[3]See, for example, I. G. Patel, "Essence of Self-Reliance," *Eastern Economist*, Jan. 5, 1973.

broadly, India's ability to defend its national integrity against adverse domestic and hostile foreign forces has depended on its ability to be self-reliant. For example, the fruits of India's green revolution were a critical asset in the 1971 conflict over Bangladesh.

But there also are conflicts among these economic objectives and reconciling them has been a long-standing preoccupation of India's economic pundits and political leaders. From a political point of view, India needed to make rapid progress on all fronts simultaneously. In practice, however, it has not been possible to meet all the development goals, and some of them have been easier to achieve than others. One fundamental problem has been that in cases where the three objectives were competitive, it has been extraordinarily difficult for public officials to set priorities because of the intensity and diversity of political pressures in India. Equally important is the dilemma of how to decentralize official responsibility to improve the efficiency of government when local governments are in the hands of people who are less inclined to press for equity than the officials in Delhi are.

Among the most critical conflicts are those linking growth and social justice through employment. For instance, deciding the timetable for introducing labor-displacing tractors and other machinery in the Punjab raises questions about (1) the relative private and social costs of alternative production techniques; (2) the efficiency of the alternative production strategies measured in food output; and (3) employment and income distribution consequences insofar as mechanization affects class, caste, and regional groups in different ways (the well-to-do farmers usually benefit most). One rough answer to this puzzle is the generalization that tractors should be used in some areas because, by speeding the turnaround time between plantings, multiple cropping will be possible. In contrast, mechanical harvesters are almost always unnecessarily capital-intensive and should be barred. Official inaction on the farm mechanization issue is not a proper response because general economic factors such as India's artificially low interest rates and overvalued exchange rate incline farmers toward mechanization. At a minimum, concern for equity via high employment requires that official policy be neutral toward labor-displacing production techniques and seek to equate market prices of the factors of production with their true social value.

Indian growth objectives conflict not only with equity but with self-reliance. An obvious example is forgoing higher investment and output in favor of military spending. At another level, the government must often decide among alternative forms of growth; for instance, the continuing debates in India about the relative merits of large- and small-scale industry and between industry and agriculture.

The pursuit of social justice is fraught with difficulty because of the complex temporal and spatial problems it raises. Time is significant, for example, because the division of national income between consumption and investment affects India's current standard of living. Similarly, the size of the future economy will be partly determined by how current national income is divided.

The Indian government is in a position to influence the current choice between investment and consumption through interest rate, fiscal, and other policies. But to what criteria should officials refer in deciding to what extent the welfare of the present generations should be sacrificed in order to improve the economic situation of their descendants? A comparable spatial question is whether the government should sacrifice the immediate development of backward areas in order to maximize production, a strategy which may trade off higher current consumption in the backward areas for a slower rate of growth there. Equity and self-reliance sometimes conflict, as in the obvious case of whether India's balance-of-payments strategy should be autarkic or whether it should seek to maximize India's real income through foreign trade based on comparative advantage.

Examples of the contradictions and questions of interpretation raised by self-reliance and other economic objectives are almost limitless. Suffice it here to say that they exist, and that attitudes toward them have often been at odds. Some Indians have chosen to dismiss them as unimportant, and others, at the opposite extreme, to portray them as insuperable obstacles to development. The truth lies between these extreme views, and we shall return to some of the basic conflicts in later chapters.

The Relevance of Population to Development

"Removal of poverty and attainment of economic self-reliance" may be the opening words in chapter 1 of the Draft Fifth Five-Year Plan, but paragraphs 2 through 10 of the same chapter are devoted to the critical subject of demography. This is tacit recognition that, whereas limiting fertility may not be a final objective of policy, it is probably the most crucial instrumental variable affecting India's progress toward social and economic welfare goals. The slow pace at which social scientists are disentangling the relationship between demographic variables and development indicates the complexity of this linkage and it would therefore be presumptuous to think that the next few pages can do anything more than summarize the current state of our understanding.[4]

It is a commonplace that human welfare is determined by what is available for consumption, the number of people, and the pattern of distribution. It is equally clear, according to the law of diminishing returns, that increasing the amount of labor relative to fixed amounts of land and capital eventually leads to declining, zero, and even negative amounts of additional production. The capacity of land to support people is determined not only by the population

[4]For a detailed description of the cost-benefit implications of population, see Warren C. Robinson and David E. Horlocher, "Population Growth and Economic Welfare," Population Council Report on Population/Family Planning No. 6, New York, 1971; Robert Cassen's forthcoming book; and George B. Simmons, "The Indian Investment in Family Planning," Population Council Report, New York, 1971.

density but by the availability of farm inputs, the state of technology, and the character of social and economic institutions. In the light of this rough macroeconomic framework, and our knowledge that the marginal productivity of Indian labor is now very low, a first-order statement can be made to the effect that India would have a higher per capita average income if its population *size* and its population *growth rate* were smaller. (It is meaningless, of course, to think of India's having a smaller population except in the special sense that a lower current growth rate will lead to a smaller future population.)

Somewhat more sophisticated are the macroeconomic models which link high rates of population growth with retarded development. The progenitor of these studies, by Coale and Hoover, dates to 1958. It and more recent research are concerned with the unfavorable effect that rapid population growth has on development by raising India's "dependency ratio" (the proportion of the total population which is unable because of youth or old age to contribute to output). These studies explain how high population growth rates hinder economic progress by (1) reducing the amount of total production available for savings and investments and (2) channeling a disproportionately large share of new investment into replication of economic and social infrastructure rather than the capital broadening projects needed to diversify the economy and to increase per capita income.[5] The tendency of high population growth rates to drive living standards toward the subsistence level looms as especially significant now that development specialists believe that potential for saving and investing resides with the populace at large and is not confined to a few wealthy families.

To postulate that India's population size is so great as to be disadvantageous is not a racist response, as is often alleged, but based on sound evidence. I have already noted the high costs of unbalanced mixtures of factors of production and the political and managerial problems which Rajni Kothari describes by the phrase "politics of scale" (page 48, Chapter 2). India's per capita aid receipts, small compared with that of other developing countries, are another often-cited result of its large size. In addition to these factors, India's scale precludes some options that are open to smaller countries. For example, if India were to try to raise its per capita exports to the level of small countries such as Singapore or South Korea by specializing in the production and export of a few commodities, it would encounter enormous obstacles owing to the disruption this would cause to world trade. (This is no excuse for India's deplorable export performance, however, as I shall explain in Chapter 9.)

The closing off of these options is especially lamentable because in many instances India has not exploited opportunities which exist because it has a large population. In particular, for a variety of economic, political, and social reasons India has not taken full advantage of potential economies of scale through long production runs. Planning for economic efficiency has had to contend with (1) the impact of Gandhian ideology favoring small enterprise; (2)

---

[5]Ansley J. Coale and Edgar M. Hoover, *Population Growth and Economic Development in Low Income Countries: A Case Study of India's Prospects* (Princeton, N.J.: Princeton University Press, 1958).

Delhi's perceived need to satisfy the political demands of states by distributing among them public sector steel mills and other industries of suboptimal size; and (3) Indian bias against private entrepreneurs which militated against large factories.

The social mechanisms through which high population growth is translated into a drag on development are not fully understood, and to the extent that this subject has been investigated, most of the research has not been empirical and the results are controversial. There is no doubt, however, that rapid population growth puts unusual strains on India's economy. Dwindling opportunities for raising the productivity of land require the migration each year of substantial numbers, some of them to the already overcrowded towns and cities. As noted in Chapter 2, the National Sample Survey and Census information indicate that joblessness and underemployment have grown. This combination of migration, urbanization, and growing unemployment has imposed incredible strains on India's social fabric and has redirected resources and energies that might otherwise have been used for development to maintaining law and order and to relief. Thus, given India's shortage of official and private management talent and currently exploitable economic resources, the cost of fast population growth on development may be many times greater than can actually be traced with the aid of conventional economic and accounting tools.

In recent years, sparked in part by mounting population in India and other developing countries, increasing attention has been directed to the issue of how population growth affects income distribution and development. Robert Cassen, for example, has investigated in a meticulous survey of the available circumstantial evidence, whether there has been any improvement in the welfare of the poorest deciles of India's population. His conclusion, based on a review of personal consumption levels, employment data, village studies, migration, and mortality rates, is that the living conditions of India's poorest have failed to improve and, in some cases, have even deteriorated.[6] Illustrative of the process through which this occurs is the case of family enlargement which leads to land division among sons and the economic inefficiency implied by the insistence of each cultivator to own his own oxen regardless of whether they are fully employed.

The conclusion, that mass welfare has not improved in India, is especially distressing in light of the growing suspicion that fertility rates are themselves a function of living conditions, i.e., that a secular decline in the birthrate is caused by—or at least is correlated with—rising standards of welfare. According to David Mandelbaum, joint family living, caste, religion, and urbanization are not the major determinants of fertility in India. What counts is the related factors of per capita income and education level; as these rise, fertility declines.[7] Perhaps the most striking and politically significant evidence supporting the existence of a link between fertility and welfare is the experience of India's states, compari-

[6]Cassen, op. cit.

[7]David G. Mandelbaum, *Human Fertility in India* (Berkeley: University of California Press, 1974), pp. 57–59.

son of which shows that the poorest generally have the fastest population growth rates. Kerala, however, which may be the most advanced state educationally, has a low rate of fertility despite its relatively low level of per capita income. If fertility rates are in fact linked to economic and educational standards, it follows that to the degree that the international community is genuinely concerned about India's reducing its population growth, aid donors should increase their assistance to India's development programs.

The most common explanation for high birthrates among the poor involves a mix of economic and social factors. In brief, the *costs* of childbearing are not fully borne by the parents but are externalized, i.e., shared with the entire community through the fiscal system and other mechanisms. In contrast, the *benefits* of having progeny are largely internalized in the sense that, as a male child matures and joins the work force, social custom causes him to become a source of family strength. According to what might be called the "family social security equation," an average man must father eight children if half of his offspring will die before maturity, half will be girls, and there must be at least two sons to support him in his old age. Since what may be rational for the individual may be intolerable for the nation as a whole, high fertility has been and will remain one of the knottiest problems confronting India.

Myrdal, in investigating the twentieth-century debate over whether India is "overpopulated," has discovered a variety of pronatalist and antinatalist views which have affected India's population policies. He also has been impressed with Indian sensitivities on this issue; foreigners can judge India to be overpopulated only at the risk of being accused of racism.[8] India, nonetheless, has had a long-standing concern about its population numbers. Although Gandhi initially opposed the idea that India was overpopulated and later was willing to acknowledge the problem only reluctantly, Nehru elicited a definite statement about the need for family planning from the Congress party's National Planning Committee as early as 1935.[9] The Indian government, in acting on this view and initiating its family planning program in 1952, was far ahead of the international community. In its First Five-Year Plan (1952), the Planning Commission included the mild conclusion that "a rapidly growing population is apt to become more a source of embarrassment than of help to a programme for raising standards of living."[10] Soon afterward, the Commission's position on population hardened; the Second Plan contained the unequivocal statement: "The conclusion is inescapable that an effective curb on population growth is an important condition for rapid improvement in incomes and in levels of living."[11]

During the first two Plans (1951–1961), Indian family planning policy was oriented toward research in such areas as motivation, communications, demography, and reproduction physiology. In the subsequent decade, as a conse-

[8]See Myrdal, op. cit., chap. 28 and app. 14.
[9]*Ibid.*, p. 1489.
[10]*First Five-Year Plan* (New Delhi: GOI, Planning Commission, 1952), p. 18.
[11]*Second Five-Year Plan* (New Delhi: GOI, Planning Commission, 1956), p. 7.

quence of growing recognition of the demographic-welfare link and India's eye-opening 1961 census, which showed population growing much faster than anticipated, the sense of urgency conveyed by Plan documents was increasingly reflected in policy. The family planning budget was increased and an active extension program to get the family planning message and contraceptive supplies to the people was initiated. The program's significance received bureaucratic recognition in 1966 when a Department of Family Planning was created in the central government, and in following years, its priority was further increased by the setting of "time bound" targets and its elevation in the Fourth Plan to the "highest priority."[12] But, despite these impressive steps, there has been lingering skepticism as to how far the central government is prepared to press beyond rhetoric and conventional approaches to reduce fertility. In 1973, for example, family planning lost more than proportionally in a round of budget cutting, even after some of the funds eliminated were later restored.[13] Moreover, the ambitious targets for reducing the birthrate stated in the Draft Fifth Plan do not appear to be supported by commensurate programs or finance.

India's population control program has had two major thrusts: it has sought in the short term to reduce the birthrate through a growing family planning effort while, simultaneously, it has attempted to have a long-run impact on fertility by changing the basic social and economic variables which determine family size. To its credit, the government started its program early, has repeatedly increased its budget, and has been in the forefront of experimentation in research and extension. The birthrate, nonetheless, has been reduced by only a small margin from its high level of about 40 per thousand of population. Responsibility for this situation, however, does not lie solely with the government; the odds against effective population limitation have been very high, given the economic advantages to families of having many children, social and political barriers to limiting family size, and the enormous technical, resource, and organizational requirements of implementing population control policies on an all-India scale. Indeed the dice were loaded against India because health-related programs—easy to justify on moral grounds and inexpensive on a per capita basis—progressively lowered the mortality rate and demanded increasingly more dramatic success on the family planning front merely to prevent the population growth rate from spiraling out of control. Reduced mortality is likely to contribute to reduced fertility in the long run, but for the interim its effect has been to increase population size.

In the final analysis India's population policy must be judged not by its objectives or logic but by its results. Because Indian policy has had such modest results thus far, it is proper to question whether the relative priority accorded family planning as compared with other government programs has been sufficient; whether the government should have devoted larger amounts of resources and management talent to family planning; and whether, if senior

[12]*India: 1974,* op. cit., p. 87.
[13]See Veit, "India's Economic Development and the Force of National Politics," op. cit.

political leaders (especially the prime minister) had publicly given the family planning program greater spiritual endorsement, this would have increased its effectiveness. In this framework, the shortcomings of India's policies should not be interpreted as a lack of official interest in fertility, but rather as the failure of family planning interests to overcome the outstanding constraints. Thus, past experience serves as clear warning that the rhetoric, assumptions, and marginal changes toward population control included in the Draft Fifth Plan will not suffice to lower India's birthrate substantially. In the absence of powerful new policies and additional funding to reduce fertility, the only way in which the Fifth Plan population growth estimates will be achieved is through a failure to decrease the mortality rate as quickly as targeted.

Policy Instruments and Attendant Tensions

It would be misleading to suggest that officials in Delhi can arbitrarily decide the course of India's development without regard to the multitude of local and exogenous forces which affect the economy. Private enterprise, especially in agriculture and other traditional sectors, has been and promises to remain somewhat independent of official policy. This was dramatically demonstrated in 1973–74 when the noncooperation of the rural community forced the government to denationalize wholesale trading in wheat. It would be wrong, however, to conclude that Delhi is a "paper tiger," that the economy is beyond its reach because of the power of state and local government and because of the extremes of size, diversity, and entrenched interests to which India is heir.

The middle ground, which I believe to be correct, puts more rather than less emphasis on Delhi's ability to make decisions affecting the national welfare, while underscoring that government efforts to give direction to the economy generate intense tensions. The growing interdependence of economic sectors as illustrated by the linkage between exports of engineering goods which earn foreign exchange and fertilizer imports which convert this international purchasing power into food for consumption by factory workers suggests that there are many points at which the government can break into the economy to influence resource allocation and to encourage or discourage certain kinds of economic behavior. For example, a government decision to build fertilizer factories not only could affect the composition and rate of Indian industrialization, but could spur farm production by increasing the availability of fertilizer. Both the payments for the new factory and the import substitution which would occur once it went into production would affect India's foreign exchange position. As an alternative to building a fertilizer plant, the government could affect the food supply by deciding between imports of (1) foreign food and (2) fertilizer to increase domestic farm yields.

Nevertheless, there are many areas where Delhi is unable to impose its will on the economy. In particular, there is a significant asymmetry between the government's positive capacity to impose development in some areas and its negative power to obstruct change. For example, officials are in a position to prevent large-scale expansion of private industry but generally are unable to force industrialists to take up unwanted investments. India is not unlike other countries in this respect.

In discussions of power a discount factor must be applied to official rhetoric and even to legislation: just as the Plans are somewhat of a mirage with respect to the policies which are passed into law, laws and officially sanctioned administrative procedures are somewhat of a mirage with respect to actual policy implementation. Indicative of the ambiguity inherent in this situation is the position of the Planning Commission, which, while unable to wrest fiscal control from India's Finance Ministry, has played an important role in shaping key development choices such as the decision to concentrate on national rather than on regional policies. Most Indian leaders have shared a bias toward national homogeneity and central control, and this has given special character to India's development efforts. In particular, the decision to impose development from above reflects an impatience and unwillingness to wait for initiatives to surface from below; it was bound to generate frictions as it challenged India's change-resistant political economy.

Macroeconomic Policies

In its pursuit of growth, equity, and self-reliance, India has used a full range of macroeconomic policies, including fiscal and monetary measures. Its experience in collecting tax and other revenues (measured by government receipts as a percentage of gross national product) is neither outstandingly good nor bad compared to other developing, and some developed, countries. What is worrisome on India's fiscal front is that there is a tendency for administrative and nondevelopment expenditures to get out of hand and to cause the government to reduce its spending on investment. Moreover, although Delhi has not been averse to budget deficits—indeed, since the Second Plan the debate has been about the deficit's size rather than its existence—India has inherited fiscal conservatism from the British. Thus, even though periods of high inflation generally can be traced directly to monsoon failures rather than to fiscal profligacy, India has tended to be too wary of budget deficits, and public investment has suffered accordingly.

India has been equally cautious in its monetary policy, where it has carefully regulated the money supply and interest rates. Delhi and the Reserve Bank in Bombay have gradually developed additional effective techniques for economic management through monetary measures, including selective credit controls. But they also have missed an opportunity by not following the experimental lead of Taiwan, Brazil, and other countries which have used their financial systems to mobilize monetary resources which otherwise would have been spent for consumption or hoarding. Rather than allowing interest rates to rise to a level where they would reflect the scarcity of capital, India has held them at low levels, sometimes so low as to make the real rate of return less than zero after adjusting the nominal interest rate for the rate of inflation.

The Not-So-Invisible Hand

Chapter 1 counterpoised the competing strategies of laissez faire, socialism, and Gandhism. It is an irony that the most alien of these to India's historical traditions, a national socialism, was to play such a dominant part in the nation's development after Independence. Implied by the phrase "socialist pattern of society" is the Indian conception that in addition to providing social services and assuring some degree of egalitarianism, the state should control both the composition and distribution of production, and strategic industries should be in the public sector. As India's economic policy has evolved, the boundaries on official scrutiny and intervention in the economy have come more and more to be only those imposed by the realities of political resistance and technical competence. In agriculture, for example, the government repeatedly has sought to control prices, transshipments of grain among states, size of landholdings, and a multitude of other factors even though the results of these policies have been very mixed. (See Chapter 8.) Although disastrous policies such as the 1973 wheat trade nationalization have been reversed, and costly but inefficient policies such as Community Development have been revamped, India's policy makers have consistently shown a preference for controls over measures which would allow market forces of supply and demand to function. Industry has been no more free of government intervention, and elaborate control mechanisms have been applied to investment, finance, profits, prices, imports, exports, and other kinds of transactions.

India's rationale for using direct controls rather than macroeconomic and market-oriented policies is multifold. One explanation, formulated in light of Pakistan's experience but equally applicable to India, is that (1) direct controls are regarded as more likely to achieve their objective; (2) civil servants are seen as more reliable than businessmen insofar as officials are thought to function in the public interest whereas businessmen are concerned only with private profits; (3) administrators are more available than the information needed to formulate macroeconomic policy; (4) some civil servants and businessmen have vested interests in perpetuating the systems of direct controls; and (5) it is believed that equity objectives are served better through direct controls.[14] Other political and social reasons to add to this list are that bureaucrats charged with business responsibilities prefer to deal with their fellow bureaucrats through a licensing system and also that control systems have served as a medium for reaching political compromises among competing economic interests.[15] Finally, according to some observers, the administrative control mechanism is an important and growing link between the need for the ruling political

[14]Gustav F. Papanek, *Pakistan's Development, Social Goals and Private Incentives* (Cambridge, Mass.: Harvard University Press, 1967).

[15]Benjamin I. Cohen, "The International Development of India and Pakistan," in E. A. G. Robinson and Michael Kidron, eds., *Economic Development in South Asia: Proceedings of a Conference Held by the International Economic Association at Kandy, Ceylon,* (New York: St. Martin's Press, 1970), pp. 552–553.

party to finance itself and its ability to bestow favors on Indian businessmen.[16]

A distinctive characteristic of India's administrative controls is the underlying rationale: not only does the state know best how decisions should be made to maximize the community welfare, but in the absence of close scrutiny, individuals will take advantage of their positions and exploit the weak with little regard for the effect of their behavior on the society. In reality, however, the selfish behavior which administrative controls are designed to counteract is characteristic of various subnational actors, ranging from individual businessmen and state governments to enterprises owned by the central government. The self-serving policies followed by many private firms are well known, but the comparable antisocial practices of official bodies are less well understood. Among the more blatant of these practices are the efforts of Indian states to obtain oil refineries, steel mills, and other symbols of modern industry, much in the style of newly independent nations. According to one seasoned observer, local officials often couch their arguments in terms of local benefits without regard to national costs or national alternatives. The use of civil disobedience in 1956 to coerce Delhi to locate an oil refinery in Assam is an instance of how, in the absence of convincing economic logic, state authorities went so far as to promote agitation to get their way.[17]

That pervasive governmental intervention in the economy elicits major resistance and generates substantial tension is not surprising. At a personal level, direct controls invite businessmen and government officials to view each other as adversaries, and their mutual mistrust leads them to attribute antisocial and self-serving motives to one another despite coinciding interests. Consequently, their relationships are played out antagonistically on the public stage and cooperatively in their more private dealings. The problem with this situation, which I discuss later in greater detail, is, first, that some of the public posturing does spill over and color actual decisions and, second, that the need to convince reluctant government officials to be more forthcoming invites corruption.

To criticize India's system of administrative controls is not to advocate unbridled free enterprise for India. Indeed, the behavior of many Indian private entrepreneurs is such as to demand public supervision. Moreover, in the absence of any large-scale experiment with other kinds of economic regimes there is no way of knowing whether these would produce superior results. Nonetheless, as will be demonstrated in the next several chapters, the frailties of the administrative control system are so great that there is a strong case for finding means to reduce official involvement in the economy.

Government Direct Participation in the Economy

Some economic activities have been regarded by Delhi as so critical to the national interest as to preclude their being left to the private sector. National

[16]See, for example, Krishan Bhatia, *Indira: A Biography of Prime Minister Gandhi* (New York: Praeger Publishers, 1974).

[17]Myron Weiner, *The Politics of Scarcity* (Chicago: University of Chicago Press, 1962), pp. 207–209.

ownership of railways, public utilities, heavy industry, and commercial banks, for example, is predicated on the dual rationale that the development impact of these activities can be strengthened through direct public control and that the fruits of their operations should be shared by the entire nation rather than a small clique of capitalists. The growth of government entrepreneurship (discussed in Chapter 9) has been limited by (1) the shortage of financial resources available for government to make new investments and to compensate shareholders of nationalized companies and (2) official concern that the technical and managerial resources needed to operate government enterprises efficiently could be developed only over time. These factors, combined with political pressures to perpetuate the private sector, have retarded but not stopped the expansion of public sector industry.

Public Versus Private Sector: A Moot Issue?

Since before Independence, an acrimonious struggle has raged in India over the relative roles of public and private sector enterprise. In 1947, the balance of power between the proponents of these alternatives was such that if the death dates of Nehru and Sardar Patel had been reversed, India might have adopted industrial policies very much in favor of private enterprise. Be that as it may, and despite numerous tactical victories by India's private sector, Delhi has gradually given a distinctive socialist tilt to its policies affecting large-scale industrial production. Meanwhile, private interests in the agricultural and small-scale sectors have been comparatively free of government controls although still very much at the mercy of official policies affecting the prices of farm inputs and outputs.

In retrospect, the process whereby the government gradually assumed control over the economy's "commanding heights" is clear, more so than it could possibly have been to the socialist-inclined leaders who implemented it. The process involves four principal elements. First was the decision, taken shortly after Independence, to concentrate new large-scale investments in the public sector and to restrain private sector investment through a licensing mechanism. Second, these policies were reinforced by the government's practice of giving preference to the public sector in the allocation of foreign exchange and scarce domestic resources. Third, nationalization of existing firms took place to a limited extent in the mid-1950s and again in 1969 and subsequent years. The fourth element, official control over the managements of privately owned firms, has been described as "backdoor nationalization" and was facilitated by India's 1969 bank nationalization. The Indian government has progressively used its near monopoly over financial resources as a means to gain a major voice in the policies of private companies.

The combined impact of these factors has been to make the issue of public versus private ownership increasingly irrelevant except insofar as it affects the distribution of income between labor and capital. Moreover, by a curious coincidence, just as control over the private sector has grown more public, there has been a trend to make public sector enterprise increasingly independent of the formal government structure. Through administrative reforms and institutional changes such as the creation of the Steel Authority of India, Ltd. (SAIL), a holding company for various public sector enterprises in the metals sector, there has been an effort to professionalize government-owned companies. The result is that there has been a convergence of the public and private sectors in the sense that with growing frequency both are run by professional managers who are motivated by the same mix of corporate and social objectives.

To the extent that this convergence will endure, the conflict over the future of large private industry has for all practical purposes been laid to rest. To say this is not tantamount to writing the obituary of the private sector because there are still a number of powerful owner-managers as well as smaller entrepreneurs who in many ways remain independent of official policy. It does suggest, however, that the importance of the public versus private sector debate—which continues to be vitriolic—has diminished and that there has been a change in the agenda of industrial policy issues. Questions which have become more prominent are (1) whether the control over production will be vested in a cadre of independent civil servants or whether the politicians will seek to exercise excessive control over company operations; (2) whether Indian industry will receive the investments and competent management it will require if it is to grow and be efficient; and, related to the above, (3) whether government direction to the industrial sector will be effected through market mechanisms or direct controls.

Two Process Variables and a Structural Change

Distinct from the objectives of development and the policy instruments discussed above is the economic process through which progress occurs. It is a truism that for India or any other country to accelerate its growth, either or both of two conditions must obtain: either (1) the ratio of investment to national income (equal to the savings ratio) must be increased and consumption's share decreased, or (2) the productivity of the nation's capital stock must be improved. If the efficiency of existing plant and equipment can be increased, a given amount of production can be obtained by using a smaller amount of capital investment. The so-called Harrod-Domar model of economic growth, initially formulated to explain Western economies but later adapted to developing countries, provides the theoretical underpinning for regarding the size and efficiency of the capital stock as critical variables.[18]

The practical significance of these two factors, which I call "process varia-

[18]See Bhagwati and Chakravarty, op. cit.

bles," is readily apparent from a reading of Plan documents. In the First Plan, for example, the savings rate was estimated to be roughly 5 to 6 percent of national income and the capital/output ratio 3:1. In conjunction, these parameters led the Planning Commission to predict a growth rate of 2 to 2.25 percent per annum.[19] The Second Plan made a more daring attempt at planning for the long term, according to which the

> proportion of investment to national income is assumed to rise from 5 per cent or so in 1950–51 to about 20 per cent by 1968–69 and to remain at that level thereafter; and the capital-output ratio was taken at 3:1 with a time lag of two years between the increase in investment and the increase in output.[20]

In reality, these variables did not perform as envisaged in the Plan, and expectations of how they would behave were revised on numerous occasions. Nonetheless, they served as bench marks for planners who used them to conceptualize the course of India's development and to evaluate economic performance. Moreover, in combination with population estimates they provided a frame for viewing how per capita growth would preceed. For example, whereas the First Plan projected that India's real national income could be doubled in 21 years, by making assumptions about fertility and mortality rates it also was able to target a doubling of per capita real income in 27 years.[21]

Giving real meaning to these process variables is infinitely more difficult than stating their existence, especially because the bulk of Indian economic policy has been devoted to bringing about a structural change—modernization. The five principal aspects of the structural change are (1) increasing opportunities and incentives for savings and investment; (2) changing the composition of investment, i.e., shifting production from machines that produce consumer items to machines that produce other machines; (3) upgrading the productivity of the capital stock by using technologies appropriate to Indian conditions and by exploiting new interindustry linkages; (4) raising the productivity of labor both directly by improving skills and indirectly through better health, nutrition, education, and related factors; and (5) shifting the composition of output so as better to serve India's priorities, i.e., producing exports, goods for communal consumption, and mass consumer goods rather than luxury items.[22]

As should now be clear, the attraction of planning is that, within the Indian framework of innumerable constraints, it promises to make maximum use of available resources. Planning also promises to synthesize India's major economic policy objectives into a composite goal and to emphasize the complementarity rather than conflicts which exist among the subparts. Thus, improved welfare for the people is seen as both the goal of modernization and the

---

[19]A. Ghosh, "The Evolution of Planning Techniques and Organization in India," *Economics of Planning*, vol. 4, no. 1 (1964), p. 33.

[20]*Second Five-Year Plan*, op. cit., p. 8.

[21]Ibid.

[22]See *Draft Fifth Five-Year Plan*, op. cit., vol. 1, pp. 8–13.

instrumental variable indispensable for its achievement. Consequently, the technical aspects of economic policy and India's efforts to raise the expectations of the masses, improve welfare, reduce caste and communal discrimination, and otherwise escape from the inertia of traditional society and the colonial experience of stagnation are but interlinked parts of a single development strategy.

The Planning Commission and the Plans

India's Planning Commission has long been a controversial body, not only because of disagreements over the substance of plans, but because of an institutional battle over its place in the government structure. Rhetorically, the Commission has often occupied stage center. Moreover, the comprehensiveness, precision, and self-confidence of Plan documents, and the centrality of the Plan in many books about India, all support the judgment of C. D. Deshmukh, a former finance minister, that "We have more or less come to accept the Planning Commission as being—like the poor it so intimately affects—always with us."[23] Even allowing for the passage of time, there is a remarkable difference between Deshmukh's view and that of Y. B. Chavan, a more recent finance minister, who is quoted as saying, "How does it matter if the [Plan] targets are unrealistic? After all, have we ever achieved targets in previous plans?"[24]

These views are not so difficult to reconcile as might appear to be the case: the role of the Planning Commission has declined; globally, there has been a growing recognition that planning is an inexact process, an art as well as a science; and there are significant differences of personality between Deshmukh and Chavan. The important point is that whereas the Plan has been a ubiquitous element in the Indian scene ever since the early 1950s, and has tended to monopolize conceptual approaches to India's development, its practical significance has varied over time. Even in its heyday, the Planning Commission's power within the government was limited and its scope for determining the shape of events outside government was still more restricted.

Nonetheless, the Planning Commission has been important: symbolically, it has been the outlet for the widespread Indian sentiment in favor of strong central control over the economy; substantively, it has affected the choice of economic policies. The Planning Commission, which Finance Minister Deshmukh heralded in his annual Budget Speech in February 1950, was the logical successor to the National Planning Committee, which Nehru had encouraged the Congress to establish in 1938 and was established by the colonial administration in 1944.[25] Moreover, it embodied a concept of planning which had earlier

---

[23]C. D. Deshmukh, op. cit., p. 69.

[24]New York Times, Dec. 10, 1973.

[25]An excellent treatise on India's planning is A. H. Hanson, *The Process of Planning* (London: Oxford University Press, 1966).

been endorsed by eight leading Indian industrialists.[26] Their so-called Bombay Plan, proposed in 1944, was most unusual because the authors transcended both their private business background and the conventional economic thinking of their era. Besides noting the contribution and responsibilities of Indian private enterprise, they laid heavy emphasis on the need to (1) provide minimum standards of living for all Indians and avoid gross inequalities in income and (2) allocate to the state both positive and negative instruments for directing the course of the national economy.[27]

Despite this historical groundwork, economic planning was anything but the vogue in the non-Communist countries after World War II, and it was regarded with suspicion by many who feared that it might not be compatible with the concept of democracy practiced in the West. Accordingly, India's movement toward a formal system of planning was cautious and deliberate. Ironically, socialist ideology played only a limited role in getting the First Plan under way in 1951; of greater immediate consequence was the feeling that planning would accelerate development, and the First Plan drew heavily on India's preparations for participation in the Commonwealth-sponsored Colombo Plan.[28] Moreover, from the outset some highly placed Indians had realized that financial and technical assistance from abroad could be critically important to India. Deshmukh assumed this in his Budget Speech of February 28, 1951, when he said:

> There is an increasing recognition by the more fortunately placed countries
> of the West and the Western Hemisphere that their help in this urgent task
> [development] is necessary and that the raising of the living standards of
> these backward areas is vital for the peace and stability of the world.[29]

In addition to the value of the Plans as a means to convince foreign governments that India needed financial aid and could use it wisely, there were other nonideological reasons for planning. These included the results which Moscow had achieved in accelerating its industrial development and the somewhat comparable benefits that wartime controls had provided for Western economies. Planning appeared not only as a logical way to improve India's economic situation quickly but was compatible with—even ideally suited to—the Brahmanical culture with its emphasis on ritual, hierarchy, and social order. Nayar has noted that a variety of unrelated political constituencies supported planning. These included "the economic technocrats at the Indian Statistical Institute and the Planning Commission, the foreign economic advisers with leftist

[26]They were J. R. D. Tata, Purshottamdas Thakurdas, G. D. Birla, Ardeshir Dalal, Shri Ram, Kastughai Lalbhai, A. D. Shroff, and John Matthai.

[27]Tarlok Singh, "The Bombay Plan Recalled," *Eastern Economist*, June 7, 1963, pp. 1178–80, and Deshmukh, op. cit., pp. 70–73.

[28]Nayar, op. cit., p. 30.

[29]Quoted in Deshmukh, op. cit., p. 79.

orientation, and the top level political élite with its recently affirmed socialist commitment."[30]

The First Plan, as I have noted, was little more than a collection of projects already under way. Nonetheless, it contained implicit Harrod-Domar calculations about the short- and long-term possibilities for increasing investment, the productivity of capital, and the rate of economic growth. Even a cursory look at the Plan shows that the competing Gandhian path to economic development and the self-reliance and social justice objectives were treated respectfully, but that the bows to cottage industries and social welfare were not sufficient to rank these goals as coequal with growth. This conclusion is confirmed by budgetary and other evidence of this and subsequent periods which shows that population planning and other social programs were usually the first casualties of adverse economic conditions.

The Second Plan was considerably less modest in its objectives and technically more sophisticated than its predecessor. Even though much of the economic progress achieved during 1951–1956 was due to good weather and other factors having nothing to do with the Plan, development in this period increased India's self-confidence in its ability to manage the economy and, after a serious debate, the government initiated a "bold" effort to accelerate development. P. C. Mahalanobis, India's foremost planner and Nehru's chief economic adviser, developed a variant of the Harrod-Domar model which distinguished two major economic sectors (capital goods and consumer goods) and was subsequently refined to deal with transactions among four sectors.[31] Another significant departure of the Second Plan from its predecessor was its shift in emphasis from a Keynesian concern for *financial* flows such as savings to *structural* and *physical* aspects of investment and interindustry linkages.[32]

The boldness of the Second Plan is indicated by its size, more than twice that of its predecessor as measured in current rupee values during a period when inflation was minimal. (See Table 7-1.) Also notable is the degree to which the Plan succeeded in its objective of promoting industrial development at the expense of some other economic sectors. Actual Plan outlays on industry and mining rose from 4.9 to 24.1 percent, while the share of agriculture, irrigation, and power declined from 44.5 to 30.6 percent. Spending on social services also diminished, from 24.1 percent of the total to 18.3 percent.

Two other features of the Second Plan were significant for later years. First was the decision to ignore the implications for foreign trade of Ricardo's doctrine of comparative advantage. This choice, which is explained more fully in Chapter 9, reduced the economy's efficiency by requiring India to develop import substitutes for a wide range of commodities, including costly capital-

---

[30]Nayar, op. cit., p. 53.

[31]These were investment goods, factory consumer goods, household industry (including agriculture), and services.

[32]Bhagwati and Chakravarty, op. cit., p. 3.

TABLE 7-1
PLAN PRIORITIES BY SECTOR*

	Agriculture and community development		Irrigation and power		Industry and mining		Transport and communications		Social services and miscellaneous		Total	
	Planned	Actual	Planned	Actual	Planned	Actual	Planned	Actual	Planned	Actual	Planned	Actual
(Billions of rupees)												
First Plan	3.6	2.9	6.5	5.8	1.9	1.0	5.7	5.2	6.2	4.8	23.8	19.6
Second Plan	5.7	5.5	9.1	8.2	8.9	11.2	13.8	12.6	10.4	8.5	48.0	46.7
Third Plan	10.7	10.9	16.6	18.3	17.8	19.7	14.9	21.1	15.0	14.9	75.0	85.8
Interim (1966–1969)	10.4	11.7	14.9	16.4	16.7	17.2	12.7	12.4	11.9	9.9	66.6	67.6
Fourth Plan†	27.3	27.4	35.3	40.8	36.3	32.4	32.4	29.8	27.7	31.5	159.0	162.0
Fifth Plan‡	47.3	...	88.7	...	89.3	...	71.1	...	77.3	...	372.5	...
(Percentage distribution)												
First Plan	15.1	14.8	28.1	29.7	7.6	4.9	23.6	26.4	25.6	24.1	100.0	100.0
Second Plan	11.8	11.7	19.0	18.9	18.6	24.1	28.9	27.0	21.7	18.3	100.0	100.0
Third Plan	14.3	12.7	22.1	22.4	23.7	22.9	19.9	24.6	20.0	17.4	100.0	100.0
Interim (1966–1969)	15.6	17.3	22.4	24.3	25.1	25.4	19.1	18.3	17.9	14.7	100.0	100.0
Fourth Plan†	17.2	16.9	22.2	25.2	22.0	20.0	20.4	18.4	17.4	19.5	100.0	100.0
Fifth Plan‡	12.7	...	23.8	...	23.9	...	19.0	...	20.7	...	100.0	...

*Pattern of Plan outlays in the public sector.

†Estimated.

‡Projected.

Sources: For First, Second, and Third Plans, India: Pocket Book of Economic Information (New Delhi: GOI, Ministry of Finance); for Third, Fourth, and Fifth Plans and interim, RBI, Report on Currency and Finance: 1973–74.

intensive industries. Second, because Mahalanobis recognized that his heavy investment strategy would not be a powerful creator of employment in the short run and that it would generate consumer demands, he also was a proponent of the labor-intensive, nonfactory consumer goods sector. Thus, in a curious way his priorities partly coincided with the ideological bias of the Gandhians, and he was able to make his economic approach acceptable to the nation.[33]

India's Third Plan made no radical departures from its predecessor. Its outstanding technical innovations were the further disaggregation of the economy by sector, an effort to assure greater consistency between supply and demand and among the various sectors, a hesitant consideration of importing as a means for relieving bottlenecks, and some use of linear programming techniques to map the dynamics of the Indian economy. In its sectoral emphasis, the Third Plan was similar to its predecessor, only on a larger scale.

In contrast to the consensus which greeted the First Plan, the Second and Third Plans had their avid supporters but also attracted much criticism. The critics regarded these Plans as faulty on grounds that they (1) assumed incorrectly that the efficiency of capital would be the same regardless of how much new investment took place or what new technologies were introduced (i.e., constant capital/output ratios); (2) overstated the possibility for increasing the rate of investment and the share of investment that could be allocated to the capital goods sector; and (3) devoted too much attention to heavy industry at the expense of agriculture. In short, both the size and underlying framework of the Plans were challenged. The unkindest professional criticism of all came retrospectively from two Indian economists who concluded that Mahalanobis's "four sector model was essentially produced to impart (unsuccessfully, as it turned out) intellectual respectability to investment allocations arrived at on other, unspecified considerations."[34]

A persuasive and rather different kind of criticism is Nayar's thesis that the bold economic strategy did not fit with India's "reconciliation" and democratic political system. According to his analysis the Plan

> was an extremely ambitious need-based rather than a resource-based plan, imposing "forced savings" on the community; . . . the emphasis on heavy industry meant the postponement of immediate "pay-offs" or "gratifications"; . . . the lack of emphasis on agriculture and consumer goods placed restraints on mass consumption; . . . the burdens and tasks assumed by the government were beyond its skills and organizational resources.[35]

Although there is no denying that India's choice of economic strategy is among the reasons why development expectations have not always been met, it is difficult to identify which of Nayar's lines of criticisms are most correct. The

[33]See Kochanek, *Congress Party of India*, op. cit., pp. 177–180.
[34]Jagdish N. Bhagwati and Padma Desai, op. cit., p. 238.
[35]Nayar, op. cit., p. 54.

Fourth Plan, which was delayed for three years to permit the Indian economy to recover from the shocks of the early and middle 1960s and the shortfalls of previous plans, contained no dramatic new technical innovations. The same is true of the provisional Fifth Plan presented in 1974. Nonetheless, the Fourth and Draft Fifth Plans were anything but carbon copies of their predecessors. Spending during the Fourth deemphasized industry in favor of agriculture and social services. The Draft Fifth Plan sought to maintain past growth objectives while redirecting attention to social justice through larger planned investments in (1) irrigation and other areas where large, strategic and sometimes rapid payoffs could be obtained and (2) social services where the economic return would be likely to require a long gestation period. A significant innovation which began with the Fourth Plan is the reappraisal of India's foreign trade options and the decision to intensify the export effort.

Despite these changes and the mystique which continues to surround the planning process, it has become increasingly apparent that the Plan does not carry as much moral authority and policy weight as in earlier years. The provisional Fifth Plan showed signs of stress long before its publication, as suggested by the sharp criticisms leveled against its approach papers in early 1973.[36] Indeed, one member of the Planning Commission, B. S. Minhas, took such exception to what he regarded as the unrealism of interindustry balances and other parameters, and the gap between Plan rhetoric and technical reality, that he took the unprecedented step of resigning from the Commission in 1973.

The stress which has characterized the Fifth Plan can be related to transitory events such as the dislocations caused by droughts and the excessive politicization of Indian public policy beginning in 1969. More basically, however, it reflects the conflict of urgent economic demands and scarce resources. The price escalation of food and fertilizer, which began in 1972, and energy, which began in late 1973, affected India more than most other countries. As an adverse blow to development it was without parallel. Unless India is able to obtain foreign financing to pay for the substantial amounts of energy and fertilizer imports which it needs—and until India develops its own fossil fuel reserves—the short- and long-term prospect for the Fifth Plan is bound to be more fantasy than reality. This is not to say that the role of planning in India will disappear. Indeed, if India's economic crisis deepens, many will argue that the necessity for planning is enhanced. What it does suggest is that to cope with its new problems, India will find it expedient to make its planning more pragmatic and to coordinate better the work of the Planning Commission with the Finance and substantive ministries. Some planning is needed in India (if not in all countries), but if planning is to be productive, the process must be flexible and accommodate the peculiarities of India's "soft" society. The basis for this diagnosis should become evident from the next three chapters on India's agricultural, industrial, and financial policies.

[36]See, for example, various articles in the February 1973 Annual Number of *Economic and Political Weekly*.

CHAPTER 8
STRATEGIES FOR AGRICULTURE

However acerb and perennial the controversy in India as to whether the government has accorded due priority to rural problems, there can be no debate about the centrality of agriculture to the nation's development. The influence of agriculture permeates India's experience with economic growth, self-sufficiency, efforts to reduce mass unemployment, search for political stability, and many other areas. The distinction between improving agrarian conditions as (1) an objective of policy and (2) an instrument of policy further underscores the significance of agriculture. In the first instance, to realize economic development in India requires that the roughly four-fifths of the population living in rural areas and directly dependent on farm conditions share in the benefits. Second, one of the preconditions for India to achieve major economic and nonmaterial national goals, including such military aims as the 1971 victory over Pakistan, has been rural development and increased farm output.

For the coming decades, there is no credible development strategy which does not highlight agrarian progress. Even if food self-sufficiency were not a basic development objective (and I shall argue later that it should be in only a limited sense), India cannot reasonably foresee building the kind of industrial millennium which would provide foreign exchange to import large amounts of food. Moreover, it cannot anticipate a rapid diminution in its 2.2 percent population growth rate, or in the growing demand for food owing to rising incomes. Thus, given its current near-subsistence level of per capita calorie consumption, India has no choice but to target and achieve sustained and at least moderate growth in farm output. Finally, underlying the economic rationale for progress in agriculture, there is a political imperative: growing unemployment, scarcity of food in the marketplace, shortages, and inflated prices for agricultural raw materials used by industry all contribute to political malaise; if economic conditions are allowed to deteriorate beyond tolerable limits, the resulting political unrest will pose a threat to the united, stable, and democratic social order which the government is committed to support.

Can India Feed Itself?

We are indebted to Malthus for underscoring that man's inability to grow enough food is among the "natural" checks on population growth. But whereas the inevitability of the Malthusian scenario appears to have been disproved by emerging social patterns in the United States and other countries, its applicability to India and many developing nations remains in question. Curiously, much of the literature on the subject of India's food-growing capacity is characterized by an anything but scientific evolution of opinion; it swings cyclically from deep pessimism to moderate and even enthusiastic optimism. The somber judgment of Sir Henry Knight that "It is true to say that the really remarkable thing about Indian food administration from 1939 to 1947 was that there was only one famine"[1] contrasts sharply, first, with exaggerated perceptions of India's food shortage (in the second half of the 1960s, for example, the Paddocks applied the concept of triage to the food deficit nations and predicted that it would become necessary to sacrifice India in order to salvage other more manageable developing countries[2]), and, second, with the ultrasanguine attitude implied by the Fourth Plan's target of an unprecedented 5 percent per year agricultural growth rate. For the next several years it would be as imprudent to rule out the possibility of famine in India as to claim that India has solved its food problem; the truth lies between these extremes, and this middle ground must be examined closely because it encompasses situations of persistent malnutrition as well as food sufficiency.

Agricultural developments in India during the past 75 years show that the concern about famine is well based. In the first half of the twentieth century while India's agricultural production stagnated, population grew at less than 1 percent per year, not very fast but faster than the food output. The simultaneous neglect of both food production and public health during this period resulted in a slow erosion of the nation's capacity to feed itself and set the stage for the much-publicized crises of recent decades.[3] To some degree the drama which has unfolded since World War II can be traced to the newly independent Indian government's policy of improving health conditions without an equally

[1]Sir Henry Knight, *Food Administration in India: 1939–1947* (Stanford, Calif.: Stanford University Press, 1954), p. 274.

[2]Paul Paddock and William Paddock, *Famine—1975!* (London: George Weidenfeld & Nicolson, Ltd:, 1968).

[3]M. L. Dantwala, "Preface to Volume of Background Papers," in *International Seminar on Comparative Experiences of Agricultural Development in Developing Countries since World War II,* The Indian Society of Agricultural Economics, 1972. For detailed analysis of long-term trends in India's food production, see S. R. Sen, "Growth and Instability in Indian Agriculture," *Agricultural Situation in India,* vol. 21, no. 10, January 1967 (Directorate of Economics and Statistics, Ministry of Food and Agriculture, Government of India), and George Blyn, *Agricultural Trends in India, 1891–1947: Output, Availability, and Productivity* (Philadelphia: University of Pennsylvania Press, 1966).

dynamic program for increasing farm output. Because the country started in 1945 from a near-subsistence position, it was doomed to a high degree of dependence on the monsoon; every time the rains played truant for two or more consecutive years, there was bound to be trouble.

India's problem in part has been the unreliability of its external environment and the difficulty of anticipating with clarity the means and timetable for increasing food output. During the 1950s, for example, more than 50 percent of the increase in food output was obtained by expanding acreage as India impressed its few remaining virgin tracts (and some other lands which for the long run should not have been deforested) for food cultivation. In contrast, since 1965 the burden of expanding food output has been shifted to increasing per acre yields, and mercifully the new technology associated with the term "green revolution" became applicable just in time for it to take up the role which expanding acreage could no longer carry and which rising population demanded. For the future, there is no question that raising productivity will play the leading role in expanding food production.

Why then has there been such frequent and hysterical concern about India's ability to feed itself? The answer to this question, which is complex but not obscure, turns on the dynamic balance between population and food output growth rates. The heady optimism which attended the birth of the green revolution has given way to a more considered understanding of its fragility— of the problems and high costs of custom-designing the general technology to differing areas, bringing about the necessary institutional and other changes needed to apply it, and making requisite investments in infrastructure and production facilities. There is no question about the long-term applicability of the green revolution to much of India and its promise for the future, but the precise timing and costs of implementing the new technology are not easily predicted, and experience to date suggests that for India as a whole it may be more correct to think in terms of a "green evolution."

The world food crisis of 1973–1975, taken in conjunction with India's continued dependence on the monsoon, implies that India's *short-term* position must be regarded as precarious.[4] Although it may be reasonable to approach India's situation with the understanding that cyclical duress and bounty are the rule and that the prospect of mass famine is not great, we cannot forget that in the story of the little boy who cried "Wolf," the beast did finally present himself, and at the most inauspicious moment when people were no longer willing to take the little boy's cries seriously. For the *longer term*, India's inexorable population growth and rising income will create a growing demand for food and will require that India devote a considerable portion of its future development effort merely to maintain the currently inadequate nutrition standards of the poor. To do less would be unthinkable; to do more appears highly desirable.

---

[4]For a discussion of assumptions regarding growth of population, GNP, food output, income, elasticity of demand, etc., see Dantwala, "Preface," op. cit., pp. 10–11.

Agriculture's Central Role

Agriculture's critical place in the economy derives, in the first instance, from the importance of achieving at least near food self-sufficiency. But a comparison of the relatively self-sustaining farm technology prevailing at the time of Independence with the more sophisticated and industry-linked system currently in use reveals that this is merely one aspect of agriculture's central role. There always has been an interdependence between India's rural and urban populations, but a quarter century ago most Indian farmers were dependent on imports from the cities to only an insignificant degree. At that time cities were much smaller and required only a limited flow of commodities from outlying rural areas. In contrast, farmers today are much more reliant on purchases of fertilizer, insecticides, irrigation machinery, and energy; indeed, many of them use special hybrid seed purchased in the market rather than seed from their own harvests. To pay for these inputs, farmers require marketing systems, transportation, storage, and consumer demand for their production. Moreover, they are only one step removed from a dependence on India's ability to gain foreign exchange through exports or foreign aid because, without this purchasing power, they would not have adequate fertilizer and energy. The counterpart of modern agriculture's dependence on the city is the urban reliance on the farm population, not just as a source of food, but as a producer of industrial raw materials and as a consumer of goods and services produced in the cities.

From a systemic point of view, agriculture's development is essential to overall economic progress. Because of its size, agriculture is the major determinant of employment. Farm productivity and rural needs affect central and local budgets on both the income and expenditure sides. Progress in agriculture has a major impact on the rate of inflation, imports, exports, and the distribution of India's national income. Viewed from the perspective of what determines agricultural development, the role of nonrural factors is critical. Among the key variables are technological progress, the amount of resources invested in agriculture-related infrastructure and agribusiness, and, more generally, the efficiency with which the Indian economy is managed. The linkages between agriculture and the rest of the economy are now so extensive that it is not possible to envision a major advance in either sector in which the other did not participate.

If it is true that India's political stability hinges on progress in agriculture, the corollary—that agricultural development is dependent on the effectiveness of political leaders and government machinery—is equally valid. The trend away from subsistence farming has created new responsibilities for government officials, and it is increasingly apparent that, if the fabric of Indian society and the Indian Union are to be preserved, government must pursue development as vigorously as the old functions of collecting taxes and maintaining law and order. Indeed, there are multiple ties between the new and traditional responsibilities as, for example, between the need to fulfill at least some of the "revolution of rising expectations" in order to maintain political stability in the countryside.

Some more mundane, but no less important, aspects of how India's agricultural and political systems are interrelated were noted in Chapter 1. The Indian Constitution's definition of agriculture as a "state" subject deprives Delhi of the authority it enjoys in industrial policy. As a result, when it comes to critical decisions such as those affecting taxation, agrarian reform, and crop procurement, the central government is in a strong position to propose policies, but it is the states which are responsible for choosing among alternatives and implementing the law. Despite the Center's superior financial position and the existing discipline with the ruling Congress party, it is only in certain areas such as the availability and pricing of farm inputs and outputs that Delhi has major jurisdiction. Good examples of the central government's impotence in rural matters are land reform and the proposal for "cooperative joint farming," which aroused strong local resistance and, despite enthusiastic support from Nehru, were not implemented by the state governments.[5]

What makes the question of who has authority for ordering the rural economy so important is that there are major differences between the policy approaches of the state and central governments. In Delhi, there is a natural tendency to see problems from a national rather than a local perspective; elected officials are somewhat more removed intellectually and politically from parochial antimodernizing influences; and there is a greater concentration of highly intelligent and experienced civil servants. Elitist agricultural interests are by no means absent in Delhi, but they are more apparent in the state capitals, and in the villages they are often dominant. In a sense, there is an inverse relationship between the closeness of government officials to Delhi and the extent to which they reflect vested rural interests. An outstanding illustration of this situation is the ability of landlords to maintain their control over the local political and economic situation by calling for police assistance in local disputes.[6]

The dilemma posed by the limited power of the central government, despite its more enlightened approach to the nation's agricultural problems, is more than just a constitutional issue. If the basic thrust of India's development strategy toward mobilizing local initiative and mass participation is to be achieved, authority must be decentralized. But how can a socialist government add to the power of inegalitarian local authorities? The problem is compounded because it is not just government officials and large landowners who have a vested interest in the status quo; most rural people, the very poorest excluded, have some political interests which could be adversely affected by change. For example, despite their lack of affluence, smaller landlords often rent out a portion of their land and feel threatened whenever legislation is

---

[5]Thorner, op. cit., pp. 34–36.

[6]For a description of how even in recent years "order was maintained by sacrificing law" in West Bengal, see *Economic and Political Weekly*, Sept. 30, 1972, p. 2009.

proposed which would limit their incomes or reduce the size of their holdings. Similarly, even tenant farmers hire day labor on occasion, and they stand to lose if minimum-wage laws are enacted, Finally, there are cultural considerations which assume economic and political significance. For instance, because peasants tend to measure their self-esteem according to the status of their most powerful clan member in the local society, they sometimes oppose agrarian reform which would benefit them directly because of the harm it would do to the standing of the caste brother to whom they look for strength.[7]

It should now be apparent that however central agriculture may be to India's development, the relationship to the country's larger economic and political ethos is very complex. Moreover, the extreme diversity of the states' agricultural situations poses an additional barrier to the making and implementing of good policy. For example, how can India hope to have a national food policy when the Punjab, with less than 2.5 percent of India's population and only a 3.2 percent share of the nation's area sown for food grains, accounts for 7.1 percent of total food grain output; and when West Bengal, with more than 8 percent of the Indian people and 5 percent of the land, accounts for 7.4 percent of total output? Developments affecting the agrarian sector are not subject to easy generalization, and whereas it is possible to specify that growth, social justice, and self-reliance have been the three principal objectives of India's economic and agrarian strategies, specific policies tend to cut across these categories. Thus, in the pages that follow, there is some effort to organize the material around India's three primary objectives, but there is also considerable overlap.

Direct Measures to Induce Agricultural Growth

Before I examine the modalities of how India increased farm input, I must enter one caveat about the speed of growth and the hazards of attributing too much significance to year-to-year changes in performance. For the period 1949–50 to 1972–73 the compound annual growth rate for food grain production was 2.1 percent; the comparable growth rate for 1950–51 to 1970–71 was 3.5 percent. The large difference between these figures suggests that the most reasonable method for estimating is a statistically unbiased regression equation, according to which the trend growth rate for the full period 1949–50 to 1973–74 amounts to 2.8 percent. The variability of the growth path is critical to development, but in the discussion which follows, the reality that India has increased its food grain output by this substantial amount over an extended period of time should not be belittled, for it is a solid achievement.

Independent India's early strategy for agriculture consisted largely of a collection of autonomous initiatives for expanding irrigation, fertilizer, and extension programs. Commenting on the planning process, in light of India's

[7]Ashok Thapar, "Where Is the Surplus Land?" *Times of India,* May 15, 1972.

World War II "Grow More Food" (G.M.F.) policy, Professor D. R. Gadgil, who later became vice chairman of the Planning Commission, has said, "Both in the formulation of consistent programmes and in the measurement of their results little change in the procedures evolved in the G.M.F. campaign has been made by the adoption of the First or the Second Five-Year Plan."[8] A leading Indian industrialist, Dr. John Matthai, was substantially in agreement with this judgment. Writing in *Times of India* in 1956, he described the First Plan as a "programme of piecemeal development." His subsequent calling of attention to three significant changes which had affected India's situation is interesting because not one of them was totally indigenous. The factors noted by Matthai were the Community Development program, which had received the support of the Ford Foundation; the general economic revival abroad, which had stimulated India's exports; and increased food supplies due to better monsoons and the American Wheat Loan.[9]

The Community Development (CD) program, an initiative taken during the First Plan, captured the imagination of politicians and development specialists at the time and later came to play a major, albeit not entirely successful, role in India's strategy. This program was exciting because it aimed at raising farm production and income through various extension techniques and also by changing attitudes, introducing rural education and health care programs, and modernizing the lives of India's rural population. In short, it made an important link between raising economic output and abolishing social, cultural, legal, and other barriers to a freer community.

During the 1950s India had access to inexpensive food imports, new lands still remained to be opened to cultivation, productivity was increased on established lands, and, at least during the first half of the decade, monsoons were better than average. For these reasons India was able to act on the then almost universally accepted belief that industrialization was the path to economic wealth and national strength and to focus its attention on the industrial aspects of development. By 1957, however, the growing problems of Indian agriculture forced a reevaluation of policies and priorities. The finding of that review was that the Community Development, cooperative, and other agricultural programs were failing to meet growth, social justice, and self-reliance objectives. Although the Community Development program had been extended to more than one-fourth of the country by 1957 and had achieved impressive results in some areas, it was lacking in many respects. One study team, chaired by Balwantray Mehta, found that CD administrators favored social services rather than economic aspects of the program because they were easier to implement and produced showier results.[10] This situation was particularly troublesome

---

[8]Gadgil, op. cit., p. 161.

[9]John Matthai, article in *Times of India,* May 16, 1956; cited in Hanson, op. cit., p. 119.

[10]Government of India, Planning Commission, *Report of the Team for the Study of Community Projects and National Extension Service,* 3 vols. (New Delhi, 1957), vol. 2, pp. 96ff.

because in many areas the quality of social services tended to disintegrate as villagers progressively assumed responsibility for the programs and outside support was reduced.[11] Even more disturbing, the Mehta committee found that there were inadequate supplies of fertilizer, improved seeds, and farm credits and that the program's greatest beneficiaries—from the point of view both of accessibility to its offerings and of ability to put them to productive use—were the large, already well-to-do owner-cultivated farms.[12]

These results were attributed by the committee to the linkage at the village level of economic and social status.[13] In effect, through their control of the political process, large landowners were able to appropriate for themselves more than a just share of the assistance coming from outside the village. A second rationale was suggested by Professor Gadgil, who argued that to become effective, the planning mechanism would have to be made much more detailed and also more sensitive to local diversity. According to Gadgil, much could be achieved in these directions through an enhanced two-way flow of information between the Center and local authorities.[14] It is an irony of history that when Gadgil later presided over the Planning Commission, the green revolution was in vogue and the emphasis on agroindustry and related areas permitted relatively little attention to the kinds of microplanning which he regarded as appropriate for Indian agriculture.

India's cooperative movement has encountered many of the same problems as Community Development. Mahatma Gandhi is prominent among those who have emphasized the economic and social virtues of formal cooperation, and since Independence, India has experimented with many small and large programs to gauge the possibilities for cooperation in the agrarian sector. By 1957, however, it was already known that cooperative credit societies were more successful than cooperatives based on the joint use of resources, cultivation of land, etc., but not even the credit societies had shown nationwide success. Moreover, in states such as Gujarat, where credit cooperatives abounded and generally remained solvent, they tended to favor the already well-to-do and to magnify income disparities. The political reasons for this and the underlying controversy between traditional forces and economic democracy were poignantly noted by Theodor Bergmann:

> Co-operation in the village faces heavy odds. The social and political order, antiquated systems of land tenure, the caste system and finally, the close ties between the upper strata and the government administration, militate against the establishment of co-operation (as the lever to improve the position of the poor). Under these conditions, massive State aid is needed to

[11]Ibid., vol. 1, p. 105.

[12]Ibid., vol. 2, p. 101.

[13]See P. C. Joshi, "Community Development Programmes: A Reappraisal," *Enquiry*, no. 3 (1960), reprinted in A. M. Khusro, ed., *Readings in Agricultural Development* (Bombay: Allied Publishers, 1968).

[14]See Gadgil, op. cit.

counter-balance the impact of vested interests. Government funds already provide part of the credit societies' share and working capital. But co-operation to carry out its giant task, needs more, not less, State help. Such help is not in accordance with the tenets of Western co-operative movement; worse than that, it implies official intervention and tutelage, possibly a severe limitation of the members' own democratic activity. The State will have to see to it that the active participation of members in co-operative management is encouraged by all means. Government intervention should be withdrawn as soon as a sufficient number of members is available for management. The best intentions, the best statutory regulations will fail to operate as long as members are unable, or fail, to exercise their rights and duties.[15]

Both the Community Development and cooperative institutions tended to operate best in the areas where they were needed least, and, with the passage of time, it became increasingly clear that however elaborate the administrative machinery of the Planning Commission, Agriculture Ministry, and state organizations down to the Block Development Office and Village Level Workers, India's backward areas were not progressing very fast and a new approach was needed to achieve real growth and genuine reform. Thus, in 1958, in response to the Balwantray Mehta committee report and other critics, the government decided to try more rather than less democracy as a means to rejuvenate the Community Development and cooperative programs. In practice, this meant the initiation of the *panchayati raj* system of local self-government (see Chapter 1) and a variety of experimental economic and social programs.

Another watershed was reached in 1959 when the report of a Ford Foundation "Food Crisis" team was submitted.[16] Heavily criticized at the time, but justified by subsequent developments, the Ford report argued that the issue on which agrarian progress would turn was whether India's millions of cultivators could be induced to adopt a multitude of small changes in their daily routines. Because it advocated that greater financial rewards should be given as a means to motivate farmers and suggested that more attention be paid to the production rather than the social aspects of agricultural programs, the Ford report was particularly controversial. Finally, based on the linkage between farm inputs and output, the report recommended adoption of a major program to improve the seed, water, fertilizer, and insecticide resources available to farmers. The Ford experts noted that the marginal output which could be derived from solo use of each of these inputs was small (in some cases it was negative), but applying large amounts of them in fixed proportions, the so-called package program, promised to increase yields vastly.

[15]Theodor Bergmann, "Co-operation in India: Selected Aspects," *Year-book of Agricultural Co-operation,* reprinted in A. M. Khusro, ed., *Readings in Agricultural Development,* op. cit., pp. 439–440.

[16]Agricultural Production Team Sponsored by the Ford Foundation; see *Ford Foundation Report on India's Food Crisis and Steps to Meet It* (New Delhi: GOI, Ministries of Food and Agriculture and of Community Development and Cooperation, 1959).

The Community Development and cooperative programs, because of both their psychological appeal and the reality that they have benefited well-to-do and politically powerful rural interests, have become rather more permanent aspects of India's development strategy than their accomplishments warrant. Nonetheless, as they failed to pay the large national dividends anticipated at the start, their share of total funds available for rural development has tended to decline, a development which is concealed by recent crash programs for relieving rural unemployment. John Mellor regards India's continuing emphasis on the CD program while the cooperative movement has tended to wither as evidence that within limits India's agricultural policies have been pragmatic.[17] In short, the continued existence of the Community Development program should be interpreted as a reflection of the Indian political system's sensitivity to the influence of vested interests, as well as to a recognition of CD's noneconomic achievements, which are not easily quantified.

What was new in India's effort to spur agricultural development after 1959 was the major augmentation in the research effort and the effort to demonstrate that the massing of various inputs, as described by the Ford Foundation team and elsewhere, would deliver the necessary output. Thus, when the experimental Intensive Agricultural District Programme (IADP) was inaugurated in 1961, it featured increasing farm output rather than improving the conditions of rural life. Consideration of the package program approach was delayed, however, until the IADP could show positive results and until the critical 1964 food crisis and 1965–1967 drought spurred implementation of the new strategy on a scale large enough to merit use of the term "green revolution."

The Green Revolution: Achievements and Limitations

The green revolution was hardly an overnight phenomenon; in reality it drew on a wide variety of elements already present in Indian agriculture. And in challenging the dismal economic prognostications of the Paddocks and others, it promised to change totally the outlook for feeding India's population and transforming the social system. In response to the green revolution's need for inputs, India stepped up its exploitation of latent resources such as groundwater and rural labor; it accelerated and innovated programs to harness hydroelectric and other energy sources needed to pump the water; it allocated more foreign exchange and initiated industrial programs for producing fertilizer and pesticides, even going so far as to permit grudgingly some new foreign investment in the fertilizer industry; the government began programs of transportation and storage to manage the enlarged output; and it stepped up its

---

[17]John W. Mellor et al., *Developing Rural India: Plan and Practice* (Ithaca, N.Y.: Cornell University Press, 1968), p. 124.

research and training programs. Perhaps most important, the government allocated better management talent to agriculture, as exemplified by the appointment of the comparatively youthful but dynamic C. Subramaniam as the nation's agricultural minister. On the basis of experience with Indian farmers which showed that they are neither lazy nor impervious to economic opportunities to improve their conditions, the government launched with considerable success an Intensive Agricultural Area Programme (IAAP) in 1965[18] and a High Yielding Varieties Programme (HYVP) in 1966. Moreover, in contrast to previous agricultural programs which for equity reasons had had an all-India thrust, the new approach concentrated on those geographic areas where it was most likely to succeed quickly.

Outstanding results were obtained in the Punjab, Haryana, and western Utter Pradesh, where a dwarf variety of wheat, developed in Mexico by Norman Borlaug for the Rockefeller Foundation, seemed ideally suited to local growing conditions. In the crop year 1967–68, for example, those farmers in the Ludhiana district of Punjab who adopted the new technology were able to increase their average per acre wheat yields from 2,108 pounds in the previous year to 4,235 pounds. Moreover, even though the market value of the new wheat varieties was slightly lower than that of indigenous crops and the cost of inputs higher, farmers were able to increase their profits by more than 70 percent.[19]

The infant green revolution could not offset the disastrous monsoons of 1965 and 1966, but beginning with the 1967–68 crop year, the situation took a dramatic turn for the better, and nationwide statistics for cereal production set new highs for four consecutive years. The transformation was so striking that "second generation" problems of food storage, transportation, and village-level income disparities became more pressing than the original problem of increasing food production. Consequently, expectations that food crisis and dependence on imported grain were over became commonplace among Indian officials and politicians, many of whom allowed themselves to be lulled into an ill-based overconfidence which blinded them to the need for taking further measures to assure future gains. Thus, India was rudely shocked when food grain production plummeted by more than 10 percent in the early 1970s and the green revolution did not prove to be the panacea that the nation's crisis-weary leaders had wished.

The first set of reasons why the benefits of the green revolution have not been available more quickly relates to the problems of moving from the general strategy to specific applications on an all-India scale. India's size and its great regional diversity were significant in this respect. The uneven geographic

[18]This was based on the Intensive Agricultural District Programme.

[19]Francine R. Frankel and Karl von Vorys, "The Political Challenge of the Green Revolution: Shifting Patterns of Peasant Participation in India and Pakistan," Policy Memorandum No. 38, Center for International Studies, Woodrow Wilson School of Public and International Affairs, Princeton University, 1972, p. 13.

impact of the green revolution is explained by a number of factors: the new hybrid wheat seeds were available before equivalent rice varieties; climate dictated that not all areas of India were appropriate for wheat cultivation and that it was much more difficult to grow rice in the dry season than during the monsoon; some areas, such as the Tanjore Valley and Andhra coast, were able to adopt the available new rice hybrids more easily than other regions; and cultivation in the Gangetic plain was dogged by an enormous drainage problem due to the flatness of the terrain. Cultural diversity among regions, India's inability to provide the entire nation with needed inputs and extension on such short notice, and other factors are also significant.

There is little doubt that geneticists eventually will develop appropriate rice hybrids, but for the short term the failure to do so is a major factor in limiting the green revolution; despite the explosion of wheat production, rice remains India's single most important food crop. The search for a rice breakthrough proved more difficult than was contemplated at first. Many early experiments with rice were not successful because the new hybrids proved very vulnerable to disease, demanded control of irrigation beyond what was available, or were otherwise unsuitable to Indian conditions. Moreover, because the subsistence nature of the Indian farmer's household economy puts great emphasis on avoiding risks, it was incumbent on government to proceed cautiously and to avoid large-scale distribution of a less than satisfactory rice variety.

The second set of reasons why the green revolution has been slow to live up to its full potential, which overlaps the first set, concerns the problems of developing particular inputs. Water, for example, has remained scarce, in part because of the shortage of management talent needed to improve administration of existing irrigation facilities and to develop new sources, such as India's largely untapped groundwater reserves. To say that a major expansion of India's farm output cannot be contemplated without a commensurate improvement in the supply of water resources is to imply that there is need not only for the finding of new water and its timely diversion into crop areas, but for solutions to such diverse problems as salinity (research), inadequate drainage (investment), and how water is to be shared among farmers (political-legal). There is little doubt that India still has large unexploited water resources, but mobilizing them for irrigation purposes is costly and time-consuming.

Equally knotty problems exist for inorganic fertilizers. Whereas production and use of this input have grown enormously, planning for fertilizer imports, domestic production, distribution, and pricing have tended to lag behind India's needs for various reasons. In building domestic fertilizer factories, for example, India has (1) accepted second-rate technology from the Soviets; (2) been extremely wary of private sector investments and collaboration agreements with foreign investors; and (3) been niggardly in appropriating budget funds. The net result of these actions is that there has been a persistent shortage of fertilizers; both growth and social justice have been sacrificed insofar as the rural elite have been advantageously placed to get more than their fair share of available fertilizer supplies. What we have said about India's water and fertilizer strategies can be applied with equal justification to research, training, extension, power, and other areas.

It is at the macroeconomic level that the third major set of reservations about India's green revolution arises. Economic planning and policy implementation suffered from misperceptions and inadequate perceptions of the specific steps needed to capitalize on the new technology. As John Mellor has put it, "Planners have made the error of not planning the next step until the last step has proven insufficient."[20] At the same time, when it came to massive action, government was peculiarly insensitive to the broader economic questions of how large investment programs would have to be timed to make available the right mix of inputs, the priority of agriculture relative to industry, the close linkage of industrial progress to rural prosperity, and the pervasive impact of farm conditions on the economy as a whole. In addition, planners tended to regard the relationships between new investment and incremental output (capital/output ratios) as fixed rather than as a target for change. Most important, by not assuring adequate food supplies to all areas of the country, they were unable to exploit what would have been an economic bonanza if they could have had each region of the country specialize in producing the crops best-suited to its agricultural conditions and thus could have rationalized the country's use of its farm resources. In short, the government's failure to assure adequate food supplies to all parts of the country led farmers to grow food rather than other crops.

Before judging India's planners too harshly, however, it must be noted that similar economic errors were made in many developing countries and that ignorance of how to proceed was common also among foreign experts from both the West and Soviet camps. There were two tiers of political barriers to what, in retrospect, appears to have been a more effective strategy. First, inertia, ideology, current conventional economic wisdom, and the fashionable standard for measuring national prestige by industrial status were all on the side of pressing the industrial priority at the expense of agriculture. Second, in rural India the political elite were skeptical about how the local power structure would be affected by the new techniques and they were often in a position to delay modernization until they were satisfied that the new strategy was not only profitable but in their political interests.

I shall address the question of social justice later in this chapter. Suffice it here to say that the green revolution has caused significant interregional disparities. It also has exacerbated local income disparities because farmers with large holdings have been able to use their superior economic and political resources to maintain and even widen their advantage over small landowners, sharecroppers, and landless laborers.[21]

[20]Mellor, op. cit., p. 97.

[21]See Francine R. Frankel, *India's Green Revolution: Economic Gains and Political Costs* (Princeton, N.J.: Princeton University Press, 1971), and Frankel and von Vorys, op. cit., which presents a similar theory for both Indian and Pakistani portions of the Punjab.

Economic disparities between dominant landowners and the majority of cultivators have been increased through a process involving replacement of traditional relations between them by commercial relations based on profit-maximizing criteria which are biased toward the already well-to-do. In taking an extreme view of the political consequences of this situation, Francine Frankel has argued that it has led to "a decline in the moral claim of landed elites to positions of authority and the breakdown of vertical patterns of peasant mobilization. Over the long run, large numbers of the landless become available for participation in the new political commitments and groups based on egalitarian values and class-struggle doctrines."[22] In effect, she has asserted that the green revolution carries with it the germs which might later lead to a "red revolution."

Another seasoned India watcher, Marcus Franda, has taken a more cautious approach to the new agricultural strategy's equity and political impacts. On the basis of his own observations, the majority opinion at the Punjab Agricultural University, and facts such as the higher incidence of land-grab movements in backward areas, Franda maintains that it is too early to conclude that the green revolution has destroyed the fabric of society or inclined the landless to a class struggle. He cites the Punjab with its increased wage levels and need to import labor from neighboring states as an example of how the rapid modernization of agriculture may benefit all classes and actually stabilize society. Franda believes, nonetheless, that there is great danger in the coexistence of rising expectations and a policy response which only partially fulfills the need to exploit the green revolution strategy to its full potential.[23]

The Meaning of 1973

A fuller picture of the forces affecting India's agricultural policies is revealed by careful analysis of the 1973 food crisis.[24] The crop response to the new agricultural strategy had been rewarding, but in evaluating output gains made during the late 1960s and early 1970s, India repeated its First Plan mistake and gave too little credit to the contribution of average and better-than-normal monsoons. Food grain production peaked at 108 million tons in 1970–71, and by the summer of 1972, the government had accumulated grain reserves of 9 million tons. An exuberant mood resulted, and many Indians presumed that

[22]Frankel and von Vorys, op. cit., p. 2.

[23]Marcus F. Franda, "Policy Response to India's Green Revolution," American University Field Staff Reports, South Asia Series, vol. 16, no. 9, 1972.

[24]For a more detailed account of these events, see my article "India's Economic Development and the Force of National Politics: The Four Seasons of Its Discontent," op. cit.

with only a modicum of government effort, domestic food production could be expected to meet India's foreseeable needs. In Delhi, it was announced that grain imports on concessional terms, which had been as large as 10 million tons in one drought year, would be discontinued at the end of 1972. Thus the seeds of the 1973 food shortage were sown on a number of fronts.

India's 1973 crisis can be characterized as a countrywide shortage of essential commodities, primarily food. It was a major blow to India's drought-affected regions and to the poor throughout the nation. It encouraged inflation, black markets, and other antisocial behavior. Not only was its impact felt throughout the Indian economy, but it induced considerable political instability as demonstrated by the deterioration in law and order and the fall of several state governments. In short, the effects of the crisis were pervasive and disruptive to India's social stability and economic development.

International politics played a muted but substantial role in the events of 1973. India's participation in the birth of Bangladesh had called for considerable economic effort. The war with Pakistan was neither long nor difficult, but the preparations for it had been a strain and its side effects, such as the burden of caring for 10 million Bengali refugees and the feeding and reconstruction of the newly independent Bangladesh, were costly to India's food resources. More important was the seeming malevolence of nature. The 1972 monsoon failed in Maharashtra as it had in the two previous years, but this time it failed over large parts of the subcontinent as well.[25] Nature also failed to provide the usual temperature levels needed to melt the Himalayan snows. The resulting insufficiency of water flowing into reservoirs reduced both the amount of water that could be released for direct irrigation and the amount of hydroelectric power available for energizing wells, running fertilizer plants, and maintaining other facilities critical to farm production.

The inevitable effect of these and other adverse factors was that in the 1972–73 crop year harvests over much of India failed completely or fell well short of potential. Food grain production is thought to have fallen to 95 to 100 million tons. We will never know the precise amount for a number of reasons, among them that state governments are responsible for reporting production. When output is high, the states exaggerate their figures in order to increase their claim on fertilizer and other inputs for the coming growing season; when the crop is bad, they underestimate their production so as to have a higher claim on relief from Delhi. Such are the problems of economic management where even the most basic facts are evasive and intentionally distorted.

The weather was cruel in 1972, but human factors also played a major role in the devastating events of 1973. Quite apart from past neglect of agriculture as evidenced by Maharashtra's lack of preparedness for drought, the absence of

[25]For a telling account of the Maharashtra drought and its broader implications, see Wolf Ladejinsky, "Drought in Maharashtra (Not in One Hundred Years)," *Economic and Political Weekly,* Feb. 17, 1973, pp. 383–396.

emergency supplies of water and power, and shortages of fertilizers[26] and tube wells, some of the government policies adopted in 1973 showed remarkable insensitivity to immediate policy needs. To its credit, Delhi reacted to the food crisis by expanding its network of fair price shops in order to sell more food at low, often subsidized, prices. But through this action it added to the already growing demand for food in response to its inexorably rising population and, in effect, it created additional claims on the food supply at the very moment of gravest scarcity. The government failed, however, to compensate for this by adding enough to supplies and distributing available grain to where it was most needed.

Moving grain to the neediest regions would have been a major difficulty under any circumstances; but it was especially complicated, in part because the government was not coping well with management of the railroad and coal industries. With respect to foreign grain, because India had announced previously that it would phase out concessional food imports, the likelihood of eliciting inexpensive food from abroad was small, even if India had been willing to reverse its stand and request it. India might have successfully employed a portion of its foreign exchange reserves to buy food but for a misreading of the United States grain situation. American grain prices appeared high in the autumn of 1972, when India recognized the need for imports, and, consequently, the government postponed taking action. But as Delhi waited, the price of wheat skyrocketed to record levels at which India could afford to buy only a fraction of its requirements, less than 2 million tons compared to 6.5 million tons which the Cabinet had authorized. World supplies of food remained so tight throughout most of 1973 that there was no alternative to the United States market until late in the year, when a bumper Soviet crop permitted the Russians to lend India 2 million tons of wheat.

Because the combined force of these factors, which would have been sufficient to cause grave difficulty on the food front, was exacerbated by inept government food policy, India sustained a full-scale crisis. The central government, to the extent that it has assumed responsibility for food grain prices, was positioned to be whipsawed from two directions: farmers asking for higher returns for their output and urban consumers who, if not placated by low food prices, threatened to demand inflationary wage increases and to cause political instability in the cities. Regulating grain prices, therefore, was a perilous occupation under the best of circumstances, and in 1973 the government erred badly by setting the official procurement price too low and keeping it too low

---

[26]As noted, the government's industrial licensing system had long operated to restrain investment, including investment in critical industries such as fertilizer. The situation was made still worse by a failure to use existing plant and equipment at anything like 100 percent of capacity. For example, in mid-1973, India's Petroleum and Chemicals Minister is reported to have deplored the total absence of any output from the Durgapur fertilizer factory, despite the project's having been mechanically completed in 1971 (see *Statesman,* July 31, 1973).

throughout the procurement season. As a result, it achieved barely 50 percent of the 8.5 million ton procurement target it had set for the spring crop.

Low prices were not the only problem adversely affecting procurement. The socialist-inclined factions of the Congress party were deeply committed to nationalization of the wholesale food trade. To placate these interests, and in response to a growing concern that grain supplies would be inadequate to meet the needs of the public distribution system, the government chose the unpropitious spring of 1973 to take over the wholesale wheat trade. Vested interests in rural India rallied to thwart the takeover by preventing food from coming to market, and an active black market developed in grain trading. But because the government had acted with virtually no advance planning, it was unable to counter this local level of resistance and, in practice, the new trade policy was in no small measure responsible for the shortfall from the procurement target and rising grain prices throughout the country.

In summary, the government did a remarkable job of alienating the Indian people and changing a serious but manageable problem into a crisis: farmers were antagonized by low procurement prices and the fear that nationalization of the wholesale trade would work to their long-term disadvantage; traders at wholesale and retail levels were upset by the disruption of markets; and consumers were seriously disturbed by high food prices and outright scarcity. Particular hardship was felt by those living in the areas most affected by drought and by the poor people who could not afford to pay the inflated grain prices which, while varying for specific areas and commodities, were universally more than 20 percent above the previous year's levels.

It bears emphasis that the government played a critical role in causing the crisis of 1973—be it in disrupting markets by nationalizing the wholesale wheat trade, or in its failure to proceed fast enough with the irrigation schemes which would have forestalled the short harvest. To its credit, Delhi eventually recognized its overextended position and later in 1973 it postponed action de facto on its plan to nationalize the wholesale trade in rice in the autumn. In doing so, however, it gave so much authority for food policy to the state governments that the continued existence of a national food policy was temporarily in doubt.[27]

If fears that the central government had opted out of major responsibility for food policy had been justified in fact, the almost certain consequence would have been long-term anarchy on the food front, as contrasted with the short-term anarchy which caused India so much pain in 1973. The probability for such a scenario was low, however, because India's leaders could not long tolerate the strains on the country's industrial economy and political structure which followed from the 1973 food crisis. Thus, although the wheat trade nationalization was reversed in 1974, Delhi took other policy measures which left little doubt that it would continue to bear responsibility for food production and distribution. Nonetheless, the rapid-fire policy reversals, from free markets

---

[27]*Economic and Political Weekly,* Sept. 22, 1973, p. 1700.

to nationalization and back to what appeared to many observers to be inadequate control, indicate the difficulty the government has in reconciling conflicting interests, choosing among alternative solutions to problems, and preventing the main thrust of policy from moving in a cyclical pattern.

The Use of Market Incentives

Most of the foregoing discussion of policies to expand farm output has involved strategies which place the government more or less directly in the production process, sometimes in ways contrary to the interests of the politically powerful and, therefore, likely to be sabotaged by them. The significance of price policy as an alternative or complementary approach is revealed by two central questions. First, what is the potential effect of price changes on Indian economic growth and the distribution of real income? (Although economic theory generally holds that the higher the price, the more farmers will produce, experience shows that in India higher food prices may on some occasions induce farmers to consume more of their own production and the amount of food available for marketing may actually fall.) Second, to what extent has Delhi used the price mechanism as an instrument of policy to affect relative prices (1) between agricultural inputs and outputs and (2) among various farm products?

Since the mid-1960s Indian planners have become somewhat more alive to the possibilities for manipulating market prices as an instrument of policy but, on balance, the government has made far from full use of this type of policy. Officials have favored direct intervention in the economic process of production and distribution, in part because of a general feeling in India that it is through the price mechanism that traders and large landowners take an unmerited slice of agricultural income and exploit unwitting and helpless small farmers. It is also generally believed that keeping farm prices low in relation to industrial prices will abet industrial development and that food prices should be kept low lest urban workers impart an inflationary bias to the economy by using their political leverage to offset rising food prices with growing wage demands. As noted by George Rosen, the government is concerned that increases in farm prices lead to (1) higher wages with consequent ill effects on India's rate of inflation, competitive position in world markets, and budget deficit; or (2) redistribution of income from the industrial sector to agriculture, which would have indeterminate effects on the overall growth rate and a likely short-term depressing effect on the industrial growth; or (3) some combination of these effects.[28]

According to Wilfrid Malenbaum, uncertainty plays a major role in discouraging government from actively using price policy. He is impressed that in the absence of reliable information about how producers and consumers react to

[28]Rosen, op. cit., pp. 149–150, 214–216.

various prices—i.e., the price elasticities of supply and demand—government can never be certain of how markets will react to price policies. He also reasons that because industrial inputs account for only a small fraction of total value added in agriculture, changes in input costs could not have much effect on the extent to which various inputs are used.[29] These are tenuous arguments, however. First, there are many safe ways in which, even without perfect knowledge of market elasticities, the government can use price policy with some expectation of success and some hope of increasing its knowledge about the markets in order to improve policy. Lack of omniscience is only sometimes a valid reason for timidity. Second, Malenbaum has used aggregate data to belittle the importance of input prices whereas, in fact, for those farms using the package program the cost of fertilizer and other inputs amounts to a significant share of the value added of their production.

In reaction to what he regards as misguided efforts to raise farm prices and redress the government's "urban bias," a noted Indian agricultural economist, M. L. Dantwala, has argued that it is not just urbanites but many of the rural poor who are dependent on the market for a significant share of their food. Thus, an increase in food prices not only affects the rural-urban relationship, but can magnify rural income disparities. While ignoring the possibility that higher farm prices might be offset by higher farm wages, Dantwala goes so far as to question whether higher farm prices would stimulate increased production.[30] His argument is not fully convincing, however, and a reader is left with the impression that he makes it less for the purpose of denigrating the importance of price than with the aim of making the Johnny-one-notes who strongly advocate price increases recognize that farm production is affected by other factors.

The case for using the price mechanism to affect the rural economy is based on numerous studies showing that Indian farmers do respond to price incentives in much the same way as farmers elsewhere. Indeed, there is now ample evidence that the profit motive is alive and healthy in rural India,[31] a conclusion which is especially important in light of the Ford Foundation's 1959 finding that farm progress depended on the actions of millions of individual cultivators and that communicating with these farmers through government extension programs was very costly and often inefficient. Changing price relationships clearly qualifies as one means for dealing with this problem without engendering large complex bureaucratic structures.

---

[29]Wilfrid Malenbaum, *Modern India's Economy* (Columbus, Ohio: Charles E. Merrill, 1971), pp. 154–157.

[30]M. L. Dantwala, "From Stagnation to Growth," *Indian Economic Journal*, vol. 19, no. 2, October–December 1970.

[31]See Mellor, op. cit., p. 121, and part 3 written by Uma J. Lele. Also see Kalpana Bardhan, "Relative Prices and Allocation of Land and Other Inputs among Competing Crops," in Khusro, ed., op. cit., p. 368.

The alternative to price policy—rationing, food zones, government fair price shops, forced procurement, credit controls, and similar measures—has been used by India to good purpose in time of food shortages, but it has not proved to be an efficient answer to short-term difficulties and has been virtually irrelevant to the basic, long-term problem of insufficient supply. India's experience with these controls has been that they induce both buyers and sellers to bypass legal channels and that they invite black markets. In addition, the controls have sometimes induced farm producers to consume a greater share of their own output and to reduce the use of inputs, thereby reducing the amount of food brought to market.[32] The positive case for India to rely more heavily on the forces of market supply and demand is made by Uma Lele. From her investigations of various Indian food grain markets, she has concluded that the existing market structures are basically sound, that there is a logical relationship among the prices for various grains and among various markets, and that seasonal fluctuations in price are consistent with storage costs and so forth.[33]

India was slow to recognize the potential role of market prices, but in a mounting crescendo of domestic and foreign criticism, it did begin to establish minimum *support prices* in 1964. In the next year, the Agricultural Prices Commission was established to advise the government on price policies, and the Food Corporation of India came into being to provide an all-India system for procuring food grains. Partly because *procurement prices* were sometimes set appreciably above support prices, India was able to accumulate a 9 million ton buffer stock of grains by the summer of 1972. But, not surprisingly, India's procurement system has worked better during periods of good harvest than during scarcity times. This is mainly because government has not been willing to ratify high market prices by raising its procurement price to a level that would attract sellers or to enforce mandatory procurement.

India's 1973 policy to nationalize wholesale wheat marketing demonstrated that the Indian government remains more than marginally concerned that price is only one among many variables for exercising control over food production. It continues to operate on the assumption that landowners and middlemen have monopoly power over farm inputs and outputs which they use to skim off a major portion of agricultural income and, incidentally, to reduce the sensitivity of farmers to changing prices.[34] But government also has become increasingly convinced of the need to make its price policies more effective. The

[32]For a full discussion of such behavior, see A. M. Khusro, "Economic Theory and Indian Agricultural Policy," in ibid., pp. 1–54, and Don Humphrey, "The Price of Food," ibid., p. 361.

[33]Uma J. Lele, *Food Grain Marketing in India: Private Performance and Public Policy* (Ithaca, N.Y.: Cornell University Press, 1971), pp. 11–12.

[34]For a fuller discussion of this subject, see Michael Lipton, "Strategy for Agriculture: Urban Bias and Rural Planning," in Paul Streeten and Michael Lipton, eds., *The Crisis of Indian Planning* (London: Oxford University Press, 1968).

Fourth Plan, for example, explicitly noted that support prices should be announced well before the sowing season, should be kept as stable as possible over time, and should apply to all grain offered for sale without any limit on quantity.[35] The principles underlying this approach, that to reduce farm risks and to ensure remunerative returns to farmers will increase production, are well founded.

Comparison of India's sectoral wholesale price indices shows that the terms of trade between agriculture and industry (ratio of farm to industrial prices) were fairly stable from Independence through the early 1960s. Subsequently, reflecting the inflationary impact on food prices of scarcity conditions, there has been a noticeable shift in the terms of trade in favor of agriculture. Before this change could become prominent, however, a number of economists took India to task for using price structures adverse to agriculture in order to favor industrial growth.[36] In taking exception to this thesis, other economists such as Ashok Mitra have asserted that agriculture has actually been favored by public policy and that the large farmers have benefited most. According to Mitra:

> About 10 per cent of the agricultural population in India constitutes a privileged minority: they own land which is more than half the total cultivated area, their per capita income is significantly higher than even in the major segments of organized industry and commerce, yet they are among the least taxed groups in the country. Even assuming that this minority contributes as much as four-fifths of the total revenue at present collected from agriculture, the tax burden is merely 5 per cent of their income. With a per capita income which is apparently 40 per cent lower, the non-agricultural population is carrying a tax burden which is twice this proportion.[37]

If, in fact, Delhi retarded the rate of agricultural growth, one major instrument for doing so was the import and public sale of foreign grain. The sizable amounts of concessionally priced cereals which the United States sold and gave away under its Food for Peace (PL-480) program, while fulfilling an important humanitarian function, also acted as an opiate on India's resource-scarce, development-minded leaders who could not easily resist allowing imports to substitute for domestic food production. Much nonsense has been uttered in passion by Indians who believe that the United States extended PL-480 assistance as a means to make India dependent, and by Americans who deny that PL-480 was in American interests. My understanding is that the dominant motivation on the part of both governments was straightforward and directed to the humanitarian and development contributions that these food shipments

[35]*Fourth Five-Year Plan* (New Delhi: GOI, Planning Commission, 1969), p. 144.

[36]See, for example, Lipton in Streeten and Lipton, op. cit.

[37]Ashok Mitra, "Tax Burden for Indian Agriculture," in Ralph Braibanti and Joseph J. Spengler, eds., *Administration and Economic Development in India* (Durham, N.C.: Duke University Press, 1963), p. 303.

could make.[38] The point remains, however, that incremental food supplies from abroad reduced the incentive for India to adopt production-increasing policies and, by enabling Delhi to hold the price of grain below what it otherwise would have been, tended to discourage agricultural investments by private farmers.

India's fiscal system also affected India's policies toward agriculture and industry. Because agriculture is a "state" subject and state capitals have been notoriously lax in imposing direct and other taxes on agriculture (in reality, farmers are often subsidized by low water and electricity rates), Delhi has sought means within the Constitution for deriving some revenue from rural India. Thus, in 1969 it introduced an excise tax on fertilizers and irrigation pumps. These levies were justified by the government on grounds that India's most successful farmers would otherwise pay very little tax, but whereas they may be tolerable when farm inputs are in short supply, they cannot be reconciled with India's long-term need to increase food production. Taxes on farm inputs—as contrasted with farm income—not only militate against India's efforts to increase acceptance of the new technology by making it relatively cheap and riskless for small farmers,[39] but fly in the face of the economic dictum that if farmers are acting rationally by equating marginal costs with marginal income, higher prices will discourage all farmers from using fertilizer and other inputs.

It should now be clear that in the absence of a comprehensive study of how taxes, tariffs, imports, monetary policy, budget spending, and other relevant factors have affected agriculture and industry, the emotion-charged question of whether agriculture has been "neglected" by policy must go unanswered. What can be said about market incentives is that (1) price policy has not been used to maximum effect; (2) differential treatment of agriculture and industry by tax and other policies vastly complicates the problem of determining the relative efficiency of economic alternatives; and (3) the agricultural and industrial sectors are so interrelated that, whereas it is possible to imagine policies which would have a differential effect on their growth rates, the real need is to formulate policies which develop both sectors by emphasizing their complementarity. In seeking a firm conclusion about the role of prices and a reply to those who worry that high food prices might lead to surplus production, there is still no better answer than that given by John Lewis in the early 1960s:

[38]To this day it is not well understood in either country that much of the food was acquired on very long-term credits, but sold almost immediately to Indian citizens through government fair price shops and private traders. In effect, India acquired an important and easy source of supplemental budget revenue which, assuming it did not lead to laxness in the levying and collection of taxes, was available to increase domestic Indian investment and social service expenditures. The soaring budget deficits which India has recorded since phasing out Title I, PL-480 imports are not conclusive proof that it had relied on the PL-480 program for domestic budget support, but it is difficult not to see some connection.

[39]Economic Survey: 1969–70, pp. 8–11.

In India, where the basic agricultural supply problem for the foreseeable future is one of food shortages, not surpluses, a program of concrete year-to-year forward price guarantees will generate little or none of the accumulated long-term problems that similar price supports have in the surplus-biased conditions of the United States.[40]

Social Justice and Land Reform

India's strategy to boost farm output is inextricably tied to issues of equity within rural India, among different regions, and between rural and urban populations. The subject is even more complex than is immediately apparent because, even as Indian society evolves from traditional to modern, relationships between urban and rural members of the same family remain important. Thus, what is significant for equity is not whether the Indian government favors industrial or agricultural development, but whether it is able to achieve growth and to distribute the benefits to the 80 percent of the population which is rural.

Those authors who have written about the tendency for poor countries to develop dualistic economic patterns in which modern industry is privileged and traditional agriculture is deprived provide a clue as to how to explain the seemingly intractable problem of agrarian poverty. An early United Nations document—which could as easily have been written in 1973—attributes poverty to the overall organization of rural society:

> Among the features of the agrarian structure which have most serious effects are the uneconomic size of farms, the maldistribution of landownership with concentration of large estates insufficiently utilised and the landlessness of a large part of the rural population; the fragmentation of holdings; the high rents and insecurity of tenure characteristic of many tenancy systems; indebtedness and lack of adequate credit facilities for the small farmer; absence of settled title to land and water; plantation economies which offer low wages and no share in management to the cultivators; taxation policies which impose undue burdens on the small farmers and farm labourers; and in general an unsatisfactory set of incentives for a rising and sustained agricultural production.[41]

Land reform which is an essential but hardly the unique ingredient of agrarian reform is regarded by many as an instrument rather than a goal of policy. As summarized in 1973 by a Planning Commission task force chaired by P. S. Appu, the objectives of agrarian reform are:

[40]See J. P. Lewis, *Quiet Crisis,* op. cit., p. 152.

[41]"Land Reform: Defects in Agrarian Structure as Obstacles to Economic Development" (United Nations, Department of Economic Affairs, 1951), quoted in H. D. Malaviya, *Land Reforms in India* (New Delhi: AICC, Indian National Congress, 1955), p. 426.

> To remove such motivational and other impediments to increase in agricultural production . . . to eliminate all elements of exploitation. These objectives were sought to be achieved by abolishing all intermediary interests between the State and the tiller of the soil, regulating rents, conferring on tenants security of tenure, and, eventually, distributing surplus land among the landless and the small holders, and bringing about the consolidation of holdings.[42]

I shall deal with the limited issue of land reform in the next several pages and reserve other issues of agrarian reform for the subsequent section.

Land reform in India is notable, not just because the transformation from semifeudal to modern rural conditions was seen as an integral part of the development process, but because this reform was attempted through democratic means.[43] Although Indian concern for land reform predates Independence, under British rule collecting taxes and maintaining law and order took precedence over social restructuring; agrarian reform, to the extent that it occurred, was directed at improving tenurial conditions rather than redistributing land. Nonetheless, the correlation between disparities of wealth and income was well understood at an early date, as evidenced by the strong wording of Article 39 of the Indian Constitution. This, in turn, was based on two debatable but strongly held assumptions about how rural wealth determines political power, income distribution, and production decisions: first, that land redistribution per se was a necessary, but by no means sufficient, condition for social justice; second, that land reform was needed to accelerate the growth of farm production.

Preventing economic exploitation is a recurrent theme in Indian policy, and the triad of landlord, trader, and moneylender were regarded as able to capitalize on the unfavorable land/population ratio and exercise a monopoly power which could be diluted only by land redistribution. Moreover, to the extent that inequitable rural conditions were due to the zamindari and other systems imposed by foreigners, there was an additional reason for land reform. But the confrontation of these compelling reasons with India's peculiar mix of Gandhian, socialist, and capitalist forces created a situation in which land reform could neither be avoided nor pressed to a truly radical—or logical, depending on one's point of view—conclusion.

Proponents of land redistribution have argued that reform will enhance the tillers' motivation by assuring them of the benefits of their efforts and will encourage them to behave as entrepreneurs, i.e., work hard, take risks, inno-

---

[42]*Report of the Task Force on Agrarian Relations,* op. cit., p. 1.

[43]The epitome of this approach to land redistribution is the Bhoodan movement, initiated in 1951 by a disciple of Mahatma Gandhi named Vinoba Bhave. A voluntary program through which the wealthy were encouraged to donate a sixth of their land to the poor, Bhoodan enjoyed some popularity but the roughly 5 million acres transferred were often of the lowest-quality land and the program has gradually lost its momentum.

vate, and invest. The case for maintaining large landholdings to maximize output, which can be stated with equal theoretical force, is based on (1) possibilities for economies of scale in the use of inputs and marketing, (2) the reduced problem of extension if only a limited number of farmers need to be educated, and (3) the assumption that unequal income distribution elicits greater aggregate savings and investment because poor people consume more of their incomes than the rich. There has been no lack of effort to establish empirically how land reform affects farm equity and growth, but the evidence presented thus far is inconclusive.[44] It is known, however, that other variables are so important to the society that land redistribution will serve equity aims only if it is complemented by structural changes which make farm inputs and credit available to small cultivators.

India's land redistribution program, which has achieved real but only limited progress, has been compared by Angus Maddison to the peeling of an onion. Under British rule the feudal society was reformed to the extent that the Mogul princes lost much of their authority and a break was made between sovereignty and landownership. But because the British ruled by maintaining an agricultural elite, the rural hierarchy survived the colonial period. The post-1947 government peeled off another layer of the onion after Independence by abolishing the zamindari and related intermediary systems,[45] but even though this brought the government into closer contact with a great many tillers of the soil, the devolution of wealth did not proceed very far. The losses were borne by a tiny number of landlords who, through various loopholes, continued to hold large estates. The benefits accrued to a larger, but still very limited, number of farmers. On balance, the lowest echelons of society such as sharecroppers and day laborers neither gained nor lost from these rounds of land reform.

This is not to say that the efforts to abolish intermediary relationships have not been largely successful. Such relationships, which prevailed in about 40 percent of the country before Independence, have now been almost totally abolished, thereby permitting about 20 million tenants to become direct landowners and facilitating the distribution of about 14 million acres. In addition, a large amount of privately owned forest, grazing, and waste land has been vested in the state.[46] However incomplete, these reforms are of very large political and economic consequence. Regardless of whether one takes the position that giving so many millions a direct stake in the system has strengthened India's infant democracy and enhanced the process of nation building, or the opposite point of view, that by creating a more broadly based but powerful rural elite the reforms have been antiegalitarian and antidemocratic (there is

[44]Dantwala, "From Stagnation to Growth," op. cit.
[45]See Maddison, *Class Structure and Economic Growth,* op. cit.
[46]*India: 1973* (New Delhi: GOI, Ministry of Information and Broadcasting, 1973), p. 213.

some justice in both points of view), the land redistribution which has already occurred is bound to be important for India's future.

Since the elimination of the zamindari and related systems, land reform has been pursued through the establishment of ceilings on the amount of land an individual or family could own. As of 1972, before the latest round of legislative changes, the ceilings ranged from 10 acres for an individual in Bihar to 336 acres for a family (defined as husband, wife, and minor children) in the desert state of Rajasthan.[47] These interstate differences were justified to some degree by differences in the quality of land and growing conditions, but they also were indicative of the varying political strength of well-to-do farm lobbies. According to the Appu task force, "As a result of the high level of ceilings, large numbers of exemptions from the law, malafide transfers and partitions, and poor implementation, the results [of land ceilings] have been meagre."[48] This conclusion is borne out by Indian statistics which show that owing to land ceilings (as distinguished from anti-intermediary legislation) only about 2.7 million acres have been declared surplus—invariably the lowest-quality land—and only 1.3 million acres are recorded as having been distributed to tillers.[49] Even worse, there is evidence that through elaborate networks of political graft and intrigue some of the land was distributed to wealthy rather than poor people.[50]

In areas where the green revolution has become a reality, the relevance of land ceilings has increased dramatically because higher potential farm profits have been reflected in higher land rents and sales values. New opportunities for mechanization and technological change also have caused large and medium-sized landowners to reassess their relations with tenants and sharecroppers. As a result, the landless have generally had their rights to till the land reduced, and although their family incomes from farming and the new tertiary industries have grown, their share of total farm income has declined. The commercialization of traditional worker-landlord relationships has resulted in a more volatile political situation, the stability of which will depend, in large part, on whether the momentum of economic growth can be maintained at a rate high enough to provide continuing growth of incomes for the majority of the population and at least subsistence incomes for the poorest. If disparities were to grow at a time when the absolute income of workers was falling, the situation would be likely to become politically untenable.

The Indian government's reaction to these new developments, which began to take shape in 1969, shows how land reform issues have generally been managed. The political decision to reduce land ceilings was taken by the Congress party in 1970 and a Central Land Reforms Committee was estab-

---

[47]Ibid., p. 214.

[48]*Report of the Task Force on Agrarian Relations*, op. cit., p. 4.

[49]*India: 1973*, op. cit., p. 214.

[50]Such was the conclusion of the Harchand Singh committee, which reported on the situation in the Punjab in 1974.

lished. The "radical" recommendations of this body, which were placed before the Indian Parliament in August 1971, appeared to be much more conservative when restated in the Agriculture Ministry's Annual Report, issued in April 1972. Only after a heated debate was the Agriculture Minister cleared of charges of having distorted and watered down the Central Land Reforms Committee's recommendations. In the process, however, it became abundantly clear that what initially had been intended to appear as a radical set of new rules was comparatively benign from the standpoint of landowners.[51] Although a formula for uniform state policies of lowered land ceilings was agreed to by the states' chief ministers in July 1972, subsequent action by various state legislatures left little doubt that considerable diversity would remain in state policies, largely because the landowners provided indignant and effective resistance to the government's initiative. Landed interests held up or mutilated implementing legislation in a number of states and resorted to a variety of evasive measures, some of them harmful to production. Among the more extraordinary steps taken by landowners were the dismantling of tube wells in order to be certain that their land could not be double-cropped and was not therefore subject to expropriation, and recourse to legal divorce by owners who continued to live with their wives but were then legally able to retain twice as much land. According to many observers the results of this latest exercise are likely to be as nominal as past efforts.[52]

The last major issue raised by land redistribution relates to the consolidation of what are often infinitesimally small and scattered landholdings. The progress of this reform has varied greatly among states, some of which have not even

[51]Wolf Ladejinsky, "New Ceiling Round and Implementation Prospects," *Economic and Political Weekly,* Review of Agriculture, September 1972, pp. A125–132.

[52]In October and November of 1972, the *Times of India* ran a series of articles which gave a dismal view of the prospects for the new land ceilings legislation. In Uttar Pradesh, over 100 members of the State Legislative Assembly were said to oppose the ceilings because their personal holdings would be affected. In Bihar the bureaucrats were alleged to be "landlord-oriented." In Rajasthan, there were complaints that even when the landless acquired holdings, they were not assisted in obtaining seed, bullocks, and other inputs needed to exploit the land. In Madhya Pradesh, illicit land transfers and phony records threatened to reduce greatly the amount of land available for redistribution. Proposed legislation in the Punjab failed to protect tenant rights. In Haryana the demand for land reform, even from the Communist party, was described as "feeble." Financial resources and land survey records were inadequate in West Bengal. Rich landlords in Assam formed fictitious cooperatives to evade the law. In Orissa, where even tribal and Harijan (outcast) political leaders were party to the farm lobby, legislation was delayed by a majority of the ruling Congress party. In Tamil Nadu, there were anxieties that the experience of past land reform legislation (in which only 10,000 acres of an expected 125,000 acres were actually acquired by the government) would be repeated because of legislative loopholes. In Mysore stiff oppostion came from within the Congress party. In Maharashtra it appeared that one side effect of the drought might be a delay in land reform.

passed enabling legislation. This nonimplementation has been a blessing in disguise, however, insofar as the states did not always take effective steps to ensure the tenancy rights of sharecroppers who, as a result of the consolidation, could no longer identify themselves with particular plots. Because landowners were often able to take advantage of consolidation to increase their share of crops harvested or to increase their profits by personally cultivating the "new" land areas, the "consolidation of holdings has often turned out to be the *coup de grâce* for the sharecroppers."[53]

The *Report of the Task Force on Agrarian Relations* was itself a coup de grace for any illusions about the effectiveness of land reform to date. The report contrasted the frail benefits achieved with the monumental needs and was unequivocal in concluding that "The over-all assessment has to be that programmes of land reform adopted since Independence have failed to bring about the required changed in the agrarian structure."[54] In describing the "Reasons for Poor Performance," the task force noted that "no tangible progress can be expected in the field of land reform in the absence of the requisite political will," and it concluded that "The sad truth is that this crucial factor has been wanting . . . as demonstrated by the large gaps between policy and legislation and between law and its implementation. In no sphere of public activity in our country since Independence has the hiatus between precept and practice, between policy pronouncements and actual execution, been as great as in the domain of land reform."[55] Reconfirming Myron Weiner's findings that there is a notable difference in attitude between government officers in Delhi and state officials, and that class conflict has not yet emerged as a major element in India's rural scene,[56] the task force was impressed by the "Absence of [political] Pressure from Below" and the laxness of state governments in legislating land reform and assuring its effective implementation by senior and junior bureaucrats who are described as having a "lukewarm, and often apathetic" attitude.

According to the task force, the identification—if not the actual coincidence—of landowners and officialdom, ranging from the village functionary to "the higher echelons of the administration has militated against reform." The report cites weak, poorly drafted, and loophole-riddled legislation which does not adequately compensate those who lose title to their land, much less provide even minimal funding for implementation, as having "hardly any chance of success," particularly given the emphasis on legal formalities common in India's judicial system and the practice of "tenacious landowners" to resort to "ingenious lawyers." In short, an "isolated law aimed at the restructuring of property relation in the rural areas has hardly any chance of success."[57] The most radical,

---

[53]*Report of the Task Force on Agrarian Relations,* op. cit., p. 6.
[54]Ibid., p. 7.
[55]Ibid.
[56]Myron Weiner, *The Politics of Scarcity,* op. cit.
[57]Ibid., p. 10.

and potentially the most vital, finding of the task force was that "a certain degree of politicisation of the poor peasantry on militant lines is a prerequisite for any successful legislative-administrative action."[58] When Mrs. Gandhi based her 1971 election strategy on an appeal to the masses, it was in recognition of this very factor, but to the extent that politicization is initiated by the leadership rather than emanating from the people, it may prove transitory and ineffective.

Sentiments similar to those of the task force were expressed in Mrs. Gandhi's 1973 interview with *Socialist India.*[59] Pressed as to why the takeover of the wholesale wheat trade had been such a failure, the Prime Minister mused that the government and the Congress party were ineffective in the absence of support from the people. She acknowledged the limits of official policies and noted that there were Congress members who had opposed the nationalization. In discussing how the peoples' needs could be articulated and made to count at the political level, she lamented that there had been looting and other irresponsible acts which complicated rather than simplified the government's task. The contradiction of roles revealed by this interview—Mrs. Gandhi, head of government and leader of the establishment, versus Mrs. Gandhi, revolutionary and leader of the people—is indicative of the complex and vital link between Indian politics and development.

Agrarian Reform Is Broader than Land Reform

For many farmers the value of agrarian reform is to be judged not by land redistribution but by the effectiveness of tenancy reforms. Tenancy and subtenancy have been widely practiced throughout India for many years, and although the legislation abolishing intermediary tenures diminished the position of the biggest absentee landlords—those who had maintained town houses and had ostentatiously lived the "good life" in India's large cities—it did not do away with landlordism. In Uttar Pradesh, for example, as recently as 1955, 10 percent of the peasant families still owned 50 percent of the land. The abolition of intermediaries which had taken place in that state was flawed for a variety of reasons. For example, ostensibly in deference to the notion that upper castes could not be expected to do manual labor because it was degrading—but more in response to political pressure—the Utter Pradesh legislation did not require landowners to till the land, much less to live in the village. Similarly, zamindars were allowed to keep lands which previously had been under their "personal" cultivation, a concession which in Utter Pradesh alone amounted to 6 million acres. Finally, the legislation provided a legal basis for sharecropping.[60]

[58]Ibid., p. 25.
[59]*Socialist India,* Aug. 11, 1973, pp. 26–33.
[60]For a detailed discussion of this legislation, see chap. 1 of Thorner and Thorner, op. cit.

In their struggles to retain titles to as much of their land as possible (the threat of grossly inadequate compensation for lands taken by the government was but one of many motivations for resisting), the ex-zamindars and new landlords used their wealth and power to convert tenancy relationships to crop-sharing arrangements.[61] They arranged for the falsification of land records—an easy and inexpensive practice in view of the immediate financial needs of local record keepers—and reallotted land to various family members. These evasive measures proved particularly significant for the nonsuccess of later government efforts to impose ceilings on landholdings and their effect was anything but welcome in the search for social justice and greater output; according to the 1973 Appu task force report:

> Tenants have, in practice, found it extremely difficult to claim successful tenancy rights because most of the leases, particularly crop-sharing arrangements, are oral and informal. Where tenancy is insecure, legal provisions regarding fair rent are useless and no tenant dares initiate action for getting fair rent fixed. This is so because the tenant who has the audacity to pray for fixation of fair rent faces the risk of certain ejectment. Thus the objective of ensuring fair rent and security of tenure still remains unattained in large parts of the country.[62]

Against the backdrop of the preceding discussion it is clear that the Community Development and agrarian reform programs have encountered the same set of barriers and that shortfalls in both programs are related. Moreover, the fate of other government programs—social services, nutritional supplementation, crash employment schemes, and longer-range efforts to get farm inputs into the hands of the poorest tillers—has been equally mixed. These programs have been responsive to critical needs, but because only a limited number of them have produced results and many have failed to benefit the target group,[63] the intended and needed support for both production and welfare aspects of development have not been fully realized.

Development has faced other obstacles in the form of legal and institutional conventions. Tenants and sharecroppers have been deterred from using modern production techniques because (1) the insecurity of their tenures does not guarantee that they will enjoy the fruits of their investments; (2) sharing formulas for output favor landlords and often are adjusted so as to prevent the

---

[61]To illustrate, between 1953 and 1955, in the Punjab "the number of tenants recorded in village land records decreased by 86 per cent—from 583,000 to a little over 80,000." See Wolf Ladejinsky, "The Green Revolution in Punjab," *Economic and Political Weekly*, June 28, 1969.

[62]*Report of the Task Force on Agrarian Relations*, op. cit., pp. 3–4.

[63]For seasoned observers it came as no shock that emergency relief projects undertaken during the 1973 Maharashtra drought were often chosen so as to upgrade the holdings of large landowners rather than for their general economic merit. See Ladejinsky, "Drought in Maharashtra," op. cit.

laborer from getting much more than a subsistence income; and (3) there is a need in some instances to attain certain minimum-size holdings to achieve scale economies. Moreover, poor peasants often experience difficulty in obtaining needed scarce inputs. When fertilizer is in short supply, for example, it tends to command black market prices at which only those who are already wealthy can afford to buy it.

In principle, the credit system could be used to ameliorate the position of the poor by making it possible for subsistence cultivators to finance investments and farm inputs and to repay loans with the increased production attributable to these expenditures. In practice, however, as recently as the late 1950s more than 85 percent of the credit used by cultivators was provided by moneylenders and other noninstitutional sources.[64] Government programs to replace local moneylenders with cooperative credit societies, commercial banks, and other regulated credit institutions have improved the situation since then, albeit these measures have met with only partial success. The credit cooperatives, which generally have been more successful than producing and marketing cooperatives, have tended to be dominated by wealthy villagers or dominant castes, and funds have not always been made available to the most needy. In 1973, revelations about the operations of credit societies in Maharashtra—one of the states where co-ops were thought to have succeeded—were a reminder of how difficult it is to help weaker members of the society.[65] Nationally, a 1974 RBI study team found that 36 percent of the loans of central cooperative banks were overdue and that the overdue rate at primary credit societies was 44 percent.[66]

Indian bankers—like most of their peers abroad—have been conservative and true to the tradition of using security rather than productivity as the criterion for making loans. Because banks granted loans on the basis of "know who" rather than "know how," the government was justified in advertising the 1969 bank nationalization as a move to get more funds to the rural areas and financially disadvantaged (see Chapter 10). In practice, the commercial banks— which were excluded for many years from agriculture by government order— have encountered internal managerial and other problems in being responsive to this challenge. For instance, analysis of one crop season in West Bengal during 1971–72 shows that the nationalized banks financed only 111 sharecroppers in the entire state.[67] Nonetheless, there is real potential for using commercial bank credit to help small farmers to break out of the well-established vicious circle according to which their crops are financed through high-interest-rate loans which must be repaid immediately after the harvest when prices are at their lowest. To the extent that the local branches of nationalized

[64]*Ford Foundation Report on India's Food Crisis,* op. cit., p. 36.

[65]*Economic and Political Weekly,* Sept. 29, 1973, pp. 1755–1756.

[66]*Report of the Study Team on Overdues of Co-operative Credit Institutions* (Bombay: Reserve Bank of India, 1974), p. 222.

[67]*Report of the Task Force on Agrarian Relations,* op. cit., p. 26.

banks are more subject to guidance by the central government than their cooperative cousins, there is hope for a major improvement in the terms on which small farmers interact with the larger economy.

Other new programs which the government expects to expand during the Fifth Plan include the Small Farmers Development Agency (to make small farmers viable) and the Marginal Farmers and Agricultural Laborers Agency (to provide additional employment opportunities for rural populations which otherwise would have no way of supplementing their farm income). India's nationalization of the wholesale wheat trade was a related, albeit clumsily timed and poorly executed step in this direction. Regardless of the intrinsic merit of this action, because it did not fulfill the expectations of its proponents and diverted attention from other difficult and essential policies, its failure was a blow to the whole reform program.

Other aspects of the rural social justice question go well beyond the specifics noted above and often involve immediate policy dilemmas. How, for example, should consumption be shared between current and future generations? The amount of production invested each year will pay dividends in the future, but it represents a reduction in what is currently available. Similarly, what are the political and economic consequences of directing agricultural resources toward low-productivity, backward regions or to wealthier areas which can give large and immediate payoffs? Should Delhi help those states which help themselves, or should it help the poorer states regardless of local government efficiency? To date, Delhi has directed its efforts in many directions and, quite wisely, has avoided committing itself to inflexible postures. Indeed, India's policy response to these difficult issues has been pragmatic and subject to frequent change and some inconsistency as national leaders sought to accommodate conflicting political interests and changes in the underlying agricultural situation. The task of formulating policy was further complicated by the lack of definitive evidence that would show the superiority of one or several approaches to the problems over the alternatives.

Whether new investments should be allocated to backward or advanced areas has been an especially vexing question for India insofar as it involves a conflict between the long-term equity of developing the poor regions and the long- and short-term equity of providing Indians living in rich and poor areas with enough food. The policy issue is whether the government should press for maximum production at the expense of some economic dualism or whether it should seek immediate fundamental changes in the nation's production struc-ture at the cost of current production. The pragmatic solution of this policy dilemma which India has pursued with some consistency has been to aim for limited production growth while committing additional funds to structural change. This problem is especially interesting because it illustrates that dualism in India is not just applicable to industry and agriculture or to indigenous and export-oriented sectors, but also involves disparities within agriculture, between various regions, and between the wealthy and poor.

The Indian economist M. L. Dantwala has posed the question of dualism in terms of whether the green revolution should be considered as an enclave phenomenon or the opening stage of a transformation of traditional agriculture. Dantwala justifiably notes that the new technology is now widely used in certain Indian states and that additional research and investment can give it all-India application. Thus, there is wisdom in his view that if the green revolution in India "is to be viewed as dualism it is at least partially benevolent and must be preferred to a more egalitarian stagnation."[68] In concluding, I can do no better than to quote Wolf Ladejinsky, a wise, longtime observer of the process of agrarian change who consistently distinguished himself by his efforts to root out the truth of what is going on in the Indian countryside:

> If substantial changes over a considerable time-space are indeed protracted, conventional wisdom suggests that a depressed peasantry would be tempted to redress its condition in its own drastic way, with economic and political consequences to match. We do not anticipate such an upheaval in the foreseeable future, partly because peasant awakening on its own has a long way to go yet, and partly because an organised peasant movement is slow in emerging. But it would be a grave error of judgment on the part of bigger owners and their supporters to bank on these conditions as an insurance against a long overdue overhaul of the agricultural structure of India. For come it will, because unfulfilled needs have a way of injecting their own dynamic for change into situations which have been long static. The only question is whether the change will take place in good time, within the due process of law, or in circumstances when an actively disgruntled peasantry takes the law into its own hands.[69]

Foreign Influence on India's Agriculture

What role have the United States and other well-to-do nations played in the green revolution and other facets of Indian agriculture? Unlike agrarian linkages between economics and politics, which are so explicit as to need no further discussion, the influence of foreign factors on Indian agriculture is ubiquitous and complex. This is so partly because foreign influences are often channeled through the Indian government, where they are blended with domestic policy and become indistinguishable; and also because of an inclination on the part of India and foreign governments to play relationships in low key and thereby to prevent them from becoming intermixed with other types of foreign policy discussions. Nonetheless, scrutiny of the behavior of governments, private organizations, and international institutions reveals important Indian ties to the outside world at a variety of levels, including ideology, technology, food imports, and capital assistance.

[68]Dantwala, "From Stagnation to Growth," op. cit., p. 182.
[69]Ladejinsky, "Land Ceilings and Land Reform" *Economic and Political Weekly,* Annual Number, February 1972, p. 408.

Foreign capital assistance—loans and grants—which has been directed to India through bilateral and international institution channels, has played a major role in helping India to upgrade its agricultural infrastructure. In contrast to the 1950s, when foreign financing was devoted largely to big investment projects such as river valley development, recent efforts to aid Indian agriculture have included general balance-of-payments support and financing of needed inputs such as fertilizer in which Indian industry was not self-sufficient. Moreover, reflecting India's growing concern for social justice, post-1970 foreign-aid-financed investments have featured reducing rural income disparities and improving agricultural markets. This innovation is particularly true for IDA loans which in response to Robert McNamara's leadership, have been designed to help India's poorest by modernizing the Indian countryside and injecting greater equity on a state-by-state basis.[70] The danger inherent in this approach is that the World Bank is seeking to change the structure of Indian society in ways that surely will be opposed by India's rural elite. (Where, for example, should one put a new agricultural marketing center when a local politician wants it in his village but World Bank locational studies show that it should be elsewhere?) The World Bank appears to have gambled that the long-term benefits of its new-style projects will exceed the political costs and that opposition to its intrusion at the local political level will be contained by Delhi in the sense that the Indian government will act as a buffer between the Bank and the local authorities and that the Bank's relations with the central government will not be adversely affected by the conflicts caused by its "radical" forays into the tradition-bound Indian countryside. Although it will be many years before this new IBRD approach can be judged, the slow disbursement rates on these loans is preliminary and circumstantial evidence of the intractability of India's farm problems.

Technical assistance is another area where foreign influence has been extensive. Thousands of Western economists, agronomists, hydrologists, educators, and other specialists have applied their skills to finding solutions to India's problems. This effort, which has involved private foreign agencies as well as official bodies, has affected virtually every aspect of India's agricultural development including but not limited to, technological developments such as the improved seed varieties pioneered by the Rockefeller Foundation and the Intensive Agricultural District Program, which was supported in its nascent and later years by the Ford Foundation.

The influence foreign ideas have exerted on India's policies is not easily divined because, in the first instance, large social theories of capitalism and socialism are common to intellectuals throughout the world; second, India usually delayed its acceptance of foreign advice for considerable time until the rationale was fully understood and the political environment was made receptive. Nonetheless, whether one looks at India's socialist-influenced cooperative

[70]*World Bank Annual Report, 1973.*

movement or the capitalist-influenced use of market-price policies, clearly traditional Indian policies have been supplemented by ideas from abroad.

As I noted in Chapters 3 to 6, foreigners pressed India in the mid-1960s to change its agricultural policy, and although many of the policy changes which did occur at that time were a blend of Indian and foreign thinking, the new strategy was fully consistent with India's interests as interpreted by Indians. To a considerable degree foreign government pressures were a regular feature of the aid relationship, and annual meetings of the India Consortium were a primary forum where they were expressed. But this is not to say that foreigners dictated Indian agricultural policy. In most cases the foreign pressure on India was no more intense than the admonitions of balance-of-payments surplus countries to deficit nations in the OECD and IMF forums. Thus, given that the balance of influence in Indian public policy is weighted on the side of implementation and administration rather than formulation, even when foreign ideas were incorporated in Indian legislation, they still had only a marginal influence on the total scene.

Another channel for foreign involvement in Indian agriculture has been food imports. Although these received the most publicity when they arrived during periods of emergency, large amounts of foreign grain (and other agricultural commodities) arrived in India during noncrisis years and were justified at the time as a supplement to India's perennially scarce food supplies. Because the United States was in a food surplus position in most years from the end of the Second World War through 1972, and because farmers, proponents of foreign aid, and other American interests strongly and constantly supported PL-480, these food shipments have been more impervious to the general direction of Indo-American relations than other types of assistance. This situation began to change, however, in the mid-1960s when, largely in response to India's mammoth import requirements, the United States expanded its grain acreage. It is again being redefined in the 1970s as world demand for food presses with increasing force on supplies and India reconsiders its need to be self-sufficient in food production.

In judging the net influence of India's food imports, negative effects such as the disincentive to domestic Indian agricultural growth must be weighed against the positive human benefits of a better-fed population and the government investments which were financed with the proceeds from selling foreign grain in domestic markets. Contrary to the cynical view that corruption and waste expanded to absorb the incremental resources attributable to food imports, the evidence is that enough of the revenues obtained by India from sales of foreign food were channeled into various development programs to have justified this policy. For the future, as global demand for food increases and as prospects for cheap food imports become increasingly bleak, the jackpot question is whether enough of India's past investments were made in agriculture and agroindustry for it to take responsibility for feeding itself.

In concert, the food import, capital assistance, technical assistance, and

ideological contributions of foreigners were large and generally supportive of
India's self-proclaimed economic objectives. To the extent that these foreign
factors have not always achieved their aims, the reasons must be sought in the
more general problems the Indian government encountered in fulfilling its
own agricultural goals; in short, a variety of weaknesses in planning and
implementing agricultural development due largely to (1) the enormousness of
the changes attempted, (2) the scarcity of physical, technical, and human
resources which could be brought to bear on the problems, and (3) the
resistance of entrenched political and other interests to social and economic
change.

In Conclusion

If agriculture is the linchpin on which the Indian nation's development turns,
there is no credible economic or political strategy which does not highlight
progress both directly in this area and in the agroindustry and infrastructure on
which it depends. Demographic trends will also be critical for the future.
Although the population growth rate may decelerate as fertility declines faster
than mortality, it is unlikely that India will achieve a zero population growth
within the twentieth century, and in the interim, the demand for food will grow
in response to both rising population and income. Because the scope for
importing food during the period will be constrained by India's shortage of
international purchasing power—if not world food shortages—the burden of
greater supply falls squarely on indigenous farm efforts. From the standpoint
of employment, the ratio of agricultural to industrial workers is so heavily
weighted toward the former that there is no conceivable rate of industrial
growth which could absorb the growing numbers in the Indian work force in
the foreseeable future. Moreover, the effort to employ more workers in the
agricultural sector will be somewhat offset by increasing mechanization. For
India, even a zero population growth—if it could be attained immediately—
would not solve this problem insofar as the appetite of those already born will
grow as they get older, as will the work force itself. For all these reasons and
many others, ranging from technical considerations of productivity to the
politics of social justice, India has good reason to concentrate a massive effort
on its agricultural development.

Judged by experience in India and elsewhere, the prognosis for accelerating
rural expansion much above the post-Independence rate is not auspicious.
Since Independence, farm output has risen by about 3 percent, a distinct
improvement from the past. But with the exhaustion of virgin land the burden
for growth has shifted to human inventiveness and management. How, under
these circumstances, can India hope to expand its rural economy at the necessary pace? What is new in the picture which will permit an improvement over
the recent past? Mercifully, there are a variety of policies, many of which India

has already adopted, which offer hope for the future. First, and hardly requiring further documentation, is the need for the far-reaching institutional and technological changes which are needed to increase production and ensure agrarian equity. The enormous potential for such changes is shown by a comparison of the low average productivity of India's agricultural resources with the productivity of equivalent resources in other countries (or even with the more advanced areas of India) and in the existing large income disparities within India. The availability or near availability of the technical factors needed to modernize agriculture in India is a hopeful sign, and the policy question here is whether they will be put to work in conjunction with the requisite investments in agriculture and agroindustries. Finally, there is the question of whether the political process can be made to serve the pressing needs for better management of the economy in general, and agrarian conditions in particular. On this score India has had such a mixed record in the past that the potential for improvement is obvious: with proper attention it should be possible to accelerate the agricultural growth rate to 4 to 5 percent a year for at least a decade.

The immediacy of India's food and employment problems is so great as to justify a greatly expanded program of labor-intensive rural works including roads, irrigation, and other construction schemes. Such a program, as noted by John Lewis, should not and need not be a "leaf-raking" exercise,[71] but should aim at increasing production. If intelligently designed, a rural works program would provide large-scale employment for the neediest sectors of Indian society and would require less capital and foreign exchange resources than alternative employment schemes. Indeed, it may have so much potential for increasing current and future food supplies that it can pay for itself in resource terms, if not fiscally. A major constraint on instituting a massive rural works program, which is often underplayed, is that this approach requires application of one of India's scarcest resources, management. Thus, even if India should choose to upgrade its rural infrastructure, the question remains whether the necessary management talent could and would be mobilized to prevent the program from falling victim to the avarice of vested interests and becoming just another source of political patronage.[72]

For the long term, the search for progress in agriculture must be pursued beyond the tactical stage. To be successful, the all-India strategy which is needed to rationalize the nation's resources must overcome a variety of technological, institutional, economic, and psychological barriers, not least of which is

[71]John P. Lewis, "Wanted in India: A Relevant Radicalism," Policy Memorandum No. 36, Center for International Studies, Woodrow Wilson School of Public and International Affairs, Princeton University, 1969.

[72]Wolf Ladejinsky, writing about the three-year drought which paralyzed Maharashtra in the early 1970s ("Drought in Maharashtra," op. cit.), has noted that relief works undertaken under those grievous conditions tended to be chosen more to assist vested interests than on their intrinsic economic merit.

the normal—and healthy—skepticism with which farmers greet government policies not only in India, but throughout the world. If the near monumental challenge of simultaneously improving the availability of agricultural inputs, transportation, markets, and so forth is met with action rather than rhetoric, India can accelerate its overall growth rate and reduce its dependence on the monsoon. The importance of the second of these objectives is obvious in the sense that inadequate rainfall in India has traditionally led to insufficient food production. What is less clear, but just as critical, is the degree to which India's dependency on the monsoon has wedded it to emergency measures which, by distracting attention from basic reform, have imparted a very inefficient stop-go pattern to the development process.

It is ironic that in concluding this chapter we must revert to the long-term importance of industrial development. Rural India demands industrial inputs and consumer goods for its development. Moreover, if India is to increase per capita incomes it will need to raise the productivity of all factors of production—labor and capital, urban and rural. Given the mix of India's land, labor, and other resources, rapid progress can best be achieved through a differentially faster growth rate in industry than in agriculture.[73] Finally, for the very, very distant future, if the international community is able to rationalize global economic resources, this will require that India be a large net importer of food and exporter of industrial products. But just as India cannot target such a relationship for the near future, there is no magic in a short-term strategy that elevates higher farm output above all other goals. Assuming that India succeeds in expanding its food production beyond the subsistence level and that it will have options between increasing food production and exports, India should be wary of resolving all policy choices in favor of food self-sufficiency.

---

[73]A discussion of the relative roles of agriculture, rural works, small-scale industry, etc. can be found in Uma J. Lele and John W. Mellor, "Jobs, Poverty, and the 'Green Revolution'," *International Affairs* (London), vol. 48, no. 1, January 1972, pp. 20–32.

CHAPTER 9
INDUSTRIAL POLICY

It is tempting to say that if India had as much industry as it has industrial policy, it would be a very well-to-do nation. To do so, however, would be to ignore the realities that since Independence India's industrial production has more than trebled and its industrial base has been broadened to produce a wide range of goods, including many highly sophisticated products. Although in 1947 India's industrial output was large in comparison with most other nations, per capita production was small by Western standards. Moreover, Indian investments were narrowly concentrated in infrastructure like the railway system and in a few manufacturing sectors such as textiles and food. Thus, the opportunities for the government to shape India's industrial evolution appeared quite large to policy makers.

The previous chapter began on the note that agricultural development is absolutely essential to India's overall progress; this chapter emphasizes the significance of industry. India's leaders and many others have thought it inconceivable that the nation's economic aspirations could be met through the progress of traditional agriculture and small-scale cottage industry alone. Indeed, since World War II, when serious planning for decolonization began, the conventional wisdom almost everywhere—Delhi, New York, Moscow, etc.—has been that the essence of development involves modern and extensive industrial capacity. Moreover, in light of India's unfavorable land/people ratio and prospective migration to the cities, industrialization was seen as a necessity for preventing unemployment among the politically strategic urban masses.

In many respects India has led other developing countries in recognizing that for economic and political reasons industrialization is one of the primary goals of modern statehood. But India has dubious credentials as a model; its greater size, higher skill levels, and more favorable natural resource base give India's aspirations to create a modern industrial society much greater potential for fulfillment than the plans of many other developing nations. Even historically,

India has had unique roots which favored industrialization. The Swadeshi ("buy Indian") movement, for example, which began in 1907 and was sparked by political dissatisfaction with British rule, has encouraged domestic production ever since. A Swadeshi view of economics complements the Gandhian approach and is reflected in current Indian policies to achieve economic self-reliance and develop cottage industries.

There are a host of major and minor themes in the Indian government's approach to industrialization, and for reasons of space I shall deal with only the most important. Small-scale and village industries which are known as the "unorganized sector," diversity among business interests, and labor productivity are among the significant subjects which are treated only in passing. Moreover, as the chapter is concerned primarily with policy, it does not purport to be a balanced appraisal of every aspect of Indian industry. Many of the achievements of large- and small-scale industry bear little relationship to policy and are not considered here. The chapter begins with private enterprise, which has been the subject of a variety of supportive, regulatory, and prohibitionary policies affecting output levels, product mix, prices, profits, inputs, investment financing, and location of industry. Certain economic functions have been regarded by India as so vital to national progress that they have been reserved for the public sector, where, presumably, there should be no gap to be bridged between private entrepreneurial and public interests. Related to these essentially domestic policies are India's systems for regulating the earning and allocation of scarce foreign exchange resources and for regulating the entry and behavior of foreign investors. I shall turn to each of these subjects in sequence, reserving for Chapter 11 a full analysis of how the totality of India's policies, resource endowment, international affairs, and politics have interacted to determine the direction and speed of India's development.

Evolution of India's Industrial Licensing and Related Policies

The Industrial Policy Resolution of 1948 set the cautious and socialist tone which has since become characteristic of India's industrial policies. India's strategy had a well-established and fairly broad-based political lineage which derived from the Lahore Resolution of the Indian National Congress (1929), the Karachi declaration of the All-India Congress Committee (1931), the Bombay Plan (1944) which had been proposed by a group of businessmen, and other pre-Independence efforts to see ahead to the day when Indians would be responsible for their own economic management. According to the Karachi Resolution, "The State shall own or control key industries and services, mineral resources, railways, waterways, shipping and other means of public transport."[1] This view, together with the decisions to regulate closely the private sector and

[1] *Resolutions on Economic Policy and Programme, 1924–1954* (New Delhi: AICC, 1954), p. 9.

to concentrate new investment on heavy industry, is central to the policies which were adopted after Independence.

India's 1948 Industrial Policy Resolution went far to implement what had been envisaged at Karachi. It established a state monopoly for arms, ammunition, atomic energy, and railways; reserved to the government responsibility for new undertakings in coal, shipbuilding, mineral oils, iron and steel, aircraft manufacture, and telecommunications equipment; and cited 18 other major industries as particularly subject to government regulation. The resolution claimed nationalization of existing industry as a state prerogative, but in spite of the opposition of radical and socialist forces, it generally ruled out nationalization for a 10-year period and was expressed in language to reassure the business community: "If it is decided that the State should acquire any unit, the fundamental rights guaranteed by the Constitution will be observed and compensation will be awarded on a fair and equitable basis." In addition to establishing a somewhat flexible division of responsibility between the public and private sectors, the 1948 resolution underscored the need to pursue development in all sectors, including agriculture and cottage industries, and promised that government would aid as well as regulate industry.

The 1948 Industrial Policy Resolution foreshadowed the formation of the Planning Commission in 1950 and the Industries (Development and Regulation) Act of 1951. The latter gave broad licensing powers to the central government while providing the states with some latitude to adopt their own regimes for regulating local industry. This act and the Essential Commodities Act of 1955, which brought pricing and distribution within the government's regulating orbit, are the principal, but by no means unique, legal basis for India's system of administrative controls.

Although the 1948 resolution had sought to instill public confidence in the government and reassure the country that the goals of industrial growth and distributive equity would be pursued through nondoctrinaire and pragmatic policies, the 1948–1956 period was marked by a sense of confrontation between business and government. Consequently, there were only limited amounts of new investment by both the private and public sectors and a general feeling of dissatisfaction with the impasse. When the Congress party met in 1955 at Avadi, it not only voted unanimously in favor of a resolution calling for "a socialist pattern of society," but heard its outgoing president, Nehru, say, "The main purpose of a socialized pattern of society is to remove the fetters to production. . . . It becomes necessary therefore to have a private sector also and to give it full play within its field."[2] Indian business remained apprehensive of socialism, but Nehru went to such pains to reassure industrialists that he obtained their cooperation, and it was no accident that in 1956 the rhetoric of socialism was accompanied by a new pragmatism in policy. Avadi was followed not only by the *bold* Second Five-Year Plan with its emphasis on investment in state-owned heavy industry, but the Industrial Policy Resolution of 1956, which,

[2]Quoted in Kidron, op. cit., p. 88.

while not worded all that differently from its 1948 predecessor, was eventually interpreted by Indian industry as a green light and therefore contributed to a sustained period of accelerated and productive investments.

The 1956 resolution recognized that industrial progress had not been satisfactory and aimed at speeding the pace by being less ambiguous about the particular roles of public and private sectors. Although it reserved an increased number of industries for the public sector, it was more emphatic in allocating responsibility in the other industries to private industry. India's subsequent industrial progress, however, depended less on the specific wording of the 1956 resolution than on the combined stimulus of rapid growth of public investment and a temporarily more favorable government attitude toward private enterprise.

At first blush it may seem a paradox that peace between the public and private sectors was achieved at a time when government investments were finally moving from the construction to the production stage and an accelerated program of new public investments was being planned for the future. In reality, the full experience of India's development since 1947 suggests that there was a reciprocal causality in the coincidental progress of public and private sectors, that at least in the short term they were more complementary than competitive.

The end of this "golden era" for Indian industry came in the mid-1960s for several reasons, most notably the misallocation of foreign exchange for new capital projects at the expense of maintenance inputs and the unbalanced development of related industries which caused bottlenecks in some sectors and excess capacity in others. India's investment pattern, which had been biased toward heavy industry and against agricultural and other mass consumer goods, was a problem, but India's acute foreign exchange scarcity, the debilitating aftereffects of the wars with China and Pakistan, and the crushing impact of India's two-year drought were also responsible. Under these conditions long-term industrial planning had diminished relevance as policy decisions were made largely on ad hoc and pragmatic grounds. Indeed, at the outset of 1969 it was a commonplace in India to say that policy lay in implementation rather than law or announced doctrine.

The trauma of 1965–1967 led to an economic and intellectual depression which gave little sign of lifting until 1969, when a political discontinuity promised to bring significant changes in its wake. Despite optimism about the economy generated by the green revolution's salubrious effect on food production, the mood in 1969 was anything but tranquil. The enduring industrial recession was disquieting, and, even more significant, political tensions within the right and left wings of the Congress, and between the Congress and other parties, had become acute. Thus, when Mrs. Gandhi took the drastic political step of splitting the Congress in the summer of 1969, her strategy was to gain full control of the government by capitalizing on the emerging agricultural surpluses and making the government's policies more definitive and popular by shifting them to the left. With respect to the relative priorities of growth and equity, Prime Minister Gandhi took issue with the position of her father and the Industrial Policy Resolution of 1948. The latter had said that "Any improvement in the economic conditions of the country postulates an increase in national wealth; a mere redistribution of existing wealth would make no essential difference to the people and would merely mean the redistribution of poverty."[3] Thus, the period following July 1969 was marked by greater efforts to translate social justice into reality through heightened control of private industry, nationalization of strategic businesses, increased spending on social services, crash employment schemes, increased tax rates on wealth and income, and related policies.

The substance of the swing left, which was well articulated in the document *Approach to the Fifth Five-Year Plan* (May 1972), remained intact in the *Draft Fifth Five-Year Plan* when that document was approved by the National Development Council in December 1973. In real terms, however, the swing left was of more limited significance insofar as the new policies were limited in scope and were in force for too short a time to measurably help India's poor. The new socialism was overtaken by events, including the costly war with Pakistan (1971), a poor monsoon (1972), and soaring international prices for petroleum, fertilizer, and food (1973–74). These developments, combined with India's enduring industrial recession and foreign exchange shortages, produced a more cautious attitude on the part of government. For example, in February 1973, when the government released a long-awaited elaboration of the industrial policy, the public judged the new document as merely a reiteration of the 1956 resolution and dismissed it as shedding little new light on how the government would actually behave in the future.[4] Another reason why the ruling party returned to a more supportive attitude toward private enterprise near the end of this period was the growing reliance on business contributions for financing elections.[5]

The political and economic uncertainties of 1973–74 produced a vitriolic policy debate. But even though radical sloganeering played an exaggerated role in the conflict, India's policies were anything but doctrinaire socialism: one expert group, led by the noted economist K. N. Raj, recommended that greater use be made of the private sector (1973); Industries Minister C. Subramaniam introduced reforms to speed the processing of industrial license applications (1973); and the government retreated from its ill-fated nationalization of the wheat trade (1974). These policies were adopted even though they were interpreted as signs of revisionism and were greeted by a chorus of criticism from the Indian left.[6] Politically, the polarization of right and left forces during

[3]Ibid., p. 85.

[4]See editorial, *Eastern Economist,* Feb. 16, 1973, p. 283.

[5]See, for example, K. Bhatia, op. cit., and S. A. Kochanek, *Business and Politics in India,* op. cit., pp. 230–239.

[6]See, for example, the acidic editorial in the *National Herald* (Oct. 20, 1973) criticizing what leftists regarded as the heresy of the Raj group.

this period weakened the chances for good policy by providing little common ground for compromise.

This brief introduction and the elaboration of Indian industrial policy which follows show that the government's approach was modified frequently in response to evolving economic and political cycles. While tactically correct, these changes were not always in the long-term interest of industrial development insofar as by disorienting company managers and depressing the price of shares traded on Indian stock exchanges, they had an adverse effect on new investment and even current production. The frequency of policy changes is of course only one among many factors complicating India's industrial development, but its significance should not be underrated. Indeed, in 1972 the Indian Parliament's Estimates Committee pleaded "That for sustained industrial growth it is imperative that industrial licensing procedures and policy should generally hold good for a reasonably long period, say a minimum of 5 years coincident with the Plan period."[7]

The Conjunction of Plan Targets and Licensing Policy

India has explicitly set quantitative and qualitative targets for a wide range of economic variables. Most relevant to industrial policy are national targets to:

¶ Encourage growth of industrial output in general
¶ Set production levels for individual companies based on their licensed capacity
¶ Set production levels for various commodities, including investment goods, exports, and mass consumption items
¶ Affect investment by sector and the choice of technology to be used
¶ Establish the relative roles of public and private sectors
¶ Avert concentration in industry and prevent private firms from developing monopoly power
¶ Encourage small-scale manufacturing
¶ Aid backward regions
¶ Affect a variety of technical, financial, and other factors pertinent to India's international economic relations

Clearly, to the extent that licensing policy was charged with the achievement of all these objectives, India's overall policy frame (discussed in Chapter 7) is of great importance. Our task here is to relate Plan targets, with the actual formulation and practice of industrial policy.

According to two leading observers of India's policies, Bhagwati and Desai,

---

[7]*Report on Industrial Licensing by the Estimates Committee (1971–72), Nineteenth Report* (New Delhi: Lok Sabha Secretariat, 1972), p. 23.

the Planning Commission's industrial targets "were not merely indicative but were treated as full-scale targets with regard to which the Industrial Licensing Committee operated and lapses from which were considered by even governmental and inquiry committees as 'failures of planning.'"[8] Although this implies the need for a close relationship between the Planning Commission and the economic ministries, in practice, coordination within the government has been less than perfect. The ministries have often made genuine contributions to Plan formulation and target setting, but the Planning Commission's influence at the more advanced stages of policy formulation has been uneven and its contribution at the implementation stage has been almost nonexistent. Indicative of the state of affairs is the nearly total absence of reference to the Planning Commission in the chapter "Economic Policy—Formulation and Implementation" in one major review by the government of its economic administration.[9] In theory there is nothing wrong with this situation, but in practice it has meant a tendency for targets to be unrealistic and a reduction in the pressure to meet targets.

A second problem raised by India's decision to use targets is the notable absence of any reliable mechanism whereby the government could compel the private sector to fulfill its share of the Plans. Whereas Delhi was legally (and, to a considerable degree, physically) competent to bar various forms of private commerce, it was the nature of government-business relations that officials were generally without positive authority to make industrialists invest, produce, or otherwise follow their directions. Moreover, shortfalls from target have not been unique to private industry. Public sector firms have been conspicuously immune to the process of translating targets into reality, as illustrated by "the colossal failure of the State Industrial Development Corporations to take any effective steps on the 120 letters of intent issued to them in the past five years for setting up industries of vital importance to the national economy."[10]

Bhagwati and Desai cite other reasons that Plan targets have been over- and underfulfilled: (1) shortfalls in various sectors of the economy (including imports) have adversely affected other sectors through a chain reaction process; (2) the licensing system has malfunctioned; (3) because targets were detailed but not exhaustive, there was production of items not initially targeted; (4) most targets applied only to the "organized" sector, but some items were produced by the "indigenous" sector; and (5) there were de minimis exemptions for some investments which sometimes were of real importance to the economy.[11]

In the mid and late 1960s the growing gap between targets and actual performance caused India to reconsider its planning techniques, especially the issue of whether the targets should be made more flexible and merely indica-

[8]Jagdish N. Bhagwati and Padma Desai, op. cit., p. 243.
[9]Report of the Study Team on Economic Administration (C. H. Bhaba, chairman), (New Delhi: GOI, Administrative Reforms Commission, 1967), pp. 208–221.
[10]Times of India, Sept. 19, 1972.
[11]Bhagwati and Desai, op. cit., pp. 243–248.

tive. It was argued that there would be more internal consistency in the progress of the economy if greater attention were paid to the relative priorities of objectives and if only "The targets of aggregate income, consumption, and investment can be considered as relatively invariant."[12] The bureaucracy and left-leaning politicians showed little sympathy for this solution and successfully opposed it.

The Licensing System in Practice

Although there have been occasional procedural changes, the government's Licensing Committee, established in 1952 and composed of representatives of the economic ministries, has generally had responsibility for the approval of investment applications. It has operated in conjunction with the Capital Goods (imports), Foreign Agreements (collaboration), and Capital Issues (finance) Committees among others, and it has had the advice of a Directorate General of Technical Development (DGTD). The operative characteristics of this system, broadly shared responsibility and ambiguous working guidelines, are such that there has been considerable latitude for excessive delays, misdirection of resources, discouragement of investment, and favorable treatment of precisely the large industrial firms which official policy aims to curb.

According to Arun Shourie's study of the Licensing Committee, the processing of an industrial investment application in the early 1970s was characterized by the following routine:

¶ An application "is passed around vertically and horizontally to as many functionaries as possible." It will be seen and initialed by as many as 20 to 30 officials in a single ministry.

¶ When the application is considered by the Licensing Committee, 30 to 40 individuals will be present and it will be one of 40 to 50 cases examined in the course of only three hours.

In Shourie's view, the whole process whereby license applications are approved is designed to operate in such a way as to make a mockery of the underlying economic objectives.[13]

The potential value of the licensing system has been further distorted by the extent to which decisions are taken ad hoc rather than according to well-defined principles. On the one hand, the government has refrained from being any more specific about its intentions than to issue one list twice a year of industries in which applications will normally be rejected and a second list of industries in which new investment is regarded as desirable.[14] On the other

---

[12]R. K. Hazari, "Industrial Planning and Licensing Policy," Final Report (New Delhi: GOI, Planning Commission, 1967).

[13]Shourie, *Controls and the Current Situation*, op. cit.

[14]Kidron, op. cit., p. 51.

hand, the government has sought to examine each proposal on its intrinsic merits, an approach which ignores the importance of priorities and weighing applications received against other proposals which have not yet come to the attention of the Licensing Committee.[15]

According to the Parliament's Estimates Committee, the technical expertise of the DGTD in handling the information provided by industry is weak and the data are often incomplete and inaccurate.[16] With respect to technoeconomic analysis, Bhagwati and Desai found that for many years "there is no evidence of any studies having been carried out by the DGTD of the optimal size, time-phasing, and location of industrial units." Moreover, studies of the DGTD show that it has been extremely negligent in monitoring the progress of investments following its issuance of licenses.[17]

To businessmen submitting license applications, there is perhaps no more frustrating experience than the wait and uncertainty which attend official review of industrial proposals. Moreover, in India's situation, where bottlenecks and failures to expand supply fast enough to meet demand carry high economic cost, official delays have major importance in the national welfare. Thus, it is distressing that despite repeated efforts to reduce the waiting time for license issuance (for example, the use of "letters of intent" as an interim measure allowing some forward movement pending issuance of the license), delays remain common. In the mid-1960s an official study team found that the government required an average of 270 days to process and issue a clearance for the import of capital goods.[18] Despite a number of "reforms" which were introduced to reduce this inordinate delay, a reappraisal of the situation in the early 1970s showed that the time elapsed in obtaining approval for import of capital goods had lengthened to 390 days and that an extra 70 days were required to place public advertisements to ascertain that the equipment needed could not be obtained from a domestic supplier. Following the 1972 report of the Estimates Committee, which criticized the multiplicity of stages at which license applications were considered and the degree to which deadlines at each stage went unmet,[19] India's new industries minister, C. Subramaniam, introduced reforms to shorten the time period drastically.[20]

The operation of India's licensing system has been complicated to some degree by the proliferation of industrial categories to which different rules

[15]Hazari, op. cit., pp. 19–20, and Swaminathan reports of 1964 and 1965.

[16]*Ninth Report of the Estimates Committee on Industrial Licensing* (New Delhi: Lok Sabha Secretariat, 1967), pp. 216–222.

[17]Bhagwati and Desai, op. cit., pp. 255–256.

[18]*Report of the Study Team on Import and Export Control Organization* (H. C. Mathur, chairman), (New Delhi: GOI, Ministry of Commerce, 1965) part 1.

[19]*Nineteenth Report of the Estimates Committee (1971–72),* op. cit., pp. 129–134.

[20]The need for close scrutiny of government reports on this subject is illustrated by data in *Economic Survey, 1973–74,* p. 29, which purport to show that most applications acted on were approved, but fail to indicate the significance of applications withdrawn or pending for long periods.

were applied. The amendments to India's industrial policy announced in February 1970, for example, introduced the notion of a "core" sector (consisting of "basic," "critical," and "strategic" industries) and a "heavy investment" sector (new investments exceeding the equivalent of $6.67 million). Following these modifications, the application of India's industrial policy required licensing authorities to distinguish among the following categories:

¶ Core sector
    Basic sector
    Strategic sector
    Critical sector
¶ Key sector
¶ Heavy sector
¶ Middle sector
¶ Small sector

Licensing authorities were required also to discriminate on the basis of whether the applicant for a license belonged to:

¶ Public sector
¶ Joint sector
¶ Private sector
¶ Cooperative sector

and an additional basis for applying different criteria to an application was whether the requested license was for:

¶ New undertaking
¶ Substantial expansion
¶ Net article
¶ Change in location

As seen by one eminent Indian economist, A. M. Khusro, "The mushrooming categories . . . are so many figments of imagination, economically justifiable only in very few cases."[21] According to Khusro, largely on account of its licensing policy India has unwisely ignored potential economies of scale as a means for achieving production efficiency.

In addtion, India's licensing system has been widely criticized for misallocating resources, undermining the efficiency and growth of the Indian economy, and causing other problems. Among the more important of these in light of India's concern with self-reliance and modernization is the effect of licensing on product design. A study by Mark Frankena noted a number of design deficien-

---

[21]A. M. Khusro, "Industrial Policy: A Critique and an Approach," mimeographed (Delhi: Institute of Economic Growth, 1972), p. 6.

cies for various Indian engineering products and cited administrative control systems as the principal cause. According to Frankena, government (1) reduced competition and allowed inefficient producers to remain profitable, (2) established price ceilings which discouraged product improvement, (3) banned new efficient technology so long as it appeared that requisite production could be maintained with existing plant and equipment, (4) biased technical choice toward the inefficient and obsolete in order to save foreign exchange or other scarce factors of production, (5) ignored scale economies, (6) arbitrarily protected cottage industries, and (7) discouraged Indian firms from learning more about efficient foreign technologies and designs. He concludes that the cumulative effect was to reduce the rate of technological change and to hamper India's transition from an import substitution policy to an export promotion policy.[22]

In the minds of many Indians one of the major purposes of administrative controls was to prevent industrial concentration and monopoly behavior by the large business houses. But when a succession of official committees were constituted during the 1960s to study the relationship, they found, ironically, that the licensing policies had actually improved the position of these so-called monopoly houses. In the first instance, the very idea of licensing tended to reduce the number of competitors in a particular industry and enlarge the possibilities for collusion and oligopoly behavior. Moreover, because the large firms had connections at high levels of government and the wherewithal to keep competent lobbyists in Delhi, submit multiple license applications, and otherwise outdo smaller firms in dealing with the licensing machinery, they were able to benefit from the control regime.[23] In response to this revelation a Monopoly and Restrictive Trade Practices Act was passed in 1969 and a Monopolies Commission was established in 1970. Early experience with this new administrative machinery, however, left some suspicion that it would merely serve as an additional hurdle in the process of obtaining industrial licenses without substantially reducing the monopoly position of India's larger private firms.[24]

The Private Sector Continued: Other Restrictions, Some Incentives, and a New Approach

In addition to various administrative controls to deal with domestic economic relations, India has licensed foreign exchange transactions such as imports, exports, and foreign investment. I shall defer discussion of these until after completing the analysis of domestic factors affecting industry.

[22]Mark Frankena, op. cit., pp. 249–264.

[23]*Report of the Committee on Distribution of Income and Levels of Living,* op. cit., Hazari, op. cit., and *Report of the Industrial Licensing Inquiry Committee* (S. Dutt, chairman), (New Delhi: GOI, Ministry of Industrial Development, 1969).

[24]*Economic and Political Weekly,* Nov. 17, 1973, p. 2033.

Locational policy, which has often been implemented through the industrial licensing mechanism, has two principal objectives: to satisfy the states that each is receiving its fair share of new industrial capacity and to divert new undertakings to the nation's more backward regions. In responding to state government initiatives and locational objectives, India's licensing policy, has shown considerable sensitivity to political considerations but also has contributed in no small way to the fragmentation of industry and the proliferation of less than optimum-size facilities.[25] This situation is unfortunate, not only because of the loss of economic efficiency, but because of the ease with which it could have been avoided if the planning and licensing authorities had predetermined the total amount of investment to be allowed in each state and thereby removed the inducement for states to compete with one another for each new investment opportunity.[26]

Indian experience with regard to the related but more difficult task of encouraging investment in backward areas has been equally unsatisfactory. According to the Estimates Committee, "During the first three Five-Year Plan periods, except for locating a few public sector projects in certain backward states, no concerted steps were taken to progressively remove disparities in the level of development between different regions in the country."[27] The Committee was disconcerted to find that in a subsequent three-year period only four licenses had been granted for development in underdeveloped areas of the populous and backward state of Uttar Pradesh.[28] The explanation for this state of affairs is that in the absence of industrial infrastructure and efficient transportation systems, private firms have been loath to accept official incentives and locate away from industrial centers. In cases where they have taken the plunge, they often have found that the government incentives did not justify the extra costs, and they have been reluctant to expand their operations. Although the Draft Fifth Plan promises a greater effort by government to rationalize investments in the neglected regions,[29] outstanding experience with public and private sector enterprises located in backward areas is so poor as to suggest that to be successful, the new government initiatives will need both to build industrial infrastructure and to change existing socioeconomic structures.

Many of India's price and distribution controls originated during the Second World War and subsequently have been used from time to time through the authority of the Defense of India Rules, Essential Commodities Act, and Industries (Development and Regulation) Act. These controls have been applied to various critical items, including steel, fertilizer, cotton textiles, paper, sugar, cement, and petroleum products. They have been used for multiple

[25]See Alan S. Manne, *Investments for Capacity Expansion: Size, Location, and Time-Phasing* (London: George Allen & Unwin, 1967), p. 146.

[26]Bhagwati and Desai, op. cit., p. 268.

[27]*Nineteenth Report of the Estimates Committee (1971–72)*, op. cit., p. 95.

[28]Ibid., p. 101.

[29]*Draft Fifth Five-Year Plan*, op. cit., vol. 2, p. 134.

purposes, such as to (1) restrain inflation, particularly for sensitive consumer goods; (2) stabilize markets in order to provide an even and equitable flow of products to all regions, throughout the year, and from year to year; (3) restrain consumption in order to minimize imports; (4) allocate scarce products for priority uses such as defense and investment; and (5) counter monopoly.[30]

In practice, the price and distribution controls preempted markets from their usual function of allocating resources and, in the view of many observers, distorted the normal production, distribution, and consumption patterns of many products. For example, one official study team found that price fixing by the Iron and Steel Controller was insensitive to relative cost and quality differences within commodity classifications and thereby deterred adjustment of the pattern of output to meet the pattern of demand, "even when there are no technical obstacles to such adjustments."[31] It is significant that another official committee, chaired by an eminent Indian economist known for his socialist views (K. N. Raj), also was highly critical of the use of controls in the steel industry. According to the Raj committee, the imperfection in the functioning of the Iron and Steel Controller's office could be traced both to the impossible task which had been entrusted to it and to the inefficiencies, lack of priorities, negligence, and corruption which characterized its operations.[32] Similar commentaries are common for most of the products to which price and distribution controls have been applied.

Supplementing the control measures already discussed is what is known as "companies legislation," i.e., laws to ensure that public corporations are managed fairly and in the public interest. Ostensibly, companies legislation is not intended to do anything more than to regulate management, protect shareholder interests, and set standards for correct corporate behavior. In practice, however, these laws have been changed so often and enforced so arbitrarily as to reduce the efficiency of the companies (public and private) which must adhere to them. Moreover, according to some observers, they are now intended "to ensure that in all important matters changes are made with the approval of Government."[33]

Balancing the government's efforts to constrain and channel the energies of big business has been its encouragement for small-scale industry. Industrial enterprises having assets of less than Rs. 750,000 ($100,000) are important not only because they account for roughly one-half of India's industrial value added, but because this sector makes a more than proportional contribution to the employment of the poor and to the output of essential consumer goods. Although government assistance to the small-scale sector has been expanded

---

[30]*Report of the Study Team on Economic Administration,* op. cit., pp. 55–56.

[31]Ibid., p. 57.

[32]*Report of the Committee on Steel Control* (New Delhi: GOI, Ministry of Steel and Heavy Industries, 1963).

[33]Madan Gopal Jajoo, "Companies Legislation in India: Plea for a Rational View," *Economic and Political Weekly,* June 9, 1973.

over time, this has not prevented a gradual decline in its position relative to large-scale industry. But even if this sector has not become the leading spirit toward development that some of its supporters would wish, official efforts to assist smaller Indian companies by reserving certain industries for them and by providing special import and credit facilities have helped make it critical to India's progress.

Like most other countries, India has sought to meet some of its economic objectives through fiscal and monetary policies which punish companies which fail to pursue officially sanctioned goals and reward those which arrange their operations to conform with what is regarded as the public good. Thus, Delhi has offered a variety of investment carrots. Among the most important indus-trial development incentives outstanding in the early 1970s were (1) tax holi-days for new enterprises; (2) partial exemption from income tax of companies in "priority industries"; (3) special depreciation allowances; and (4) income tax credits to offset the costs of new investments.[34] Some of these have failed to elicit the desired company response (e.g., tax relief to firms investing in backward areas), others have not been fully effective because of frequent changes in the benefits and conditions attending their use, and still others have been perverted by company lawyers and accountants and have served merely to reduce corporate tax liability. Nevertheless, the incentives have had some marginal success in encouraging productive investment, but because India's economic situation has been marked by such contrary factors as near confisca-tory tax levels, black markets, labor indiscipline, and scarce industrial licenses, they have accomplished less than their potential.

The flagrant disregard of some private companies for the social interest— and official suspicions that most Indian firms were managed in this way— contributed to the progressive implementation of controls over private indus-try. The close alliance between much of Indian business and the Congress party which had existed before Independence gradually gave way to a mood of conflict and mutual distrust. Bureaucrats and political leaders were frustrated because official controls and high taxes seemed to have little effect in channel-ing the behavior of entrepreneurs into desired patterns. Businessmen, in turn, were dissatisfied not only with what they regarded as inept and radical official policies which hampered their profits and expansion, but with the failure of the government to assure faster economic growth.

The political events of 1969 and the government's new flirtation with nation-alization were disturbing to private industry. Businessmen were especially bothered by bank nationalization because this gave the government a near monopoly over financial resources and made private companies more depen-dent and subject to government pressures than in the past. Delhi recognized its new power and devoted considerable attention to the question of how, by monitoring the flow of bank credit to industry, it might affect the behavior of

[34]For a more detailed description, see *Seminar on World Partnership in the Second Development Decade*, op. cit., pp. 66–69 and 81–89.

private companies. The idea that the government should nominate public officials to serve on the boards of directors of some private companies was suggested and in some cases implemented. Moreover, according to the new policy the government reserved for itself the right to convert its holdings of company debt into equity in cases where it felt that the firm was not operating in the public interest. This threat of "backdoor nationalization" rekindled the debate over the proper role of private large-scale industry and deterred some new investment.

By discouraging both bureaucrats and businessmen from taking decisions which would increase investment, the conflict between proponents and critics of the private sector was almost universally recognized as an impediment to development goals. To break the impasse, and to meld the best features of public and private sectors, it was proposed in 1972 that a "joint sector" of mixed public and private ownership be established to operate in oligopoly-prone industries. The proposal elicited a mixed reaction from the Indian business community, but the nation's leading industrialist, J. R. D. Tata, endorsed the idea and, in a memorandum to the government, made far-reaching proposals for its adoption. Tata suggested that the capacity of the Tata Iron and Steel Company (TISCO) be doubled and that this should be achieved through a joint venture. This idea attracted considerable interest, but it was eventually rejected, chiefly because of the political opposition of socialists.[35] Subsequently, although the notion of joint sector enterprise remained alive and even was noted in the Draft Fifth Plan, the Tata case was regarded as an inauspicious sign for its future.

The Status of Public Sector Enterprise

The cold shoulder accorded by Delhi to the joint sector proposal is indicative of the political leadership's strong sentiment in favor of state ownership of large business.

The Indian government's preference for the public rather than the private sector can be traced by the growing share of national investment which has been directed to government enterprise. As Table 9-1 shows, public sector investment has increased steadily, from 46.4 percent of total investment during the First Plan to a projected 66.0 percent in the Fifth Plan. As I have noted, there was both ideological and pragmatic justification for the prevailing opinion that public sector enterprise should extend beyond strategic industries (mainly defense) and natural monopoly activities (such as the railroads). This view was well rooted in India's pre-Independence economic debate, and many Indian leaders believed that it would help the economy to grow faster and improve the

[35]J. R. D. Tata, "Suggestions for Accelerating Industrial Growth," Memorandum to the Government of India, dated May 17, 1972, published in *Mainstream,* vol. 10, nos. 51 and 52 (Aug. 19, 1972).

TABLE **9-1**
PUBLIC VERSUS PRIVATE SECTOR INVESTMENT

	Total investment (billions of rupees)	Private sector (percent of total)	Public sector (percent of total)
First Plan, 1951–1956	33,600	53.6	46.4
Second Plan, 1956–1961	68,310	45.4	54.6
Third Plan, 1961–1966	113,190	37.1	62.9
Interim, 1966–1969	NA‡	NA	NA
Fourth Plan, 1969–1974*	226,350	39.7	60.3
Fifth Plan, 1974–1979†	475,610	34.0	66.0

*Estimated.

†Proposed.

‡NA = not available.

Sources: *India: 1974*, pp. 158 and 164; *Draft Fifth Five-Year Plan, 1974–79* (New Delhi: GOI, Planning Commission, 1974), vol. 1, p. 41.

distribution of development benefits by depriving India's economic magnates of their privileged position in the society and power over the national economy.

Nehru generally took a pragmatic view of the private sector. While recognizing that it did not always operate in the public interest and was not the paragon of efficiency that it claimed to be, he regarded it as a potential resource for development, especially valuable in the early post-Independence years when the public sector had only limited management and other resources for initiating new enterprises. Nehru's views conflicted sharply with the perceptions of the Congress party left-wing and other doctrinaire socialists, but because they led to some of the same policy conclusions espoused by the Gandhians who were suspicious of bigness and central control over the economy, they were politically acceptable. Thus, Nehru's 1948 Industrial Policy Resolution generally eschewed nationalization for a period of 10 years, and when nationalization was used in 1955, its object was the Imperial Bank, which accounted for about one-third of total commercial bank demand deposits and, while not a central bank per se, often acted as the government's fiscal agent. In this case and the few other instances where Nehru did choose to take over private companies (airlines and life insurance), even the Federation of British Industries could not help but agree that his action had been necessary and desirable.[36]

The principal bases for the growth of India's public sector, therefore, were (1) the expansion of the nation's very extensive railroad system and similar infrastructure which were already government-owned in 1947 and (2) the

[36]See *India: A Survey for British Industrial Firms*, published by the Federation of British Industries, cited in Vera M. Dean, *New Patterns of Democracy in India* (Cambridge, Mass.: Harvard University Press, 1969), p. 128.

government's large and sustained post-Independence investments in core sector industries such as petroleum, chemicals, iron and steel, and heavy engineering. These investments, which attracted great attention during the decade 1955–1965 (Second and Third Plans), were concentrated in the capital goods sectors on the theory that in this way India would move with maximum speed to become a modern industrial and self-reliant nation. With few exceptions, each of these investments was based on a heavy dependence on technology from one or several foreign aid donors and involved the Indian economy in a complex activity in which it had had little earlier experience.

Since the Third Plan ended in 1966, India has suffered more or less constantly from industrial recession, budgetary stringency, and shortage of foreign exchange. Consequently, there has been somewhat less concern for new investments and more emphasis on bringing planned investments on-stream and retrenching to improve the operating efficiency of units already in production. Moreover, India's renewed interest in social justice and self-reliance as policy objectives coincided with the bifurcation of the Congress in 1969 and contributed to the country's first major experiment with nationalization. The takeover of India's 14 largest private commercial banks in 1969 was followed by nationalization of coking coal companies and general insurance (1971), the Indian Iron and Steel Company (1972), the Copper Corporation (1972), and noncoking coal and the wholesale wheat trade (1973). Operating results in these new public sector activities were not encouraging at first, and the wholesale wheat trade proved to be indigestible and was returned to private hands in 1974. This at least temporarily interrupted the momentum of the nationalization movement but left little prospect for any other denationalizations.

It is not easy to sketch a profile of the public sector because existing data on "departmental undertakings" (enterprises directly managed by various Delhi ministries), "nondepartmental undertakings" (activities owned by the central government but managed by corporations), and state-owned business are incomplete. Estimates for 1969 show the central government had investments in 91 economic enterprises (departmental and nondepartmental) valued at Rs. 53.4 billion ($7.1 billion).[37] As shown by Table 9-2, the public sector's significance within the Indian economy has grown considerably; the share of total government activities (entrepreneurial and administrative) in net national product has almost doubled in 20 years. Public sector enterprise would show a comparable growth rate but for a revision in the statistical presentation which makes it look even more dynamic. For the future, the public sector is projected to continue to increase in relation to the private sector and the gross national product as a whole. The Draft Fifth Plan projects that it will grow from 14.7 percent of GNP in 1973 to 18.2 percent in 1978–79 and to 20.7 percent in 1985–86.[38]

The share of national income attributable to public sector enterprise may

[37]*Yearbook of Public Sector: 1970* (Bombay: Commerce, 1970), p. 9.
[38]*Draft Fifth Five-Year Plan,* vol. 1, op. cit., p. 12.

TABLE **9-2**

CHANGING SHARE OF THE PUBLIC SECTOR IN NET DOMESTIC PRODUCT (percent)

Year	Public sector enterprise	Government administrative	Total public sector
1950–51	3.0	4.5	7.5
1955–56	4.2	5.7	9.9
1960–61	4.0	6.4	10.4
1965–66	6.7	6.5	13.2
1970–71*	7.7	7.1	14.8

*Provisional.

Sources: India: 1974, p. 134; and Yearbook of Public Sector: 1970 (Bombay: Commerce, 1970), p. 137.

appear small in relation to the amount of investment which it has received (Tables 9-1 and 9-2), but it would be misleading to conclude that government enterprise is insignificant or unproductive. The public sector was initially small compared to the private sector, and it therefore took a concentrated and extended investment effort to increase its output capacity. It has been slow to assume its potential position in the national economy owing to delays in completing investments and putting them into operation, and the even more adverse effect of the post-1966 industrial recession on the heavy industries where government investment is concentrated. Indeed, for a country in India's circumstances, where indigenous agricultural and industrial enterprise played such a large role, the public sector could not be expected to dominate the economic landscape overnight. The significant feature of public sector enterprise is that it has taken a commanding position in the industrial economy and accounts for well over 50 percent of activity in such strategic areas as steel, heavy engineering, petroleum, and finance. Not only has it grown rapidly and diversified extensively, but the public sector has mastered a wide variety of sophisticated industrial and scientific skills including the manufacture of jet aircraft, complex chemicals, and heavy engineering goods.

Performance of the Public Sector

It is no easy matter to measure how the public sector has affected development, partly because government enterprise has been used to serve a variety of public goals and the costs and benefits it has engendered are not strictly comparable to those of private industry. For instance, when public sector companies have intentionally kept their prices low to reduce inflation, their profits measured by conventional accounting methods have been understated compared with their net social contribution. Similarly, operating profits have been overstated (losses understated) in cases where the government chose to capitalize operating losses or to finance its enterprises at concessional or zero rates of interest. Thus, in applying some traditional tests of industrial efficiency to India's public sector, the results must be interpreted as circumstantial evidence rather than the final word.

Whatever one may say to qualify the significance of profit and loss statements, this accounting convention commands a gravitational attraction for analysts of the public sector, including the government itself. Because many government-owned enterprises hold oligopoly or monopoly positions within their own industries, and because the special favorable and adverse factors affecting their operations tend to offset one another, these firms are expected to produce a reasonable return on capital invested. In fact, the financial performance of the public sector has been very mixed and, on average, returns on capital invested have been low (Table 9-3). Government-owned companies engaged in trading, petroleum, and shipping have usually managed to produce good profits. These have been largely offset, however, by losses in steel, heavy machinery, mining, and pharmaceuticals. The enormity of the red ink is indicated by the extent to which the equity positions of some companies have eroded and sometimes become negative. As of 1973, accumulated deficits as a percentage of equity capital amount to 34.4 percent for Hindustan Steel Ltd., 54.6 percent for the Heavy Engineering Corporations Ltd., 115.3 percent for Heavy Electricals (India) Ltd., and 181.1 percent for the Mining and Allied Machinery Corporations Ltd.[39]

In seeking the cause for these financial results, it sometimes is possible to go beyond vague assertions of extenuating circumstances to a consideration of particular aspects of company operations. For example, there is evidence that inventory levels of many government-owned companies are unduly large in relation to operating levels.[40] Moreover, a comparison of Annual Reports of India's Bureau of Public Enterprise and RBI Surveys shows that the inventory/sales ratios of government undertakings often exceed those of comparable private sector companies by a margin of 2 to 1.

The public sector also has maintained a generally poor record of capacity utilization. Among the exogenous factors responsible for this situation are (1) the industrial recession, (2) the shortage of foreign exchange for importing industrial raw materials and replacement parts, (3) the proliferation of undersized firms in response to regional and other pressures on the licensing system, and (4) the indivisibility of certain large investments, the full output of which cannot be exported or consumed at home. But by any absolute or relative standard, or by historical comparison, the proportion of India's publicly owned industrial capacity which has been idle appears to have been excessive for an extended period of time. In the two year period 1966–67 to 1967–68, for example, average production/installed capacity ratios were iron ore (32 per-

[39]*Economic Times* (Bombay), Sept. 11, 1973, p. 7.
[40]Bhagwati and Desai note that they amount to signfiicantly more than a year's future needs; op. cit., p. 165.

TABLE 9–3
RETURN ON OPERATIONAL PUBLIC SECTOR INVESTMENTS*

Fiscal year	Number of running undertakings	Capital employed: loans and equity (Rs. crores)	Return: interest plus profits (Rs. crores)	Total return to total capital employed (percent)	Nondepartmental undertakings	
					Total return to total capital employed (percent)	Of which: profits after payment of tax and interest (percent)
1962–63	50	3,241.9	146.2	4.51	1.2	(−1.4)
1963–64	55	3,690.1	194.1	5.26	2.9	(1.9)
1964–65	62	4,339.6	171.2	3.95	2.7	(1.7)
1965–66	65	5,151.9	192.0	3.73	2.3	(1.2)
1966–67	67	5,963.7	172.1	2.89	1.6	(−0.8)
1967–68	77	6,679.9	154.0	2.31	1.3	(−2.6)
1968–69	84	7,324.4	230.9	3.15	1.8	(−2.0)
1969–70	99	7,715.9	305.5	3.95	3.1	(−0.2)
1970–71	105	8,242.9	316.2	3.84	2.8	(−0.2)
1971–72	108	8,705.8	359.9	4.13	2.7	(1.0)

*Excludes financial institutions. Departmental undertakings, which consist mainly of the railways, posts, and telegraphs, account for roughly 60 percent of total capital employed in IFY 1962–63 and 45 percent of the IFY 1971–72 total. Nondepartmental investments are less oriented toward infrastructure and include mainly manufacturing and commercial activities.

Source: Yearbook of Public Sector, 1973–74 (Bombay: Commerce), pp. 57 and 80.

cent), steel (76 percent), boilers (22 percent), heavy engineering structurals (32 percent), and machine tools (45 percent).[41] During this and subsequent periods production levels fell short of domestic demand, even for critically needed items such as coal, steel, and fertilizers.

Another indicator of the difficulties that the public sector has encountered, on which we need not dwell, is the steady stream of case history and analytic criticism which appears in press reports and elsewhere, even from sources sympathetic toward socialism and the government. Suffice it to say that the sources of the evidence have been official reports, statements by members of the ruling Congress party, and other reliable informants. The problems revealed by the profit and loss statements, inventory practices, capacity utilization, and case histories, especially because they are long-standing, are an impressive body of evidence suggesting that however much India's public sector has spearheaded industrialization and modernization, it also has been a major source of economic inefficiency and a restraint on development.

Faulty management, which is one, but certainly not the only, reason why the public sector has failed to live up to the expectations of its proponents, must be interpreted at two levels, national economic policy and official control over public sector enterprise. I have previously described some of the more prominent aspects of how the economy has been mismanaged, especially how India has been vulnerable to political and ideological motivations to establish prestigious but technically inappropriate facilities and to adopt other economic development strategies which are preordained to be inefficient. Also important has been the government's attitude toward the public sector which Bhagwati and Desai have aptly described as "schizophrenic," as wavering between "neutrality" toward the private sector and doctrinaire socialism, as a mix between appointing successful capitalists to manage state-owned firms and leftists such as K. D. Malaviya as chairman of the public sector Heavy Electricals Corporation.[42]

Before turning to how government-owned enterprises have been mismanaged, we should note that just as inefficient company operations are reflected in disappointing profit and loss statements of firms and harm the overall economy, they are created by adverse conditions in the national economy. In short, the problems of the public sector are as much systemic as they are particular to individual firms. Moreover, they are caused by selfish and ill-advised private decisions and general resource scarcities as much as by faulty economic policy.

Among the difficulties which have beset the management of public sector enterprise have been the following:

1. There has been great reluctance at the company and government levels to introduce modern management tools such as cost-benefit analy-

---

[41]*Yearbook of Public Sector,* 1970, op. cit., pp. 162–164.
[42]Bhagwati and Desai, op. cit., p. 147.

sis. Only in recent years has the government begun to confront economic alternatives with more than the crudest forms of analysis.

2. Company officials and various enterprises have been excessively open to criticism on the floor of Parliament. According to one study, a single company, Indian Airlines Corporation, was the subject of an average of 200 parliamentary questions each year.[43] Officials of public sector companies are hardly likely to innovate or depart from rigid SOPs under such circumstances.

3. The public sector has had great difficulty in its labor relations. Because the government is basically sympathetic to the needs of workers, it has tried to meet demands for higher wages and other benefits. State-owned factories have become overstaffed, however, and, especially in recent years, there has been a growing militancy among workers which has been expressed in the form of demonstrations, slowdowns, strikes, and even sabotage of plant and equipment. Having fostered a blue-collar elite, the government has yet to devise means to deal with its demands, albeit the firmness shown in 1974 to the railway workers' strike shows that when the requisite political will is present, the government can enforce considerable discipline.

4. Quite apart from labor relations in the public sector, which have been at least as bad as those in private industry, choosing managers for government enterprises has proved to be a colossal personnel problem. There has been a continuing competition between bureaucrats and men with technical skills for top management positions, and the post of chief executive officer has been allowed to go unfilled for extended periods of time in many companies.[44] Moreover, with few exceptions those chosen for senior positions are technicians with little management ability and administrative skills or bureaucrats inexperienced in both the technical

[43]*Report of the Study Team on Public Sector Undertakings* (New Delhi: GOI, Administrative Reforms Commission, 1967), p. 47.

[44]The Sept. 23, 1972, issue of *Economic and Political Weekly* told the bizarre story of how the managing director and other functional directors of the Fertilizer Corporation of India (FCI) offered to resign because the reluctance of an Empanelling Committee to approve their recommendations for general manager appointments at production units had caused all nine units to be without permanent heads for two years. At the heart of the dispute between the FCI and the committee was a 1968 change in procedure for making senior appointments in the public sector. This change militated against the appointment of bureaucrats, but by not fully removing them from the appointments process, it created a situation where bureaucratic intransigence could hinder effective management. Another telling comment on the management of public corporations came in 1972 from Prakash Tandon, chairman of the State Trading Corporation (STC). Tandon, an acknowledged expert in management, asserted that the STC could do a better job by halving its employment roles. Not surprisingly, he was not allowed to remove much of the deadwood in the STC.

and business aspects of their responsibilities.[45] Thus, management is ill-prepared to impart economic efficiency to the public sector, and, as seen by one senior civil servant, the behavior of government managers often combines a mix of (1) apathy, risk and responsibility avoidance, delay, red tape, and lack of imagination with (2) self-serving behavior motivated by the prospect of financial, social, or political elevation.[46]

There are a number of outstanding examples of how particular public sector companies have excelled in their particular fields. Despite initial reservations on the part of some aid donor countries, Air India has grown to be a large, profitable, and efficient company with standards comparable to those of other international air carriers. Since it was incorporated in 1953, Hindustan Machine Tools has located five operating units in various parts of the country, manufactured a wide range of precision tools and watches, and developed important export markets for these products. The scientific and technical achievements of the Departments of Atomic Energy and Space place India in a class by itself: no other developing country and only a few of the wealthier nations can match its research and applied expertise.

These operations are not typical of the public sector, however, and the favorable impression they convey must be balanced against the existence of less effective public sector investments. The Neyveli project in Tamil Nadu is an example par excellence of the potential for public sector enterprise and the cruel disappointment that some of these investments have caused. Based on an enormous lignite deposit, this integrated investment was intended to employ more than 10,000 workers and to serve a variety of priority needs, including production of electric power, fertilizer, and charcoal briquets. The Neyveli scheme is especially interesting because it was designed to be highly mechanized. As the lignite was to be mined by giant excavators and the ore moved about on large conveyor belts, Neyveli was dependent on costly and sophisticated equipment purchased from Germany and other aid donors including the Soviet Union.

However logical the planning for Neyveli, and despite the decision to import the best equipment regardless of cost, the operations of this public sector project (which was started in 1956) have been nothing short of disastrous. Management inefficiency, poor maintenance of equipment, and a wrong choice of mining and transportation equipment are among the reasons why Neyveli deteriorated so far that in the early 1970s barely enough lignite was produced to keep the power plant operating at 25 percent of rated capacity. After satisfying the electrical requirement for producing further inadequate amounts of lignite, there was hardly any electricity left over for use in the Tamil Nadu

[45]See, for example, Phiroze B. Medhora, "Managerial Reforms in India's Public Sector," *South Asian Review*, vol. 7, no. 1, October 1973, pp. 17–29.

[46]Dass, op. cit.

grid. Moreover, there was scarcely any lignite for use as raw material in the fertilizer and briqueting factories. The inevitable result of the Neyveli muddle was that in 1973 the Finance Ministry, Planning Commission, and Ministry of Steel and Mines, which were jointly responsible for the project, were all skeptical of investing additional resources to bring lignite production up to what was intended.[47] In short, inefficient project design and management had created the conditions for inefficient production for the indefinite future.

In seeking to improve the management of the public sector, the government has appointed a series of special committees and has frequently endorsed and tried to implement their recommendations. A recent development in this respect—and also one of the more revolutionary—was the establishment in January 1973 of the Steel Authority of India, Ltd. (SAIL). This was a holding company for India's public and joint sector steel facilities and related input industries like coking coal, iron ore, and manganese ore. If SAIL is even moderately successful in (1) coordinating the technical and economic development of India's steel industry and (2) providing a management environment with the right mix of executive autonomy from, and responsibility to, government, it is likely that similar holding companies will be established in other industrial sectors.

Just as the causes of public sector inefficiency lie both within and outside the enterprises themselves, the consequences of the public sector must be measured according to both narrow and broad criteria. With respect to economic growth, it is difficult to escape the conclusion that by fostering public enterprise, India has been profligate with physical, budgetary, and foreign exchange resources. It has pursued a concept of development which has not always been appropriate for the nation's basic needs and insisted on a style of industrial organization which has shown itself to be highly inefficient. Moreover, little can be claimed for the public sector's role in furthering social justice. Both management and labor in the public sector have secured special privileges equivalent to or even superior to those offered by private industry. Even with respect to self-reliance, there is no convincing evidence to assert that roughly the same results or better could not have been achieved with less direct official intervention in the economy. But because of the very uneven quality of private company management and economic statesmanship, it is only on the basis of a subjective judgment that one can conclude that a less-fettered private sector could have done a better job.

The Primacy of Import Substitution over Export Promotion

India emerged from World War II with a healthy store of international monetary reserves. Moreover, because the commodity price boom caused by

---

[47]See *Economic and Political Weekly*, Apr. 14, 1973, p. 700.

the Korean war and the time span between the planning and implementation of investments sheltered India from the recognition of its difficult foreign exchange position until after the mid-1950s, Delhi allocated substantial amounts of external assets during this period for imports of consumer rather than investment goods. As seen by one official body:

> In retrospect, the Committee would like to state that the large foreign exchange reserves, built up at considerable sacrifice during World War II, were a valuable asset which could have been used, in the early years of planning, to strengthen the agroindustrial base of the economy. This was, unfortunately, not done and till about the end of the First Plan large amounts of foreign exchange were frittered away, year after year, on imports of non-essential goods which the country might well have done without.[48]

Although the draconian import control regime which India instituted to cope with the exchange crisis of 1956–57 was relaxed during the Third Plan and further liberalized after the 1966 devaluation, the luxury of ample foreign exchange reserves has never returned. For India, the distinction between domestic production and imports was not new. The Swadeshi movement had aimed at substituting home production for imports both to stimulate the Indian economy and to punish Britain for its holding colonial sway. In addition, Gandhians had constantly pleaded for greater attention to cottage industries and the desirability of community self-sufficiency. Thus, what was new about India's post-1957 foreign exchange regime was the cause, an enduring balance-of-payments crisis.

More basically, and in contrast to China's policies since its break with Moscow, the Indian government ruled out autarky as an approach to its economic problems. After an initial hesitancy, it decided to import both to supplement domestic resources and to obtain critically needed goods which either could not be produced in India or could be produced only at very high cost. The resultant gap between the demand for imports and the amount of foreign goods India could afford to purchase, and the policies India used to equate import demand and supply, became prominent influences on the course of India's development. The significance of foreign exchange problems and policies used to deal with them are often understated because in the long run policies to suppress fundamental balance-of-payments disequilibrium are invariably effective and disguise the extent of unrequited import demand. Some idea of how significant these problems have been for India is revealed by the import substitution, export promotion, foreign investment, and foreign assistance policies, all of which were at least partly directed at compensating for or ameliorating the insufficiency of imports.

When, in the 1950s, the need to shore up India's balance-of-payments

---

[48]*Report on Foreign Exchange by the Estimates Committee (1967–68), Thirtieth Report* (New Delhi: Lok Sabha Secretariat, 1968), p. 310.

position with a more dynamic foreign trade policy became apparent, India's leaders were not without their predispositions as to whether policy should emphasize import substitution or export promotion. Whereas they regarded extreme autarky as unacceptable, import substitution had strong appeal because of India's favorable mix of (1) undeveloped raw industrial resources such as coal and iron ore, (2) economic and technical skill levels which were varied and impressive by less-developed country standards, (3) the large size of the Indian market which would support large-scale production efficiency, (4) the inclusion of many easily produced consumer items among India's imports in the early 1950s, and (5) the willingness of foreign governments to assist in the development of Indian industry. Another significant reason why India chose the import substitution option was that this coincided with the conventional wisdom of the 1950s. At the time, economists, political analysts, government leaders, and other elites throughout the world were in agreement that this was the correct path for developing countries.

In addition to the logic just stated, the choice of import substitution in preference to export promotion was justified by other reasons related to India's larger objectives of growth, equity, and self-reliance. These factors, only some of which were valid, were not only interrelated but in many instances were identical to the justifications for India's domestic policies, such as industrial licensing.

1. *Growth:* In a sense India's decision to go for import substitution was predetermined by the prior decision to industrialize, diversify the economy, and concentrate on capital goods manufacture. Because Mahalanobis's background had been in physics and statistics, the working model he developed for India was insensitive to the flexibility that foreign trade could impart to the economy, and the Plan, therefore, paid comparatively little attention to this area. In part, import substitution was preferred to export promotion because government officials found it easier to limit planning to the domestic economy and to avoid consideration of foreign supply and demand factors, most of which lay beyond the reach of Indian policy. Further support for this strategy came from historical evidence to the effect that in a number of countries long-term import substitution and industrial growth were positively correlated.[49] Two other economic reasons for the choice were, first, that production for import substitution might have a greater development impact because of the particular mix of factors of production available in India and the kinds of production for which they were best suited and, second, that discouraging imports would signal businessmen that they would have a protected market and would encourage them to invest.[50]

2. *Equity:* As previously noted, Indian leaders were loath to abandon the

[49]H. B. Chenery, "Patterns of Industrial Growth," *American Economic Review,* September 1960, pp. 639–641 and 651.

[50]Benjamin I. Cohen, "The International Development of India and Pakistan," in Robinson and Kidron, eds., op. cit., pp. 550–551.

distribution of costs and benefits from economic activity to the forces of what were rightly regarded as imperfect markets. Bureaucratic control was seen as the surest way to transfer plans into reality and as the proper response to exploitation by domestic monopolists and foreign neocolonialists, alike. Within this thought framework Indian policy makers perceived that export promotion might be akin to pushing on a string and therefore favored what they regarded as the more reliable alternative of spurring domestic output by limiting imports.

3. *Self-reliance:* Because India's leaders (1) resented their nation's economic dependence during the colonial period, (2) were senstitive to what they regarded as elements of neocolonialism in the post-World War II period, and (3) longed for the prestige and power that industrialized countries appeared to have, they strongly favored import substitution. These motivations were buttressed by the view, widely held in the 1950s, that world markets would be inhospitable to exports from developing countries and that insuperable barriers to trade existed or would be instituted to restrain the growth of the developing countries' exports. Consequently, it did not seem unreasonable to adopt import substitution as a "second best" strategy.

4. *Risk Aversion:* The additional argument, that producing for an existing and protected Indian market would be more "surprise-free" than producing for world markets, was convincing to many officials of both India and aid-giving nations.

The cumulative weight of these factors was so great that it is hardly surprising that India, like many other developing countries, did opt for import substitution rather than export promotion and that this approach was pursued long after it had showed itself to be inadequate to meet its objectives.

India's Foreign Trade Regime

It is noteworthy that over time India's foreign trade has been conducted increasingly through government agencies. The State Trading Corporation (STC) was established in 1956, and by 1973 more than half of India's imports either had been canalized through the STC and other public trading agencies or were acquired directly on government account. Similarly, about one-fifth of exports were handled by the public sector.[51] Among the reasons why the Indian government wished to canalize foreign trade through official bodies were its wishes to (1) tighten official control over the commodity mix, quantity, and quality of items imported; (2) assure a fair distribution of imports to small-scale industry and others who might otherwise have little access to foreign goods; (3) obtain price concessions on imports through quantity purchases; (4) promote exports; and (5) facilitate bilateral trading arrangements, albeit these did not always require government-to-government sales.

[51]*Economic Survey: 1972–73*, p. 76.

In spite of government statements to the contrary, many aspects of India's trade policy have not changed substantially since it was formulated in the late 1950s. Policy received its biggest shake-up after the 1966 devaluation, when a major effort went into import liberalization and a greater emphasis was placed on exporting. The 1966 strategy, which called for increased imports, to be financed in the short term by more foreign aid and in the long term by greater exports, had only a limited impact as discussed later in this chapter.

In outline, India's policy has required that all imports be licensed, with different procedures applicable, depending on whether the prospective importer (1) belongs to the public or private sector; (2) is a trader or actual user of the commodity; and (3) belongs to a priority category such as a small-scale industry or an exporting firm. The system further distinguishes imports of capital goods from raw materials, spares, components, and consumer items. Finally, licenses are allocated not only by industry but by firm and sometimes even by plant.[52]

The administration of the import regime involves a large number of Delhi agencies, including the Ministries of Finance and Foreign Trade, various functional ministries, the Directorate General of Technical Development (DGTD), the Chief Comptroller of Imports and Exports, and sometimes the STC and others. The two principal criteria applied to applications are, first, whether the item is needed by the Indian economy and, second, whether it is unavailable from any domestic Indian source (the so-called clearance from the indigenous angle). Items which can be produced in India in adequate amounts are placed on the "banned list," and imports are allowed only under extraordinary circumstances. In addition to licensing, import substitution is pursued through the imposition of high tariffs and negotiated agreements with importers who are urged to find domestic Indian suppliers to meet their needs.[53] The

[52] In Indian fiscal year 1972–73 the pattern of import licenses issued was as follows:

Category	Rupee value of licenses (crores)	Percentage of total
Established importers	55.3	2.98
Actual users	376.0	20.26
DGTD units	171.2	9.23
Small-scale industry	86.4	4.65
Registered exporters	136.0	7.33
Capital goods	268.0	14.44
Customs clearance permits	58.1	3.13
State trading agencies	620.9	33.46
Other	83.8	4.52
TOTAL	1,855.7	100.00

Source: Economic Survey: 1973–74, p. 42.

[53] For a more detailed description of import and export regimes, see Anne O. Krueger, "The Benefits and Costs of Import Substitution in India: A Microeconomic Study," IBRD monograph, Washington, D.C., October 1970, and Bhagwati and Srinivasan, forthcoming.

threat that an import item might be placed on the banned list serves as a powerful incentive for Indian enterprise to find ways to meet its needs through indigenous production.

In fashioning an export promotion policy, India has had to take account of a difficulty similar to that which plagued United States exports in the 1960s and early 1970s: its large sheltered home market has been highly profitable, and with the exception of a limited number of traditional export items, there has been little profit motive for domestic firms to seek foreign sales actively. Indeed, in some instances India has discouraged exports by imposing export taxes to siphon off some export revenues for the government and through promotional schemes designed to increase domestic consumption of some goods (including tea) which would otherwise have been exported.[54]

India's policies to overcome its export inertia have evolved gradually and include both incentives and punishments. The principal rewards offered to exporters are rebate of duties paid on the import content of items exported, cash subsidies, special import entitlements for specified commodities (usually in free foreign exchange and in excess of import replacement needs), and other benefits such as preferential finance. To complement these incentives, the government has compelled firms to export through measures such as (1) setting export targets as a condition for the approval of industrial licenses and (2) requiring that all firms in a particular industry export a certain percentage of their total output.

Consequences of the Foreign Trade Policy

India's foreign trade regime has suffered from many of the same problems that affected the domestic industrial licensing policy. Excessive delays, shortages of critical materials, insufficiency of foreign exchange, inadequate information on which to base allocation decisions, corruption, and a host of other difficulties have opened a chasm between the way the program was intended to operate and the actual situation. Rather than dwell on these operational difficulties, however, I shall concentrate on the program's impact on the Indian economy.

A first cut at evaluation leads to the trade data and the question of how successful the import substitution and export promotion programs have been. As shown in Table 9-4, India's sustained effort to substitute domestic for foreign production, combined with its emphasis on heavy industry, has dramatically changed the composition of its imports. Excepting cereals, consumer items have been eliminated in favor of capital goods, raw materials, and intermediate manufactures. Moreover, Indian data show that the significance

---

[54]See Manmohan Singh, *India's Export Trends* (Oxford: Clarendon Press, 1964), and Benjamin I. Cohen, "The Stagnation of Indian Exports: 1951–1961," *Quarterly Journal of Economics,* vol. LXXVIII, November 1964, pp. 604–620.

TABLE **9–4**
COMPOSITION OF INDIA'S IMPORTS (millions of dollars)

Commodity	1951–52	1960–61	1970–71	1973–74
Consumer goods	607.5	600.0	284.0	630.8
(Cereals)	(483.6)	(600.0)	(284.0)	(630.8)
Raw materials and industrial				
intermediates	660.2	1,629.8	1,189.1	2,195.6
(Fibers)	nss*	(335.2)	(168.9)	(123.7)
(Petroleum products)	nss	(229.1)	(181.2)	(747.7)
(Fertilizer)	nss	(49.1)	(133.2)	(519.0)
(Chemicals)	nss	(246.8)	(155.5)	(140.4)
(Iron and steel)	nss	(405.3)	(196.0)	(324.6)
Capital goods	374.0	1,177.1	538.7	867.3
Unclassified other	. . .	362.7	168.1	200.8
TOTAL	1,641.8	3,769.5	2,178.9	3,894.5

*nss: not shown separately.

Note: Columns may not total, owing to rounding.

Sources: Economic Survey, various issues; and *Report on Foreign Exchange by the Estimates Committee (Thirtieth Report),* (New Delhi: Lok Sabha Secretariat, 1968), pp. 37–38.

of imports relative to total estimated supplies in a wide variety of basic industries is now quite small.[55]

Import substitution has been regarded by India as a dynamic process; as domestic self-sufficiency is reached in one item, attention is turned to others. This is illustrated by the effort to eliminate imports of consumer goods in the First Plan and the shift of emphasis to capital goods in the period 1956–1963.[56] In many areas import substitution has proceeded up the technological ladder and the composition of imports has changed accordingly. Nonetheless, the tendency for officials to be overoptimistic about domestic economic prospects contributed to the anomalous and costly situation of 1973–74 when more than one-third of India's imports consisted of crude and partly refined petroleum, fertilizer, and food, all items which India's import substitution policy, if more successfully applied, could have made unnecessary. Accordingly, for the Fifth Plan period, India has targeted grains, petroleum and products, and fertilizer along with metals, machinery, and equipment as the areas where it will concentrate its import substitution policy.[57]

Analysis of India's export indices shows that both price and volume have

[55]*Economic Survey: 1973–74,* p. 100.

[56]For a comprehensive analysis, see Padma Desai, *Import Substitution in the Indian Economy* (Delhi: Hindustan Publishing Co., 1972).

[57]*Draft Fifth Five-Year Plan,* vol. 1, op. cit., p. 75.

been lacking in vitality. The compound annual growth rate for the value of exports over the extended period 1950–1973 amounts to 4.2 percent. Even considering that the export promotion program received little attention until the late 1950s and did not begin in earnest until the second half of the 1960s, the 6.3 percent growth rate for 1960–1973 is disappointing in light of burgeoning international trade and inflation in that period. As a consequence of its laggard export performance, India's share of total world exports has fallen steadily and by a large amount, from 2.0 percent in 1950 to 0.6 percent in 1973.[58]

The reason some economists have cited to explain this situation, barriers of rich nations to imports from developing countries, is not credible in light of (1) the extraordinary export performance of some countries (Taiwan, South Korea, Malaysia, and Brazil) which have increased their shares of world trade and (2) India's declining position in jute, tea, and other markets where it is a major supplier. Nonetheless, the changing commodity composition of India's exports (Table 9-5) reveals some cause for optimism about the future. In particular, the stagnation of traditional exports such as tea and jute has been more than offset by the vigorous growth of iron ore, leather, and engineering products. Exports of such "nontraditional" products, which thus far are only a

[58]Data based on various issues of the International Monetary Fund's *International Financial Statistics.*

TABLE 9–5
COMPOSITION OF INDIA'S EXPORTS (millions of dollars)

Commodity	1950–51	1960–61	1970–71	1973–74
Jute	803.7	447.1	253.9	303.1
Tea	305.8	408.9	197.7	193.2
Cotton fabrics*	231.3	190.3	100.4	256.2
Iron ore	3.4	56.3	156.4	177.1
Oil cakes	. . .	47.3	73.9	227.5
Leather products	85.5	82.5	96.3	228.4
Cashews	29.8	62.6	69.4	99.2
Engineering products	. . .	28.1	173.9	268.4
Fish and products	12.6	15.3	41.1	117.9
Total (includes others)	1,987.4	2,183.6	2,046.9	3,310.9

*1951–52 includes yarn.

Note: Columns may not total, owing to rounding.

Sources: Economic Survey, various issues; *Report on Foreign Exchange by the Estimates Committee (1967–68), Thirtieth Report* (New Delhi: Lok Sabha Secretariat, 1968), pp. 40–41; and *Data on the Indian Economy: 1951 to 1969* (New Delhi: Ford Foundation, 1970), table 7.04.

fraction of potential, have risen rapidly and by 1973–74 they accounted for 17 percent of total foreign sales.

The second level at which we must investigate the consequences of India's foreign trade policy is the systemic one of how, in conjunction with industrial licensing and other policies, it affected India's development. The import substitution strategy not only benefited India by contributing to diversification of the economy, but eliminated the need for importing foreign consumer goods other than food and substantially reduced India's reliance on imports of many critical products. Could these benefits have been achieved through alternative strategies? What are their costs? Would India be better off importing some consumer items and paying for them with increased exports? It is the answers to this kind of question which make analysts dubious about the net value of India's strategy.

Whether India's foreign trade policy is evaluated (1) according to technical economic criteria such as efficiency (allocation of resources and ability to minimize costs) and impact on domestic savings[59] or (2) from the vantage of India's triad of growth, equity, and self-reliance, the conclusion is that India has gone well beyond what "infant industry" logic would justify. Through its extreme protectionist policies India has raised the cost structure and lowered the efficiency of domestic industry to such an extent that the economy has become insensitive to the price and other signals which, under other conditions, would serve India's growth and distribution objectives as well as capitalize on its international comparative advantage. Specifically, the foreign trade regime as implemented has contributed to the following interrelated problems:

1. In practice, Indian policies have supported monopoly behavior by domestic firms, public and private sector. New private enterprises have not been started because it has been so difficult to obtain the necessary import licenses for capital goods, raw materials, and industrial intermediates. Smaller firms which could not afford to "chase licenses" through the Delhi bureaucracy often have been forced to go out of business or to curtail their expansion plans. Public and private firms alike have been induced by the foreign trade regime to restrict production and set high prices on consumer goods, measures adverse to both economic growth and social justice. Other side effects of the monopoly practices which the system virtually guaranteed were a reduction in operating efficiency and a disincentive to innovate. Together, these factors were eventually reflected in lower rates of investment and slower development.

2. The foreign trade regime has been operated so as to encourage expansion of capacity rather than efficient utilization of existing plant and equipment. Because merchandise obtained through import licenses is worth more in India than the international price (even after customs duties), the acquisition of import licenses has become a business objective in and of itself. The entrepreneur who obtains one can either earn a monopoly profit by reselling it or

[59]For an explanation of this framework, see John H. Power, "Import Substitution as an Industrialization Strategy," in *Philippine Economic Journal*, vol. 5, no. 2, 1966.

import the goods and use them to bolster the profits of his own manufacturing operations. Because some import licenses are allocated on the basis of rated production capacity, even socially and economically unproductive investments are of value to the businessman. Notably, even the foreign aid relationship has contributed to this problem; donor governments often have insisted that their funds be used for specific projects, thereby leaving India to choose between no aid and surplus capacity.[60]

3. The loss of efficiency associated with India's complicated and imperfect trade regime is regarded by many economists as staggering.[61] They hold foreign trade policies responsible for costly delays in needed investment and current production; the tendency for inventories to be either excessive or scanty, depending on whether the current foreign exchange situation is easy or tight; the extraordinary requirement of public and private management talent required to administer the system; and the incentive for firms to locate near Delhi, where their executives can stay in close touch with key government officials. Moreover, the large volume of bogus applications for import licenses and the slipshod and sometimes corrupt administration of foreign trade policy lead one to suspect that the imperfection of this system may be greater than the imperfection of the market system it seeks to replace.

4. There is particular reason to believe that India's foreign trade regime does not even optimize the nation's foreign exchange position. For example, the export promotion system is somewhat of a shotgun approach; sometimes it gives incentives to firms which do not need them, and in other cases it fails to provide adequate incentives. Moreover, according to one study there are some export activities which, because of the high import content of goods exported and low price received from the foreign purchaser, actually have had a negative effect on India's foreign exchange position. This is possible because, in calculating its profit, the exporting firm adds to the selling price the value of cash and other export incentives such as import entitlements.[62]

5. Finally, the foreign trade regime has had an anti-investment and anti-growth bias. The construction of plant and installation of equipment in factories that will not be utilized cannot truly be regarded as investment. Indeed, such activities use funds which might otherwise be devoted to productive capital schemes. In addition, the failure of the government to equate the domestic value of imports with the costs to importers has resulted in a loss of budget revenues which, alternatively, could have been devoted to public investment.

One indicator of the imperfection of India's foreign trade policy is the gap

---

[60]Edward S. Mason, "Economic Development in India and Pakistan," Occasional Paper in International Affairs No. 13, Center for International Affairs, Harvard University, September 1966, p. 41.

[61]In particular, see Manmohan Singh, Bhagwati and Desai, Benjamin Cohen in Robinson and Kidron, eds., op. cit.

[62]Krueger, The Benefits and Costs of Import Substitution in India, op. cit., p. 114.

between the official exchange rate of the Indian rupee and the rupee's real value in international trade (i.e., the rupee's effective exchange rate as indicated by the domestic resource cost of India's production for export markets and the rupee value of imported goods). According to one study of 34 commodities in the automobile and ancillary industries, in comparison to the official exchange rate of Rs. 7.5 = $1.00, the effective exchange rates derived from domestic resource costs for each commodity were substantially higher, the median being Rs. 18.2 = $1.00.[63] This finding is supported by a number of other studies covering a variety of commodities. Because of the widespread sensitivity to exchange rate changes which was especially strong before the freeing of rates in the 1970s, some of these studies have not been made public and there has been only limited discussion of how the exchange rate could be used as a means for obtaining domestic and international economic goals.

The 1966 Devaluation and Thereafter

The question of how India's exchange rate is affected by its foreign trade regime became critical in 1966, when a major effort was made to back away from the unsatisfactory policies of the past. The par value of the rupee was reduced from Rs. 4.76 = $1.00 to Rs. 7.5 = $1.00. Devaluation was accompanied by a rationalization-cum-liberalization of the foreign trade control system. The purpose of this change was to encourage the Indian economy to become more responsive to basic economic factors, first, by shifting away from governmental controls to a greater reliance on market forces and, second, by redesigning official policies to substitute rifle for shotgun approaches. Among other measures, the new import policy (1) specified 59 priority industries (many of them involved in manufacture for export) for which liberalized procedures would be implemented; (2) lowered import duties for a number of items in order to bring prices in India more in line with international prices; (3) took special steps to spur Indian production and to prevent inflation by importing fertilizers and other needed products; (4) abolished most export incentives for "nontraditional" items; and (5) imposed export duties on a number of "traditional" exports such as jute and tea in order to garner the new profitability of these industries for the government exchequer.[64] The quid pro quo for the new policy package and the incentive on which its success depended was the India Consortium's "quick promise and implementation of 900 million dollars of new-project aid."[65]

It is extremely difficult to evaluate how the policies announced during June 1966 and thereafter actually affected India's domestic economy and balance of

[63]Ibid., p. 110.
[64]*Thirtieth Report of the Estimates Committee*, op. cit., pp. 91–93.
[65]Ibid., p. 89.

payments. As noted by Bhagwati and a number of his collaborators, because a number of changes were made in trade policy at that time, the devaluation's de facto size was considerably smaller than the de jure adjustment would indicate.[66] The 1966 monsoon failure is but one of many unanticipated factors which, by perpetuating the supply shortages and price pressures which the devaluation was intended to ameliorate, tended to undo it before its effect could be felt and also complicated analysis. A similar effect is attributable to the Indian government's fiscal conservatism and concern with inflation, which led it to restrain monetary expansion and fiscal expenditures.[67] The brunt of this retrenchment fell on capital investment rather than current spending. In addition, officials were wedded to their predevaluation ways, and even before 1966 had ended, the government had introduced new export incentives and moved to reestablish something like the former, bureaucratically controlled foreign trade regime. In practice, the government showed itself unable to renounce the principle of "clearance from the indigenous angle," in no small part because the continuing industrial recession and attending excess domestic capacity made it politically difficult to reduce protection and allow imports.

Consequently, India was unable to make optimum use of the new aid monies which were put at its disposal,[68] and by 1974, signs of the liberalization were barely recognizable. The cumulative effect of these and other adverse factors was to erode seriously the relationship between India and the Consortium and to reduce the amount of foreign funds available through aid channels. The Indian sentiment (right or wrong) that the Consortium had reneged in financing the devaluation was critical here, as it led Indian officials to opt for policies which would spare them from foreign interference in India's economic affairs.

From a domestic political point of view, devaluation was an unmitigated disaster.[69] Coming less than one year before a national election, and in the absence of definitive evidence that it was either necessary or a success, devaluation became a divisive election issue. The frail new government of Prime Minister Gandhi was subjected to criticism by (1) those who felt the devaluation had been taken to appease anti-Indian, foreign interests; (2) other Indians who for intellectual reasons disagreed with the underlying economic rationale; and (3) some Congress leaders who resented not having been consulted about its desirability and others who feared that they might lose patronage as a result of the trade liberalization. Most opposition parties—right and left—joined with

---

[66]Bhagwati and Srinivasan estimated the de facto devaluation at 21.6 percent compared to the de jure magnitude of 57.5 percent. See Jagdish N. Bhagwati, "The Exchange Rate Policy—II," *Statesman*, May 5, 1972.

[67]See *Thirtieth Report of the Estimates Committee,* op. cit., pp. 92–114.

[68]Bhagwati and Desai, op. cit., pp. 484–485.

[69]For a full treatment of this subject, see the series of articles by J. Bhagwati, K. Sunderam, and N. Srinivasan in the Sept. 2, 9, and 16, 1972, issues of *Economic and Political Weekly*.

the majority of the press and India's economist community to condemn the change in the rupee's international value. Moreover, because it was publicly supported only by the business-oriented Swatantra party and a few other groups with limited weight, devaluation became identified with the right of the Indian political spectrum and this served as a further cause for its denigration.

The misunderstanding of the economic imperatives behind devaluation and the political opportunism which led to its being the subject of intense and widespread criticism might have been contained by the government but for the involvement of foreign interests. For several years prior to 1966 there had been pressure from abroad for India to devalue. This, in turn, had elicited powerful antidevaluation propaganda from the Indian government. For reasons not obvious, but partly linked to the countering of the foreign pressure, few Indian economists had publicly advocated devaluation in the period immediately preceding 1966, thereby making the debate over its necessity one-sided. Thus, when devaluation was announced and it was also made public that the Consortium would increase its assistance to India, it took no great imagination to make scapegoats of the IMF, IBRD, United States, and Corsortium. Moreover, so long as devaluation could be identified as an imported evil, there was less reason for Indians to identify with it and to work to make it a success.

In retrospect, it is difficult to find evidence that the 1966 devaluation served its intended purposes, but it is even more difficult to believe that India could have adjusted its balance-of-payments policies to maintain its old exchange rate. It is regrettable that the trade liberalization experiment was swamped by a variety of unforeseen and unmanageable events and that the political reaction it engendered was so overwhelmingly negative as to reduce the scope for future efforts to liberalize policy. The critical point here is not that the import substitution strategy was without merit, but that in India it was applied with such extreme dogmatism as to engender outlandish and unnecessary costs and to blind the Indian policy eye to other more efficient policies. India can hasten its development by achieving a greater exposure to the world economy, but this implies the need for it to take greater advantage of its economic comparative advantage than it has in the past. This, in turn, would require India to adopt a foreign trade and foreign exchange policy more alive to market forces than what can be achieved with an overvalued exchange rate and panoply of administrative controls.

The Special Case of Foreign Private Investment

Few issues in India's economic development strategy have been as controversial as the treatment of private foreign investment. As the apparent embodiment of the old colonialism, foreign investment was doomed to be the living repository of a long heritage of frustrated ambitions and resentments. As if this unsavory lineage were not enough, foreign investment also has fallen heir to current dissatisfactions stemming from India's failure to achieve various economic and political objectives at home and abroad. Thus, that foreign enterprise in India has continued to exist and even to expand somewhat is a reflection of its value to India's development and a tribute to the objectivity of those Indian leaders who braved the political storms in order to support its continued life.

Ideologically, foreign private investment has attracted criticism from various sources: leftists objected to private enterprise in any guise, domestic or foreign; Gandhians took exception to most large-scale activities; and nationalists, who were opposed to all foreign participation in the Indian economy, were particularly hostile to foreign exploitation of India's natural resources. According to a recent survey by the Indian Institute of Public Opinion, even if foreign investors are linked in Indian thinking with India's political subservience during the colonial period, "the prejudice against foreign investments is shared more by 'leftist ideologues' in the ruling party and by small but more vocal leftist parties than by the people at large."[70]

Because pro-Communists perceive private foreign investment as forging an important link in India's relations with the West, they have lost no opportunities to undermine its place in the economy. The position of Indian businessmen is more complex. Initially they were reluctant to share the Indian market with foreign investors, but as they gradually recognized that through foreign collaborations they could obtain various licenses and grow faster, they became more supportive.

The Indian government's approach to private foreign investment shows many of the same, schizophrenic characteristics as its attitude toward domestic industrial licensing and import substitution. In practice, this has been reflected in the alternating welcome and unwelcome signals issued by the government and by the conditional acceptance, fraught with red tape and delays, which has been accorded foreign investors during the welcome periods.

The Industrial Policy Resolution of 1948, which featured the conditions for permitting foreign investment rather than the potential for external business to aid the Indian economy, was interpreted as offering small scope for foreign capital. Asaf Ali, India's first ambassador to the United States, is quoted as having said that there was "no more than a limited field for private enterprise in an Independent India."[71] In contrast, Prime Minister Nehru's statement in Parliament on April 6, 1949, appeared considerably more liberal. The principles enunciated by Nehru on that occasion have remained operative, albeit the basic decision to encourage or disallow foreign investment and the procedures

[70]Indian Institute of Public Opinion, Blue Supplement to vol. XIX, no. 11, p. III.
[71]Kidron, op. cit. p. 97, quoting the *New York Times,* Apr. 17, 1947.

with which foreign investors have had to comply have been changed drastically from time to time to suit current Indian economic conditions. According to Nehru:

> (1) The government would encourage foreign investment;
> (2) Foreign investors, once admitted, would be treated in law and policy as domestic investors;
> (3) Foreign investors would be free to remit profits and repatriate capital, subject to Indian balance-of-payments constraints;
> (4) Compensation would be given in case of nationalization;
> (5) Investments normally would be established with majority ownership and management control in Indian hands; but
> (6) The Indian government would remain flexible in negotiating the conditions of foreign investment.[72]

The public reaction to Nehru's policy was decidedly negative, and major criticism was leveled at it by socialist politicians and the business community. The latter was in an ambivalent position insofar as it regarded any bow to the private sector as welcome, but objected to the entry of foreign competitors. This situation persisted until 1955 and very little private investment of any kind took place in the interim.[73] It is more than an irony that the Industrial Policy Resolution of 1956, which heralded the golden era of India's industrial development, signaled the most fruitful period not only of public and private Indian investment but also of foreign private capital inflow. Illustrative of the more liberal attitude toward external investors is the number of foreign collaboration agreements approved by the government; they rose from 81 in 1957 to a high of 403 in 1961 and 1964, and subsequently fell to an average of less than 200 per year.[74]

The government established an Indian Investment Centre in 1961 and a Foreign Investment Board in 1968 to clarify the conditions in which foreign investors would be permitted entry and to speed applications. These institutions have had only limited significance, however, because they generally have not been able to remove the disincentive to foreign investment posed by India's slow economic growth rate and the administrative rigors of doing business in India. And, despite the Investment Centre, in scrutinizing each new application for (1) whether the investment offers an economic benefit which could not be obtained using domestic resources ("clearance from the indigenous angle" in a new guise), (2) the essentiality of the commodity to be produced, and (3) balance-of-payments effects, the Indian government has been extremely loath to issue approvals.

---

[72]Nehru's statement is reproduced as Annex V of the Administrative Reforms Commission's *Report of the Study Team on Economic Administration,* op. cit., pp. 306–307.

[73]Kidron, op. cit., pp. 101–112.

[74]V. N. Balasubramanyam, *International Transfer of Technology to India* (New York: Praeger, 1973), p. 35.

Although new guidelines for would-be foreign investors have been issued from time to time, most recently in 1961, 1968, and 1973, India's relations with the international economic community have been marked by misunderstanding and the failure of both business and government to communicate with one another. This situation is illustrated by the negotiations for a massive fertilizer program conducted from November 1963 through July 1965 between the government of India and a consortium of private foreign investors led by the Bechtel Company of the United States. According to Ashok Kapoor, and quite apart from the merits of the Bechtel proposal, not all aspects of the government's guidelines on foreign investment were taken seriously by either party, and this caused the negotiators to have incorrect expectations about what terms might be agreeable. Kapoor ends his description of this arduous and disappointing negotiation on the upbeat—but unsubstantiated—note that both the companies and India learned from it, and that tangible benefits may follow in the future.[75]

In practice, India has sought to minimize foreign penetration of its economy and to channel foreign investment into such priority areas as high technology, import substituting products, and exporting industries. This understandable selectivity has brought about a significant change in the profile of foreign investment in India. The British stake in Indian industry, for example, has remained larger than that of any other country, but it is no longer preponderant. Also apparent is the shift in the character of investment illustrated in Table 9-6. Recent investments have been concentrated in "nontraditional" industries such as petroleum and engineering rather than "traditional" areas such as commerce and plantations.

The Foreign Exchange Regulation Act of 1973 sought to curb what India regarded as an excessive remittance of profits abroad by, among other measures, charging the RBI to obtain greater control over foreign investors and seeking to reduce the equity positions of foreign companies in their Indian subsidiaries.[76] The act was written so loosely, however, as to lead the *Economic and Political Weekly* to lament that it provides "Loopholes not guidelines" and that "the Reserve Bank's omnipotence, however, is more apparent than real."[77] In the final analysis, the 1973 legislation did nothing more than reflect India's long-standing mixed sentiments toward foreign capital, an ambivalence which became unusually clear in a series of 1974 decisions affecting the petroleum industry. In 1974, despite India's critical shortage of foreign exchange and the need to mobilize new resources to compensate for the dramatic escalation of fossil fuel prices which endangered its development, the government decided that the technical and other benefits it was receiving from Exxon did not justify

[75]Ashok Kapoor, *International Business Negotiations: A Study of India* (New York: New York University Press, 1970), pp. 261–262.

[76]*Business Week,* Dec. 14, 1973, pp. 34–35.

[77]*Economic and Political Weekly,* vol. 8, no. 152, Dec. 29, 1973, p. 2279.

TABLE **9–6**
BOOK VALUE OF FOREIGN INVESTMENT IN INDIA (percent)

Industry	1948 (2.6 billion rupees)	1967 (6.5 billion rupees)
Plantations	20.4	16.4
Mining	4.5	0.7
Petroleum	8.7	19.5
Services	38.6	14.2
Manufacturing	27.8	49.0
(Food, beverages, and tobacco)	(14.2)	(10.8)
(Textiles)	(39.4)	(5.0)
(Transport equipment)	(1.4)	(7.1)
(Metals and products)	(11.3)	(15.3)
(Chemicals)	(11.3)	(29.3)
TOTAL	100.0	100.0

Source: Adapted from V. N. Balasubramanyam, *International Transfer of Technology to India* (New York: Praeger Publishers, 1973), p. 32.

the domestic and external costs of allowing this multinational to maintain a subsidiary in India. It therefore negotiated a takeover of the local firm. In a more or less separate decision, the government acknowledged that it did not have the resources to explore for deep-sea petroleum reserves. But, rather than choose one of the leading international firms to search in the Bombay High region of the Arabian Sea, where the best prospects existed, it contracted to have two less-experienced foreign companies explore sites in areas where the prospects were less good. Meanwhile, the search for oil in the Bombay High was pressed with other resources, but not until 1975 was the pace commensurate with the priority of finding and extracting large amounts of petroleum in the shortest time possible.

It is striking how little is known about the true economic costs and benefits of foreign private investment in India and elsewhere. The problem is defined by the inherent weakness of hypothetical arguments, data gaps stemming from country and company secrecy, and difficulties in distinguishing costs and benefits as measured by the company accounts from the larger social impact of company operations.

Foreign investment has had a net beneficial effect on India's economic growth insofar as it has supplemented rather than displaced Indian investment, and it has increased output and employment. It is not known, however, how much these achievements exceed any net balance-of-payments drain which would reduce potential for growth in other sectors of the economy. With respect to social justice, to the extent that foreign-augmented investment levels have increased both the supply of commodities on the market and created new jobs and incomes, external investment has been justified. But, to the degree that foreign investment has strengthened the position of local monopolies, as found by the Dutt committee, it has been contrary to India's social justice objective.[78] Moreover, by contributing to the development of a dualistic or "enclave" economy, foreign investment has increased disparities and has been disruptive of the society.[79] Although Indian officials have recognized the threat of dualism as particularly real in the case of foreign investment (albeit not irrelevant to domestic private and public sector investment), they have advanced no effective policy to deal with dualism other than to disapprove proposed new foreign investments.

As for self-reliance, the presence of a foreign-owned factory in India would appear to be an asset to the Indian economy, if not a political and economic hostage. Officials in India, however, have been more concerned with possible dependency, the balance-of-payments costs that foreign investment may engender, and the degree to which foreign companies may ignore India's national interest in their operations. It would be naïve to deny the potential and actual grounds for this concern but just as naïve to assume that foreign companies will show more antisocial behavior than domestic companies. Moreover, in light of the controls available to a sovereign nation and the sophistication of Indian officials, it would be implausible to think that the Indian government could not and has not prevented or curbed the worst abuses of company power. The record shows that whereas some foreign companies have tried to take advantage of their strong positions, and on occasion have succeeded, India's fears on the score of foreign control over its industry have not been justified and, for the most part, foreign companies have acted responsibly.

There are three principal areas in which foreign investment is potentially important to India: transfer of technology, import of capital, and balance of payments. Thus, recent studies which show that foreign investors tend to use more capital and less labor than is economically and socially justifiable support the case for careful screening of proposed foreign investments.[80] It is also well known that the second-rate and outdated technology imported by India have, in some instances, been ideally suited to Indian economic conditions and, on other occasions, have proved uneconomic. The decisions to acquire these technologies, which have been made by both private firms and government, raise the question of whether the cost of obtaining technology through direct investment is less than through alternative means. The case against technical

[78]*Report of the Industrial Licensing Inquiry Committee*, op. cit., p. 71.

[79]See Hans W. Singer, "The Distribution of Gains between Investing and Borrowing Countries," *American Economic Review, Papers and Proceedings*, vol. 11, no. 2, May 1950.

[80]See, for example, Louis T. Wells, Jr., *Economic Man and Engineering Man: Choice of Technology in a Low Wage Country*, Economic Development Report No. 226, Center for International Affairs, Harvard University, November 1972. Also, James Pickett et al., "The Choice of Technology, Economic Efficiency, and Employment in Developing Countries," a study by the Overseas Development Unit, University of Strathclyde, Glasgow, 1973.

collaboration agreements (the policy India has favored in many instances) is based on the following facts: (1) foreign firms are psychologically less willing and bureaucratically less able to transfer complex technology in cases where they have no equity interest; (2) technical collaboration agreements generally underestimate the full costs of transferring the technology; and (3) the terms of transfer agreements often assume administrative, technical, and labor skills not fully available in India.[81] In short, only by involving a foreign company in a direct equity investment can it be made to feel sufficiently committed to deal with the almost inevitable follow-on problems which attend technical transfers.

Economists have yet to give a satisfying answer to the question of how the capital transferred through foreign private investment affects the economy of the recipient country because, to a considerable degree, the recipient country's larger economy determines the productivity of investments and other impacts. One issue which has attracted great attention—whether India is better off receiving private investment or foreign public aid monies—is hardly relevant, given the shortfall of foreign aid from India's large absorptive capacity for foreign capital. The two have been more complementary than alternative, and practically no choice would exist unless aid possibilities were greatly increased.

On the complex issue of how foreign investment has affected the balance of payments, it is bizarre that in the late 1960s, at a time when India was disapproving foreign investment applications on the grounds that these would adversely affect its foreign exchange position, the United States initiated a program to improve its own balance of payments by restricting American investment abroad. The situation, as seen by India, is illustrated by an RBI study which developed a model to measure the balance-of-payments effects of foreign investment over varying periods of time. On the basis of reasonable assumptions about profit rates (16 percent) and the split between profit remittance abroad and reinvestment (50:50), the model showed that the cumulative effect of a 100-rupee investment over 20 years would be a gross repatriation of dividends amounting to Rs. 260, i.e., a net balance-of-payments loss of Rs. 160.[82]

Regrettably, by omitting several key variables the RBI model gives a wrong impression.[83] The model took no account of the fact that foreign equity

[81]Balasubramanyam, op. cit., p. 136.

[82]S. S. Tarapore, "Some Aspects of Foreign Investment Policy," *RBI Bulletin*, May 1966.

[83]An early study of the economic consequences of foreign investment by Judd Polk, Irene Meister, and Lawrence A. Veit, "U.S. Production Abroad and the Balance of Payments" (The Conference Board, 1965), found on the basis of close work with major United States investors that the balance-of-payments effects could be positive or negative, but were usually insignificant in comparison with the increased production associated with foreign investment. The most complex econometric study of this subject is by G. Hufbauer and F. M. Adler, *Overseas Manufacturing Investment and the Balance of Payments* (Washington, D.C.: U.S. Department of the Treasury, 1968), which was equally indecisive in providing an answer to the balance-of-payments question.

investment either (1) increases India's international monetary reserves on which it receives interest in hard currencies or (2) saves India from having to dig into its scarce foreign exchange reserves to buy the requisite technology and capital goods needed to undertake the new operations. In addition, and in many cases much more important, the RBI study failed to consider import substitution and export generation which may result from foreign investment. These factors are likely to be of sufficient magnitude to swamp the cost to India of allowing repatriation of earnings on foreign investment.

The counter argument is that about 50 percent of India's foreign investment agreements include export-restriction clauses and these reduce India's export potential.[84] This is a dated argument, however, because in recent years the Indian government has not only followed a policy of minimizing export-restriction clauses, but required investors to commit themselves to export minimum amounts of their production. On balance, therefore, it should be possible for India, by carefully scrutinizing and negotiating new investment proposals, to harness these in support of its domestic development and international payments positions.

The Bechtel-proposed fertilizer program exemplifies the kind of foreign investment which would probably have greatly benefited India if agreement could have been reached on terms. Even more dramatic is the case of the Tenneco Company's offer to explore for petroleum in the deep waters of the Bombay High. In the mid-1960s complex and costly deep-sea drilling technology was available only from United States companies. When seismographic work done by the Soviet Union showed the likelihood of finding petroleum in this area, Tenneco offered to assume all costs and risks of exploration, provide the drilling rig, and train Indian technicians in return for 20 percent of any crude oil discovered. Although at that time there was no alternative way to explore for this oil (the Soviet Union made an exasperating and unhelpful offer to develop the technology jointly with the Indians at India's expense), Indian officials decided against the Tenneco offer. The reason was "partly because of political sensitivity of the Government of India and partly because it was not willing to commit a share of the crude to a foreign company for an unspecified period of time."[85] If the Tenneco offer had been approved, India might have been able to achieve self-sufficiency in petroleum and the acute economic crisis which developed in 1974 could probably have been avoided.

Thus, by vacillating between excessive zeal in denying entry to foreign investors and by neglecting to define its objectives more precisely and to act more forcefully, India appears to have missed a number of opportunities to use foreign companies to serve national interests. Moreover, the bureaucratic attention which has been paid to ritual and symbolic issues such as financial and managerial Indianization has been constructive but excessive insofar as it has

---

[84]*Foreign Collaboration in Indian Industry, Survey Report* (Bombay: RBI, 1968), pp. 106–108.

[85]*Overseas Hindustan Times,* June 6, 1974.

distracted attention from the prime problems of efficiency, growth, and bal-ance-of-payments earnings. The practical consequences of this situation are suggested by the comparatively small role of foreign investors in India and the larger international presence in more dynamic developing countries. In assess-ing the prospect for foreign private investment in India, one could easily be misled by official rhetoric which, as in the past 25 years, continues to encourage foreign investors only to disappoint them at the licensing gate. In reality, India's foreign investment policy is likely to conform with its more general attitude toward the private sector, and unless there is a fundamental reversal of the policies India has followed since Independence, the scope for private foreign investment may change marginally but it is bound to remain prevailingly small.

The development of this chapter has followed a rather more consistent pattern than might have been anticipated. Whereas I have not taken exception to India's objective of industrialization, and have only tangentially questioned the emphasis on heavy industry, India's strategy for gaining these objectives appears to have been remarkably unsuited to its social and political character. India's policies toward the public and private sectors—toward domestic and foreign business relationships—have engendered inefficiency, fostered monop-oly and privilege, and otherwise failed to meet its economic objectives. Chapter 11 will return to this subject and consider India's industrial strategy in the broader context of how it interacted with social, political, and other economic factors in determining the course of development.

CHAPTER **10**
THE POLITICAL ECONOMY OF
BANK NATIONALIZATION

On July 19, 1969, the President of India signed a historic ordinance which nationalized India's 14 largest private commercial banks. Taken at face value, the ordinance was a major step in the Indian government's efforts to harness the nation's economic resources for development. To even the most casual follower of the Indian scene, however, it also was a daring move on the part of Indira Gandhi to resolve an important and immediate political problem; a move calculated to transform her titular leadership of the ruling Congress party into a genuine suzerainty. At still another level, bank nationalization was loaded with deeper meaning in that it reflected a shift leftward in India's political center of gravity, a movement of the economy toward a more egalitarian and doctrinaire socialist approach. Indian policy toward its commercial banks involves so many disparate ideological, political, managerial, and basic economic issues as to be illustrative of how Indian policy is made and implemented. At another level, banking policy is a critical ingredient of India's development strategy.

The Pros and Cons of Nationalization

One need not search far in India's ideological background to discover why in 1969 bank nationalization was regarded by Indian socialists as a priority objective. On the one hand, countries such as France and Italy had government-owned banks and they had demonstrated that public ownership could be applied successfully to the financial sector. On the other hand, leftists had long complained that India's business leaders controlled the banking system and thereby had preempted the national wealth for their own selfish objectives and further increased income disparities. For years there had been agitation favoring bank nationalization, not just by political leaders but also by bank workers (one of India's principal bank labor unions was Communist-controlled), journalists, intellectuals, and academics. In December 1954, for example, in conjunction with the movement to adopt a "socialist pattern of society" as a political objective of the Indian government and the Congress party, an effort was made to have all commercial banks nationalized.[1] It was vigorously opposed, however, and the only change undertaken during this period was the nationalization of the State Bank of India (formerly the Imperial Bank) in 1955. This was no great victory for the socialists because the Imperial Bank had served as banker to the government and its takeover did not set a precedent that would assure the future takeover of other private banks. Moreover socialists were not appeased because the major portion of commercial bank deposits remained in the private sector.

The political case against bank nationalization in 1969 was made by bank shareholders, bank officials, favored borrowers, others who preferred the status quo because they were benefiting from the system, and a small group who for practical or ideological reasons felt that the bulk of the banking system should remain under private control. In a characteristically Indian way, opposition to bank nationalization was rooted not only in class distinction, but in regional diversity. For instance, well-banked states like the Punjab fought to ensure that the savings of the Punjabi people would not be siphoned off for investment in poorer areas. As it turned out, such arguments were self-defeating because they raised disparity consciousness and evoked counterattacks by the poorer and less well-banked states.

The main burden of the economic case for bank nationalization rested on a judgment that bank operations, with respect to both mobilization of new savings and the pattern of lending, were not fully meeting their potential contribution to the development process. Even though commercial banks more than doubled the number of bank branches in the period 1955–1967, from 3,182 to 6,985, more than two-thirds of the new branches were established in centers where banking facilities already existed.[2] Because banks were still sparsely located in rural India, agrarian families did not have the option of placing their money with banks and, as a result, either consumed a greater proportion of their incomes than they would have if banks were available or hoarded commodities in order to preserve their wealth. As for the lending side of the banks' portfolios, the All-India Rural Credit Survey had emphatically noted as early as 1954 that adequate finance was not available to the weaker members of the agricultural sector.[3] In 1969, it was commonly believed that priority areas such as agriculture, small-scale industry, and exporters were denied their fair share of bank loans and that this was retarding investment.

Also important in the economic justification for bank nationalization was a concern for equity. The Dutt committee had revealed the close affiliation of major Indian banking houses to the "Larger Industrial Houses" (in some cases

---

[1]Kidron, op. cit., p. 133.
[2]*Report of the All-India Rural Credit Review Committee*, op. cit., p. 330.
[3]*All-India Rural Credit Survey*, vol. 2, *The General Report* (Bombay: RBI, 1954).

banks were controlled by industrialists), and it had shown how this relationship contributed to monopoly.[4] In addition, because Indian banking practices tended to be very orthodox, loans were made on the basis of security rather than the profit potential of the schemes they were to finance. This meant that funds often were available for commodity speculation but not for real investment. Typical of the "unwashed" orthodox banker's skepticism of modern banking and reluctance to take any risks is the lament contained in the *Bulletin* of one of the 14 nationalized banks (incidentially, long after nationalization):

> The land laws of various states are so complicated that it is difficult to verify the ownership rights of the farmers who apply for loans. The farmers' main asset is the land and unless the ownership right on the land is verifiable, it would be difficult for the commercial banks to consider loan facilities. It is not only that the land will form a security to the banks, but to assess the credit needs . . . , the production base of land . . . should also be known.[5]

The problem before 1969 was not just that poor people could not obtain credit. An elaborate network existed whereby those who were able to obtain bank loans made funds available to less credit-worthy borrowers who, in turn, reloaned the funds until they reached the lower echelons. The disadvantage of this system was that it engendered relationships of personal dependency and that the most needy people—not necessarily the worst credit risks—paid the highest (exorbitant) rates of interest.

The economic case against bank nationalization was also strong. Opponents questioned whether government ownership would have any impact on the Larger Industrial Houses. For evidence, they pointed to the Dutt committee's finding that in the period 1956–1965 these firms had managed to obtain more than their fair share of financial assistance from public sector institutions, including the State Bank.[6] Similarly, they noted that the State Bank's performance with regard to opening new branches and making loans to priority sectors and the poor was not conspicuously better than that of the private commercial banks. Opponents of nationalization noted that commercial bank lending to priority sectors such as agriculture was low because in previous years the government had favored cooperatives and discouraged commercial banks from actively seeking business in rural areas. In addition, they pointed to the progress private banks were making in responding to the newly recognized role of banks and the potential for accelerating the pace through the system of "social control" which had been put into operation early in 1969. They weighed the possible advantages of bank nationalization against what, to many of them, looked like the imminent dangers of bureaucratic inefficiency, interference in the banking system by politicians for both political and personal pecuniary

---

[4]*Report of the Industrial Licensing Inquiry Committee,* op. cit., Main Report, p. 17, and appendix to vol. 2, p. 93.

[5]*Bank of India Bulletin,* vol. 9, no. 4, April 1971, p. 55.

[6]*Main Report,* op. cit., p. 149.

reasons, graft, and an adverse psychological effect on potential investors (domestic and foreign).

Crisis and Response

The forces for and against bank nationalization were so evenly balanced that any change in the status quo required a major change in India's political environment. This explains why only the Imperial Bank was taken over in 1955. Moreover, when the AICC met in Ernakulam in September 1966, and leftist congressmen lobbied to have bank nationalization made part of the party platform in the 1967 general elections, their insistent demand was met by a compromise ("social control" of banks) which "seemed a verbal trick designed to satisfy the party's left wingers without overly antagonizing the right wing and its constituents in the business community."[7] For at least one seasoned Indian observer, however, the handwriting was on the wall, and it was just a matter of time before the euphemism "social control" would be translated into nationalization.[8]

In 1967 the Congress was in deep trouble because of the faltering economy and growing political disaffection. The party's Election Manifesto, reflecting Ernakulam, stated that "It is necessary to bring most of these banking institutions under social control in order to serve the cause of economic growth and fulfill our social purposes more effectively."[9] But in the bitterly contested elections of 1967 neither this declaration nor any other could save the Congress from suffering a startling reversal at the polls. Mrs. Gandhi's response to this setback was to turn leftward and to embrace the highly vocal "Young Turks" in the Congress. In May 1967, at the New Delhi meeting of the Congress Working Committee, she obtained support for accelerating the process of implementing socialist democracy through a 10-point program which included social control of banks, nationalization of general insurance, enhanced government control over imports, exports, and the food grain trade, and a variety of other left-leaning measures.

Following approval of the 10-point program by the All-India Congress Committee later in the year, the government acted to provide a legal framework for social control through passage of the Banking Laws Amendment Act of 1968. More or less simultaneously, a National Credit Council (NCC) was organized under the finance minister, Morarji Desai, and various subgroups of the NCC were established to study the problems of the banking system and to make recommendations for improvements. Most important among these was the Study Group on Organized Framework for Implementation of Social

[7]*New York Times,* Sept. 27, 1966.
[8]*Eastern Economist,* Sept. 23, 1966, p. 560.
[9]See Congress Party Election Manifesto in *General Elections in India, 1967* (New Delhi: Government of India, 1967), p. 173.

Objectives. Under the tutelage of D. R. Gadgil, who had moved from his role as chief critic of the Planning Commission to its vice chairmanship, the work of this study group contributed heavily to the financial strategy India adopted after the banks were nationalized.

Under the 1968 Banking Laws Amendment Act, the boards of directors of the private commercial banks were reconstituted to make them more efficient and also to dilute the influence of large business houses. In February 1969, when the "social control" scheme came into force, the banks were pressed to expand into what were regarded as "nontraditional" activities. They were obligated to make agricultural loans, expand their branches in rural areas, undertake loans to other priority sectors such as small traders and transport operators, and intensify their efforts to mobilize new deposits.

The social control program did not have a whirlwind start. In part this was because of the apathy and antagonism of bank owners and managers, but normal problems of initiating a new scheme and the absence of adequate preparation were also factors. Nonetheless, the almost unanimous opinion of bankers and Delhi bureaucrats in the summer of 1969 was that the scheme was being introduced according to the expected timetable and that it was beginning to cause the desired changes in the banking structure. It therefore came as a great surprise when, at the July 1969 session of the AICC, Mrs. Gandhi declared her dissatisfaction with the social control program and stated: "It is widely recognized that the operations of the banking system should be informed by a larger social purpose and . . . that the desired regulation and rate of progress consistent with the urgency of our problems could be secured only through nationalization."[10]

The Prime Minister went on to ask for a far-reaching revision of India's economic policies, to include the substitution of bank nationalization for social control and a stiffening of the industrial licensing and other policies to curb the powers of India's largest companies. Her economic objective, to realign the banking system's priorities with those of the government, was manifestly clear as evidenced by her words and her suggestion that the requirement for minimal bank assets invested in government securities be raised to 30 percent from its then current level of 25 percent. Her political goal, to seize unchallenged control of the party, also was clear, and many believed it to be her first priority. The unanswered question—which may remain unresolved—is whether the Prime Minister intended bank nationalization to spearhead a decisive move toward socialism, or whether this was merely a convenient feint to serve more immediate economic and political needs.

In 1969, the leadership of the Congress was known as the "Syndicate" because it included a small group of "bosses" with power derived from various local political machines. It was highly conservative and unique insofar as at no other time since the Constitution was put in force had India had a collective

---

[10]Quoted in S. A. Pandit, "Nationalization of Banks in India," *Finance and Development,* vol. 10, no. 1, March 1973, p. 33.

leadership. The Syndicate opposed Mrs. Gandi's bank nationalization proposal but acquiesced when their opposition to it threatened to cause a split in the party. Indeed in an effort to heal the rift between Mrs. Gandhi and the right wing, the conservative deputy prime minister and finance minister, Morarji Desai, moved the resolution endorsing the Prime Minister's new economic policy. The Syndicate, meanwhile, had chosen to fight on another front, the choice of a Congress candidate to run in the Indian presidential election which was to be held in August. Disregarding the Prime Minister's preference for the candidature of V. V. Giri (the then acting president) or Jagjivan Ram (one of her supporters), the Syndicate decided in favor of Sanjiva Reddy, who at the time was Speaker in the lower house of Parliament and a known opponent of Mrs. Gandhi. Although the Congress Working Committee had unanimously adopted the resolution supporting the Prime Minister's economic proposals, the choice of Reddy was too obvious a challenge to her authority to go unmet. It appeared as a possible first step in a Syndicate effort to remove her from office and, if ignored, would place in high office a man who could raise impediments to the Prime Minister's program.

In rising to the political problem of Congress party leadership, Mrs. Gandhi chose to relieve Morarji Desai of his post as finance minister, ostensibly because he could not be expected to implement a policy (bank nationalization) with which he did not agree. Desai, who had resisted nationalization on the grounds that the social control mechanism had only just come into force and that it should be given another two years to prove its value, found himself in a highly embarrassing situation. On July 16, he resigned the deputy prime ministership.

By combining the issues of whether the Congress should move leftward and whether her position as prime minister gave her authority within the Party, Mrs. Gandhi polarized the Congress and won over her opposition. Right-wing elements of the party accused her of manipulating the economic program for self-serving purposes and of disregarding the preference of the party leadership. She counterattacked by accusing them of having a retrograde view of their responsibilities and of refusing to implement the socioeconomic program long recognized by the party and exemplified by the idea of a "socialist pattern of society."

Opposition parties were united in welcoming the demise of Morarji Desai as a step toward further weakening of the Congress, but they were sharply divided on the bank nationalization issue. Conservative criticism of bank nationalization from outside the Congress was even more vitriolic than from within. The Jan Sangh (Hindu nationalist) and Swatantra (business-oriented) parties attacked the new policy as a step toward communism, and Communist party support for Mrs. Gandhi on this issue did little to allay their concern. The Jan Sangh objected to "the concentration of economic power in the hands of those who are already in control of the state apparatus."[11] Minoo Masani, the leader of the Swatantra party and at one time generally regarded as a future Indian prime

---

[11]*Indian Recorder and Digest,* August 1969, p. 10.

minister, expressed concern about the reaction of Indian and foreign business-men to bank nationalization: "Nationalization has so far meant bureaucratic inefficiency, political influence, corruption, and financial losses."[12] In contrast, the Central Secretariat of the Communist Party of India (Moscow-oriented) characterized the situation as "The beginning of a new significant stage in the fight against monopoly capital and the forces of right reaction inside the country," and extended the support of the party to "these bold and timely steps taken by the Prime Minister."[13]

After Morarji Desai's resignation, Mrs. Gandhi proceeded to take personal charge of the Finance portfolio, and on July 19 she called an emergency meeting of the Cabinet at which it was decided that bank nationalization should be implemented immediately. Because Parliament was in recess, the legal procedure for acting was a presidential ordinance—evidence as to why the choice of a Congress candidate for the presidency was so critical. Before nightfall, Acting President V. V. Giri had put his signature to the document and the Prime Minister had gone on national radio to explain the decision to the Indian people. Her statement that evening emphasized the importance of bank nationalization to the economic needs of the people and the necessity for the government to improve their position by controlling "the commanding heights of the economy" through state ownership. It presaged the Congress party strategy and use of the *garibi hatao* ("abolish poverty") slogan in the 1971 general election.

When bank nationalization legislation came before the Parliament on July 25, conservative forces within the Congress failed to oppose it. They feared that by doing so they would appear socially backward. In addition they clung to a residual hope that by appeasing the Prime Minister the rift could be healed. Finally, some of them regarded conciliation and moderation as offering the best chance for the success of Sanjiva Reddy in the presidential election. Thus, the proposed legislation nationalizing banks was passed without any serious chal-lenge. But even though the spirit of compromise which had characterized the internal ethos of the Congress in the past was on their side, the Syndicate had failed to reckon with the go-for-broke strategy of Mrs. Gandhi. The Prime Minister, having rejected the Reddy candidacy, decreed that Congress electors had the right to vote freely and according to their consciences. On August 16, her candidate, V. V. Giri, was elected president by a narrow margin.

These rapid-fire events were followed by a period of maneuver, self-justifica-tion, and rationalization by both right- and left-wing elements of the Congress. As the Syndicate was unable either to topple the Prime Minister or to make her compromise her left-leaning position, it became only a matter of time until the Congress split and a new chapter in Indian political history began. Most of the entries in this new chapter were written by the socialist wing of the party, which, with the aid of non-Congress leftist parties, proceeded to move against large

[12]*London Times,* July 25, 1969.
[13]Quoted in the *Indian Recorder and Digest,* August 1969, p. 9.

private companies, the purses and privileges of the former princely rulers, and other established private interests.

Bank Nationalization and Indian Politics

Bank nationalization is important because at the very least the events of 1969 represented an inflection point leading in the short term to more salient socialism. They may also prove to be a turning point in the long-run direction of India's economic policy. Moreover, the conjunction of high politics and high economics encompassed by bank nationalization tells us a great deal about the factors affecting India's development. These events would not be nearly as important but for the fact that both the economic and political issues involved were critically important to development.

We have identified compromise as an outstanding feature of the Indian political system, and it is therefore significant that on the bank nationalization issue the Prime Minister was unwilling to compromise. The strategic weakness of Morarji Desai and the Syndicate, from the time of the Ernakulam agreement on "social control" through the endorsement in July 1969 of Mrs. Gandhi's economic policy proposal, was their assumption that the rift with the Prime Minister could be healed. What they failed to appreciate was the character of Mrs. Gandhi and her view that a major political change within the government and the party was required to give her real authority and to deal with the nation's pressing economic problems.

Significantly, the Indian spirit of compromise and willingness to elevate economic pragmatism over doctrinaire politics were reasserted in instances where there was no threat to the Prime Minister's political power. In particular, they can be seen in the decision to allow the smaller Indian commercial banks and the branches of foreign banks to remain in private hands. The Banking Commission (1972) dismissed the importance of foreign banks: "They may be allowed to continue as at present since their branch expansion is in any case limited to port towns and since their share in the total banking business in India is fast diminishing".[14] The more immediate reasons for allowing the foreign banks to remain in business, which the Prime Minister gave Parliament on July 21, 1969, were (1) that they played a specialized role in facilitating foreign trade and tourism through their international facilities and (2) that their takeover would have engendered a hostile reaction abroad which, in turn, would have inhibited India's receipts of needed foreign loans and investments.[15] Whether this was a correct judgment of foreign opinion is questionable, but it did reflect a caution which was prudent in the light of the earlier public-private controversy between India and foreign aid donors. As a result of bank nationalization, foreign branch banks were placed in a holding pattern; their operations had to

---

[14]*Report of the Banking Commission,* op. cit., p. 393.
[15]*London Times,* July 22, 1969.

be in low profile, but for all practical purposes they continued to carry on their normal business and to make profits in India.

Another characteristic of Indian political economy which is illustrated by the bank nationalization episode is what might be called the "lure of the left." Private ownership has an inherent disadvantage in India and other countries where the majority of the population is too poor to have any investment capital. Working-class Indians enthusiastically greeted bank nationalization as heralding an era of affluence for the masses; they interpreted national ownership of banks as giving them a right to the money deposited in the banks, and countless mammoth processions passed by the Prime Minister's home to support her action.[16] In these circumstances, it is no wonder that there is a continuing pressure for radicalization of India's economic policies and heavy reliance on sloganeering as the language of political communication.

The sequence of events related to bank nationalization also illustrates both the commitment to democracy and the flexibility of the Indian political system. The Indian Constitution recognized the holding of private property as a fundamental right, and the possibility that this right had been abridged by bank nationalization caused the Indian Supreme Court to issue a stay order on July 22, 1969. When, in February 1970, the Supreme Court voted by a margin of 10 to 1 to delcare the Bank Nationalization Act unconstitutional, its finding was greeted by Mrs. Gandhi and her followers with no small amount of consternation.

Although it took little more than a technical change of language and a larger compensation to the former owners of the banks to rewrite the legislation so as to make it acceptable to the judiciary, the Supreme Court's negative judgment served as the occasion for several weeks of intense agitation by all political elements. The Jan Sangh and Swatantra parties repeated their earlier criticisms of bank nationalization, and they were joined to some extent by voices from the conservative wing of the Congress. Morarji Desai and his followers criticized Mrs. Gandhi for having nationalized the banks with excessive haste. At the other end of the political spectrum, the bank workers' unions lobbied vehemently and demonstrated publicly for extension of the nationalization to all banks, including foreign branches in India. The Prime Minister's party actively defended its legislative record and, while making no major changes in the new bank nationalization law, inched closer to the radical view that the Fundamental Rights provisions should be deleted from the Constitution and that the Supreme Court was a reactionary body standing in the way of social progress.

Subsequently, over the strenuous objections of Indian conservatives, legislation amending the Constitution was approved by Parliament in 1971. The Twenty-fourth Amendment, referred to by the Prime Minister as "a milestone in the march of the Indian people toward democracy, secularism, and a just and

---

[16]See Frank Moraes, *Witness to an Era: India, 1920 to the Present Day* (New York: Holt, Rinehart and Winston, 1973), p. 259.

human society,"[17] sought to give sole authority for deciding compensation to the legislative branch of government and to make this a nonjusticiable subject. A further weakening of the judicial branch occurred in 1973, when the Prime Minister, seeking to obtain a Supreme Court more amenable to her own political views, took the unprecedented step of choosing the new chief justice on a basis other than seniority. This evoked an outcry from conservatives and others, such as the venerable freedom fighter and spiritual leader Jayaprakash Narayan, who were concerned about what appeared to be tampering with the democratic process. The only concrete opposition to this action, however, was the indignant resignation of the justices who had been passed over.

Finally, and linked to the above, is the importance of the symbolic versus substantive aspects of bank nationalization. This daring policy was a rallying point in Mrs. Gandhi's 1971 election platform, but thereafter it tended to recede as a political issue toward the more limited position which it had occupied during most of the pre-Independence years. In contrast, the political changes to which it had been central—the split of the Congress, a leftward movement in India's rhetoric and policy, a shift of political power from the states to the Center, and a movement to alter the Constitution and the Supreme Court's attitude—were in their infant stages and promised to have a profound effect on the future course of India's development. According to John Lewis, "bank nationalization was not and is not a first-order issue, one way or the other—any more than the other economic reform proposals."[18] This may be true insofar as Mrs. Gandhi might have chosen any one of her 10 points to serve as the vehicle for the political realignment and did not realize the latent power in the bank nationalization move. But is it misleading in the sense that bank nationalization had potentially more real economic content than most of the other points and that it promised to change the pace and the texture of Indian development. It is instructive, therefore, to trace the implementation of India's bank nationalization and to see whether its potential for accelerating develop- ment has been realized.

The Proof of the Pudding

As in the case of many of the socialist schemes in the Congress platform, no serious earlier thought had been given to how bank nationalization should be implemented. Thus, after the event, there was a hasty scramble to staff a Banking Department in the Ministry of Finance and to establish the individual responsibilities of the Ministry and the Reserve Bank of India. In practice, remarkably good coordination between Finance and the RBI was achieved, in no small part owing to Mrs. Gandhi's drafting a man in whom she had confidence, R. K. Hazari, as deputy governor of the RBI. Hazari, who had

[17]*Indian Recorder and Digest,* September 1971, p. 7.
[18]John P. Lewis, "Wanted in India: A Relevant Radicalism," op. cit., p. 3.

taught economics at the University of Bombay and who as editor of *Economic and Political Weekly* had been a strong advocate of the takeover, proved to be a hardened pragmatist in dealing with the problems at hand.

Although supervisory government machinery was established quickly and authority for management of the nationalized banks was shifted from the 14 boards of directors to a like number of government-appointed custodians, the break with the past was not as great as might be imagined because the custodian for each bank had previously served as the chairman of its board of directors. In mid-1970 the government appointed temporary management committees to aid the custodians in policy matters, and later that year it was decided that, when appointed, the board of each bank should include representatives of the government, the RBI, bank management and workers, and customers. In late 1972 the intricate political task of choosing these individuals was resolved; 3½ years after nationalization, the banks were given permanent top management.

Together, the RBI and the Finance Ministry sought to redefine the objectives of the "social control" program and, with the aid of various old and new advisory groups, to decide how policies should be implemented. The challenge and content of their task had been clearly outlined by the Prime Minister in her July 19 broadcast:

> What is sought to be achieved through the present decision to nationalise the major banks is to accelerate the achievements of our objectives. The purpose of expanding bank credit to priority areas which have hitherto been somewhat neglected as also (1) the removal of control by a few, (2) provision of adequate credit for agriculture and small industry and exports, (3) the giving of a professional bent to bank management, (4) the encouragement of new classes of entrepreneurs, and (5) the provision of adequate training as well as reasonable terms of service for bank staff still remain and will call for continuous efforts over a long time. Nationalisation is necessary for the speedy achievement of these objectives, but the measure by itself will not achieve these objectives.[19]

In practice, this was interpreted as requiring several measures, which we shall review. First among them was enlargement of the banking system, particularly through the opening of bank offices in smaller, rural, and backward areas, and especially in those areas which had no banks. Table 10-1 shows that the growth in the number of bank branches has been nothing less than extraordinary; the number of these offices increased by almost 100 percent in the course of only four years. Moreover, whereas in mid-1969 only 22 percent of the banks were classified as being in rural centers (places with a population of less than 10,000), by mid-1973 the share of rural banks had grown to 36 percent.[20] In 1974, the Lok Sabha's Estimates Committee criticized the government because during

[19]Quoted in *Report of the Banking Commission,* op. cit., p. 4.
[20]RBI, *Report on Currency and Finance, 1972–73,* p. 118.

TABLE **10–1**
TRENDS IN INDIAN BANKING

	July 1969	June 1970	June 1971	June 1972	June 1973
I. *Number of bank offices:*					
State bank*	2,465	2,935	3,519	3,958	4,430
14 nationalized banks	4,168	5,318	6,368	7,189	8,109
Private commercial banks	1,688	1,878	2,126	2,475	2,823
TOTAL	8,321	10,131	12,013	13,622	15,362
II. *Deposits (billions of rupees):*					
State bank*	12,385†	(44,260)	17,044	21,234	25,160
14 nationalized banks	26,334†		35,088	42,013	50,540
Private commercial banks	7,739†	8,490	10,021	12,074	14,480
TOTAL	46,458†	52,750	62,153	75,322	90,180
III. *Public sector bank advances— outstanding to priority sectors (billions of rupees):*					
Agriculture	1,623†	3,016	3,410	3,885	4,461
Small-scale industry	2,511†	3,695	4,422	5,271	6,427
Road transport	55†	244	398	504	625
Small business	194†	644	720	774	950
Professional self-employed	19†	66	86	122	212
Education	8†	21	37	29	32
TOTAL	4,410†	7,687	9,073	10,585	12,707

*Including its subsidiaries.

†End of June 1969.

Sources: RBI, *Report on Currency and Finance, 1972–73,* pp. 111–112, 118; *Economic Survey, 1973–74,* p. 83; various issues of the *RBI Bulletin; Report of the Banking Commission,* p. 46.

these four years the opening of bank branches had decelerated and regional disparities in the availability of bank offices had not been eliminated.[21] In light of the data cited above, however, this criticism appears ill-founded or, at very least, premature.

After nationalization, the banks were charged with deposit mobilization on the premise that this would increase saving and discourage consumption. Although technically correct that the option of depositing money in a bank could increase personal savings, the process of substituting deposits for consumption was likely to be less important than the process of substituting

[21]*Extension of Credit Facilities to Weaker Sections of Society and for Development of Backward Areas,* Sixty-second Report of the Estimates Committee (1973–74), Fifth Lok Sabha (New Delhi: Lok Sabha Secretariat, 1974), pp. 31–36.

deposits for saving done through hoarding of commodities. Moreover, to the extent that commercial bank deposits were increased at the expense of cash or other financial asset holdings, they promised to have no real benefit for the economy. What I am suggesting is that the importance of deposit mobilization was exaggerated by the policy makers. Be that as it may, it is interesting to see how the deposit mobilization effort fared. At first blush, the recorded increase in public sector bank deposits (see Table 10-1) suggests that the measures taken after bank nationalization paid handsome dividends. But when these figures are interpreted in the light of the extraordinary inflation and creation of new money during the period, and when it is noted that private bank deposits grew equally fast despite various constraints which were not applicable to public sector banks, the performance of the public sector banks is no longer impressive.

In restructuring the nationalized banks' asset portfolios, the government's object was twofold. The negative aspect was to deprive India's large industrial and trading houses of their privileged access to capital. In fact, private investment was not very ebullient during these years, and credit policy appears to have met liberally the capital demands of large private companies. Although their share of total bank loans declined, there is no evidence that bank credit was withheld from the Larger Industrial Houses. Indeed, according to the Estimates Committee, the government and RBI neglected their duty by insufficient vigilance to assure that loans to this sector were not "diverted for un-social or un-productive purposes".[22]

The positive objective of the new lending policy was to align bank credit portfolios with the socioeconomic goals of the nation. This required accelerated lending to the weaker and priority sectors, including agriculture, small-scale industry, artisans, transport operators (taxis, scooters, trucks, etc.), and exporters. Here, as in the case of deposit mobilization, the statistics are misleadingly optimistic (see Table 10-1). On the one hand, the base from which the growth of advances to priority sectors is measured is small. On the other hand, classification of loans is a matter of judgment and is subject to manipulation by various levels of bank officials who are anxious to please senior officers and, ultimately, their political masters. As seen by the Estimates Committee, some of the growth of the loans to priority sectors is illusory. Moreover, owing to the "lack of systematic followup" by the banks, the Estimates Committee was "not convinced that the nationalized banks have been able to meet the genuine requirements of credit of weaker sections of society in whose name the nationalization scheme had been implemented."[23]

In tracing how the policy of portfolio diversification has not always directed money to targeted sectors, Ashok Mitra, former chief economic adviser to the government and a pronounced leftist, has noted the proclivity of big business to open small-scale operations "so as to siphon away bank funds ostensibly

---

[22]*Sixty-second Report of the Estimates Committee,* op. cit., p. 22.
[23]Ibid., p. 18.

intended for the poor artisans." He also has called attention to the pattern of rural lending in which the major beneficiaries are the already well-to-do peasants rather than the truly disadvantaged.[24] While the evidence, such as it is, lends support to this kind of statement, there are not enough facts to make the judgment conclusive. Moreover, there are extenuating circumstances which suggest that the program may fail to achieve its goals directly but succeed through a complex indirect process. The role of financial intermediaries is a case in point. Since 1931 when the Indian Central Banking Enquiry Committee estimated that indigenous bankers accounted for more than 90 percent of the total bank credit in the country,[25] the organized banking sector has made enormous progress and its relative position has grown. Nonetheless, for all but the wealthy and privileged, credit still is provided by the large landowners, traders, and the privileged classes whom Mitra cites as benefiting directly from bank nationalization. The hidden, but very real, link in this story is that as more credit becomes available to the rural elite, they are better able to increase their loans to the poor. Moreover, in cases where an aggressive bank has been established, it often has had the effect of causing indigenous bankers and others to reduce the rate of interest they charge the poor.

A disturbing aspect of the postnationalization banking situation is the extent to which loans to priority sectors have not been repaid. Information on this subject is elusive because bankers quite naturally are loath to reclassify overdue loan collections as bad debts. Nonetheless, in private many Indian bankers express concern that whereas large borrowers in the priority sectors will prove to be good credit risks, many of the smaller loans may never be repaid. Circumstantial evidence to support this worry comes from the Estimates Committee's finding that the recovery rate for loans to agriculture was only 50.7 percent, and that it was as low as 21.3 percent in West Bengal.[26] The larger difficulties which have overtaken Indian banking since nationalization are suggested by the faltering profitability of banks even though the spread between borrowing and lending rates has widened from 4½ percent in 1969 to 7 percent in 1974.[27]

How should bank nationalization be evaluated? Ashok Mitra has commented acidly:

> The nationalization of the banks served the purpose for which it was intended. A slogan was given a body. A pretence was provided with a cover. A crowd, which is the populace of India, was provided with a cause for emotion. The fact that, in today's grey light, it may be revealed as a fakery to some does not diminish the original allure of the cause. Alongside with

[24]See *Economic and Political Weekly,* July 28, 1973, p. 1312.
[25]*History of the Reserve Bank of India, 1935–51* (Bombay: Reserve Bank of India, 1970), pp. 111–112.
[26]Ibid., p. 80.
[27]Christie Davies, "The Shady Side of Nationalization in India," *Banker,* October 1974.

Bangladesh and the break-up of Pakistan in 1971, bank nationalization carved out the primrose path to power and glory for the government installed in New Delhi.[28]

Mitra goes on to mock the politicians and economists by asserting that bank nationalization has the characteristics of Pareto optimality; no one has been harmed (former bank owners, bank laborers and officials, depositors, and wealthy industrial interests), and some small-scale businessmen and rural interests are marginally better off.[29] The weaker sector of society—India's poor —do not count in such calculations.

Mitra's criticism is not without merit. The Estimates Committee was highly critical of the government for delaying too long before it introduced new bank policies.[30] Further harm was done by the government's tardiness in appointing full-time boards of directors for the banks, its tolerance of blatant indiscipline on the part of bank workers, the waste caused by its headlong rush to open new bank branches without first considering the availability of trained managers, and the unacceptable repayment performance among some of the new borrowers. Do such criticisms lend too little weight to the potential benefits of giving the commercial banks a development responsibility? Surely the increased savings, new borrowing opportunities for people previously regarded by banks as uncreditworthy, and nationwide lowering of interest rates are not to be regarded as inconsequential. The fact of the matter is that bank nationalization is a process rather than an event; some entries—plus and minus—have been made on the scoreboard, but the contest is far from over.

At another level, the evaluation of bank nationalization cannot be confined to the important but narrow question of whether bank policy was successfully redesigned. The difficulties encountered in bank nationalization are more generally a function of India's broader development problems. For example, without reform of land tenancy rights, or in the absence of adequate fertilizer supplies, the availability of credit is of only subsidiary importance. Indeed, it is precisely in those states which are developing fastest (Punjab, Gujarat, and others) that the absolute amount of credit per farmer and the distribution of credit to low-income families is most satisfactory. Thus, the future economic payoff from bank nationalization rests not only with the government's wisdom in its choice of deposit mobilization and credit measures, but also with the range of its development policies in which banking can play a crucial but only a complementary role. Finally, from a political viewpoint, the significance of bank nationalization is that, in contrast to the enormous benefit it provided Mrs. Gandhi in 1969 and the next several years, a failure to deliver the promised economic fruits in the long run may make it a grave liability.

[28]*Economic and Political Weekly,* July 28, 1973, p. 1312.
[29]Ibid.
[30]*Sixty-second Report of the Estimates Committee,* op. cit., p. 5.

PART IV
CONCLUSION

CHAPTER 11
INDIA'S ECONOMIC DEVELOPMENT

India's debate on economic policy predates Independence by many years and has characteristically been lively. Nevertheless, the termination of colonial rule in 1947 was a watershed. Political independence forged the links between discussion, decision, and action; it quickened the debate and banished all trace of the esoteric that had marked some earlier deliberations; it brought democracy and extended the forum for decision from internal Congress party review to the all-India level; and in later years, because many nations wished to see what they regarded as pluralistic Indian democracy outperform monolithic Chinese totalitarianism, it thrust the issue of India's development onto a global stage as a drama in which audience participation was a vital ingredient of the performance.

How can we judge India's economic performance? This task, to which previous chapters have been leading, is complicated by substantive and procedural difficulties. For example, what criteria should be used to measure the relative significance of factors which India could affect by its policies and those that lay beyond its reach? Or what remedial steps can be taken to bypass the basic problems of misleading and missing data? As there are no fully satisfactory answers, my procedure is to examine Indian development according to four standards: historical precedent, the need for progress, the potential for development (given existing social and economic conditions), and the political rhetoric of the period. Based on this analysis, the second part of the chapter seeks to give a coherent, if eclectic, explanation of the process which has governed the Indian economy's evolution.

Four Views of India's Economic Performance

The bare facts of India's progress as measured by commonly used economic indicators were presented in Chapter 2 and elsewhere. In summary, conventional GNP estimates show India to be growing at an average annual rate of 3.0 to 3.5 percent. This is based on a trend growth rate for food grains of 2.8 percent (enough to improve nutrition standards marginally, given the population growth rate of 2.1 percent) and a roughly 6 percent growth rate for industrial production. These averages conceal large interstate and even intrastate differences. Although Indian industry has been profoundly enlarged and diversified, the significance of agriculture remains predominant. The distribution of income between rich and poor (regionally or within communities) has remained grossly unequal and, in some cases, income and asset disparities have widened. Finally, as indicated by India's chronic balance-of-payments problem and import suppression policies, foreign exchange scarcity has been a major constraint on development ever since the late 1950s. Before I proceed to interpret these results, a digression to distinguish several relevant analytic problems is in order.

Gross national income (GNI), or variants thereof, is frequently taken as the single most important statistic of an economy's size, and changes in GNI are regarded as the prime indicator of growth. It is widely recognized, however, that the techniques of national income accounting are crude and difficult to apply in less-developed countries. For example, not only is it more difficult to assemble reliable data on how much production takes place outside the market economy in developing countries, but a larger proportion of their GNI is generated in this way. Such problems are less significant for periodic comparisons within a single country (for example, India's progress during the decade of the 1950s and the following decade) than they are for assessing absolute standards of welfare at a particular time or for intercountry comparisons. But, for conceptual as well as statistical reasons GNI is a misleading growth indicator and an especially poor one for measuring structural change.

In seeking to circumvent the weaknesses of GNI analysis, the authors of one economic study took changes in entrepreneurial ability, modern investment, skills, factory employment, and technology as the relevant growth measures. Their calculations showed a composite growth of these indicators of 7 percent per annum for the period 1954–1964, an amount twice the 3.5 percent annual increase registered for GNI.[1] Moreover, when K. N. Raj studied the small-scale manufacturing sector, he found evidence of a 5 percent growth rate for this sector, as compared with the national income data which showed it growing at only 1 percent for the period he surveyed.[2] These studies of one of India's more dynamic sectors point up the dangers of analysis based on highly aggregated statistics and on the conceptually faulty national income procedure. They

[1]V. V. Bhatt and V. V. Divatra, "On Measuring the Pace of Development," *Quarterly Review*, Banca Nazionale del Lavoro, nos. 8 and 9, June 1969.
[2]K. N. Raj, *Indian Economic Growth: Performance and Prospects* (Bombay: Allied Publishers, 1965).

may also indicate structural changes that will allow India to accelerate its progress in the future. They do not, however, require one to adopt a view of India's overall development substantially different from that suggested by the national income data.

Although there can be little argument that with a rising population the conditions for achieving social justice must include both the growth and equitable distribution of national product, the social sciences do not provide a methodology for measuring the relative importance of these factors. Thus, whereas situations of no growth and no narrowing of disparities are almost universally less desirable than those with both growth and declining disparities, there are no objective criteria to decide whether it is better to have no growth and better income distribution or substantial growth and a widening of income disparities. Writing in the early 1950s, Simon Kuznets prophetically saw that the gap between rich and poor within nations might grow temporarily as a by-product of the process of development. Recent statistical analysis suggests the correctness of this view. But this widening of disparities need not cause alarm when it is recognized that, if the experience of OECD countries is repeated, the disparities will eventually decline as still higher levels of affluence are attained.[3] Nonetheless, there is no way of knowing whether the OECD pattern will be repeated in the now developing countries or whether the social pressures created by the disparities can be contained in the interim. Because of its mix of socialism and democracy, India is more subject than other countries to confrontations between the opposing advocates of growth and equity policies. For historical reasons it may also be better able than other nations to accommodate disparities.

The analysis of national self-reliance raises knotty problems insofar as this objective is ambiguous: there is no Indian consensus as to where, between the poles of autarky and eliminating foreign aid, the target should be set. Moreover, there is no single objective measure of progress, in part because of the need to define international self-reliance with respect to some minimal level of domestice self-sufficiency. Perhaps the most vexing dilemma raised by self-reliance is the trade-off between national autonomy and development. It entails, to quote Richard Cooper,

> the expense of giving up a certain amount of national independence, or autonomy, in setting and pursuing economic objectives. National *autonomy*, as used here to mean the ability to frame and carry out objectives of domestic economic policy which may diverge widely from those of other countries, should not be confused with the notion of *sovereignty*, which represents the formal ability of countries or other political units to make

[3]For a discussion of this subject in the light of recent developments, see John H. Adler, "Development and Income Distribution," *Finance and Development*, September 1973, pp. 2–5. Statistical evidence is provided by Irving B. Kravis, "A World of Unequal Incomes," *Annals of the American Academy of Political and Social Science*, September 1973.

their own decisions—and to renounce decisions previously made—but not necessarily to achieve their objectives.[4]

Performance in the Light of India's Pre-Independence Experience

A dramatic and unambiguous comparison can be drawn between the Indian economy's development prior to and since Independence. Although the reasons are hotly debated, India's growth in the half century prior to 1947 was anything but dynamic—less than 1 percent per annum. As population was growing at close to 1 percent per annum during this period, the standard of individual welfare probably declined by some small amount. In contrast, since 1947 India's economic and population growth rates have accelerated to over 3 and 2 percent, respectively.[5] Thus, whatever else one may say about India's recent economic performance, there has been an impressive improvement in the growth rate and an increase of roughly 25 percent in the average per capita national output.

Satisfaction with these gains must be tempered, however, because they have been unevenly shared. Differential income and population growth rates have shifted income distribution patterns among persons and regions to such a degree that these and accompanying social trends are calculated to have left a few sectors of Indian society even worse off than before Independence.[6] Although the coexistence of poverty and wealth has always been a source of social tension, the conspicuous consumption of India's nouveau riche has greatly complicated the problem. Productivity aside, because many of the new elite are unable to justify their higher incomes on the basis of traditional social conventions such as membership in princely families, high caste, and so forth, their wealth is deeply resented by the less-well-to-do and is a divisive factor in Indian society.

Data on per capita consumption of basic commodities such as food grains, sugar, and cloth suggest that the poorer classes generally have not participated in India's growth. As shown in Table 2-11 (page 78), per capita availability (domestic production plus imports) of basic commodities has been relatively stagnant. In contrast, even though the poor have not obtained a fair share of the government-provided social services, improving literacy rates and increased average life-spans are evidence that these public programs have reached them.[7]

Many village studies show that although there has been concrete progress,

[4]Richard N. Cooper, *The Economics of Interdependence: Economic Policy in the Atlantic Community* (New York: Published for the Council on Foreign Relations by McGraw-Hill, 1968), p. 4.

[5]See Maddison, *Class Structure and Economic Growth,* op. cit., pp. 76, 166–168.

[6]Dandekar and Rath, op. cit.

[7]See Pranab K. Bardhan, "India," in Hollis Chenery et al., *Redistribution with Growth* (London: Published for the World Bank and the Institute of Development Studies by Oxford University Press, 1974), pp. 255–262.

the quality of life of the poor remains unsatisfactory and, in many respects, unmodernized. It is important to look at the exceptions, however, first, because they encompass politically strategic constituencies such as urban populations and nouveau riche farmers and, second, because they include entire states such as the Punjab and Gujarat. Indeed some regions have progressed so far that personal mobility has been increased and jati, caste, and other "traditional" distinctions have declined in significance. By rendering the society more flexible, this modernization process has both opened new development opportunities and posed the danger of political discord. The conflict between urban and rural interests, for example, requires new kinds of political management if it is not to become disruptive to future development.

India's situation with respect to economic self-reliance has been so altered by Independence that it is difficult to make comparisons. In the production of military hardware, for example, India has established a manufacturing capacity for both traditional and sophisticated weapons.But when India was part of the British Empire, there was little need for such facilities. Thus, whereas there is no question about the technical achievement implied by military manufactures, there is question as to whether these should be regarded as a social cost or a benefit. Ironically, the major use of military production has been against an area with which India was territorially linked until 1947.

The situation of nondefense industry is no less complex. Since Independence, India has experienced unprecedented industrialization and import substitution. But, despite a declining ratio of imports to gross national product (the ratio of industrial imports to domestic industrial output has also grown smaller), India is still reliant on imports, and the derived need to export has not been alleviated. If anything, India's foreign exchange gap now looms larger than in earlier years because of unanticipated limitations on the import substitution strategy and the commitment to maintain the higher, post-1947 economic growth rate. The situation may be even less favorable in the sense that before Independence a fair portion of import demand was for consumer items which, in times of stringency, could be foregone. Today, in place of consumer goods, India imports food, raw materials, and capital equipment that are vital to keep its population fed and factories running. Thus, any serious reduction in the quantity of imports (such as that implied by the soaring petroleum, fertilizer, and food prices of 1973–75 threatens dire consequences for all sectors of its economy.

The conclusion that India is still heavily reliant on international trade for meeting its basic employment and consumption needs is inescapable. This is tempered, however, by two facts: first, to a greater degree than growth and equity, self-sufficiency is a symbolic goal and its achievement in the short term is less important for meeting the physical needs of consumers or for assuring political stability; and second, since 1947 India has significantly developed physical and human resources with potential to provide a greater degree of self-reliance in the future.

The Need for Economic Development

Contrary to the impression of those misinformed Westerners who dismiss Indian poverty as the result of spiritual otherworldliness, the vast majority of India's elite and poor keenly desire development. Nonetheless, the social law which appears most applicable to India is the dreary formulation of Malthus that living standards tend toward subsistence. Although Malthus's theory is belied by the experience of many Western and Asian nations, the difficulty which India and some other countries have in escaping from the subsistence pattern is disconcerting: the acceleration of India's population growth has made trivial what might otherwise have been a substantial increase in per capita living standards. On the more optimistic side, most observers agree that India's shift from near stagnancy to a small but creditable rate of economic growth took place despite and not because of the accelerated population growth rate.[8] Indeed, the mainstream of opinion is that the achievement of lower fertility and higher per capita GNP would be mutually reinforcing and, because birthrates for the poor are comparatively high, would probably also serve to advance social justice.

The need for development arises not only from real but from psychological sources. While the Indian people have experienced a revolution of rising expectations, their economic position has been so strained that the hopes of many could be satisfied in the short run merely if they were to receive some assurance that their welfare would not deteriorate. And, although the political mobilization of its population has proceeded slowly, fulfillment of at least some of the expectations and hopes kindled by political promises cannot be delayed indefinitely without risking the future of consitutional democracy. It may be that in the first 25 years after Independence India's national leaders devoted so much of their attention to political problems—internal and foreign—that they had inadequate energy to deal with economic difficulties. For the future, however, there must be a reordering of priorities with more concern for economic issues.[9]

Because the motivation for obtaining self-reliance is as much political as it is economic, the significance of this goal is not always as apparent to foreigners as it is to nationals. India, which is no exception to this generalization, has shown an especially strong desire for greater self-reliance in all areas, including food and defense output. The rationality of India's concern is illustrated by such events as the soaring international grain and fertilizer prices of 1973–74 and its 1960s experience when the United States and others used emergency food shipments as a lever for changing its domestic policies. Nonetheless, although India must be respected for seeking a middle ground between autarky and

---

[8]This point is disputed by neo-Swadeshi analysts such as Subramaniam Swamy, who reason that the extra population is needed to enhance demand for products and the supply of labor. See Swamy, op. cit.

[9]I have argued this point at greater length in my article "India: Today, Tonight, and Tomorrow Morning," *Pacific Community*, January 1974.

dependence, it is disappointing that 25 years after Independence India's economy, remaining hazardously close to the subsistence level, is still in need of foreign assistance, requires substantial food imports, and is painfully sensitive to domestic and foreign disturbances, including the vagaries of the monsoon.

The Potential for Development

The reader has every right to be skeptical of an analysis which seeks to pronounce on the potential versus the real rate of growth of an economy. Displaying determination and skepticism in about equal parts, Angus Maddison has made such an analysis, and his results and methodology bear summary. According to Maddison, India sustained a growth rate of 3.3 percent for the period 1950–1965. This compares with an average growth of 5.5 percent for a sample of countries he considered. As he sees it, India's relatively poor performance is explained by an inherently lower growth potential than other countries (a handicap of one to two percentage points) and the failure of Indian policy to induce the economy to run at full potential (about one percentage point). The reasons he cites for the handicap are (1) the low level of income, which itself militates against efforts to mobilize savings for investment; (2) India's low per capita level of foreign aid receipts compared to smaller developing countries; (3) poor natural resources; (4) the adverse effect of military expenditure, which was roughly equal as a share of GNP to many other developing countries but nevertheless higher than in the pre-Independence period; and (5) institutional constraints.[10]

The weakness of Maddison's presentation is that, by laying more emphasis on India's handicaps than on its advantages, he understates the failure of policy. Maddison himself recognizes that "None of the first four reasons are overwhelming disadvantages."[11] Recent economic studies, for example, show that the poor as well as the rich are potential savers when proper incentives are offered. (See pages 81 to 84). Because of artificially low rates of interest, barriers to investment, and other factors in India, the failure to mobilize savings for investment seems as much a failure of policy as it is an inherent economic weakness.

As for the contribution of foreign aid, it is quite true that per capita receipts in India have been lower than in other countries, but this is balanced to some degree by their having been provided on better terms and over a longer period of time (see pages 340 to 341). It is also true that because of India's low domestic savings rate, foreign capital played a proportionally larger role in net capital formation (about 20 percent in the Third Five-Year Plan period) than in other countries. Finally, the significance of foreign aid is rendered suspect because of the experience of China, where, largely in the absence of foreign aid, the

---

[10]Maddison, *Class Structure and Economic Growth,* op. cit., pp. 78–81, and Angus Maddison, *Economic Progress and Policy in Developing Countries* (New York: W. W. Norton, 1970), chap. 2.

[11]Maddison, *Class Structure and Economic Growth,* op. cit., p. 81.

growth rate has been at least comparable to India's and where a modicum of economic social justice and considerable self-reliance have been achieved. This is not to say that China would not have progressed faster if it had received foreign assistance, only that it was able to develop by virtue of its own domestic resources and economic policies.

On the question of India's natural resources Maddison is wary because, as he notes, "By comparison with Latin America or Africa there is heavy pressure of population on the land,"[12] but other Asian countries such as Japan, Korea, and Taiwan have overcome this obstacle. Maddison reaches the erroneous conclusion that India is comparatively underendowed with natural resources because, by devoting too little attention to nonagricultural resources, he has overlooked India's wealth of coal, petroleum, iron ore, and other assets.

Although institutional constraints are undoubtedly significant in the formulation and implementation of policy, Maddison may have overstated their importance. India is not alone among developing countries in having to overcome the inertia of "traditional" society, the opposition of vested interests, and the counterinitiatives of local interest groups. To regard institutional constraints as a special handicap without some objective measure of how these affect India and other developing countries is questionable. It implies a cultural determinism which in reality may not exist. And it ignores the remarkable progress which has been made in the Punjab and other Indian states.

Finally, Maddison's analysis is incomplete because it fails to consider some of India's major assets. Particularly important among these are the nationalism which has helped India to cope with emergencies, the excellence of its legal system, the administrative and technical skills already extant in 1947, and the advantages that large size affords for economies of scale and industrial diversification. Additional evidence to support the position that India's handicaps have been less significant than policy failures comes from a critical appraisal of the Indian economy. Surely, such factors as the low ratios of capacity utilization found in Indian industry and the inefficient exploitation of proved mineral resources suggest that India is not using its assets to best advantage. This conclusion is reinforced by the consistency with which India has been able to improve its performance in time of crises, be it the 1965–1967 drought or the feeding of 10 million Bengali refugees in 1971.

For India the linkage between growth and social justice has been especially critical to the issue of real versus potential development. In practice, many Indians have regarded economic growth as the quid pro quo for meeting equity goals, as the critical ingredient without which the rich would be unwilling to lessen their opposition to political decisions which would narrow income disparities. An accurate description of this relation has been given by Phiroze Medhora, an economist and deputy general manager of the semipublic Industrial Credit and Investment Corporation of India(ICICI). According to Medhora's political and economic calculations, the 5.5 percent growth rate targeted in the Draft Fifth Plan would not permit achievement of India's major objective,

[12]Ibid., p. 79.

minimum consumption for all. He argues that, for political reasons, the only potentially successful strategy in a country as poor as India is to increase the welfare of both the 40 percent of the population below the subsistence level and the next 50 percent, who also are very poor. On strictly economic grounds, Medhora regards the possibility for concurrently increasing GNP by 5.5 percent and raising the lowest 40 percent of the population to the subsistence level as suspect. This would imply an increase of one-third in food production during the Fifth Plan which could be achieved only by reducing investment and devoting a greater share of national income to consumption. Medhora is also suspicious of the joint attainment of social justice and a 5.5 percent growth rate because he feels that efforts to help the least-privileged will tend to raise birthrates and lower death rates in the short run, thereby creating the need for still more growth merely to maintain minimum living standards.[13]

In Medhora's view, the way to avoid this predicament is through a planned 7 to 7.5 percent growth rate. He regards this as feasible and contingent only on the government's resource mobilization efforts and skill in fashioning economic policies to improve management and economic efficiency in the public and private sectors. At the core of Medhora's argument is the notion that human activity must be motivated, that the cooperation of the more skilled members of the community must be enlisted, and that the principal way to mobilize human effort in a democracy is by offering financial incentives.[14] In passing, it should be noted that when a seasoned observer of the Indian economy like Medhora recommends a 7 to 7.5 percent growth target, it is further evidence that a gap exists between India's actual economic performance and potential.

With respect to how India has capitalized on its potential for achieving self-reliance, nonessential imports of consumer items have been largely eliminated from the import bill. There are still some imports of raw materials and capital equipment which will eventually find their place in the production of consumer goods, but these are not unduly large or unreasonable. What is bothersome about the commodity composition of Indian imports is that many items would be unnecessary if India set higher priority on its agricultural sector, made better use of its installed industrial capacity (especially steel, fertilizer, and energy), and were more aggressive in developing indigenous natural resources. As noted in Chapter 9, it is lamentable that in 1973–74 more than one-third of Indian imports were of petroleum, fertilizer, and food, all commodities for which the import substitution possibilities were great. It is a commonplace that better domestic economic performance would have enabled India to use its foreign exchange purchasing power to import more capital equipment and more of the raw materials needed by its industries and thereby to accelerate its growth rate. Similarly, India's balance-of-payments position could have been greatly strengthened by a more effective export regime. India need not have

[13]Phiroze B. Medhora, "Planning: Next Move," *Eastern Economist,* Dec. 15, 1972, pp. 1228–1233.

[14]Phiroze B. Medhora, "Approach to the Fifth Plan," *Economic and Political Weekly,* vol. 7, no. 28, July 8, 1972, pp. 1319–1329.

lost its share of world markets for commodities such as jute and tea to the extent that it has, and India could have increased its exports of nontraditional commodities such as iron ore at a much faster rate.

The relevance of India's large and growing—but not extraordinary by developing-country standards—international debt burden to its potential for self-reliance is, at best, tangential. Multinational rescheduling has taken the place of default. It seems unlikely therefore that a country as poor and as indebted as India will either default or provide a substantial net flow of commodities to repay the foreign assistance it has received from the rich. Moreover, the real, as contrasted with the nominal, burden of international debt has been greatly reduced by world inflation. In short, the significance of India's external debt has become increasingly suspect. Nevertheless, in the absence of a global hyperinflation or other unanticipated developments, the financial and psychological burden of India's annual debt service is great, and one day debt service may exceed the inflow of new foreign assistance. Should such a situation occur, it could cause serious political tensions between India and aid donors and require reconsideration of their economic and aid relationships.

Rhetoric and Reality

No analysis of India's development would be complete without at least passing reference to how actual performance compares with what has been promised by the government. As I have noted, salient features of the Indian scene are the setting of development targets and the extravagant claims of what will be accomplished in the future. Formal government targets and statements by officials can be rationalized in various ways: as the spark needed to quicken aspirations and mobilize resources for development, as a genuine blueprint for the economy, or as the traditional smoke screen of promises common to politicians and bureaucrats throughout the world. Bardhan, for example, has concluded from his analysis of how the elite have evaded asset redistribution, and have garnered the major share of the benefits from public investment and other social schemes for themselves, that the formulating of reform schemes and their nonfulfillment are part of the same political-economic process.[15]

By far the largest departures of rhetoric from reality can be traced to ad hoc statements and political promises. These gaps, however, are both less important and less amenable to measurement and analysis than the related shortfalls of performance from official targets such as those of the Five-Year Plans. Because targets, once established, lead independent lives and influence policy, they are a critical factor in the government's management of the national economy.

A comparison of selected Plan objectives and recorded achievements (Table 11-1) reveals progressively larger shortfalls in various target areas. Only the First Plan, which set no formal income target and was largely only a collection of projects begun before 1951, came close to achieving its stated goals. Perform-

[15]Bardhan, op. cit., p. 261.

TABLE 11-1
PLAN TARGETS AND ACHIEVEMENTS

	First Plan, 1951–1956		Second Plan, 1956–1961		Third Plan, 1961–1966		Fourth Plan, 1969–1974		Fifth Plan, 1974–1979
	Target	Actual	Target	Actual	Target	Actual	Target	Actual	Target
Production									
1. Food grains (million tons)	62.7	65.8	75.0	82.0	100.0	72.3	129.0	103.6	140.0
2. Oilseeds (million tons)	5.6	5.6	7.0	7.0	9.8	6.3	10.5	8.7	12.5
3. Sugar (million tons)	6.4	6.0	7.1	11.2	10.0	12.1	15.0	14.5	17.0
4. Cotton (million bales)	4.2	4.0	5.5	5.3	7.0	4.8	8.0	5.8	8.0
5. Steel (million tons)	1.7	1.3	4.3	2.4	6.8	4.5	8.1	4.5	9.4
6. Coal (million tons)	39.6	38.4	60.0	55.7	98.5	66.7	93.5	75.5	135.0
7. Iron ore (million tons)	4.1	4.3	12.5	11.0	30.0	18.1	51.4	22.8	58.0
8. Aluminum (thousand tons)	12.2	7.3	25.0	18.3	80.0	62.1	220.0	147.9	370.0
9. Nitrogenous fertilizer (thousand tons of nitrogen)	90	79	290	101	800	232	2,500	1,060	4,000
10. Crude petroleum (million tons)	...	...	3.9	0.4	6.0	3.0	8.5	7.2	12.0
11. Cement (million tons)	4.9	4.6	13.0	8.0	13.2	10.8	18.0	14.7	25.0
12. Bicycle tires (millions)	...	5.8	11.8	11.1	31.0	18.5	35.0	23.1	30.0
13. Electric power (billion kilowatt-hours)	...	10.8	22.0	20.1	45.0	36.8	86.0	64.6	120
14. Power installed capacity (million kilowatt-hours)	3.5	3.4	6.9	5.7	12.7	10.2	23.0	16.2*	33.0
Other indicators									
15. National income growth (percent)	2+	3.7	5.0	4.1	5.0	2.5	5.7	3.0	5.5
16. Savings/GNP (percent)	6.75	7.0	9.7	8.5	11.5	11.1	13.2	10.0	15.7
17. Investment/GNP (percent)	8.0	7.3	10.7	11.0	14.0	13.4	14.5	11.0	16.3
18. Exports (percent change)	2.0	0.3	0.6	1.1	4.0	4.1	7.0	12.8	7.6
19. Irrigated area (million hectares, net)	24.3	22.8	27.5	24.6	36.4	26.4	43.0†	42.9†	54.3†
20. Students in schools (million)	29.9	32.1	42.1	44.7	63.9	64.8	96.4	87.3	110.0
21. Hospital beds (thousands)	117.2	125.0	155.0	185.6	240.0	240.1	281.6	281.6	321.6

*End of calendar year 1973.

†Gross.

Sources: Various Plan documents; *India. Pocket Book of Economic Information. 1972* (Delhi: GOI, Ministry of Finance, 1972); and *Economic Survey.*

ance under the Third Plan (admittedly affected by war and drought) was so poor that a three-year Plan holiday was needed before long-term planning could be resumed. Despite this pause, the Fourth Plan did less to fulfill its growth, equity, and self-reliance goals than any of the prior Plans, and in 1974 the base from which the Fifth Plan was to be launched looked so precarious that serious consideration was given to declaring another Plan holiday.

There is no simple interpretation of how India's development has been affected by these shortfalls of performance from what I have called rhetoric, but which could just as readily be dignified as officially proposed, professionally designed, and nationally accepted targets. The dilemma exists because there are no a priori grounds on which to judge whether the benefits from raising incentives and awakening expectations outweigh the costs of the centrifugal forces which are set in motion when hopes are not realized. This issue cannot be looked at in the abstract; it requires consideration in the larger perspective of the suitability of India's chosen strategy to Indian conditions.

Toward an Approach to an Explanation

Factors affecting India's development experience do not fall into discrete, unrelated categories, and thus it is hardly surprising that different observers emphasize different facets according to their own subjective judgments, even though they share the same body of objective facts about India. My aim in the rest of this chapter is to single out what I regard as the major determinants of Indian development. To clarify the logic of this analysis, however, I must first repeat several commonplace caveats which are critical and apply generally to most developing countries.

1. The multiple causes of India's particular experience arise not only from the set of variables peculiar to one or another branch of the social sciences and humanities (i.e., insufficient economic investment, political diversity, social customs, attitudes and outlooks, and so forth), but from all of them operating conjointly. This is a truism which workers in each discipline know well, to be sure, but one which they repeatedly forget or ignore as they formulate their explanations.

2. Linkages exist at countless levels. Variables affect one another directly and through circuitous channels, but almost without exception, they are mutually causal. The intensity of that mutual causality may be weak or strong and varies over time in response to particular events and to changes—structural, technical, and environmental. The impact on development of India's military situation illustrates this interacting causality well. The cost of military preparedness not only has been a *constant* factor and has *grown* over time, but has followed a *cyclical* pattern in response to periodic wars. More subtle is the influence of climate, which, although it is generally assumed to be constant over time but subject to extreme variation from one year to the next, is also shifting. Meteorologists now suspect that the world's climate is changing (for the worse); man

has increased his capability to modify the weather; and to the extent that modern technology produces better seeds for drylands and irrigation is improved, man has reduced the significance of climate as a variable affecting agriculture.

3. The determinants of development fall at, or range between, two poles, depending on the extent to which India can affect them. At one extreme are variables of geography, for example. Given past and current levels of knowledge about social and physical engineering, these factors lie beyond India's control. (They are exogenous variables.) At the other extreme are variables, such as the amount to be invested in new public sector steel plants, over which India has more or less complete control (endogenous variables). Differences of interpretation over India's development experience can often be traced to differences of opinion about where on the exogenous-endogenous scale such variables as foreign aid and culture should be placed.

4. It is easier to distinguish between extreme *forms* of development and underdevelopment than to define the *process* of development. Moreover, just as broad interpretations of development are more meaningful than narrow ones, so they are more difficult to define. Evidence for judging how a particular nation is progressing over a limited period usually is very mixed, especially in India's complex situation.

These caveats, which derive from India's experience as described in previous chapters, lead to a view of development which is uncomfortably imprecise, eclectic, even amorphous. No single variable can be said to be the principal determinant of India's evolution because all variables are linked systemically. Just as a car is unable to run without ignition, battery, pistons, transmission, tires, and hundreds of other parts, so India cannot develop unless social, economic, international affairs, and domestic policy are favorably aligned. But the determinants of development are not all of equal importance, and the remainder of this chapter, therefore, is a recapitulation of how important factors vary in significance and how they react among themselves to produce a distinctly Indian pattern of development. Although I pay considerable attention to policy formulation and implementation in this analysis, this does not imply that policy is invariably more significant than other factors. In reality, policy does not exist in a vacuum; it is determined not only by autonomous pragmatic decisions, but by a constellation of ideological, political, cultural, and other systemically related forces.

Economic Assets and Liabilities

Brazil began a decade of growth in 1964 which gave rise to the witticism that there have been three postwar economic miracles: the first of these, Germany, was based on hard work; the second, Japan, was due to extraordinary savings; and the third, Brazil, was truly a miracle. This quip, obviously not to be taken at its face value, highlights the two possible routes to economic development. There is no escape from the tautology that output is determined by the size of a nation's capital investment and the productivity of its labor in exploiting nature-given and man-made resources. The conventional wisdom, that the prerequisite for a country to develop is control over natural resources (domestic in the case of the United States, colonial in the case of Britain), has fallen gradually into ill repute in response to the eveidence that resource-rich countries like Ceylon and Indonesia do not necessarily progress whereas resource-scarce nations such as Japan and South Korea have overcome this handicap. Nonetheless, the recent economic dynamism of Nigeria, Malaysia, and Iran is such that the relevance of natural resources to economic growth should not be understated. It is significant that even on a per capita basis, India's land and mineral wealth fall somewhere in a midway range between scarcity and abundance.

What is striking about India's resources—a situation common to most less-developed countries—is the extent to which they remain underutilized. Symptomatic are India's slow development of its extensive iron ore deposits despite assured export markets, tardiness in arranging for exploration of potentially large petroleum reserves, and the absence—much more exploitation—of comprehensive hydrological surveys of what is believed to be an enormous renewable water resource below the Gangetic plain. Among the reasons why India has not developed resources faster are (1) shortcomings of physical infrastructure and human skills endemic in less-developed countries; (2) domestic budgetary scarcities; (3) foreign exchange shortages; (4) reluctance to export raw materials, such as iron ore, which India will some day be able to convert to finished products at home; and (5) extreme wariness of foreign investors.

India's position with respect to infrastructure and human resources, while more favorable than that of many other developing countries, has hardly been comfortable. Not only were the communications, transportation, and other basic facilities extant in 1947 costly to maintain and still more costly to expand, but India had very scanty assets in research and development, accounting, marketing, and other critical areas. That India has had only moderate success in employing highly educated, skilled, and unskilled members of its labor force is both a function of the middling pace of development and a reason why the economy has not grown faster. India's position in this area is unique, not only because of its size, but because of the relative abundance of managerial, administrative, and technical skills which already existed at the time of Independence. Nonetheless, because of size, cultural mores, and political factors, India has encountered great difficulties in (1) matching skill levels with the needs of the economy; (2) obtaining interregional labor mobility; (3) removing people from jobs for which they are not qualified; (4) inducing agricultural engineers, doctors, and other specialists to work in rural and backward areas; and (5) staffing public sector enterprises with management specialists instead of civil service generalists and engineers.

Demographic trends have had, and will continue to have, a pervasive economic effect. In the short term, by absorbing resources which might otherwise have been devoted to enhancing the welfare of a smaller population, the material needs of the growing number of Indian children have acted as a constraint on capital formation. It is not a priori determinate whether their productivity, when these children become workers, will be higher than the productivity of the investment they displace, or whether the total size of India's future gross national product will be greater or smaller as a result of population growth. But by adversely affecting the already strained ratios of land and resources to people, this population increase is certain to reduce the marginal productivity of labor and thereby depress the growth of per capita incomes. To the extent that the inevitable reduction in India's population growth rate is accomplished soon and by reducing the birthrate, rather than through an increase in mortality, the proportion of active workers in the population will grow and the economic effect will be more conducive to development. Although competition among various caste and religious factions has often been cited as a reason why it is so difficult to reduce fertility in India, the vicious economic circle created by poverty appears to be an even more important determinant. Population growth promises to be an intractable problem for many years to come, and the primary burden it imposes will necessarily be borne by India rather than the international community.

The two faces of capital formation, saving and investment, are affected both by basic economic and sociopolitical factors and by development strategy. Indian planning and policy have both been deeply influenced by the neo-Keynesian approach of the Harrod-Domar model, which, through the concept of "incremental capital/output ratios," explicitly links additions of investment to growing production. When this framework was applied to the special problems of developing countries by Sir Arthur Lewis, W. W. Rostow, and others, it gave rise to the logic that accelerating rates of investment and production would lead to a process of self-sustaining growth, commonly known as "takeoff."[16] It is significant to India's experience that savings and investment are closely linked, not only in the social-accounting sense that they are the respective sources and uses of resources not consumed, but in the operational world where individuals, companies, and governments all save and invest and where, just as a lack of savings may inhibit investment, a poor investment climate may induce higher consumption at the expense of savings.

According to recent investigations, problems in mobilizing savings in India and other developing countries are not primarily due either to the low level of per capita income or to the income distribution.[17] A combination of economic, institutional, and political factors is responsible. For example, the low rates of interest paid by banks and other deposit-accepting institutions and the scarcity of banks in rural India have discouraged savings and induced individuals to hoard commodities. India's potential for collecting savings from the poor is

[16]See Arthur Lewis, *The Theory of Economic Growth* (London: George Allen and Unwin, 1959), and W. W. Rostow, *The Stages of Economic Growth* (Cambridge: Cambridge University Press, 1960).

[17]See H. S. Houthakker, "On Some Determinants of Savings in Developed and Underdeveloped Countries," in Robinson and Kidron, eds., op. cit., pp. 212–224, and D. W. Johnson and J. S. Y. Chiu, "The Savings-Income Relation in Underdeveloped and Developed Countries," *Economic Journal*, vol. LXVIII, no. 2, June 1968, pp. 321–323.

strikingly demonstrated by the history of the atypical Syndicate Bank, which was formed with a capitalization of only 8,000 rupees in 1925. The Syndicate used a "Pygmy Plan" and other devices to collect small deposits in both rural and urban areas. Its growth was so rapid that it was one of the 14 largest private commercial banks nationalized in 1969.[18]

Another barrier to the expansion of India's capital stock has been the nonavailability of loans to would-be investors. This is a complicated story involving (1) the timidity of most commercial banks in rural areas; (2) the Indian government's decision to allot the burden of the task of rural lending to the only sometimes effective cooperatives; and (3) the orthodoxy of financial institutions which tended to lend to well-established customers regardless of how the money was to be used but to refrain from lending to individuals who were less well known or who could offer no collateral. Thus, India's limited supply of loanable funds has often financed consumption or hoarding rather than productive investment, and even since 1969, commercial banks have made only slow progress in redressing this situation.

The contribution of state and central government fiscal policy to India's savings and investment experience is not outstandingly good or bad. Although states have been lax in taxing agriculture, offical revenues have grown by a substantial amount. They would be considerably higher, however, if the massive tax evasion and huge losses of some public sector enterprises could be eliminated. On the expenditure side, central and state governments have allowed administrative costs, especially wages for civil servants, to escalate and divert resources from investment. Because of (1) the reciprocal relationships between changes in production and investment and between economic growth and increased savings and (2) official policy to reserve a greater share of investment for the public sector, the Indian government's inability to exercise greater control over finances has adversely affected the pace of development.

Foreign exchange scarcity is another among the critical constraints on economic progress. Quite apart from India's commercial policies, which I discuss later in this chapter, a number of "structural" factors have eroded India's ability to earn foreign exchange by exporting. Among the most important of these were (1) the post-Korean war decline in world demand for some of India's major commodity exports, which lowered both the price and volume of these; (2) the subsequent, relatively stagnant world demand for many of India's traditional exports such as coir; (3) increased rivalry from other countries in export markets such as for tea; and (4) rising competition from synthetics which reduced demand for products such as jute. India not only suffered a gradual deterioration in its terms of trade but was among the most vulnerable nations to the situation of the early 1970s when colossal price increases for petroleum, food, and fertilizer, together with generally inflated prices of industrial products, threatened to undermine totally its foreign exchange position and to cause

[18]See Selden Menefee, *The Pais of Manipal* (Bombay: Asia Publishing House, 1969) chaps. 7, 16, and 17.

a disastrous shortfall in the domestic availability of food and other essential commodities.

Uncertainty, the last major factor affecting the economy I shall discuss here, is qualitatively different from the other factors but no less relevant. Year-to-year variations in the rainfall pattern, an outstanding source of uncertainty, are reflected in inefficiency as they cause the supply of essential commodities to fluctuate from inadequate to generous. Offsetting policies, such as keeping buffer stocks and emergency relief for drought and flood areas, require costly facilities, invariably lead to some waste and spoilage of food stocks, and divert scarce private and official management talent from long-term development. Another kind of uncertainty is that created in the minds of private entrepreneurs by official policies: to the extent that businessmen have felt threatened by various government programs, they have been inclined to take short-term profits rather than to make the kind of investments which the economy needed. The deterioration of the Kerala tea estates, which began when the state government announced its intention to nationalize but did not follow through, is an outstanding example. Other uncertainties troubling India have been the threat of war with its neighbors, instability of foreign demand for its exports, and foreign aid as donors have generally been unwilling to make long-term commitments. India has acted to reduce the effect of uncertainty, but to fully offset this factor has not always been possible, and countervailing measures usually have been at the expense of development.

Political Economy Revisited

India's diversity and its well-established capacity to deal with cleavages sometimes impede development, as suggested by the situation of Center-state relations, but they also serve as social glue binding together society and nation. Diversity and a capacity for mixing tradition and inflexibility with modernity and adaptation are not uncharacteristic of developing countries. But in Indian culture the interaction among these forces has shaped development in ways quite unlike that of other countries.

The impact of cultural factors, while undoubtedly inimical to development, has been overstated by Myrdal and others. I say this not only because social mores have given India strength in times of adversity, but also because placing the main burden for explaining nondevelopment on culture suggests that basic economic and political factors are somehow not significant. It also is objectionable as it implies a cultural determinism and absence of free will which I find intellectually abhorrent, and because it contradicts the reality that at various times and in various Indian regions development has proceeded very satisfactorily.

To the extent that culture does impede development, its effect is enmeshed with other factors such as politics. Indeed, there is no way of saying with any certainty whether India's policies are bad because they are not suited to the social climate or whether it is the particular Indian culture which causes inappropriate policies to be adopted. Stanley Heginbotham believes that his research into the process of modernization reveals a significant misfit between the dharmic order of society and the role and authority requirements of efficient government. According to Heginbotham, many of the bureaucratic problems that are "attributed to unknown malevolent forces or some basic flaw in Indian character" are actually due to a separation of the functions of policy formulation and implementation. He regards this artificial and impractical division as culture-based but also due to political factors.[19] Other examples where culture has caused Indians to react to some economic problems with nonsubstantive, ritual and symbolic behavior, include (1) a general preoccupation with monopoly per se rather than with the real evil of monopolistic trade practices; (2) an extreme reluctance to change the rupee's international exchange rate, even when it was hopelessly overvalued; and (3) a governmental tendency to interpret new bank branches and deposits as proxies for new savings.

It is easy to either understate or exaggerate the contribution of political factors to economic progress and the impact of the economy on the political structure; and their high degree of interdependence does not diminish the significance of other forces. In various instances, India has met economic objectives in spite of political problems and also missed economic opportunities even though political circumstances were favorable. Without belittling the ability of state and local governments to alter Delhi's plans, it must be recognized that the locus of political power is at the center. Moreover, even though industrialists, labor leaders, the press, intellectuals, rural interests, and others play roles of varying importance depending on the issue at hand, government policy is largely the creation of politicians and bureaucrats. To put it bluntly, the fruits of development, if any are to be had, must be reaped with the cooperation, if not on the initiative, of India's central administration. The elite which manages this establishment not only determines living conditions for the urban population, the rate of industrialization, and India's foreign policy, but also makes decisions affecting food prices, irrigation, development of hybrid seed, and bank lending. Hybrid seed, fertilizer, and power are essential to rural progress, but they will not appear spontaneously, and local interests generally are unable to provide them.

As I noted in Chapter 1, the scantiness of physical goods to satisfy even subsistence needs has put extreme pressure on the exercise of government and greatly complicated the decision-making process. Faced with the alternative of a reduced standard of living, elite groups have struggled hard to maintain their privileged position in the society, and for some individuals the search for power and patronage have become goals in themselves. Other sources of political weakness—the difficulties of bringing democracy to an inexperienced and largely illiterate society, extreme pluralism, large size, and so forth—have also

[19]Stanley J. Heginbotham, *Cultures in Conflict: The Four Faces of Indian Bureaucracy* (New York: Columbia University Press, 1975).

been detrimental to the government's ability to press for the development to which it is committed. These barriers to development would be substantially reduced if India were to abandon its democratic and socially minded efforts to offer both economic and political participation to all adult citizens. They would not disappear, however, and there is no certainty that new barriers to development would not arise if India adopted a more authoritarian system of government.

International Factors

According to Ainslie Embree, if India has not actually been aggressive toward other nations, historically it has been inclined toward expansionism and has been deeply concerned that its neighbors not be strong.[20] To the extent that Embree is correct, Great Power intervention in the subcontinent may have strained existing tensions between India and Pakistan but cannot be regarded as the cause. Nonetheless, by arming these South Asian rivals, Washington and Moscow undoubtedly enlarged the possibility for, and the cost of, warfare between them. Indeed, when the costs of regional conflicts are reckoned in real resource, budgetary, and foreign exchange effects, and also in the energies and attention of political leaders, it is clear that international involvement in South Asia has been a significant constraint on development.

Regrettably, the burden of maintaining the kind of South Asian regional order India desires shows little sign of being lightened, even after the 1971 split-up of Pakistan. India is certain to remain vigilant in its posture as Pakistan recoups its military strength. Moreover, India has not only obligated itself to support Bangladesh, but would feel threatened by internal instability there or in any other country in South Asia, including Pakistan. India's relationship with China is wary; for as long as there is no genuine reduction in the mutual distrust, India will be bound to position troops along the Himalayan border and to incur costly defense expenditures. When India detonated a nuclear device in 1974, it was widely censured for having diverted resources from development. This criticism was largely unjustified because, however much India's crossing of the nuclear threshold was to be regretted, the cost of its having done so was trivial in comparison with the size of its economy and in light of its more general nuclear program. So long as India does not undertake large programs to develop delivery systems for its weapons, the cost of its nuclear capacity will remain small.

It is beyond the scope of this book to evaluate the international political role which India has played unilaterally and in concert with other "nonaligned" nations. It does bear note, however, that India's unwillingness to align itself in the cold war probably delayed the flow of substantial aid from the Soviet Union

[20]Ainslie T. Embree, "The Diplomacy of Dependency: Content and Style in Nineteenth Century Foreign Relations in India," paper prepared for the Conference on Leadership, School of Oriental and African Studies, London, March 1974.

and the West until the mid-1950s. This loss may or may not have been redressed by India's ability to command assistance from *both* sides in subsequent years, but I suspect that the net economic effect of these offsetting factors is near zero.

In contrast, India's international economic diplomacy has balanced doctrinaire and pragmatic concerns in such a way as to produce substantial net benefits. Even before Independence, India supported the multilateral-institution approach of Bretton Woods; as demonstrated by IDA, UNCTAD, and the India Consortium, it has been in the forefront of efforts to extend the benefits of liberal internationalism to the developing countries. The results of these efforts have been mixed, as suggested by the contrast between UNCTAD's slow progress on trade issues and the fact that IDA has grown so important that in 1975 roughly half of India's gross foreign assistance receipts came from this source. India's investment in these activities has not been costly and, although many of the demands of the developing countries remain unsatisfied, even UNCTAD has already proved to be rewarding.

India's foreign trade strategy, although characteristic of the way many developing countries approached balance-of-payments policy, was ill-conceived: international markets were not so hostile to Indian exports as to justify the one-sided emphasis on import substitution which prevailed through the mid-1960s. Given the number of developing countries which have sustained annual growth rates for their exports well in excess of 10 percent, Indian concern about barriers to trade looks like a self-fulfilling prophecy. Although the export achievements of selected developing countries are disparaged sometimes on grounds that the outstanding performers are small nations, this is an illogical explanation as developed-country trade barriers are generally not geared to the size of exporting nations. Indeed, it is incongruous that in 1973 Hong Kong, Singapore, and South Korea each exported more than India and that many developing countries had larger per capita exports than India. This suggests that the proper explanation for India's nonpenetration of exports markets is not to be found in the trade barriers of rich countries but in Delhi's own policies.

On occasion, India has been faulted for not having accepted more of the private long-term loans which the international financial community could have provided. This criticism is unfair, however, as servicing such loans would have imposed a costly foreign exchange burden. Only if, by borrowing more, India could have improved the operation of its domestic economy and earned substantially more foreign exchange—questionable assumptions—would recourse to such funds have been wise. In fact, India has been censured by the Consortium for having used medium-term supplier credits (often in conjunction with foreign aid) to import essential commodities such as fertilizer. The case of foreign private equity investment is somewhat different because this kind of foreign capital is more directly related to India's capacity to improve its domestic economy. India accepted only a fraction of the projects which were offered, in part because many foreign company proposals were not responsive to the needs of the Indian economy, but also because of India's generally negative attitude toward private investment, as discussed below.

It has often been alleged that, compared to many developing countries, India has been handicapped by small per capita receipts of foreign assistance. For example, data prepared by the OECD's Development Assistance Committee for 1968–1970 show that of 94 developing countries India ranked thirteenth in aid as a percentage of imports, sixty-third in aid as a percentage of domestic GNP, and eighty-first in per capita aid receipts.[21] Nonetheless, India has not been as short-changed relative to other aid recipients as is generally believed. Data pertaining to United States foreign grants and credits for the period July 1945 through December 1971 show that cumulative per capita aid to India (gross aid divided by the 1971 population) amounted to slightly more than $16, compared with an average of $21 per capita for African and Western Hemisphere recipients. Western aid to India has not only been better sustained over time, but has also been supplemented by assistance from the Soviet bloc, an incremental and strategic support which has not been available to all developing countries. Moreover, India has figured prominently as a user of local currency repayments (a large portion of which have been forgiven), grants, debt rescheduling, soft loans through IDA, and other mechanisms intended to reduce the burden of aid for very poor countries. The grant equivalent of its foreign assistance receipts is notably better than that of many other nations; for the period 1965–1972, for example, IBRD data show the grant equivalent of aid to India at about 75 percent.[22]

On balance, therefore, it does not appear that India has been conspicuously disadvantaged in comparison with other aid recipients; indeed, a careful statistical analysis might show it has been treated more favorably than many. Be that as it may, the amount of foreign assistance which India could have absorbed was much higher than what was actually made available, and there is no denying that India's growth was curtailed by persistent shortages of international purchasing power. It is hazardous to speculate on whether more foreign money would have been forthcoming if India has not felt compelled to balance acceptance of foreign assistance with protestations and demonstrations that this aid should not compromise its independence. But although this element of India's diplomacy undoubtedly had an adverse effect on foreign sympathy, gross aid flows have been maintained through a gradual shift from bilateral to multilateral sources. It is nonetheless likely that the quantity and quality of aid could have been greater still if Indian and foreign officials could have initiated and sustained a greater sense of mutuality in their quest for Indian economic development.

In summary, related cold war and regional South Asian conflicts have had a significant and unambiguously negative effect on Indian development. In

[21]Edwin M. Martin, *1971 Review of Development Assistance* (Paris: OECD, 1971), pp. 194–195,

[22]*World Bank Annual Report, 1974* (Washington, D.C.: IBRD, 1974), p. 97.

contrast, India's international economic diplomacy appears to have produced mixed—probably positive—benefits. But for reasons to which I shall turn, India has not profited to the extent possible from participation in international trade, investment, and aid relationships.

India's Own Strategy: The Better Is
Enemy of the Good

There is nothing remarkable about India's choice of goals in aspiring to be modern, socialist, democratic, and independent. Nevertheless, the famine-prone, laissez faire, and colonial experience in the century before Independence was bound to make progress toward these objectives difficult. India's emphasis on growth, equity, and self-reliance as the principal means to attain its overall goals is equally unexceptional. Even the most controversial, self-reliance, has been justified by the adverse effect of South Asian wars, closure of the Suez Canal, depressed prices for India's traditional exports, and skyrocketing prices for imports. There may be some question about whether population limitation should be regarded as a basic objective or merely part of the strategy, but India is on firm ground in recognizing that the economics and politics of population control are *sui generis* and in treating fertility as a separate issue. In any case, India has expended considerable effort to reduce birthrates even though its population explosion was not foreseen in 1947.

Procedurally, India's strategy has required government to shoulder far-reaching responsibility for the progress of the economy through an elaborate system of centralized planning and broad directive and regulatory powers. But because the system has not fully paid the anticipated dividends, its value must be questioned. Was it realistic to assume that informed human decision could serve Indian development better than a market mechanism geared to private profit? Could the political process in Delhi respond to competing claims from states, companies, and other interests and satisfy them with compromises which would be economically efficient? Did policy makers have adequate information and technical resources to fix functional, temporal, and spatial priorities? Would the Indian economy respond to the central government's directives, and could the loss of constructive local initiatives as a result of centralization be kept minimal?

Although the short answer to all these questions is "no," there is no certainty that India would have fared better under another type of regime. What is clear is that, in practice, India's approach to regulating the economy was not fully compatible with the nation's (1) political system, (2) size, diversity and poverty, (3) scarcity of experienced managers and economists, and (4) weak communications network. The question of procedure is deeply concerned not only with economic relationships, such as how to bridge the gap between the abstraction of the Planning Commission's econometric models and the harsh reality of a monsoon-oriented, tradition-bound society, but with political factors. In agrarian reform, for example, very little progress has been made because those in power do not have the political will and those in need have not yet assumed the political power. Thus, by taking advantage of the fragmented state-central authority structure, vested interests have maintained their political and economic hegemony. Even when agrarian reform initiatives have been pressed by the government, they have made little headway because of the ability of the rural elite to write restrictive clauses into the legislation, control the judicial and administrative machinery, and reduce the funds appropriated for implementing the legislation to unreasonably small amounts.

In substance, although Indian economic policy has addressed many issues simultaneously, some measures have been more significant than others.

1. When, in the 1950s, India chose to accelerate industrialization, this decision implied a confidence in the agricultural base which was regarded as justified by the growth of farm output during the First Plan. In retrospect, it is clear that the succession of good crops in the early 1950s was due to several better-than-normal monsoons rather than to any basic improvement in the farm economy. If in planning for its economy, India had more fully recognized the precariousness of its food situation by placing marginally greater emphasis on agriculture and agroindustry, it would probably have spared itself subsequent crises and dependence on foreign food. In practice, even though Indian officials were acutely aware of the need for rural progress and agriculture was hardly ignored by policy, industrialization had a magnetic appeal for policy makers, and except at times of food scarcity, almost all other goals were treated as poor cousins. The cyclical pattern of attention to agriculture that resulted from according second-order priority to an area which, when neglected, caused first-order crises is illustrated by the evolution of policy after the mid-1960s drought. Undoubtedly some enduring progress was made after the drought as the food shortage focused greater attention on agriculture in the second half of the 1960s. But when these policies were rewarded with record growth of food production, the government's effort flagged. Thus, in the early 1970s, when India again encountered bad monsoons, farmers were already beset with seed, fertilizer, power, and pricing problems; production suffered accordingly.[23] The lesson to draw from this experience—that India should give high, if not top, priority to assuring that adequate food will be available regardless of weather—is more easily recited than implemented. India badly needs a *green evolution,* with all the sustained attention and massive resources that this implies; but Indian officials, like officials elsewhere, remain responsive to the *green revolution* psychology with all its hazards of stop-go policies and the periodic need for emergency relief.

Assuming that India had put greater resources into agriculture, what sector of the economy would have been the loser? No definitive reply is possible, but undoubtedly some—perhaps even more than 100 percent—of the resources

---

[23]The havoc caused by India's agricultural policies is an important warning that the concept of unbalanced growth which Hirschman and others have sometimes advocated should not be pressed to extremes. See Albert O. Hirschman, *The Strategy of Economic Development* (New Haven, Conn.: Yale University Press, 1958).

could have come from relief programs which would not have been needed if farm output had been increased. The validity of this point is supported by a comparison of the costs of drought relief in Maharashtra in the early 1970s and the prophylactic measures which could have reduced the state's vulnerability to drought and rendered the relief unnecessary.[24] Be that as it may, the policy changes required to give India a more comfortable food position are so basic that to set the issue in terms of agriculture versus industry is misleading. Moreover, the reorientation of India's strategy to stress energy and agroindustries at the expense of heavy engineering could have been done in the 1960s with no deleterious effect on India's efforts to spur defense production, create industrial employment, substitute domestic production for imports, or generally establish a modern industrial nation.

2. India's praiseworthy concern for social justice, which has had a major influence on the attitudes of the World Bank and others interested in development, must be judged by its practical impact on the distribution of assets, income disparities, and mass welfare. As noted by Bardhan and others, India has had only limited success in each of these areas.[25] In rural India, for example, when the upper crust of Indian landlords (zamindars) was removed soon after Independence, it was replaced by a somewhat larger but still highly inegalitarian elite of well-to-do landowners who have gradually consolidated their political and economic power. Data on income distribution show no narrowing of disparities and suggest that in some areas they have actually grown larger. Finally, as social services have been extended to rural India, they have transformed social patterns gradually rather than radically, and elites have obtained more than a fair share of the benefits.

In large part, the difficulty in promoting equity in rural India stems from population growth; to repeat a commonplace, every generation demands its own land reform. It also is due to the laxness of central and state governments in pressing the issue and to the political weakness of the rural poor. Looked at from another angle, the intractability of wealth and welfare disparities reflects the mutual dependence of the Congress party and the well-to-do farmers. It is significant that although the Community Development, cooperative, and related programs have improved rural conditions to some degree, their direct focus on social goals has sometimes diverted attention from the basic need to increase agricultural output, which itself has major social implications. Although poor farmers have had the most trouble in maintaining their ownership and tenurial rights in states where agricultural growth has proceeded fastest, India's experience to date is that so long as growth was maintained, they participated in the rising standard of living.

3. India's decision to stress rapid industrialization, heavy industry, and public sector enterprise was almost as critical to policy as its choice of growth, equity, and self-reliance. The attraction of this approach was not just psychological. For example, to the extent that India could process its extensive mineral deposits at

[24]See Ladjinsky, *Drought in Maharashtra*, op. cit.
[25]Bardhan, op. cit.

home, it would not only spur industrial progress and import substitution but also enhance the value of exports. In addition, the logic of investing in heavy engineering was economic; this sector was expected to produce machinery which, in turn, would produce more machines and consumer goods. As such, it promised to serve both the growth and self-reliance objectives.

The weaknesses of India's industrial strategy were that (1) the skill levels and industrial sophistication needed for heavy engineering were not always available in India, (2) large machines generally can be used to produce only a limited range of products, (3) domestic and foreign markets for the output of some of India's heavy industries were of limited size, and (4) the underutilization of these machines made them uneconomic. The problems became most apparent when, in the mid-1960s, the pace of India's development slowed and the resulting decline in new investment (in 1970 the output of capital goods industries was less than in 1965) turned the heavy engineering sector into an unexpected albatross.[26] Following the Third Plan, the Indian economy suffered from a self-made structural problem of insufficient *supply* of consumer goods and a related insufficient *demand* for capital goods. If instead of investing in heavy industry, India had concentrated on mining, light manufacturing, economic infrastructure, and agriculture, its economy probably would have had greater resilience; it would have resumed its growth sooner; there would have been more current output to satisfy the poor during the recession, and the foreign exchange situation would have been easier.[27]

In retrospect, it is clear that the decision to concentrate new investments in the public sector also had its practical shortcomings. Phiroze Medhora has doubtless overstated the case when he writes that the

> lack of competitiveness of Indian industry arises not out of any economic factors but entirely of the incompetent management of the units in the public sector. The policy of putting bureaucrats into public sector units not only led to uneconomic production costs and low output, but has also led to the discrediting of public sector enterprise in the country and outside. It is futile to blame planning for this phenomenon.[28]

But India's experience with public sector enterprise has been decidedly bittersweet. When it reacted to budgetary pressure, the government generally cut little from administrative and defense spending but constrained development investments. The consequence of this pattern is illustrated by India's steel shortage in the 1970s, which Medhora traces directly to the tight budget situation of 1964 when the government halted most iron and steel development except for the Bokaro plant.[29] In short, the government's practice of first ruling out private investment in certain key economic sectors, and then cutting public

---

[26]See Brahmananda, op. cit., p. 23.

[27]Ibid., pp. 23–27.

[28]Phiroze B. Medhora, "Industrial Development: A Quarter Century Review," *Commerce*, Aug. 19, 1972, pp. 47–49.

[29]Ibid., p. 49.

investment in these areas, gave India's industrial strategy an unintended anti-investment and antiproduction bias.

4. Related to India's industrial strategy was its decision to stress import substitution more than export promotion. Some individuals cite the declining share of imports in India's total supply of various consumer and investment goods as evidence that the strategy has succeeded. In reality, just the opposite conclusion is suggested by the pervasive complaint in India that foreign exchange shortages have caused government to constrain imports and that this, in turn, has inhibited the domestic economy's progress. Although there is no a priori standard for determining the optimum relationship between imports and domestic supply, it is almost certain that if the Indian economy had grown faster, imports would also have expanded more quickly. Indeed, many economists and technicians are now agreed that India pursued industrial diversification and "clearance from the indigenous angle" to uneconomic extremes; that the economy would have been more flexible if India had made a greater effort to increase its exports and benefit from international trade. Finally, the import strategy in combination with the domestic licensing regime has provided excessive protection for most Indian industries and, by insulating them from the fresh air of foreign competition, has helped to make them extraordinarily inefficient.

5. India's policy to minimize foreign private equity investment in its economy is readily explained by historical and political factors, by the unreasonable demands of some established and other would-be investors, and by misconceptions about the potential balance-of-payments costs to India. Be that as it may, India's position appears shortsighted in light of the favorable experiences that countries as diverse as South Korea, Malaysia, and Brazil have had with foreign investors. Moreover, it ignores the logic that a country should try to employ its labor force productively by obtaining the requisite capital and technology from abroad if it is not available from domestic sources. It is ironic that although India has gradually learned how to relegate foreign investors to a role which serves national development needs at a reasonable cost and without forfeiting Indian sovereignty, there is little prospect that India will change the substance of its investment policies to admit new enterprises.

6. Since World War II, a variety of factors including new nationhood, concern for development, food shortage, and East-West confrontation, have induced rich and poor countries to establish economic aid relationships. Schools, hospitals, factories, dams, and hybrid seeds are the tangible evidence that foreign aid can be effective. But India's abiding poverty, its hodgepodge of factories (each based on the unique technology of a different aid donor), and its mounting external debt burden are among the problems which suggest that foreign assistance has had its shortcomings. What is bothersome about foreign aid is not just that it has engendered more negative political tensions than are desirable, but that it has not been as efficient an instrument for promoting economic development as was once expected. Because foreign aid comes in various forms and from various national donors, it is anything but a homogeneous commodity. Even so, there have been a few major instances, such as the

"package program" for agriculture, and many smaller occasions when external assistance played a critical role in India's development. Nevertheless, the suspicion remains that if domestic conditions in India had been more conducive to economic progress, the value of foreign aid would have been vastly greater.

The Ingredients Mixed

It is impossible to analyze the determinants of Indian development and the results without also touching on the social process through which they are linked. But because that process takes on a life of its own as both a cause and an outcome, it deserves some further elaboration. The vital significance of social and other factors which lie behind and affect the impact of policy actions cannot be ignored. Policy, however, has always been a unique factor because, unlike culture and resources, it can be varied. Moreover, insofar as the lead time for policy to affect the society is often very long, the longer the time period considered, the greater its significance becomes.

Before turning to a more strictly economic interpretation of how the economy works, we should note a psychological aspect of policy. Experienced observers of India are familiar with a pattern which R. Venkateranam, a lawyer who served as industries minister in Tamil Nadu before becoming a member of the Planning Commission in 1966, characterizes as "the better is enemy of the good."[30] The situation this phrase refers to is an all too pervasive combination of good intention and inadequate pragmatism at the formulation and implementation stages of policy.

As an example of muddled policy formulation Venkateranam cites the late 1960s debate over how to meet Uttar Pradesh's energy needs. Initially, it was proposed that a system of medium-size hydroelectric power stations be installed. This could have been accomplished within about two years, using almost 100 percent indigenous Indian technology and manufactures. Most prominent among the counterproposals was the suggestion that a single nuclear-powered generating station should be built. If undertaken, this investment would not only have been vastly more costly, but would not have been completed for 10 years and would have required heavy Indian reliance on imported machinery and technology. Most significant, since the debate between alternative proposals was fought to a draw, Uttar Pradesh received less new power-generating capacity than needed; this proved a major factor in the industrial and agricultural recession of the early 1970s.

The critical importance of pragmatic policy implementation is illustrated by Venkateranam's own experience as industries minister. By his own account, he was frustrated on his first day in office when he found that the staff recommendation on every industrial license application on his desk was "Do not approve." The three points he made to his staff on this occasion were (1) that surely some

---

[30]The phrase comes from Voltaire's *La Begueule,* where it is attributed to "a wise Italian."

applications were acceptable as submitted or with minor modification; (2) that government should explain its disapprovals because, even though this would give businessmen more grounds to quarrel with official decisions, it would help them to understand the state's policies and submit more acceptable applications in the future; and (3) that because Tamil Nadu favored industrialization, when officials could not approve private investment proposals, they should recommend alternative projects which could be approved. Although Venkateranam's approach was radically different from normal operating procedure, it was adopted while he was minister and is generally credited with having provided Tamil Nadu with an unsurpassed period of industrial progress.

The relevance of this experience to implementation is that it challenges the wisdom of India's comprehensive official planning and control. Venkateranam was a rarity. When he left Madras, his successors from the locally based DMK government failed to keep the bureaucratic reforms he had introduced. Moreover, in the all-India world of the Planning Commission, Venkateranam was unable to accomplish a fraction of what he had done at the state level. It can only be stated hypothetically that India would benefit from a shift in its policy approach away from administrative controls and centralized management. Nonetheless, there is enough evidence to suggest that Indian development would accelerate under a system which continued to provide official direction to the economy but did so through market intervention and also permitted greater private participation.

The more traditional analysis of how India's development has been affected by the gap between the pretensions of policy and the social and other realities which undermined official efforts to impose a particular pattern on India's development has to do with the economics of monopoly, the political economy of extralegal economic transactions, and the sociology of alienation. The starting point, as seen by Mahbub ul Haq, is as follows:

> Once direct controls were introduced, they bred like mushrooms. In order to control the final price of cotton cloth, the Government started controlling the price of raw cotton, the dealer's margin, the manufacturer's costs, the distributor's profits, and a whole lot of related activities. And as the direct controls started replacing the market, the pyramid kept on building, till the government officials sitting on top of it did not know any longer what on earth they were controlling.[31]

Although Pakistan's experience inspired this passage, Haq has been widely quoted in India, where his criticisms are regarded as equally applicable.

Evidence does not support India's premises for using administrative controls—that they were needed to overcome the social and economic disabilities of the poor and that, in contrast to the ignorant, self-seeking, and disingenuous private citizen, the average government official is competent, motivated and

---

[31]Mahbub ul Haq, *The Strategy of Economic Planning* (Karachi: Oxford University Press, 1966), p. 51.

honest.[32] At the technical level, government economists and planners often are inadequately informed and ill-equipped with tools to cope with the complexities of India's real world of conflicting political objectives and major economic uncertainties. Planners are no more omniscient than the policy makers and implementers are omnipotent. That the "law and order" emphasis in the training of government officers has only recently been supplemented by a concern for development is but one reason why many Indian bureaucrats are notably ill-prepared for the economic tasks for which they are responsible. Moreover, there is almost no precedent for enhancing official expertise by bringing experienced businessmen or academics into the government for limited periods of service.

According to a number of Indians, the technical weaknesses of India's bureaucracy have been compounded by insufficient or errant motivation on the part of many officials. The Indian Civil Service is notorious for its reliance on seniority rather than performance as the criterion for promotion, and in contrast to the potentially dire consequences for any bureaucrat who incurs the displeasure of a minister, there is generally no penalty for general inefficiency. As a result, officials do not meet deadlines, they seek the clearances of a maximum number of fellow bureaucrats so as to avoid personal responsibility, and they indulge otherwise in bureaucratic practices not conducive to development. According to Arun Shourie's view of bureaucrats:

> As they are not managers, as they are not directly affected by the progress or lack of progress in a plant or an industry and as they cannot be penalized for their errors and delays they function without any notions about costs and benefits. They examine each case as it would be examined by a criminal judge—without any thought about the opportunity costs of their examination. They insist on the formal enforcement of rules and procedures without any notion of the net benefit to the economy of this compliance.[33]

Shourie cites in illustration the Kota fertilizer expansion scheme, where, because blind application of the "clearance from the indigenous angle" precluded the import of Rs. 3.1 million worth of equipment, completion of the project was delayed for a year and production of Rs. 70 million worth of fertilizer was lost.[34]

At another level, the monopoly profits created by the widespread use of administrative controls are an invitation for poorly paid bureaucrats to augment their incomes by according preferential treatment to applicants who are willing to allow officials to share in the profits. According to one of India's most vociferous critics, Nirad Chaudhuri,

> An Indian's faith in bribes is infinite and unshakable. Not only is bribing believed to be an infalliable remedy for all workaday inconveniences—a

[32]For an intensive look at the bureaucrat and controls in India, see Shourie, "Controls and the Current Situation," op. cit.

[33]Ibid., p. 1485.

[34]Ibid., p. 1483.

> belief justified by experience—it is also regarded as an equally effective
> means of managing high affairs of state, but in this instance without the
> same warranty.[35]

Chaudhuri has overstated the case, but an acquaintance with daily life in India, along with evidence from parliamentary debates and official government reports on the subject, leaves no doubt as to the pervasiveness of petty and large-scale corruption of public servants, of tax evasion, and of other illicit behavior by private citizens and government employees.

India's administrative controls have helped to create monopoly conditions which corroborate fully the textbook theory of how imperfect markets lead to high prices and low output. A long and well-documented literature shows that the behavior of India's monopolists and oligopolists, while rational from the perspective of company profits, has been highly disadvantageous to the national economy's efficiency, growth, and equity. Regulatory measures affecting imports, new investment, the allocation of scarce commodities, and many other areas have created such a large gap between market prices and actual values, and the profits from exploiting that gap have been so large, that they have caused major distortions in India's economy.

The conjunction of bureaucratic controls, progressive tax structures in which the highest rates are almost confiscatory, and other restrictive economic policies has resulted in a situation even worse than monopoly. An economic order based on extralegal transactions and financed with "black money" (funds which, because they have been earned illegally, cannot be declared for tax purposes and must therefore be spent illegally) has come to exist side by side with the licit economy, and it has grown at an accelerating rate. The imposition of administrative controls has initiated a vicious circle insofar as government measures to control black money have created not only penalties for illegal transactions but also new rewards for evasion. Further, to the extent that the controls have not been effective, they have begotten new, more elaborate and extensive controls.

Little research has been done on the subject of corruption, in part because the natural tendency for both participants in, and official investigators of, illegal transactions is to be discreet. Consequently, there is only scanty evidence as to whether corruption in India (1) is worse than in other countries, (2) is on the increase, or (3) serves an economic allocative function beneficial to the society.

In 1964 an official committee under the chairmanship of K. Santhanam reported to the Home Ministry on corruption in India. The committee was shocked not only by the moral evil of illicit practices, but also by the ease with which it was able to trace the existence of corruption back through the millennia of Indian history and sideways to other developing and developed nations. Without seeking to condone what it regarded as an unmitigated evil, the committee gave reasons as to why corruption existed and had grown. In

[35]Nirad Chaudhuri, *The Autobiography of an Unknown Indian* (Berkeley: University of California Press, 1968), p. 104.

particular, it noted that by assuming new roles in the economic sphere, government had opened new opportunities for extralegal practices by officials.[36]

The Santhanam report mixed its description and analysis with considerable moralizing. In sharp contrast to its ethical approach is the political view that corruption serves an important social function. According to Myron Weiner:

> Equal opportunity to corrupt is often more important than the amount of corruption, and therefore that an increase in *bakshish* is in the long run less serious than an increase in corruption by ascriptive criteria. So long as the businessman and the peasant can obtain what they want from local administrators through the payment of money, there is less likely to be popular discontent than if those who can and wish to make payments discover that caste and family connections are more decisive. For in that case, those of lower status backgrounds but rising economic success will find themselves blocked, and political disaffection is likely to increase.[37]

This line of argument may be valid if the proportion of extralegal to licit transactions is constant. If corruption is growing faster than the general economy, however, there is bound to be a critical point where it seriously affects government revenues and makes citizens so cynical as to threaten the downfall of government and perhaps also democracy. It is therefore critical whether Weiner's stable equilibrium is likely or whether there is a process whereby corruption is institutionalized, receives the unofficial blessing of society, and escalates to ever higher and politically intolerable levels. Experience with India to date and history suggest that either situation can exist. At a more basic level, Weiner's thesis, that corruption serves a beneficial political and economic function, is in conflict with Myrdal's view that corruption is one of the key "forces that help to preserve the 'soft state' with its low degree of social discipline" and poor prospects for development.[38] With these views of how corruption affects the economy, it is significant that not only politicians and journalists, but Santhanam, Myrdal, and other serious analysts agree that since Independence corruption has increased as a factor affecting the Indian economy.

This conclusion is supported by fragmentary evidence such as the findings of an official study team under the chairmanship of M. G. Kaul. Based on a careful investigation of India's foreign exchange situation in the early 1970s, the Kaul report conservatively estimated the amount of illegal international transactions in one year to be roughly $320 million, equal to more than 15 percent of India's recorded exports.[39] The sophistication of the illegal operators—and the study team which reported on their activities—is indicated by

[36]*Report of the Committee on Prevention of Corruption* (K. Santhanam, chairman), (New Delhi: GOI, Ministry of Home Affairs, 1964).

[37]Weiner, *Politics of Scarcity*, op. cit., p. 236.

[38]See Myrdal, op. cit., p. 952.

[39]*Report of the Study Team on Leakage of Foreign Exchange through Invoice Manipulation* (M. G. Kaul, chairman), (New Delhi: GOI, Ministry of Finance, 1971).

Table 11-2, which shows the sources and uses of the $320 million (equivalent of Rs. 2,400 million). The Kaul report shows the wide variety of means whereby illegal transactions take place. An exporter, for example, has several options, depending on his objectives. If he chooses to be honest, he can submit a straightforward export invoice to the authorities; if he wishes to obtain a larger than justified import entitlement, he can overinvoice, or if his goal is to accumulate a foreign exchange balance abroad, he can underinvoice.

Such circumstantial but convincing evidence that corruption is growing is especially significant in that the economic effects are anything but benign. The common belief among Westerners, that corruption is merely a device for lubricating administrative machinery and an indispensable safety valve for satisfying some of the more powerful demands of economic elites, is not only cynical but also misses the point of how costly corruption can be to the economy. The costs of illegal transactions go well beyond the salary of the "Delhi representative" who is retained to see to it that the government moves files with alacrity and makes the "right" decision. This has often been demonstrated; most recently, with respect to the economic distortions which India's quantitative restrictions on its international trade have introduced.[40]

[40]Anne O. Krueger, "The Political Economy of the Rent-seeking Society," *American Economic Review,* vol. 64, no. 3, June 1974, pp. 291–303.

TABLE **11–2**

SOURCES AND USES OF ILLEGAL FOREIGN EXCHANGE (millions of rupees)*

Sources:	
Deflection of remittances to India	1,000–1,200
Underinvoicing of exports	400– 500
Overinvoicing of imports	100– 150
Miscellaneous trade manipulations	50
Smuggling of silver, narcotics, antiques, etc.	400– 450
Receipts from foreign tourists	150
	2,100–2,500
Uses:	
Illegal imports	1,600–1,700
Tourism for Indians abroad	350– 400
Underinvoicing of imports, overinvoicing of exports, and foreign investments	250– 300
	2,200–2,400

*Rs. 10 million = $1.3 million.

Source: Derived from the *Report of the Study Team on Leakage of Foreign Exchange through Invoice Manipulation* (M. G. Kaul, chairman) (New Delhi: GOI, Ministry of Finance).

Corruption must not be viewed only in the perspective of monopoly, inefficiency, bottlenecks, inflexibility, politicization, and inordinate delays to which it is related. It must also be seen as an integral part of India's political economy, as a symptom of the system as much as a determinant of its character. In this context, growing corruption coincides with what many Indian and foreign observers perceive as a disintegration of India's political economy since 1965. In reacting to this situation, the government increasingly made use of (1) socialist rhetoric and sloganeering of an ever more radical nature and (2) hastily conceived crash programs and political gestures designed to appease the growing dissatisfaction without actually eradicating the cause of the problem. But because neither response could effectively deal with India's real problems, and because India has undergone a series of unlucky events, its social fabric has come under increasing duress. Private businessmen, more and more unwilling and unable to cope with government controls, have reverted to extralegal devices; farmers have become more concerned with averting risks than with raising output; labor has become both less efficient at work and more militant in its attitude toward management; and government employees (white- and blue-collar workers) have increasingly put their own personal interests ahead of the nation's, even to the point of engaging in industrial sabotage.

Thus, the growing malaise in India, epitomized in 1975 by J. P. Narayan's protest movement and Mrs. Gandhi's harsh reaction, is significant not only as a cause and effect of slow and unbalanced economic development, but also as a bellwether of India's domestic political future and place in the world community. As I shall suggest in the Epilogue, to project this gloomy mood into the future would be imprudent. India has repeatedly demonstrated a capacity to endure hardship and to recover its vitality. This is true for both the short-term cycles which have affected India since Independence and the longer-term historical movements. Moreover, too glum a prognosis would ignore the islands of progress in industry and elsewhere which already amount to a substantial asset for further development and have continued to expand despite the general stagnation. Finally, although there are few aspects of the social system that India's political leaders can afford to ignore, by concentrating policy on priority areas and permitting pragmatism to rule over ideology, there is great scope for transforming some of India's old vicious circles into a new virtuous circle of development.

CHAPTER 12
INDIA'S SECOND REVOLUTION

India's social and economic evolution has acute interest not only for participants, but for scholars, statesmen, and foreigners concerned with public affairs. Will India's future progress follow the pattern established during the past quarter century? What roles do socialism and radical thinking play in the Indian experience? What are the prospects for Indian democracy in light of its economic outlook and, reciprocally, how will the political situation affect the economy? In projecting domestic political and economic trends, what can be said about India's future as a nation? Will it coalesce, or will centrifugal forces gain the upper hand? How will India's domestic characteristics affect its place in the emerging world order? And what are the implications of India's situation for United States policy?

INDIA: PAST, PRESENT, AND FUTURE

Since 1947, India's situation has oscillated from hopeful to grim more frequently and more extremely than the human mind can comfortably comprehend.[1] Not surprisingly, therefore, attitudes toward India's prospects have fluctuated even more widely, ranging from the ultragloomy forecast that it will become necessary to practice a form of international economic triage in which India is treated as a hopeless case, to ultraoptimistic predictions that the green revolution will soon obviate the need for concessionally priced grain imports.

[1]For a lengthier analysis of this subject, see my "India: Today, Tonight, and Tomorrow Morning,"op. cit., and "India's Economic Development and the Force of National Politics,"op. cit.

Regrettably, large and frequent shifts in attitude, from euphoria to despair, have tended to camouflage the true state of India's political economy.

In 1973–74, attitudes toward India's economic situation were once again in a gloomy phase. The economy was afflicted with nature-sent trials in the form of bad weather, homemade hardships due to ill-conceived and poorly implemented policies, and crises induced by such foreign factors as skyrocketing prices of food, fertilizer, petroleum, and other essential imports. Given the income distribution pattern, its economy was unable to provide minimal living standards for large numbers of the poor. And true to the pattern in past periods of hardship, Indians sought protection for themselves by hoarding grain, raising prices, striking for large wage increases. These and other responses, taken together, exacerbated the lot of the poor and, more generally, harmed the economy and complicated the process of restoring growth. Although the uncontrollable transitory factors which so profoundly depressed India during this period will become more favorable in time, the relentless expansion of population now threatens to preempt much if not all future economic growth. Indeed, if the Indian population continues to increase by more than 1 million each month and world food stocks remain low, the possibility of serious famine becomes a probability which, until now, has been sensed by only a minority of observers.

India's political situation, while hardly cause for cheer, is somewhat less bleak than its short-term economic position. Although the services of the Indian Army were needed in 1973 to quell an uprising of the armed constabulary in Uttar Pradesh, external security and the domestic political system are not currently subject to serious challenge. I say this even though (1) voting abuses and corruption are all too common and appear to be on the increase; (2) the Bihar, Gujarat, Andhra Pradesh, Uttar Pradesh, and other state governments have fallen since the 1972 election; and (3) the popular protest movement against political corruption which J. P. Narayan has launched has begun to attract adherents throughout the nation. These are signals of political malaise even though they must also be interpreted as signs that India's nascent democracy remains a vital force. Coincident with a generally reduced discipline within the Congress party and the nation at large, they suggest that the future course of politics will not always be stable and, on occasion, may be unpleasant.

Even if one discounts for the likelihood that India was merely in the trough of one of its cycles—by early 1975 India had yet to recover from 1973, which Mrs. Gandhi described as the most difficult year in India's history[2]—the long-term situation still appears perilous. The opinion of India's former president, V. V. Giri, is instructive. Speaking at Lucknow in 1973, while in office, he reminded his audience that in the 1920s Mahatma Gandhi had warned against seven social evils: politics without principles; wealth without work; pleasure without conscience; knowledge without character; commerce without morality; science

[2]*New York Times,* Aug. 20, 1973.

without humanity; and worship without sacrifice. "Today," he warned, "these sins are present in our society in a more virulent form. . . . Unless and until we take immediate steps to remove them, lock, stock, and barrel, we cannot survive as a nation."[3] What is significant about President Giri's speech is that it was motivated by his perception, right or wrong, of underlying trends in Indian society rather than by a superficial appraisal of the current situation.

How did India's leaders allow their country to enter such dangerous straits? The broad explanation that I find convincing—one which absolves Indian leaders from some but not all responsibility—emphasizes two related factors: first, the scarcity of resources (human, material, and financial) to satisfy all the demands posed by domestic and foreign problems; and, second, the government's failure to create a more effective system for managing the economy.

The first of these reasons is, in essence, a matter of priorities. To the Western visitor, as to many Indians, poverty in India is so acute and omnipresent that it is difficult to regard the more intangible political task of nation building as taking precedence over economic progress. But in reality, India has accorded first priority to noneconomic issues. In the opinion of its leaders, India has experienced domestic and external political challenges in the past quarter century which it could have ignored only at the cost of its status as a sovereign nation. Coping with mass migrations, persistent violence and three outbreaks of war with Pakistan, the smoldering feud with China which reached battle pitch in 1962, and domestic tensions arising from regional, caste, class, and religious diversity—all this has drained India's development effort of real resources and the political attention which it would have received under less pressing circumstances.

The subject of how government has managed the economy greatly qualifies two major components of Indian public policy, socialism and planning. It is noteworthy that in practice it was the procedural aspect, as contrasted with the substantive content, of socialism which was more a burden than a benefit for the economy. Few Indians oppose the principles of improved welfare for all and of narrowing disparities, only the administrative measures taken to secure these goals. Moreover, India's unhappy experience with socialistic policies does not prove that socialism per se is bad. It might appear that India can take solace in the fact that few non-European socialist economies have flourished; indeed, the governments of some Western centrally planned economies, finding that there are limits to this approach, have experimented gingerly with reforms, including capitalist motivational techniques. But to say that socialism has performed badly elsewhere is hardly comforting in view of India's gargantuan economic problems and their political overtones.

The situation of Indian socialism is roughly comparable to that of Indian planning insofar as hypothetical benefits are only sometimes reflected in the actual course of events. In retrospect, if India had managed the resources that

[3]*New Statesman*, Sept. 14, 1973, p. 337.

were available for its economic development with less doctrinaire concern for socialism, planning, and heavy industry, with more sensitivity to the cultural barriers to change, and with a greater effort to shield economic processes from the interference of all monopoly forces—public and private—its development would have been faster and even the poor would have participated in the growth.

Despite the uneven pace at which development has proceeded, external conflicts, centrifugal forces stemming from domestic diversity, and the difficulties of governing such a large and growing population, it is remarkable that India has grown politically stronger. The principal reason—which also explains why India shows no sign of coming apart—is the nation's extraordinary capacity for adaptation. The time-honored system of intermediating political demands by the Center so that, by the time Delhi's will is acted on by local authorities, decisions are palatable to the polity, has operated during the Mogul, colonial, and modern eras. Except during the Independence movement, the Indian body politic has not been accustomed to make demands on government and has had little expectation that benefits would be forthcoming. And, since 1947, the pursuit of constitutional government and popular legitimacy have also supported national unity.

But the post-Independence period differs fundamentally from its predecessors. Interventions by the government now are made in the name of the people rather than of the nation or the ruling class. The population has begun to respond to democracy and no longer regards the slogans and pieties in the sky offered by political leaders as totally irrelevant. People have begun to think it legitimate to make demands on government—and sometimes even to expect that their demands will be satisfied. Confronted by these changes, India's "soft" political system still appears able to hold the nation together, but not fully adequate to the task of mobilizing resources for rapid economic development. "Stalemate" is the word which best describes the current scene. Nationalistic and modernizing interests have made some progress, but the power of kinship and other subnational, extrapolitical relationships remains strong and the influence of vested interests high.

These factors, combined with the Indian penchant for relying on bureaucratic decision, have created a peculiar situation in which effective government usually occurs only in times of crisis. Long-run problems such as economic development do not receive the care and attention they deserve. Indeed, when India's praiseworthy record of crisis management is compared with its dreary experience in solving more mundane problems, it seems that a variant of Parkinson's law is at work, according to which the government expands its efficiency to the point where it is able to ameliorate—but not always solve—only its most pressing problems. If this is true, it is particularly unfortunate because as the Indian economy develops more sophistication and interlinkages, the need for more effective, but not more extensive, government oversight increases.

India's erratic record in matters of economic development combines elements of correct action, no action, wrong action, and inconsistent action. Although indifference and the pursuit of vested interests partly explain why this is the case, such an explanation ignores the high motivation of many Indians to address the country's economic problems and is patently inadequate. The more plausible, multicausal explanation is that, in addition to indifference and entrenched interests, there are weaknesses in India's ability to perceive and articulate its problems and to move through a democratic process to find remedial policies and means for implementing them. The villains of the piece include, but are not limited to, wrongly motivated individuals; well-intentioned but misguided judgment; and the impersonal fact that when conflicting points of view interact, the resulting compromises may ill serve any of the interests represented.

The cyclical patterns which seem to characterize the Indian economy and economic policy are not conducive to development. Thus, it is important to assess whether they are inevitable; whether the material and intellectual factors responsible for them can be contained or more productively rechanneled; and whether the cycles have been changing in intensity, tending toward more gradual and less disruptive changes or toward more violent vicissitudes.

Although the swing left which began in 1969 and marked Mrs. Gandhi's ascendance to power was advertised as a definitive shift toward more populist policies, subsequent developments suggest that it was merely another inflection point in the cycle and no more loaded with special meaning than previous socialist initiatives. Be that as it may, the Indian economy has been undergoing important structural changes which virtually guarantee that in the future the cyclical pattern will be altered. India's population has soared. The economy has grown, but too slowly and unevenly to satisfy mass demands. In its increasing diveristy, sophistication, and size, the economy has greater interindustry linkages, and these place new strains on the government's economic management apparatus. Economic disparities at the village and regional levels may or may not have widened, but the willingness of poor people to accept their economic status has declined, even is such backward states as Bihar.[4] New vested interests have emerged and precipitated new struggles between the private and public interests.

The most alarming structural change now envisaged for the year 2000 is that the already cruel mismatch among population numbers, employment opportunities, and food supplies will grow infinitely worse. According to a panel of experts convened under government auspices to trace where current demographic trends will lead,

> a good look at the requirements of the year 2000 A.D. present before us a
> picture of definite chaos. No matter in which direction we look, the popula-

---

[4]See, for example, F. Tomasson Jannuzi, *Agrarian Crisis in India: The Case of Bihar* (Austin: University of Texas Press, 1974), p. 168.

tion problem looks like our Waterloo. What perhaps needs to be done quickly is harnessing of the post-industrial technology to our present know-how so that we may be able to restore some normalcy.[5]

While attracting many adherents, this view is far from universal among Indians and may make the classic error of ignoring India's capacity to endure adversity. But like President Giri's speech about India's socioeconomic fabric, it addresses a fundamental and vital problem. As some Indians now realize, to cite "economic stagnation" as the root cause of India's troubles is "facile" and "dishonest." According to one perceptive article,

> The shattering revelation that the economic capacities built up over our 25 years of independent existence are less than 50 percent utilized in so many vital areas points to the real truth. . . . The first casualty of populist anarchy has been productivity. The second casualty has been the maintenance of the assets built up over 25 years. And now we are entering the phase of dislocation and closure of units of all description.[6]

Salvation under these circumstances is not easily attained. Although the case for political change is overwhelming, it is far from certain whether India has more to gain by trimming its policy sails more carefully or by setting an altogether new course for the economy. In either instance, despite the wide dispersion of power both within and outside government, there is no question that in 1975 and for the foreseeable future, Indira Gandhi is more strategically placed to change the course of events than any other person. The Prime Minister's public statements are impressive testimony that she is painfully aware of India's problems and the difficulties which obstruct solutions—undoubtedly more so than the foreign observers who carp at her with such regularity. The record of her actions and their consequences, however, has been anything but impressive. This gap has promoted speculation as to whether Mrs. Gandhi is herself so bourgeois as to be disinclined to lead her country to a new, more socialist order. Some observers have questioned whether the Prime Minister has boxed herself in, whether she has based her political standing on a leftist dogma from which she is now unable to deviate because of past commitments and current fears that her government would collapse without the radical backing she receives from the left wing of the Congress party and the Moscow-oriented branch of the Communist Party of India. As seen by the *Economic and Political Weekly*,

> The Prime Minister is here a prisoner of her own dilemma. The dilemma stems from the gathering of economic forces which she has assembled under the umbrella of the Congress, and whose short-term avarice cuts into the

[5] National Committee on Science and Technology Panel on Futurology, "First Draft of the Base Document on Futurology," mimeographed, New Delhi, 1974.

[6] *Economic and Political Weekly*, June 2, 1973, p. 966.

prospects of the nation's economic progress. Each of these forces wants to be subsidised at the expense of the State; none wants to pay any additional tithe to the State. Each of them has got used to being a beneficiary of an unrequited system of spoils. With Indira Gandhi's diminished political prowess, it would now be most difficult to introduce a different behavioural pattern. . . . In terms of rough and ready class alignments, Indira Gandhi's political infrastructure continues to be based on the support of the upper peasantry and the bulk of the urban bourgeoisie. These classes, in their turn, have made use of her populist image to swing in their favour a sizeable segment of the electorate. Her strategy of leaning on radical slogans succeeded in offering opiates to large groups on rural masses, industrial workers and the urban middle class; at the same time her pragmatism ensured that the gravy continued to flow to the kulaks and the urban industrialists.[7]

An alternative explanation holds that the Prime Minister and her government appear so powerless to cure India's difficulties because they have an inadequate understanding of the situation and of the policies to deal with it effectively. In an interview in 1973, Mrs. Gandhi said of economic policy, "We do need an entirely new approach. . . . I have been saying that we need a *financial wizard* [emphasis added] who could get us out of this rut and onto an entirely different system."[8] Her remark may seem to reflect intellectual flexibility, but in the subsequent 18 months she neither appointed any dynamic personalities to positions of authority nor initiated any radical policy changes. Moreover, that a *deus ex machina* or a financial wizard should determine economic policy, that such an agent could substitute for political will and leadership, are really distressing notions when expressed by the Prime Minister. It is all the more remarkable that, despite the many reversals which India's economy has sustained since 1969, Mrs. Gandhi's "image remains untarnished. Her popularity is so great that the have-nots regard her as their only benefactor."[9] If, as suggested by this judgment, Indira Gandhi can continue in office despite the failings of her administration, and if she proves unable to initiate a new approach, then India's near-term prospects are not sanguine.

India and the World Community

Partisans of the Prime Minister and her government see the situation in a different light. They regard India's problems as so formidable as to have been beyond solution during the past several years. Consequently, they are less critical of the content and implementation of policy. For instance, Mrs. Gandhi and her colleagues are convinced that the positive gains already achieved by

[7]June 16, 1973, p. 1057.
[8]*Socialist India,* op. cit., p. 29.
[9]*Overseas Hindustan Times,* Sept. 6, 1973.

bank nationalization outweigh the problems, and they are optimistic that the financial community will abet growth and equity in the future. To take another example, although India has made only limited progress to date in the area of family planning, officials defend past policy. They note that there has been a large increase in funds appropriated for reducing fertility and also that Mrs. Gandhi has given unprecedented attention to this issue by discussing it in her 1974 Independence Day speech and by writing about it to every *sarpanch* (village headman) in India.

In addition to arguments like these, based on good intentions and the intractability of India's problems, the New Left in the West and many Indians are agreed that the source of India's difficulties is the behavior of the well-to-do nations. More than 25 years after Independence it is still common for Indian speakers to reflect on how pre-1947 policies affect India's current situation. In 1973, for example, Mrs. Gandhi said:

> Problems of hunger and nutrition, economic development and education are a consequence of the long period spent under subjection. Any kind of mercantile, industrial, and intellectual enterprise which was inconvenient to the colonial rulers was discouraged and the evolution from within our traditional societies was perforce inhibited.[10]

Blame for India's current problems is placed not merely on the lingering effect of the West's pre-Independence policies, but even more on what Indians regard as the evils of "dependence" and "neocolonialism".[11] In a variety of trade, investment, and financial relationships India regards itself as the object of unfair Western policies. Moreover, many Indians believe that foreign aid and other programs designed to compensate for the handicaps developing countries face in the international economy are grossly inadequate and, to the extent that these programs also embody political goals, unfair.

However justified the views regarding the malign effects of colonialism and neocolonialism, Indian economic progress has clearly been much hampered by various world developments. Changing technology, for example, by reducing world demand for India's raw material exports and making the international terms of trade less favorable to India, has undermined India's foreign exchange position and had a profoundly negative effect on its development. In addition, setbacks to Indian development have arisen in the Third World itself. To leave aside for the moment the controversy over whether the wars with Pakistan were a result of the conflict among the Great Powers or merely a by-product, India's war with China, the need to promote South Asian stability by shoring up

[10]See text of Indira Gandhi's address to the One-Asia Assembly, Indian Embassy, Washington, D.C., Press Release No. 621, Jan. 7, 1973.

[11]On the subject of how the international monetary system discriminates against developing countries, see, for example, my article, "Development and the International Monetary System," op. cit.

Bangladesh, and the steep escalation of international oil prices, all had their origins in the Third World.

Regardless of whether one places primary responsibility for India's economic situation on domestic demons or foreign devils, there can be no question that the burden of slow growth is principally borne by its own people. But the leitmotiv of our age has been our awareness of how the world order has been reshaped and interlinked by rising economic wealth, technological advances in communications, the increasing ability of distant peoples to change the course of one another's lives, and the growing importance of transnational relations. How applicable is this admittedly rather grandiose formulation of international affairs when it is superimposed on India's foreign relations? Have geographically remote countries been adversely affected by India's slow development? Is development significant, not merely for India's strength, but also because it influences the political, economic, and ethical interests of foreigners?

To begin with political factors, obviously the pace and sectoral composition of development are determinants of India's international power and prestige. But political power is heterogenous and so, outward appearances aside, there is no incongruity between the Indian army's inability to press forward during the 1965 war with Pakistan for lack of petrol and India's detonation of a nuclear device beneath the Rajasthan desert in 1974. Similarly, India's diminished but still active position of leadership within the Third World is compatible with India's inability to enforce its will in international issues, including those which involve other developing nations. Clearly, if its development were proceeding at a faster pace, India would have the military and political power to act more decisively in regional affairs, even in the style of what Samuel Huntington calls a "local leviathan."[12] It would also make Indian attitudes on international issues of greater significance to the world community. Unlike population, where large size and fast growth are apt to be as much a liability as an asset, high per capita income in combination with large size is almost invariably a positive factor in determining a country's political strength.[13]

Rapid economic development would directly benefit India's international position by creating economic surpluses that could be diverted from domestic consumption to foreign policy goals. By strengthening the domestic political situation, it would also further increase the credibility of India's international policies and reduce the need for India to commit domestic resources in order to have its way internationally. This is significant because in the past, major

[12]Samuel P. Huntington, "The Role of Foreign Assistance," *National War College Forum,* Summer 1973. Whether more forceful behavior in South Asia would be desirable from a non-Indian point of view is debatable in view of India's already heavy involvement with its neighbor states, but this is a question beyond the scope of this book.

[13]See my essay, "India's Population and International Affairs," in Marcus F. Franda, ed., *Responses to Population Growth in India* (New York: Praeger Publishers, 1975).

domestic problems have weakened India's position in international affairs by absorbing the leadership's energies and by making its tenure less secure. Although India's problematic development experience cannot be isolated as the critical factor driving the nation either to international cooperation or to confrontation (for example, it is unlikely that it was a determinant of India's decision to go nuclear), the pace of its development and its preparedness to make constructive contributions to the world order are positively related.

International migration is an intriguing example of how domestic social issues can spill over and cause difficulties in the arena of foreign affairs. The future rate of Indian emigration will be affected by domestic conditions and the willingness of other countries to issue visas. But, while population growth fuels the pressure for Indians to emigrate, host nations do consider the demographic and economic characteristics of the countries from which they receive migrants, and the specter of rampant poverty and population numbers in countries like India is bound to deter them from adopting liberal immigration policies. When most of the Asians holding British passports were expelled from Uganda in 1972 by Idi Amin, the repercussions extended far beyond the lives of the migrants. How a frustrated competition for scarce resources within India may some day lead to domestic turbulence and cause problems abroad is unclear, but in an age when international terrorism and confrontation between have and have-not nations are all too common, both its probabilty and the potential costs are too high to be treated with indifference.[14]

As for the future, the scope of expanding various kinds of foreign economic relationships with India is far broader than their current limited scale suggests. There is great potential for India to accelerate its economic growth by increasing its foreign trade and allowing more foreign investment. Conversely, a stepped-up growth rate not only would make more efficient and fuller use of Indian resources, but also would make India a more dynamic trading partner. In short, there is no doubt that by combining foreign capital with Indian labor, and through other economic ties, Indian and foreign welfare can be promoted simultaneously.

Some Westerners would argue that the expanded trade and investment relationships suggested above are naïve and would not be in the West's interest. Their concern that jobs would be "exported" is largely misplaced, however, because India's need for imports is much greater than its current international purchasing power. Increased buying from India would almost certainly be followed by equally large sales to India, thus creating jobs to offset those lost by larger Western imports of Indian goods. Granted, this would require a redeployment of the West's labor force, which would hurt some sectors while

[14]See, for example, Hedley Bull, "Violence and Development," in Robert E. Hunter and John E. Rielly, eds., *Development Today: A New Look at U.S. Relations with the Poor Countries* (New York: Praeger Publishers in cooperation with the Overseas Development Council, 1972).

benefiting others, but in the long term, it would enable Westerners and Indians alike to achieve higher living standards with equal or less human effort.

The argument is sometimes made that it is not in the West's interest for India to develop because the world's natural resource and ecological tolerances are already strained. This argument is selfish to the point that most of its authors feel obliged to cloak it in moral terms. It is also faulty because it naively assumes that current international disparities and Indian poverty can be perpetuated indefinitely and that the dynamics of development will never bring about a better balance between India's population size and its gross national product. The real environmental question is one of timing, whether the joint process of improving the welfare of Indians and reducing population growth will be fast or slow. And, in light of the evidence that economic progress and lower birthrates go hand in hand, it would appear that rapid Indian economic progress is in everyone's interest.

Although the net amounts of foreign assistance now available to India are small, the economic implications for the West and India of this relationship cannot be slighted. The status of aid has been so clouded by the confusions and common disappointments of the past that it is impossible to forecast whether a faster rate of Indian development would induce donors to increase, hold steady, or reduce the flow of concessional capital to India. In any case, because (1) India has such great need for assistance, (2) the potential usefulness of foreign aid remains large, and (3) donors are inclined to help, a positive net inflow of capital is likely to persist for some time to come.

Use of the work "interdependence" implies that even if relationships are asymmetrical, dependence is a two-way street and that to some degree the United States economy and others depend on India. There is no commodity, like petroleum, for which India is positioned to disrupt world markets; but acting with other countries, India does have some marginal amount of "commodity power" in iron ore, tropical products, and other areas. Of greater significance, however, is India's capacity to support or to undercut such Bretton Woods institutions as the GATT, IBRD, and IMF. The significance of Indian development to the management of systemic international economic relationships is highlighted by the range of Indian positions on various issues. In 1972, for example, in a dramatic appearance in Stockholm at the United Nations Conference on the Human Environment, Mrs. Gandhi took the position that world pollution stemmed more from profligate resource use by the West than from excessive population growth in India and other developing countries. Moreover, she implied that India would not accord high priority to demographic and environmental objectives unless the have nations made a greater effort to eradicate world poverty through a more egalitarian sharing of international production.[15] For reasons not fully explained, when India's Health and Family Planning Minister Karan Singh addressed the United Nations World

---

[15]Mrs. Gandhi's speech is reproduced in *Socialist India,* June 24, 1972.

Population Conference at Bucharest in 1974, he was no less adamant about the need for a more equitable international distribution of incomes, but he did not threaten that India would predicate its population policies on how the well-to-do nations responded to other Indian positions.[16]

All too often in matters of public policy, ethical considerations are either given short shrift or are embellished and used to cloak baser motives. Be that as it may, and despite the wide diversity of views, ethics is still a major considera-tion in Indian development. Western attitudes toward the developing countries have been conceived in many dissimilar forms, including the "white man's burden," foreign aid, and leaving developing countries alone to preserve their "cultural authenticity." Yet there is a common strand running through these conceptions—a morally inspired and geographically unbounded concern for improving the human condition. To move from such a concern to action, however, poses a problem for those inspired by moral issues. In the real world of priorities and imperfections, pursuit of one objective may occasion inatten-tion to others, and good intentions do not always lead to the intended good results. For many generations, India has been a focus of international humani-tarian concern because of its size and poverty. This is not to deny that some foreigners have been alienated by (1) the prospect of close relations with any nations having such staggering problems as India, (2) the slow pace at which Indian conditions have been improved, and (3) the amorality—or immorality, depending on one's point of view—of income disparities and other forms of social injustice in India. (Here, too, by expanding the potential for, and the sensitivity and response to, international relationships, modern communica-tions and technological innovations have had humanitarian as well as economic and political impacts.)

Collectively, these political, economic, and moral factors are a more than sufficient reason to explain why the international community has been, and continues to be, so deeply concerned with Indian development. In addition, the prospect is that India will have some influence on a wide range of issues, including international peace-keeping, arms proliferation, population control, the international trade and payments system, and seabed management. These particular issues are reason enough for the United States and other Western countries to concern themselves with India's economic progress. They are pale, however, in comparison with the benefit to the West if its most cherished goals—human material welfare and democracy—can be successfully pro-moted.

Implications for American Policy

Putting India's development into proper perspective for United States policy is no easier than specifying how the potential American contribution to India's

[16]Government of India, Department of Family Planning, New Delhi, 1974.

progress should be weighed in Indian policy. Just as foreign aid (broadly conceived) is but one of many factors affecting India's domestic developmental and foreign policies, the specific issue of how the United States might abet India's development is but one aspect of bilateral relations, as well as of America's attitude toward developing countries at large. The nature of the relationship between these narrow and broad policy issues is subject to great controversy, and I do not propose to undertake any comprehensive explication of United States foreign policy. To supplement the policy implications which appear throughout the book, what I shall do here, in a manner appropriate for an American writing about Indian development, is to draw on the body of this book (especially Chapters 3 to 6) to see how Indian development fits into the framework of American foreign policy. Just as issues, events, and personalities all can, and do, change rapidly, policy prescriptions can become obsolescent alarmingly fast. Accordingly, I shall treat this subject at a general level.

Many observers believe that, viewed in the global context of United States foreign policy, India is not central to the United States on political, security, or economic grounds. Indian development not only is remote from United States interests, but is an area where, despite our costly commitments of money and manpower, we have fallen well short of our objectives. Senator Fulbright, for example, has said that Indians "would have been better served if we had let them alone and forced them to face up to their own plotical and economic problems."[17] Clearly, the mood of the 1970s is quite unlike that of the 1950s and 1960s. For those Americans who believe that we should not involve ourselves deeply in India, limiting our activities to symbolic gestures of good will and skillful diplomacy to play down areas of disagreement, the Soviet-American detente and our growing recognition of pressing economic and political problems at home are significant additional reasons for holding aloof.

A subconscious, and sometimes conscious, element influencing those who would minimize United States attention to the subcontinent's development is the frustrating course which Indo-American relations have followed since 1947. Owing to a variety of misperceptions and misguided policies in both India and the United States, responsible officials have all too rarely been able to suppress conflicts and emphasize common views. And, even though the major Indo-American disagreements have centered on issues of international politics, differences on economic matters have also been frequent. In practice, there has been no practical way to dissociate either nation's political policy from its foreign economic policy.[18] The point here is that although it is almost inconceivable in the next decade for the United States and India to become either close allies or be at war, if they continue to adopt international political positions as

[17]U.S. Congress, *Congressional Record Senate*, Feb. 7, 1974, p. 15422.

[18]For an analysis of the material and psychological reasons why Indo-American relations have typically been strained, see Barnds, "India and America at Odds," op. cit.

incompatible as those of the past, the scope for mutually beneficial economic relations is bound to be commensurately limited.

Assuming that the United States does wish to assist Indian development, it can adopt policies for (1) transferring material and other resources to India through bilateral and multinational channels and (2) helping India to devote a greater share of its own domestic resources to development. The second path includes such diverse elements as American restraint in arming Pakistan (which would permit India to curb its military spending) and American leverage to induce India to adopt policies which accelerate development. If the past is any guide to the future, it appears unlikely that any of these elements of policy will be operative in any substantial way, and so it is sensible to discuss only the first path, namely, resource transfer.

In the past, international trade has made only a limited contribution to development because of Indian as well as American policies. As the potentialities of world trade have gradually been recognized, however, India has animated its export promotion policies and America, along with the OECD countries, has reduced its tariff and nontariff barriers to imports. India should gain from the new scheme of generalized preferences included in the 1974 Trade Act but will have to share these benefits with other developing countries. Indeed, because American barriers to developing country exports are generally not large, and because the United States will probably continue to adhere to the most-favored-nation principle, it is unlikely that India will get much help through changes in conventional trade policy. The critical question here is whether the United States will adopt a cooperative attitude toward commodity agreements (pricing, buffer stocks, financing, and so forth). If it were to do so, this could emerge as the single most important American policy for assisting India and other developing countries. However, to say that the potential benefits of the generalized preferences schemes now operating and proposed are limited, is not to downgrade the existing opportunities for India to increase its exports, or to belittle the significance of exporting to its domestic development.

In many ways the most efficient vehicle for transferring resources for development is private equity investment. That notwithstanding, India's confirmed skepticism about private entrepreneurs and foreigners is not likely to be overcome, and the prospect for more foreign equity capital in India is almost certain to remain bleak. In these circumstances, United States policies to assure the public accountability of companies with international operations will be welcome; but, aside from information about investment in India, insurance against expropriation, and similar programs now in operation, there is little that American policy can do. Even a United States tax credit for American companies investing in developing countries will be irrelevant so long as India discourages foreign equity capital. If Indian policy should change, however, the possibility for the United States government to play a role would be vastly enhanced and, through administrative as much as legislative action, the amount and variety of American investment in India could be increased at what I suspect would be an astounding rate.

The opportunities for transferring financial resources to India through transactions involving private portfolio capital are real and, this far, almost unexplored. India must, perforce, restrict supplier credits and other international borrowing, but the limit on its use of foreign capital is set mainly by its capacity to service debt. Thus, if the United States, through direct subsidy, tax credit, or other means were to decrease the cost of United States private capital, India would command increased resources for development. If American congressional sentiment toward foreign assistance remains as prevailingly negative as in recent years, the prospect for this kind of policy will be slim. But, if there is a rebirth of interest in international development, the inevitable search for new ways to get the job done and the traditional United States preference for the private sector suggest that such a policy might prove to be a viable alternative to the bureaucrat-oriented, government-to-government capital transfers of the past.

Although the reputation of conventional foreign assistance has been so corroded that some observers are now convinced that the base material is not genuine sterling, the vast majority of Indians and Americans—this writer included—continue to believe that, even if the metal is debased, it is a valuable policy instrument, especially when used in conjunction with other development measures. The Indo-American aid relationship was seriously injured by the events of 1971, but it was not totally destroyed, as is sometimes believed. Moreover, its eventual resuscitation is a near certainty, first, because India is bound to have mammoth emergency and longer-run economic problems and, second, because the United States can help India with technical assistance, commodity aid (especially food), and capital loans and grants. It is largely the yawning gap between what is economically desirable between India and America and what is politically possible between Delhi and Washington that complicates the task of predicting the timing for, and the format of, a new bilateral aid relationship.

The question of how a new relationship can be structured so as to be less irritating to both sides leads directly to the issue of style. There is probably no way in the foreseeable future whereby the United States or India will feel comfortable with what the other regards as its rightful place in international affairs. Recognition of this handicap, therefore, is a first step toward the greater sensitivity and tolerance needed on both sides to mobilize greater American support for Indian development. More candor on the part of Indian and American officials, both in relations with each other and in domestic political discussions, would also prove helpful as it would reduce misunderstandings and avoid disappointments. The successful negotiation for a settlement of the "excess rupee problem" is an outstanding example of how sensitivity and candor can overcome problems which otherwise would be very troublesome.

Similarly, it is to be hoped that the overly close identification of American economists with India's macro- and microeconomic policies in the 1960s will not be repeated. United States officials cannot evade their responsibility to assure taxpayers that foreign aid is used to hasten growth and social justice, but our experience is that outsiders have only a marginal capacity to promote these objectives when they are not shared by the aid recipient governments. Just as militant behavior on India's part (commodity cartels, nuclear blackmail, and so forth) would be a disservice to the world community and ineffective as an economic instrument, so overbearing United States postures on how India and other developing countries should manage their economies would heighten international tensions and probably fail. In short, our experiences should have convinced us by now that it is better to have no foreign aid program in India than to put money into what we regard as unjustifiable channels or to accompany our flow of funds with a flow of unwanted advice.

It has often been suggested that by framing Indo-American economic relations in a multilateral context, policy makers would improve them. This approach would seem to deemphasize Indian economic dependence, highlight areas of common concern, and insulate development policies somewhat from bilateral political conflicts. There is a danger, however, in thinking that multilateral aid will be a panacea for all the ills of bilateral economic arrangements. Public officials and private citizens are not easily hoodwinked by the use of international institutions to accomplish what is unfeasible bilaterally, and there is only limited scope for using the IBRD and other world bodies in ways which legislatures and voters of member countries regard as contrary to their interests. Indeed, the danger posed to the India Consortium by the effort in 1972 to convince American to increase its debt rescheduling for India at a time when its aid program was in limbo, is an example of how, by pressing ahead despite bilateral differences, the World Bank risked involving disinterested countries and endangered its future position.

In the final analysis, the relevance of America's foreign policies is dwarfed by the preeminence of India's domestic policies. Bilateral and multilateral relationships are by no means insignificant. But, just as there is no conceivable international strategy to speed India's progress if its own economic management and efforts are deficient, so the Chinese experience suggests that although India stands to benefit from outside help, it could more than compensate for the loss of foreign aid by adopting more effective domestic policies. In short, the paradise of developing countries is a world where foreign aid and good domestic policies act as complements rather than substituting for one another.

As the economic policy debate in India continues to rage, timing and luck are not to be discounted as factors bearing on whether in the next years or decades a human tragedy of monumental proportions will take place. The potential for large-scale famine and social unrest has been widely perceived in India and abroad, although even to project the current state of India's duress into the

future would be to make a profoundly gloomy statement. Under these circumstances the forces leading India to seek help abroad and attracting the international community to respond positively are certain to be powerful. For them to
be irresistible, however, it is incumbent upon India to break with the patterns of
the past quarter century. If India can mobilize itself for the task of consistent
and broad-scale economic development, and if foreign countries can recognize
the significance of Indian development to the world community and act accordingly, then what Asoka Mehta refers to as "India's second revolution" will move
much closer to reality in less than a generation.

EPILOGUE

In June 1975, Prime Minister Indira Gandhi declared a state of national emergency, and a new chapter was opened in India's development odyssey. The crisis had its proximate cause in a ruling by the Allahabad High Court. In finding Mrs. Gandhi guilty of a minor election offense, the Court threatened to deprive her of her premiership. This legal challenge to Mrs. Gandhi was even greater than might normally have been the case: it was made in the broader political context of a state of nationwide social decay and economic stagnation which dated from 1970–71.

The measures Mrs. Gandhi took to quash these explicit and implicit threats to her continued rule were authoritarian, so much so that they had the almost immediate impact of halting dissent in India and raising a storm of criticism by liberals outside the country. Civil liberties normally guaranteed by the Indian Constitution were suspended. Thousands of opposition leaders, including some members of Parliament and some dissident members of the ruling Congress party, were jailed. Likewise, many thousands suspected of committing economic crimes were arrested and denied recourse to normal legal process. Strict censorship was imposed, and some journalists were jailed.

Concurrently, the Prime Minister moved to legitimate her position and to arouse popular support for her actions. New legislation to legalize ex post facto the actions for which she had been taken to court was challenged in the Supreme Court and found valid. In addition, in a move which the Court found unconstitutional, Parliament sought to amend the Constitution in such a way as to promote itself above the judicial branch of government. Finally, to attract support from the Indian masses, Mrs. Gandhi laid heavy emphasis on the economic reasons for declaring the emergency: initially, on the potential immediate gains from ending hoarding, black markets, smuggling, and so forth; later, on a 20-point program of reforms designed to decrease social and economic disparities. Characteristically, the announcement of a socialist program was accompanied by unpublicized decisions to permit some private Indian companies to expand their operations.

This cursory review of the 1975 crisis does scant justice to the breadth and complexity of the situation. Such treatment is appropriate, however, insofar as the meaning of these developments will only be fully clear when they can be placed in a historical perspective which includes 1976 and later years. Be that as it may, the events of 1975 cannot be ignored. Moreover, although they occurred several months after the body of this book had been completed, they reflect the pattern of Indian development which I have analyzed, and they raise afresh some of the most haunting questions about India's mode of existence.

Is it true, as some would say, that for the Indian executive and Parliament, economic subjects are subservient to more purely political issues? As a corollary, have successive Indian governments tended to pay so little attention to development—either by choice or owing to the intrusion of problems commanding higher priority—to almost guarantee that economic ills would grow to the point where they would cause political difficulties? By underscoring the relations between democracy, economic efficiency, social justice, and national self-reliance throughout this volume, I have given at least a tentative answer to these questions.

The link between politics and economics can be brought into focus if one imagines India's chief executive officer as both prime minister and chairman of the Planning Commission.

The chief executives, in their political role, have surmounted a host of serious internal and external threats to national integrity, but they have not succeeded very well in bettering the living conditions of India's poor. As the gap between the aspirations of the masses and the promises of government grows larger, the society's stability becomes more tenuous. Thus, one of the choices before India's future chiefs is between devoting a greater share of their energies and the nation's resources to development or precipitating a major change in the sociopolitical system. Because many internal conflicts have been defused and the weakening of Pakistan in 1971 greatly reduced the external threat, it now appears possible for Indian leaders to concentrate on economic issues. It is by no means clear, however, whether they will choose to do so or, if they do, whether they will choose democratic or authoritarian means.

Can India hope to be more successful in the economic sphere without adopting a different, more authoritarian political system? The conflicts between democracy and development, and between diversity and central control, are ones that I have approached from many different angles, and their resolution is by no means a matter for a priori reasoning. Aside from what many are too quick to forget—that democracy has value in its own right—there are substantial economic benefits in allowing free expression and encouraging local initiative. But without the discipline which authoritarian government promises to provide, how can the power of local interests inimical to growth with social justice be broken? Or, to approach the issue from another direction, is social justice greater in democracy with stagnation or in authoritarianism with economic growth? My suspicion is that to a degree, these questions are less relevant than they might seem. The kind of social discipline that makes societies progress is not the private preserve of the democrats or the autocrats. In reality, each type of government has its moments in history, and also its time when it is ineffective. If, as seems possible, Mrs. Gandhi senses the political and economic advantages of democracy and eventually acts to return India to more democratic forms, the crisis will not have been entirely fruitless. This is not to excuse Mrs. Gandhi for the poor quality of her prior economic management, which contributed significantly to the crisis, but merely to say that the events of 1975 may be only temporary and that some good may come from them.

In reality, despite a renewed torrent of leftist promises, the economic policies implemented in the months immediately following June 1975 were generally pragmatic. Why did Mrs. Gandhi use, at least temporarily, leftist rhetoric merely as the veneer for a policy which aided private industry and gave freer reign to market forces? Is it possible that the Prime Minister suddenly recognized that some actions taken in the name of social justice actually could have the effect of reducing welfare for all? Or, as appears more likely from the historical record, was the swing away from socialist and ideological policies already underway at that time? The cyclical patterns which roughly describe the evolution of India's economy and its economic policy making may not fit into a fully logical explanation of how societies operate, but such patterns exist and cannot be ignored. If these policies are extrapolated, the short-term outlook for India—both in terms of policy and actual economic development—is favorable. It would be a heroic act of faith, however, to predict that the progress will be sustained for many years.

The authoritarian policies of 1975 must also be judged in operational terms. Were they justified by the de facto abridgement of social justice inherent in the indiscipline and the inequities of the preceding period? Will the "emergency" measures improve the Indian economy beyond what bountiful rains will provide, or are they merely an instrument for keeping Mrs. Gandhi in power? Indeed, for the great majority of Indian people, is the new situation fundamentally different from earlier periods when democracy was as much a shadow as a reality?

There are no simple answers. It is my suspicion that the events of 1975 were an aberration. In the post-Independence period, the economic and political fabric of India had never been so strained, and 1975 was the inevitable climax of a social cycle which typically had moved with dizzying rapidity between the extremes of progress and retrogression. Strong and varied forces are still at work in India today. These include a genuine dedication to constitutional democracy, the power of local elites, and a spirit of compromise. In concert, these forces are likely to prevail over press censorship and other temporary authoritarian measures and, thereby, to redirect India's political life into more familiar channels. Together, they may sometimes impede growth or social justice. But, in the long run, they may prevent India from entering deeper into a vicious circle of authoritarianism. In short, India's future welfare may depend on a middle course which avoids stagnation or radicalism by combining the traditional and the modern in order to sustain a development revolution.

SELECTED BIBLIOGRAPHY

I. Books and Monographs

Adelman, Irma, and Cynthia T. Morris. *Economic Growth and Social Equity in Developing Countries* (Stanford, Calif.: Stanford University Press, 1973).

Appleby, Paul. *Public Administration in India: Report of a Survey* (New Delhi: Government of India, Cabinet Secretariat, 1953).

Apter, David E. *The Politics of Modernization* (Chicago: University of Chicago Press, 1965).

Bagchi, Amiya K. *Private Investment in India, 1900–1939* (London: Cambridge South Asian Studies 10, 1972).

Bailey, F. G. *Politics and Social Change: Orissa in 1959* (Berkeley: University of California Press, 1963).

Balasubramanyam, V. N. *International Transfer of Technology to India* (New York: Praeger Publishers, 1973).

Baldwin, David A. *Economic Development and American Foreign Policy: 1943–62* (Chicago: University of Chicago Press, 1966).

Barnds, William J. *India, Pakistan, and the Great Powers* (New York: Praeger Books for the Council on Foreign Relations, 1972).

————. "The South Asian Regional System," chapter in James Rosenau et al., eds., *World Politics* (forthcoming).

————. "Soviet Influence in India: A Search for the Spoils That Go 'with Victory,'" chapter in *Soviet and Chinese Influence in the Third World* (New York: Praeger Publishers, 1975).

Bauer, P. T. *Dissent on Development: Studies and Debates in Development Economics* (London: George Weidenfeld & Nicolson, Ltd., 1971).

————. *Indian Economic Policy and Development* (New York: Praeger Books, 1961).

Benoit, Emile. *Defense and Economic Growth in Developing Countries* (Lexington, Mass.: D. C. Heath and Co., 1973).

Berliner, Joseph S. *Soviet Economic Aid* (New York: Praeger Books for the Council on Foreign Relations, 1958).

Bhagwati, Jagdish N. *Economics of Underdeveloped Countries* (New York: McGraw-Hill, 1966).

———. "The Theory and Practice of Commercial Policy: Departures from Unified Exchange Rates," Special Paper in International Finance No. 8, Princeton University, International Finance Section, January 1968.

——— and Padma Desai. *India: Planning for Industrialization and Trade Policies since 1951* (London and New York: Oxford University Press, for the OECD, 1970).

Bhatia, Krishan. *Indira: A Biography of Prime Minister Gandhi* (New York: Praeger Books, 1974).

———. *The Ordeal of Nationhood* (New York: Atheneum, 1971).

Bhatt, V. V. *Two Decades of Development: The Indian Experiment* (Bombay: Vora, 1973).

Blyn, George. *Agricultural Trends in India, 1891–1947: Output, Availability, and Productivity* (Philadelphia: University of Pennsylvania Press, 1966).

Bowles, Chester. *Ambassador's Report* (New York: Harper and Brothers, 1954).

Braibanti, Ralph, and Joseph J. Spengler, eds. *Administration and Economic Development in India* (Durham, N.C.: Duke University Press, 1963).

——— and———. *Tradition, Values, and Socio-Economic Development* (Durham, N.C.: Duke University Press, 1965).

Brass, Paul. "Political Parties of the Radical Left in South Asian Politics," chapter in Paul R. Brass and Marcus F. Franda, eds., *Radical Politics in South Asia* (Cambridge, Mass.: MIT Press, 1973).

Brecher, Michael. *Nehru: A Political Biography,* abridged ed. (Boston: Beacon Press, 1962).

Brown, W. Norman. *The United States and India, Pakistan, Bangladesh* (Cambridge, Mass.: Harvard University Press, 1973).

Carras, Mary C. *The Dynamics of Indian Political Factions: A Study of District Councils in the State of Maharashtra* (Cambridge: Cambridge University Press, 1972).

Carter, James Richard. *The Net Cost of Soviet Foreign Aid* (New York: Praeger Special Studies in International Economics and Development, 1969).

Chandrasekar, Sripati. *American Aid to Indian Economic Development, 1951–1963* (New York: Praeger Books, 1965).

Coale, Ansley J., and Edgar M. Hoover. *Population Growth and Economic Development in Low Income Countries: A Case Study of India's Prospects* (Princeton, N.J.: Princeton University Press, 1958).

Dagli, Vadilal, ed. *Twenty-five Years of Independence: A Survey of Indian Economy* (Bombay: Vora, 1973).

Dantwala, M. L. "Preface to Volume of Background Papers," in *International Seminar on Comparative Experience of Agricultural Development in Developing Countries since World War II,* The Indian Society of Agricultural Economics, 1972.

Datar, Asha L. *India's Economic Relations with the U.S.S.R. and Eastern Europe, 1953 to 1969* (Cambridge: Cambridge University Press, 1972).

Davis, Kingsley. *The Population of India and Pakistan* (Princeton, N.J.: Princeton University Press, 1951).

Dean, Vera Michael. *New Patterns of Democracy in India* (Cambridge, Mass.: Harvard University Press, 1969).

Desai, A. R., ed. *Essays on Modernization of Underdeveloped Countries,* 2 vols. (New York: Humanities Press, 1972).

Desai, Padma. *The Bokaro Steel Plant: A Study of Soviet Economic Assistance* (London and Amsterdam: North-Holland Publishing Co., 1972).

———. *Import Substitution in the Indian Economy, 1951–1963* (New Delhi: Hindustan Press, 1972).

Deshmukh, C. D. *Economic Development in India, 1945–1956: A Personal Retrospect* (Bombay: Asia Publishing House, 1957).

Eldridge, P. J. *The Politics of Foreign Aid in India* (New York: Schocken Books, 1969).

Epstein, Trude S. *Economic Development and Social Change in South India* (Manchester: Manchester University Press, 1962).

Fisher, Margaret W., and Joan V. Bondurant. *Indian Approaches to a Socialist Society*, Indian Press Digests Monograph Series No. 2, Institute of International Studies, University of California at Berkeley, July 1956.

Ford Foundation. *Data on the Indian Economy: 1951 to 1969* (New Delhi: Ford Foundation, 1970).

Franda, Marcus F. "Militant Hindu Opposition to Family Planning in India," American Universities Field Staff Reports, South Asia Series, vol. 16, no. 11, September 1972.

———. "Policy Response to India's Green Revolution," American Universities Field Staff Reports, South Asia Series, vol. 16, no. 9, 1972.

———. "Population Politics in South Asia: Population Pressures and the Beginnings of Bangladesh," American Universities Field Staff Reports, South Asia Series, vol. 16, no. 4, part 3, April 1972.

Frankel, Francine R. *India's Green Revolution: Economic Gains and Political Costs* (Princeton, N.J.: Princeton University Press, 1971).

——— and Karl von Vorys. "The Political Challenge of the Green Revolution: Shifting Patterns of Peasant Participation in India and Pakistan," Policy Memorandum No. 38, Center for International Studies, Woodrow Wilson School of Public and International Affairs, Princeton University, 1972.

Frykenberg, Robert E. "Traditional Process of Power in South India: An Historical Analysis of Local Influence," chapter in Reinhard Bendix, ed., *State and Society* (Berkeley: University of California Press, 1968).

———, ed. *Land Control and Social Structure in Indian History* (Madison: University of Wisconsin Press, 1969).

Gadgil, D. R. *Planning and Economic Policy in India* (New York: Asia Publishing House; and Poona: The Gokhale Institute of Politics and Economics, 1961).

Ghose, Sankar. *Socialism and Communism in India* (Bombay: Allied Publishers, 1971).

Goldman, Marshall I. *Soviet Foreign Aid* (New York: Praeger Publishers, 1967).

Hanson, A. H. *The Process of Planning: A Study of India's Five-Year Plans, 1950–1964* (London: Oxford University Press, 1966).

——— and Janet Douglas. *India's Democracy* (New York: W. W. Norton, 1972).

Haq, Mahbub ul. *The Strategy of Economic Planning* (Karachi: Oxford University Press, 1966).

———. "Tied Credits: A Quantitative Analysis," paper in *Capital Movements and Economic Development: Proceedings of a Conference Held by the International Economic Association*, John H. Adler and Paul W. Kuznets, eds. (New York: St. Martin's Press, 1967).

Hardgrave, Robert L., Jr. *India: Government and Politics in a Developing Nation* (New York: Harcourt, Brace & World, 1970).

Harrison, Selig S. *India: The Most Dangerous Decades* (Princeton, N.J.: Princeton University Press, 1960).

Hazari, R. K., et al. "Public International Development Financing in India," Report No. 9, Public International Development Financing Research Project, Columbia University School of Law, New York, July 1964.

Heginbotham, Stanley J. *Cultures in Conflict: The Four Faces of Indian Bureaucracy* (New York: Columbia University Press, 1975).

Hirschman, Albert O. *The Strategy of Economic Development* (New Haven, Conn.: Yale University Press, 1958).

Honovar, R. M. "Industrial Efficiency and Aid-Tying," mimeographed, (Washington, D.C.: World Bank Economic Development Institute, 1967).

Huntington, Samuel P. *Political Order and Changing Societies* (New Haven, Conn.: Yale University Press, 1968).

Independence and After: A Collection of Speeches by Jawaharlal Nehru, 1946–1949 (New York: The John Day Co., 1950).

Jannuzi, F. Tomasson. *Agrarian Crisis in India: The Case of Bihar* (Austin: University of Texas Press, 1974).

Joshi, P. C. "Community Development Programme: A Reappraisal," originally published in *Enquiry*, no. 3, 1960; reprinted as a chapter in A. M. Khusro, ed., *Readings in Agricultural Development* (Bombay: Allied Publishers, 1968).

Jukes, Geoffrey. *The Soviet Union in Asia* (Berkeley: University of California Press, 1973).

Kahin, George McT. *The Asian-African Conference: Bandung, Indonesia, 1955* (Ithaca, N.Y.: Cornell University Press, 1956).

Kapoor, Ashok. *International Business Negotiations: A Study of India* (New York: New York University Press, 1970).

Kapp, H. W. *Hindu Culture, Economic Development, and Economic Planning in India* (Bombay: Asia Publishing Co., 1963).

Kautsky, John. *Moscow and the Communist Party in India* (Cambridge, Mass.: MIT Press, 1956).

――――. *The Political Consequences of Modernization* (New York: John Wiley & Sons, Inc., 1972).

Kharve, D. D. *The New Brahmans* (Berkeley: University of California Press, 1963).

Khusro, A. M. "Economic Theory and Indian Agricultural Policy," chapter in A. M. Khusro, ed., *Readings in Agricultural Development* (Bombay: Allied Publishers, 1968).

Kidron, Michael. *Foreign Investments in India* (London: Oxford University Press, 1965).

Knight, Sir Henry. *Food Administration in India: 1939–1947* (Stanford, Calif.: Stanford University Press, 1954).

Kochanek, Stanley A. *Business and Politics in India* (Los Angeles and Berkeley: University of California Press, 1974).

――――. *The Congress Party of India: The Dynamics of One-Party Democracy* (Princeton, N.J.: Princeton University Press, 1968).

Kothari, Rajni. *Politics in India* (New Delhi: Orient Longmans, Ltd., 1970).

Krishna, Raj. "Unemployment in India," Presidential Address to the Indian Society of Agricultural Economics, 1972; reprinted by the Agricultural Development Council, New York, 1972.

Krueger, Anne O. "The Benefits and Costs of Import Substitution in India: A Microeconomic Study," IBRD monograph, Washington D.C., 1970.

Lal, Deepak. "The Costs of Aid Tying: A Study of India's Chemical Industry," UNCTAD Secretariat, Geneva, 1968.

Lamb, Beatrice. *India: A World in Transition*, 3d ed. (New York: Praeger, 1968).

Lambert, Richard D. *Workers, Factories, and Social Change in India* (Princeton, N.J.: Princeton University Press, 1963).

Lee, Douglas H. K. *Climate and Economic Development in the Tropics* (New York: Harper, for the Council on Foreign Relations, 1957).

Lele, Uma J. *Food Grain Marketing in India: Private Performance and Public Policy* (Ithaca, N.Y.: Cornell University Press, 1971).

Lewis, John P. *Quiet Crisis in India: Economic Development and American Policy* (Washington, D.C.: The Brookings Institution, 1962).

――――. "Wanted in India: A Relevant Radicalism," Policy Memorandum No. 36, Center for International Studies, Woodrow Wilson School of Public and International Affairs, Princeton University, 1969.

―――― and Ishan Kapur, eds. *The World Bank Group, Multilateral Aid, and the 1970s* (Lexington, Mass.: D. C. Heath and Co., 1973).

Lynch, Owen M. *The Politics of Untouchability: Social Mobility and Social Change in a City of India* (New York: Columbia University Press, 1969).

McLane, Charles B. *Soviet-Asian Relations* (New York: Central Asian Research Center and Columbia University Press, 1974).

Maddison, Angus. *Class Structure and Economic Growth: India and Pakistan since the Moghuls* (New York: W. W. Norton, 1971).

——. *Economic Progress and Policy in Developing Countries* (New York: W. W. Norton, 1970).

Mahalanobis, P. C. *Talks on Planning* (New York: Asia Publishing House; and Calcutta: The Indian Statistical Institute, 1961).

Malaviya, H. D. *Land Reforms in India* (New Delhi: AICC, Indian National Congress, 1955).

Malenbaum, Wilfrid. *East and West in India's Development* (Washington, D.C.: National Planning Association, 1959).

——. *Modern India's Economy* (Columbus, Ohio: Charles E Merrill Co., 1971).

——. *Prospects for Indian Development* (New York: The Free Press of Glencoe, 1962).

Mandelbaum, David G. *Human Fertility in India* (Berkeley: University of California Press, 1974).

——. *Society in India* (Berkeley: University of California Press, 1970).

Manne, Alan S. *Investments for Capacity Expansion: Size, Location, and Time-Phasing* (London: George Allen & Unwin, 1967).

Mason, Edward S. "Economic Development in India and Pakistan," Occasional Paper in International Affairs No. 13, Center for International Affairs, Harvard University, September 1966.

—— and Robert E. Asher. *The World Bank since Bretton Woods* (Washington, D.C.: The Brookings Institution, 1973).

Mehta, Asoka. *Economic Planning in India* (New Delhi: Young India Publications, 1970).

Mellor, John W., et al. *Developing Rural India: Plan and Practice* (Ithaca, N.Y.: Cornell University Press, 1968).

Menefee, Selden. *The Pais of Manipal* (Bombay: Asia Publishing House, 1969).

Menon, V. P. *The Transfer of Power* (Princeton, N.J.: Princeton University Press, 1957).

Minhas, B. S. "Rural Poverty, Land Redistribution, and Development Strategy," paper presented at the Seminar on Employment and Income Distribution, New Delhi, 1970.

Monteiro, John B. *Corruption · Control of Maladministration* (Bombay: Manaktalas, 1966).

Moraes, Frank. *Witness to an Era: India, 1920 to the Present Day* (New York: Holt, Rinehart and Winston, 1973).

Morris-Jones, W. H. *The Government and Politics of India* (New York: Anchor Books by arrangement with Hutchinson & Co., London, 1967).

Myrdal, Gunnar. *Asian Drama: An Inquiry into the Poverty of Nations*, 3 vols. (New York: Pantheon Books, 1968).

Nanda, B. R., ed. *Socialism in India* (New Delhi: Vikas Publications, 1972).

Narain, Dharm. *Impact of Price Movements on Areas under Selected Crops in India* (Cambridge: Cambridge University Press, 1965).

Nayar, Baldev Raj. *The Modernization Imperative and Indian Planning* (New Delhi: Vikas Publications, 1972).

Neale, Walter C. *Economic Change in Rural India* (New Haven, Conn.: Yale University Press, 1962).

——. *India: The Search for Unity, Democracy, and Progress* (New York: Van Nostrand Co., Inc., 1965).

Nehru, Jawaharlal. *The Discovery of India* (New York: The John Day Co., 1946).

Nicolson, Norman K. "The Indian Council of Ministers: An Analysis of Legislative and Organizational Careers," paper presented at the 25th Annual Meeting of the Association for Asian Studies, Chicago, April 1973.

Norman, Dorothy, ed. *Nehru: The First Sixty Years,* 2 vols. (New York: The John Day Co., 1965).

Paddock, Paul, and William Paddock. *Famine—1975!* (London: George Weidenfeld & Nicolson, Ltd., 1968).

Palmer, Norman D. *The Indian Political Process* (Boston: Houghton Mifflin, 1961).

———. *South Asia and United States Policy* (Boston: Houghton Mifflin, 1966).

Park, Richard L., and Irene Tinker, eds. *Leadership and Political Institutions in India* (New York: Greenwood Press Publishers, 1969).

Partners in Development: Report of the Commission on International Development (Lester B. Pearson, chairman), (New York: Praeger Books, 1969).

Patel, I. G. "Aid Relationship for the Seventies," chapter in Barbara Ward, ed., *The Widening Gap: Development in the 1970s* (New York: Columbia University Press, 1971).

———. *Foreign Aid* (Bombay: Allied Publishers for the Institute of Public Enterprise, 1968).

Pickett, James, et al. "The Choice of Technology, Economic Efficiency, and Employment in Developing Countries," study by the Overseas Development Unit, University of Strathclyde, Glasgow, 1973.

Population of Less-developed Countries (Paris: OECD Development Center, 1967).

Prasad, Kamita. *Role of Money Supply in a Developing Economy* (Bombay: Allied Publishers, 1969).

Pylee, M. V. *Constitutional Government in India,* 2d rev. ed. (New York: Asia Publishing House, 1965).

Raj, K. N. *Indian Economic Growth: Performance and Prospects* (Bombay: Allied Publishers, 1965).

———. "Some Issues Concerning Investment and Savings in the Indian Economy," paper in E. A. G. Robinson and Michael Kidron, eds., *Economic Development in South Asia: Proceedings of a Conference Held by the International Economic Association at Kandy, Ceylon* (New York: St. Martin's Press, 1970).

Rao, M. S. A. *Tradition, Rationality and Change: Essays in Sociology of Economic Development and Social Change* (Bombay: Popular Prakashan, 1972).

Rao, V. K. R. V., and Dharm Narain. *Foreign Aid and India's Economic Development* (New York: Asia Publishing House, 1963).

Reddaway, W. B. *The Development of the Indian Economy* (Homewood, Ill.: Richard D. Irwin, Inc., 1962).

Reid, Escott. *Strengthening the World Bank* (Chicago: Adlai Stevenson Institute of International Affairs, 1973).

Repetto, Robert C. *Time in India's Development Programme* (Cambridge, Mass.: Harvard University Press, 1971).

Robinson, E. A. G., and Michael Kidron, eds. *Economic Development in South Asia: Proceedings of a Conference Held by the International Economic Association at Kandy, Ceylon* (New York: St Martin's Press, 1970).

Robinson, Warren C., and David E. Horlocher. "Population Growth and Economic Welfare," Population Council Report on Population/Family Planning No. 6, New York, 1971.

Rose, Saul. *Socialism in Southern Asia* (New York: Oxford University Press, 1959).

Rosen, George. *Democracy and Economic Change in India* (Berkeley: University of California Press, 1966).

Rudolph, Lloyd I., and Suzanne H. Rudolph. *The Modernity of Tradition* (Chicago: University of Chicago Press, 1967).

——— and———, eds. *Education and Politics in India: Studies in Organization, Society, and Policy* (Cambridge, Mass.: Harvard University Press, 1973).

Seminar on World Partnership in the Second Development Decade, 3–4 December, 1971 (New Delhi: Indian Investment Centre, 1972).

Sen, Sunanda. *India's Bilateral Payments and Trade Agreements, 1947–48 to 1963–64* (Calcutta: Bookland Private, Ltd., 1965).

———. "The Structure of India's Bilateral Payments Agreements," Economic Essays (Bombay: Asia Publishers, 1965).

Sigmund, Paul E. *The Ideologies of the Developing Nations,* 2d rev. ed. (New York: Praeger Publishers, 1972).

Simmons, George B. "The Indian Investment in Family Planning," Population Council Report, New York, 1971.

Singer, Milton, ed. *Traditional India: Structure and Change* (Philadelphia: American Folklore Society, 1959).

———. *When a Great Tradition Modernizes: An Anthropological Approach to Indian Civilization* (New York: Praeger Publishers, 1972).

Singh, Manmohan. *India's Export Trends* (Oxford: Clarendon Press, 1964).

Singh, Patwant. *India and the Future of Asia* (New York: Alfred A. Knopf, 1966).

Spear, Sir Percival. *The Oxford History of Modern India, 1740–1947,* 2 vols. (New York: Oxford University Press, 1965).

Srinivas, M. N. *Social Change in Modern India* (Berkeley: University of California Press, 1966).

Srinivasan, K. *Productivity and Social Environment* (New York: Asia Publishing House, 1964).

Stein, Arthur. *India and the Soviet Union: The Nehru Era* (Chicago: University of Chicago Press, 1969).

Stern, Robert W. *The Process of Opposition in India* (Chicago: University of Chicago Press, 1973).

Streeten, Paul L. *The Frontiers of Development Studies* (New York: John Wiley & Sons, 1972).

——— and Michael Lipton, eds. *The Crisis of Indian Planning* (London: Oxford University Press, 1968).

Swamy, Subramanian. *Indian Economic Planning: An Alternative Approach* (New Delhi: Vikas Publications, 1971).

Talbot, Phillips, and S. L. Poplai. *India and America: A Study of Their Relations* (New York: Harper and Brothers for the Council on Foreign Relations, 1958).

Tansky, Leo. *U.S. and U.S.S.R. Aid to Developing Countries: A Comparative Study of India, Turkey, and the U.A.R.* (New York: Praeger Publishers, 1967).

Thorner, Daniel. *Agricultural Cooperatives in India: A Field Report* (New York: Asia Publishing House, 1964).

——— and Alice Thorner. *Land and Labor in India* (New York: Asia Publishing House, 1962).

United Nations Conference on Trade and Development (UNCTAD). "Case Study Prepared by the UNCTAD Secretariat on Trade and Economic Relations between India and the Socialist Countries of Eastern Europe," TD/B/129, July 21, 1967.

Uphoff, Norman T., and Warren F. Ilchman, eds. *The Political Economy of Development* (Berkeley: University of California Press, 1972).

Vakil, C. N., and P. R. Brahmananda. *Planning for an Expanding Economy* (Bombay: Vora, 1956).

Vartikar, V. S. *Commercial Policy and Economic Development in India* (New York: Praeger Special Studies in International Economics and Development, 1969).

Ward, Barbara. *India and the West* (New York: W. W. Norton and Co., 1961).

Weiner, Myron. *Party Building in a New Nation* (Chicago: University of Chicago Press, 1967).

———. *Party Politics in India* (Princeton, N.J.: Princeton University Press, 1957).
———. *The Politics of Scarcity* (Chicago: University of Chicago Press, 1962).
Wells, Louis T., Jr. *Economic Man and Engineering Man: Choice of Technology in a Low Wage Country,* Economic Development Report No. 226, Center for International Affairs, Harvard University, November 1972.
Wolf, Charles, Jr. *Foreign Aid: Theory and Practice in Southern Asia* (Princeton, N.J.: Princeton University Press, 1960).
Yearbook of Public Sector (Bombay: Commerce, 1970).
Zinkin, Maurice. *Development for Free Asia* (New York: Oxford University Press, 1963).

II. Government of India Publications

Administrative Reforms Commission. *Interim Report on the Machinery for Planning,* New Delhi, 1967.
———. *Report of the Study Team on Centre-State Relations,* 3 vols., New Delhi, 1968.
———. *Report of the Study Team on Economic Administration* (C. H. Bhaba, chairman), New Delhi, 1967.
———. *Report of the Study Team on Public Sector Undertakings,* New Delhi, 1967.
All-India Congress Committee. *Resolutions on Economic Policy and Programme, 1924–1954,* New Delhi, 1954.
Constituent Assembly (Legislative) Debates, February 17, 1948, New Delhi, 1948.
Economic Survey, New Delhi; annual publication.
Estimates Committee (1966–67). *Industrial Licensing, Ninth Report* (New Delhi: Lok Sabha Secretariat, 1967).
——— (1967–68). *Foreign Exchange, Thirtieth Report* (New Delhi: Lok Sabha Secretariat, 1968).
——— (1971–72). *Industrial Licensing, Nineteenth Report* (New Delhi: Lok Sabha Secretariat, 1972).
——— (1973–74). *Extension of Credit Facilities to Weaker Sections of Society and for Development of Backward Areas, Sixty-second Report* (New Delhi: Lok Sabha Secretariat, 1974).
Explanatory Memorandum on the Budget of the Central Government, New Delhi; annual publication.
Government of Tamil Nadu. *Report of the Centre-State Relations Inquiry Committee* (P. V. Rajamannar, chairman), Madras, 1971.
Indian Statistical Institute. *National Sample Survey, Seventeenth Round,* Report Nos. 140 (1966) and 176 (1967), New Delhi.
Ministry of Agriculture. *Indian Agriculture in Brief,* 13th ed. (New Delhi: Directorate of Economics and Statistics, 1974).
Ministry of Commerce. *Report of the Study Team on Import and Export Control Organization* (H. C. Mathur, chairman), New Delhi, 1965.
Ministry of Finance. *External Assistance,* New Delhi; annual publication.
———. *India: Pocket Book of Economic Information,* New Delhi; annual publication.
———. *Indian Economic Statistics,* New Delhi, August 1973.
———. *Report of the Study Team on Leakage of Foreign Exchange through Invoice Manipulation* (M. G. Kaul, chairman), New Delhi, 1971.
Ministries of Food and Agriculture and of Community Development and Cooperation. *Ford Foundation Report on India's Food Crisis and Steps to Meet It,* New Delhi, 1959.

Ministry of Foreign Trade. *Annual Report,* New Delhi.

Ministry of Home Affairs. *Report of the Committee on Prevention of Corruption* (K. San-thanam, chairman), New Delhi, 1964.

Ministry of Industrial Development, *Report of the Industrial Licensing Inquiry Committee* (S. Dutt, chairman), New Delhi, 1969.

Ministry of Information and Broadcasting. *India,* New Delhi; annual publication.

———. *Social Background of India's Administrators,* New Delhi, 1971.

Ministry of Labour. *Employment Review,* New Delhi, June 1971.

Ministry of Planning. *Monthly Abstract of Statistics* (New Delhi: Central Statistical Organization, Department of Statistics).

Ministry of Steel and Heavy Industries. *Report of the Committee on Steel Control* (K. N. Raj, chairman), New Delhi, 1963.

National Committee on Science and Technology Panel on Futurology. "First Draft of the Base Document on Futurology," mimeographed, New Delhi, 1974.

Planning Commission. *Basic Statistics Relating to the Indian Economy, 1950–51 to 1969–70,* New Delhi, 1971.

———. *The Corporate Private Sector Concentration Ownership and Control* (R. K. Hazari, chairman), New Delhi, 1966.

———. *Draft Fifth Five-Year Plan, 1974–79,* 2 vols., New Delhi, 1974.

———. *Fifth Five-Year Plan,* 2 vols., New Delhi, 1974.

———. *First Five-Year Plan,* New Delhi, 1952.

———. *Fourth Five-Year Plan,* New Delhi, 1969.

———. *Fourth Plan Mid-term Appraisal,* 2 vols., New Delhi, 1971.

———. *Industrial Planning and Licensing Policy, Final Report* (R. K. Hazari, chairman), New Delhi, 1967.

———. *The New India: Progress through Democracy* (New York and London: Macmillan & Co., 1958).

———. *Report of the Committee on Distribution of Income and Levels of Living* (P. C. Mahalanobis, chairman), New Delhi, 1964.

———. *Report of the Task Force on Agrarian Relations,* New Delhi, 1973.

———. *Report of the Team for the Study of Community Projects and National Extension Service,* 3 vols., New Delhi, 1957.

———. *Second Five-Year Plan,* New Delhi, 1956.

———. *Third Five-Year Plan,* New Delhi, 1960.

Report of Expert Group on PL-480 Transactions, New Delhi, 1969.

Report of the Banking Commission, New Delhi, 1972.

Report of the Finance Commission, New Delhi; periodic publication.

Report of the Indian Central Banking Inquiry Committee, Bombay, 1931.

Report of the National Planning Committee (K. T. Shah, ed.), Bombay, 1949.

Reserve Bank of India. *All-India Rural Credit Survey, 1951–52,* Bombay, 1952.

———. *All-India Rural Credit Survey, 1954,* Bombay, 1954.

———. *Bulletin;* monthly publication.

———. *Foreign Collaboration in Indian Industry, Survey Report of the Reserve Bank of India,* Bombay, 1968.

———. *History of the Reserve Bank of India, 1935–51,* Bombay, 1970.

———. *Organizational Framework for the Implementation of Social Objectives* (Report of a Study Group of the National Credit Council), Bombay, 1969.

———. *Report of the All-India Rural Credit Review Committee,* Bombay, 1969.

———. *Report of the Study Team on Overdues of Co-operative Credit Institutions,* Bombay, 1974.

———. *Report on Currency and Finance,* Bombay; annual publication.

III. Articles

Adelman, Irma, and Cynthia T. Morris. "An Anatomy of Income Distribution Patterns in Developing Countries," *Development Digest*, vol. 9, no. 4, October 1971.

Adler, John H. "Development and Income Distribution," *Finance and Development*, vol. 10, no. 3, September 1973.

Arora, Satish K. "Social Background of the Fifth Lok Sabha," *Economic and Political Weekly*, Special Number, August 1973.

Barnds, William J. "Friends and Neighbors," *Foreign Affairs*, vol. 46, no. 3, April 1968.

———. "India and America at Odds," *International Affairs* (London), vol. 49, no. 3, July 1973.

Bhagwati, Jagdish N. "The Exchange Rate Policy—II," *Statesman* (Calcutta), May 5, 1972.

———. "The Tying of Aid," UNCTAD TD/7/Supplement 4, Agenda Item 126 (ii), New Delhi, February 1968.

——— and Sukhamoy Chakravarty. "Contributions to Indian Economic Analysis: A Survey," *American Economic Review*, vol. 59, no. 4, part 2, September 1969.

——— and Anne O. Krueger. "Exchange Control, Liberalization, and Economic Development," *American Economic Review, Papers and Proceedings of the 85th Annual Meeting of the American Economic Association, Toronto, Ontario, December 1972*, May 1973.

——— et al. "Political Response to the 1966 Devaluation," *Economic and Political Weekly*, Sept. 2, 9, and 16, 1972.

Bhatt, V. V. "A Century and a Half of Economic Stagnation in India," *Economic Weekly*, Special Number, July 1963.

——— and V. V. Divatra. "On Measuring the Pace of Development," *Quarterly Review*, Banca Nazionale del Lavora (Rome), nos. 8 and 9, June 1969.

Bowles, Chester. "The Developing Nations' Greatest Need," *New York Times Magazine*, Apr. 12, 1964.

Cassen, Robert H. "Population Growth in India: Reflexions on the 1971 Census," *Environment and Change*, December 1973.

Chenery, Hollis B. "Patterns of Industrial Growth," *American Economic Review*, September 1960.

Clarkson, Stephen. "Non-Impact of Soviet Writing on Indian Thinking and Policy," *Economic and Political Weekly*, Apr. 14, 1973.

Cohen, Benjamin I. "The Stagnation of Indian Exports, 1951–1961," *Quarterly Journal of Economics*, vol. LXXVIII, no. 4, November 1964, pp. 604–620.

Dandekar, V. M., and N. Rath. "Poverty in India: Dimensions and Trends," *Economic and Political Weekly*, Jan. 2 and 9, 1971.

Dantwala, M. L. "From Stagnation to Growth," text of Presidential Address to the 53d Annual Conference of the Indian Economic Association, Gauhati, December 1970; reprinted in *Indian Economic Journal*, vol. 19, no. 2, October–December 1970.

Dass, K. K. "Crumbling Administration," *Seminar*, January 1973, pp. 56–59.

Embree, Ainslie T. "Pluralism and National Integration: The Indian Experience," *Journal of International Affairs*, vol. 27, no. 1, January 1973, pp. 41–52.

Frankena, Mark. "The Industrial and Trade Control Regime and Product Designs in India," *Economic Development and Cultural Change*, vol. 22, no. 2, January 1974, pp. 249–264.

Ganguli, B. N. "Defense Production and Defense Expenditure," *Economic Weekly*, Annual Number, February 1963.

Ghosh, Arun. "The Evolution of Planning Techniques and Organization in India," *Economics of Planning*, vol. 4, no. 1, 1964.

Huntington, Samuel P. "The Role of Foreign Assistance," *National War College Forum,* Summer 1973.

"Impact of Enlarged EEC on India's Exports," *India Economic Bulletin,* March 1972.

"India's Economic Development and Balance of Payments," pamphlet by the IBRD, reprinted in *Monthly Review* of the Federal Reserve Bank of New York, vol. 43, no. 4, April 1961.

Jajoo, Madan Gopal. "Companies Legislation in India: Plea for a Rational View," *Economic and Political Weekly,* June 9, 1973.

Jha, L. K. "Democracy and Socialism in India," *India News* (New York), Apr. 6, 1973.

Johnson, D. W., and J. S. Y. Chiu. "The Saving-Income Relation in Underdeveloped and Developed Countries," *Economic Journal* (London), vol. LXVIII, no. 2, June 1968.

Kennedy, John F. "If India Fails," *Progressive,* January 1958.

Kothari, Rajni. "The Congress 'System' in India," *Asian Survey,* no. 4, December 1964, pp. 1161–1173.

———. "Political Reconstruction of Bangladesh: Reflections on Building a New State in the Seventies," *Economic and Political Weekly,* Apr. 29, 1972.

Kravis, Irving B. "A World of Unequal Incomes," *Annals of the American Academy of Political and Social Science,* September 1973.

Krueger, Anne O. "The Political Economy of the Rent-seeking Society," *American Economic Review, Papers and Proceedings,* vol. 64, no. 3, June 1974.

Ladejinsky, Wolf. "Drought in Maharashtra (Not in One Hundred Years)," *Economic and Political Weekly,* Feb. 17, 1973, pp. 383–396.

———. "The Green Revolution in Punjab," *Economic and Political Weekly,* June 28, 1969.

———. "Land Ceilings and Land Reform," *Economic and Political Weekly,* Annual Number, February 1972.

———. "New Ceiling Round and Implementation Prospects," *Economic and Political Weekly,* Review of Agriculture, September 1972, pp. A125–132.

Lele, Uma J., and John W. Mellor. "Jobs, Poverty, and the 'Green Revolution,'" *International Affairs* (London), vol. 48, no. 1, January 1972.

Lewis, William A. "Economic Development with Unlimited Supplies of Labor," *Manchester School of Economic and Social Studies,* May 1964.

Lindblom, Charles E. "Has India an Economic Future?" *Foreign Affairs,* vol. 44, no. 2, January 1966.

Lipton, Michael, and Peter Tulloch. "India and the Enlarged European Community," *Journal of International Affairs,* vol. 50, no. 1, January 1974.

Loomba, Joanne F. "U.S. Aid to India, 1951–1967: A Study in Decision Making," *India Quarterly Journal of International Affairs,* vol. 28, no. 4, December 1972.

Medhora, Phiroze B. "Approach to the Fifth Plan," *Economic and Political Weekly,* vol. 7, no. 28, July 8, 1972.

———. "Industrial Development: A Quarter Century Review," *Commerce* (Bombay), Aug. 19, 1972.

———. "Managerial Reforms in India's Public Sector," *South Asian Review,* vol. 7, no. 1, October 1973.

———. "Planning: Next Move," *Eastern Economist,* Dec. 15, 1972.

Mitra, Phani. "India Reverts: The Economic Factors," *South Asian Review,* vol. 6, no. 4, July 1973.

Narayan, Jayaprakash. "A Plea for Gandhism," *Vigil,* 1953, p. 8.

Pandit, Shrikrishna A. "Nationalization of Banks in India," *Finance and Development,* vol. 10, no. 1, March 1973.

Patel, I. G. "Essence of Self-Reliance," *Eastern Economist,* Jan. 5, 1973.

Power, John H. "Import Substitution as an Industrialization Strategy," *Philippine Economic Journal,* vol. 5, no. 2, 1966.

Rao, B. Shiva. "The Future of Indian Democracy," *Foreign Affairs*, vol. 39, no. 1, October 1960.

Rao, R. V. R. Chandrasekhara. "Indo-Soviet Economic Relations," *Asian Survey*, vol. 13, no. 8, August 1973, pp. 796–798.

Rosario, J. A. "India's Trade with the Socialist World," *Economic and Political Weekly*, Feb. 24, 1968.

"Rupee Payments Agreements: A Balance Sheet," *Economic Weekly*, Oct. 28, 1961.

Schultze, Charles L. "The Economic Content of National Security Policy," *Foreign Affairs*, vol. 51, no. 3, April 1973.

Sen, S. R. "Growth and Instability in Indian Agriculture," *Agricultural Situation in India*, vol. 21, no. 10, January 1967.

Sen, Sunanda. "A Note on India's Balance of Payments with the Soviet Union," *Arthaniti*, vol. 4, no. 2, July 1961, pp. 138–146.

———. "Rationale of India's Bilateral Payments Agreements," *Arthaniti*, vol. 5, no. 1, January 1962, pp. 39–56.

Sen Gupta, Bhabani. "Moscow, Peking, and the Indian Political Scene after Nehru," *Orbis*, vol. 12, no. 2, Summer 1968.

Shah, Manubhai, "Economics of Rupee Trade," *Eastern Economist*, Nov. 10 and 17, 1967.

Shenoy, B. R. "Aid to India from the World Bank Group," *Il Politico* (University of Pavia), vol. 36, no. 3, 1971.

———. "Monetary Impact of PL-480 Finance," *Eastern Economist*, Silver Jubilee Number, July 26, 1968.

Sheth, D. L. "Profiles of Party Support in 1967," *Economic and Political Weekly*, Annual Number, January 1971.

Shourie, Arun. "Controls and the Current Situation: Why Not Let the Hounds Run?" *Economic and Political Weekly*, Special Number, August 1973.

———. "On Citing the Scriptures," *Economic and Political Weekly*, Aug. 25, 1973.

Singh, Manmohan. "India and the European Common Market," *Journal of Common Market Studies*, vol. 1, no. 3, 1962.

Singh, Tarlok. "The Bombay Plan Recalled," *Eastern Economist*, June 7, 1963.

Subhan, Malcolm. "An 'Empty Shell' for India," *Far Eastern Economic Review*, Apr. 30, 1973.

Tarapore, S. S. "Some Aspects of Foreign Investment Policy," *Reserve Bank of India Bulletin*, May 1966.

Tata, J. R. D. "Suggestions for Accelerating Industrial Growth," Memorandum to the Government of India, dated May 17, 1972; reprinted in *Mainstream*, vol. 10, nos. 51 and 52, Aug. 19, 1972.

Thapar, Ashok. "Where Is the Surplus Land?" *Times of India*, May 15, 1972.

Valkenier, Elizabeth Kridl. "New Trends in Soviet Economic Relations with the Third World," *World Politics*, vol. 22, no. 3, April 1970.

Varma, Kewal. "Congress Leftists in Dogfight," *Financial Express* (Bombay), June 21, 1972.

Veit, Lawrence A. "Development and the International Monetary System," *International Development Review*, vol. 16, no. 3, Fall 1974.

———. "India: Today, Tonight, and Tomorrow Morning," *Pacific Community*, vol. 5, no. 2, January 1974.

———. "India's Economic Development and the Force of National Politics: The Four Seasons of Its Discontent," *Asia*, Supplement No. 1, Fall 1974.

———. "India's Population and International Affairs," paper prepared for the Wingspread Conference on the Social and Cultural Responses to Population Change in India, November 1974; in Marcus F. Franda, ed., *Responses to Population Growth in India* (New York: Praeger Publishers, 1975).

Verghese, B. K. "Rupee Payment Arrangements: An Appraisal," *Economic Weekly,* Special Number, July 1963.

IV. Newspapers and Journals

Asian Survey (University of California); quarterly publication
Commerce (Bombay)
Eastern Economist (New Delhi); weekly publication
Economic and Political Weekly (Bombay)
Economic Weekly (Bombay)
Economist (London); weekly publication
Far Eastern Economic Review (Hong Kong); weekly publication
Financial Express (Bombay); daily publication
Financial Times (Bombay); daily publication
Foreign Affairs (New York); quarterly publication
India News (New York); weekly publication
Indian Economic Journal
Indian Recorder and Digest (New Delhi, Diwan Chand Institute of National Affairs); monthly publication
Overseas Hindustan Times (Washington, D.C.); weekly publication
Pacific Community (Tokyo); quarterly publication
Socialist India
South Asian Review
Statesman (Calcutta); daily publication
Times of India (New Delhi); daily publication

V. United States Government Publications

Arya, P. N. "A Study of India's Bilateral Trade and Payments Arrangements, 1951–1968," mimeographed, (New Delhi: USAID, Nov. 12, 1968).
Comptroller-General of the United States. "Report to the Congress: Opportunities for Better Use of the U.S.-Owned Excess Foreign Currency in India," Jan. 29, 1971.
Congressional Record, Senate, 85th Congress, 2d Session, vol. 104, part 4, Mar. 25, 1958 (Washington, D.C.: Government Printing Office, 1958).
"Foreign Currency Availabilities and Uses," *The Budget of the U.S. Government for Fiscal Year Ending June 30, 1961* (Washington, D.C.: Government Printing Office, 1960).
India Emergency Assistance Act, 1951 (Hearings before the Committee on Foreign Relations, House of Representatives, 82d Congress, 1st Session, Feb. 20–23, 1951), (Washington, D.C.: Government Printing Office, 1951).
Indian Rupee Settlement Agreement (Hearing before the Subcommittee on Near East and South Asia of the Committee on Foreign Relations, House of Representatives, 93d Congress, 2d Session, Jan. 29, 1974), (Washington, D.C.: Government Printing Office, 1974).
Legislation on Foreign Relations (House of Representatives, Committee on Foreign Relations), (Washington, D.C.: Government Printing Office, 1973).
Testimony of Bureau of the Budget Director Kermit Gordon before the Subcommittee of the Committee on Appropriations, House of Representatives, 89th Congress, Final Session (Washington, D.C.: Government Printing Office, 1965).

INDEX